Flashbulb Memories

We all have memories of highly emotional personal and public events that may have happened some years ago but which are felt as strongly as if they happened yesterday. We remember where they happened, the people who were with us, and seemingly irrelevant details such as the weather, particular sounds or specific clothes. Why do we remember these things? Is it because such events are so deeply emotional or so unexpected or because people talk about them so many times? Why are these "flashbulb memories" so vivid and lasting?

Flashbulb Memories: New Issues and New Perspectives explores these questions in the first book on flashbulb memories (FBMs) for more than a decade. It considers the many developments over the last 10 years, including new models of FBM formation, advances in statistical methods and neuroscience, and two key public events, the death of Princess Diana and the September 11th attacks in the US, which can help test FBM. The book examines the status of FBMs as "special" or "ordinary" memory formations, and the expert contributors represent a balance between those that favour each approach. It also investigates controversial topics of research such as:

- Are emotional, cognitive, or social factors highly relevant for the formation of FBMs?
- How can sociological, historical, and cultural issues help us to understand the process of FBMs?
- What are the differences between FBMs, memories for traumatic experiences, and highly vivid personal memories?
- How can we provide a valid and reliable measure for FBMs?

This book gathers together specialists in the field in order to make significant progress in this area of research which has remained divisive for the past 30 years. It will provide essential reading for researchers in FBM and also be of interest to those in related areas such as social psychology, cognitive psychology, cross-cultural psychology, sociology, political sciences and history as well as clinicians dealing with those who have strong FBMs after personal traumatic events.

Olivier Luminet is Research Associate at the Belgian National Fund for Scientific Research (FNRS-FRS), as well as Associate Professor at the Catholic University of Louvain (UCL), Belgium and at the Free University of Brussels (ULB), Belgium.

Antonietta Curci is Associate Professor at the University of Bari in Italy.

Flashbulb Memories

New issues and new perspectives

**Edited by
Olivier Luminet
and Antonietta Curci**

Psychology Press
Taylor & Francis Group
HOVE AND NEW YORK

First published 2009
by Psychology Press
27 Church Road, Hove, East Sussex BN3 2FA

Simultaneously published in the USA and Canada
by Psychology Press
270 Madison Avenue, New York, NY 10016

*Psychology Press is an imprint of the Taylor & Francis Group, an
Informa business*

Copyright © 2009 Psychology Press

Typeset in Times by
RefineCatch Limited, Bungay, Suffolk
Printed and bound in Great Britain by
TJ International Ltd, Padstow, Cornwall
Cover design by Sandra Heath

This publication has been produced with paper manufactured to strict
environmental standards and with pulp derived from sustainable
forests.

British Library Cataloguing in Publication Data
A catalogue record for this book is available from the British Library

Library of Congress Cataloging in Publication Data
Flashbulb memories : new issues and new perspectives / edited by
Olivier Luminet and Antonietta Curci
      p. cm.
   Includes bibliographical references and index.
   ISBN 978–1–84169–672–0 (hbk)
   1. Flashbulb memory.   I. Luminet, Olivier, 1969–   II. Curci
Antonietta, 1969–
   BF378.F55F53 2009
   153.1′3–dc22

                                                      2008027312

ISBN 978–1–84169–672–0 (hbk)

Contents

List of contributors

William Aue, Department of Psychology, Syracuse University, Syracuse, NY 13244, USA. william.aue@gmail.com

Çağla Aydın, Department of Human Development, Cornell University, Martha Van Rensselaer Hall, Ithaca, NY 14853-4401, USA. ca94@cornell.edu

Guglielmo Bellelli, Department of Psychology, University of Bari, Piazza Umberto I, 1, 70121 Bari, Italy. g.bellelli@psico.uniba.it

Dorthe Berntsen, Department of Psychology, University of Aarhus, Jens Chr. Skous Vej 4, Nobelparken, 8000 Aarhus C, Denmark. dorthe@psy.au.dk

Jennifer G. Bohanek, Center for Developmental Science, University of North Carolina at Chapel Hill, Campus Box 8115, 100 East Franklin Street, Chapel Hill, NC 27599-8115, USA. Jennifer_Bohanek@unc.edu

John N. Bohannon III, Department of Psychology, Butler University, Indianapolis, IN 46208, USA. bohannon@butler.edu

Andrew E. Budson, Center for Translational Cognitive Neuroscience, Geriatric Research Education Clinical Center, Edith Nourse Rogers Memorial Veterans Hospital, 200 Springs Road, Bedford, MA 01730, USA. abudson@bu.edu

Antonietta Curci, Department of Psychology, University of Bari, Piazza Umberto I, 1, 70121 Bari, Italy. a.curci@psico.uniba.it

Robyn Fivush, Department of Psychology, Emory University, Atlanta, GA 30322, USA. psyrf@emory.edu

Carl A. Gold, Center for Translational Cognitive Neuroscience, Geriatric Research Education Clinical Center, Edith Nourse Rogers Memorial Veterans Hospital, 200 Springs Road, Bedford, MA 01730, USA. goldca@umdnj.edu

William Hirst, Department of Psychology, New School for Social Research, 55 W 13th Street, New York, NY 10011, USA. hirst@newschool.edu

Megan Julian, Department of Psychology, University of Pittsburgh, Sennott Square, 3rd floor, 210 S. Bouquet St., Pittsburgh, PA 15260, USA. meganjulian@gmail.com

Olivier Luminet, Department of Psychology, Research Group on Emotion, Cognition, and Health, Université Catholique de Louvain, 10, Place Cardinal Mercier, B-1348 Louvain-la-Neuve, Belgium. Olivier.Luminet@uclouvain.be

Kelly Marin, Manhattan College, 292 Central Park West #2C, New York, NY 10024, USA. kmarin@emory.edu

Jessica McDermott Sales, Emory University School of Public Health, 4682 Stone Lane, Stone Mountain, GA 30083, USA. jmcderm@emory.edu

Robert Meksin, Department of Psychology, New School for Social Research, 55 W 13th Street, New York, NY 10011, USA. MeksinR@gmail.com

Dario Páez, Department of Social Psychology and Methodology, Faculty of Psychology, University of the Basque Country, Av. de Tolosa, 70, San Sebastian 20018, Spain. pspparod@ehu.es

David B. Pillemer, Department of Psychology, University of New Hampshire, Durham, NH 03824, USA. david.pillemer@unh.edu

Bernard Rimé, Department of Psychology, Research Group on Emotion, Cognition, and Health, Université Catholique de Louvain, Belgium, 10, Place Cardinal Mercier. B-1348 Louvain-la-Neuve, Belgium. Bernard.Rime@uclouvain.be

David C. Rubin, Duke University, Psychology and Neuroscience, Campus Box 90086, Durham, NC 27708-0086, USA. david.rubin@duke.edu

Jennifer M. Talarico, Department of Psychology, Lafayette College, 307 Oechsle Hall, Easton, PA 18042, USA. talaricj@lafayette.edu

Qi Wang, Department of Human Development, Cornell University, Martha Van Rensselaer Hall, Ithaca, NY 14853-4401, USA. qw23@cornell.edu

Daniel B. Wright, Psychology Department, Florida International University, 11200 S.W. 8th Street, Miami, FL 33199, USA. dwright@fiu.edu

Acknowledgements

The history of a book is always a collective adventure, the result of the hard work of several people. Most of these individuals are involved in this project, and we thank all of them for sharing our enthusiasm and dedication to it. There are some additional people who were very important in making this book possible and whom we would like to thank.

The first is Catrin Finkenauer. Without her enthusiasm to conduct a study related to the flashbulb memory (FBM) for the sudden death of the Belgian King Baudouin in 1993 it is likely that one of the editors of the present book (OL) would not have started investigating these questions. But it was simply impossible to stay indifferent or uninterested by the topic after a meeting with Catrin! He will always remember those dozen hours spent together, building structural equation models or arguing about different theoretical issues. There are no words to describe Catrin's state when she learned that the paper describing this study had been accepted for *Memory and Cognition* and OL has a very detailed FBM of this event! It was under the encouragement of Catrin that the second editor of the present book (AC) first applied the structural equation modelling (SEM) approach to data collected on memory for President Mitterrand's death. The effort we made on that project, the hundreds of outputs we checked, the hours spent in discussing our findings, led her to feel the urge to explore other methodological and statistical possibilities to model FBM data.

The second person to thank is Martin Conway. Martin has always been a very supportive colleague since we first corresponded in early 1994. He always encouraged us to pursue this work. Thank you Martin for your active participation in the meeting held in 2002 in Polignano a Mare (Bari, Italy) during which many important questions related to the modelling of FBM for the 9/11 attacks were discussed in the wonderful natural setting of a Mediterranean beach. Many thanks also to Ticu Constantin, Albina Shayevich, Ineke Wessel, Masao Yogo, Tia Hansen, and Yumi Shimojima who were the other participants of this unforgettable meeting. Thanks also to Elizabeth Marsh and Faruk Gencoz who were actively involved in the data collection and writing concerning the 9/11 terrorist attacks. We are also deeply grateful to Tiziana Lanciano, who took the boring task of checking the references and manuscripts, and preparing them for the final steps of the editorial process. Finally, we gratefully acknowledge the help of all the undergraduate and postgraduate students who enthusiastically cooperated in the many data collections concerning FBM, making available all the empirical material upon which the conclusions of this book have been built.

We also have more specific acknowledgements that we each would like to address. For the first editor (OL), Lydia Gisle is also strongly associated with the first steps of this research on FBM, as most of the time they were three in Catrin Finkenauer's office. We also had a very nice collaboration on another paper looking at group differences related to the death of the former French president François Mitterrand. Thanks also to Pierre Philippot and Martial van der Linden (at the Catholic University of Louvain at that time) who initiated a seminar on autobiographical memory in the autumn of 1993. The seminar was an excellent incentive for starting the study related to the Belgian king's death. Thank you Martial for insisting so much on collecting data on a large sample and for helping us in getting so many questionnaires completed in that study and in many later ones. Finally, this research project would not have been possible without the generous support of the Belgian National Fund for Scientific Research (FRS-FNRS) which gave OL three grants related to the study of FBM (1.5.128.03, 1.5.078.06, and 1.5.158.08).

I (OL) would also like to thank close relatives. First, my parents who greatly contributed to my passion for psychological matters. Thank you so much for all the confidence you showed in my abilities. Then, my wonderful new family, my wife Annette, and two fantastic children, Leah and Pablo. I would also like to dedicate this book to the memory of Hugh Wagner. Hugh was such a generous and brilliant colleague and friend.

From the second editor (AC), the first thanks are addressed to Guglielmo Bellelli for proposing that I write my PhD thesis on FBM, many years ago. As often happens, I felt this topic was a bit removed from my interests as a young postgraduate student, and could not understand the determination of my supervisor in considering this issue. As I progressed in my PhD research work I radically changed my mind, so that I now have to thank him for his determination. A great many times I have been faced with roadblocks in running FBM projects or writing on this topic. The generous advice of Bernard Rimé, his passionate curiosity about all scientific material, and his expertise in research work have often given me the motivation to overcome these obstacles.

I (AC) would like to thank my family, friends, colleagues, and students for being the co-protagonists of many FBMs of relevant benchmark events in my personal and professional life. I would like to dedicate this work to my mother's patience and in memory of my father.

Introduction

Olivier Luminet and Antonietta Curci

I was watching TV by myself. It was a Sunday evening in spring. The weather was quite warm, although very humid, and the sky was dark. Tension could be felt on the screen. In the next few minutes, the journalist was going to announce who had won the election and who would be leading France for the next 7 years. Then, there was an advert sequence that seemed to be never-ending. Although I was only 12, I was already very interested in political matters and was familiar with many aspects of French politics.

Suddenly, the music became louder and progressively the image of the two candidates started to grow on the screen. It became quickly obvious that the image that would grow faster would be the one of the winner. It was like I could no longer breathe. Finally, the music receded to the background and the journalist announced in a very formal manner that François Mitterrand had won the election and was going to be the next president of France. This news came as a complete surprise for me as most people thought that, as usual, the candidate of the right-wing party was going to win, despite polls that were very encouraging for the Socialist candidate. I intensely felt the strong positive emotions that came with the announcement. I remember that I screamed as loudly as I had when the Belgian national soccer team scored during a World Cup game. I also felt an urgent need to tell my family about the unbelievable news. I started to run in the house before realizing that my father was outside in my mother's Renault 4 car that he was going to pull into the garage. I opened the front door ran up beside the driver's window. My father probably saw me arriving very fast as he stopped the car. He immediately opened the window in order to understand what kind of news would have led to my very agitated state. I came up next to him and screamed *"Mitterrand a gagné!"* (Mitterand has won!). Although he was not in such an ecstatic state as I was, I remember his expression of happiness and relief.

Then, during dinner, all conversation was focused on the changes that were expected following his election and the impact it could have not only in France but also in neighbouring countries such as Belgium. The end of the death penalty, new rights for workers, and more freedom for the media were among these topics.

You will certainly all have examples of this type that include very high vividness for the circumstances that surround the announcement of a public news event (be it political, sporting, or cultural in nature). Sometimes the event was so vivid that you remember the words that were said, smells that were present, or other apparently unimportant details such as the weather or the clothes that you were wearing. It is likely that the memory was associated with an event that was experienced as highly surprising, that involved strong positive or negative emotions, that was personally important, and with strong consequences. It is also quite likely that the events you remember the best were those for which you had already some previous knowledge and strong attitudes about. It is further likely that the event occurred when you were a teenager. Another typical feature is that although the event occurred 10–20 years ago or more, you are very confident about all the details you report, even if another person who was with you that day disagrees with you. These memories are called *flashbulb memories* (abbreviated to FBMs in this book). They have intrigued psychologists for a long time, although systematic investigations started only at the end of the 1970s with the famous study published by Brown and Kulik (1977).

The topic of FBM generated a great number of publications in the 1980s and early 1990s. Then the enthusiasm vanished, partly because some studies showed that what was thought to be a special memory mechanism was more ordinary than had been speculated, and that these memories, although very vivid and related to high levels of confidence, were often not very consistent or long lasting. The reduced interest for the topic is reflected by the absence of recent books that cover the literature on FBM. The book *Flashbulb memories* by Martin Conway was published more than 10 years ago. The edited book by E. Winograd and U. Neisser, *Affect and accuracy in recall: Studies of flashbulb memories*, was published in 1992. Other books that have connections with FBM did not cover the topic in full detail and most of them were published more than 10 years ago (e.g., *Theoretical perspectives on autobiographical memory* by Conway, Rubin, Spinnler, & Wagenaar, 1992; *The construction of autobiographical memories* by Rubin, 1995; or *Remembering our past. Studies in autobiographical memory* by Rubin, 1996).

However, the absence of recent books does not reflect the current state of the literature. We will name just a few of these recent advancements. First, new models of FBM formation have been proposed and tested (Finkenauer et al., 1998; Er, 2003). Second, much progress in statistical methods has been made (e.g., Curci, 2005). Third, two public events that supposedly met the conditions needed for the creation of FBM (high novelty and surprise, high personal importance/consequentiality, intense feeling states, and extended rehearsal) have been investigated in a rather systematic way by researchers. These events were the death of Princess Diana in 1997, and the September 11th attacks in the US in 2001. The fact that the same events were investigated by many different research groups allowed for a better understanding of the key variables involved in the process of FBM formation. Fourth, this flourishing literature allowed psychologists to examine with new arguments one central issue in FBM—whether it is a reconstructive process based on rehearsal or a consistent and accurate memory that has biological underpinnings.

The present book has the goal of summarizing many of these recent advancements and adopts a broad perspective on these topics. With such a broad perspective in mind, we expect that the content will be interesting for a large number of researchers in various fields of psychology (social, cognitive, cross-cultural, . . .). The fact that we have included clinical issues could also make this book interesting for practitioners who have to deal with people who have FBMs related to personal traumatic events. We also expect that the content will be appealing for other fields of social sciences such as sociology, political sciences, or history. Some chapters (see Chapters 9, 10, and 11) make explicit links with these disciplines. We will now briefly describe the four sections of the book.

METHODS, STATISTICS, AND MODELLING ISSUES

The first section of the book is dedicated to conceptual questions. We think that this is a crucial issue, as some of the sharpest criticisms of previous FBM research were related to methodological or statistical weaknesses and to the lack of model testing. The three chapters of this section show that recent improvements can hold a promising future.

In Chapter 1, Curci raises the fact that FBM researchers often search for or develop theories without appropriate concerns for methodological issues. The author addresses the question by comparing two types of measurement models used for the assessment of FBMs: categorical (i.e., latent class analysis) and dimensional (i.e., latent trait analysis) models. She explains in a very clear way and with useful examples the mathematical assumptions that underlie these approaches. References to empirical data are used to show that a categorical measurement model is more appropriate to account for FBM data. The issues developed in the first part of the chapter are not restricted to methodological and mathematical domains. They have important implications for better understanding of the nature of FBMs, and more largely for modelling autobiographical memory. This is the aim of the last part of the chapter in which it is shown that dimensional measurement models would fit well with ordinary autobiographical data, while FBMs would be better modelled through a categorical approach.

In Chapter 2, Wright calls for more concerns related to methodological issues in FBM research. He claims that the way the original paper by Brown and Kulik was designed hampered further fruitful developments in understanding the mechanisms that explain high memorability of certain news events. This claim for methodological concerns includes both conceptual and measurement issues. For instance, it is necessary to have in mind the population of events to investigate. It is also necessary to understand the implications of using latent variable models. Wright also makes important suggestions about associative vs causal statements in FBM research. A last issue relates to the importance of combining the traditional single event approach that looks for consistency in FBMs with studies that compare different events in order to examine whether there is some generalizability in memory formation. His chapter will force us to contemplate the appropriateness of the methods that we use to answer research questions relevant to FBM investigation.

There is an overall consensus on the contribution of emotional, cognitive, and social factors to the formation of FBM. There is much less agreement, however, on the way these variables relate to each other and on their direct or indirect effect on FBM. In Chapter 3, Luminet suggests that using structural equation modelling (SEM; Bollen, 1989) is a promising method to compare different models of FBM formation. In the SEM approach, theoretically grounded proposals are tested against empirical data. The author reviews four models that are proposed for the formation of FBM (Brown & Kulik, 1977; Conway et al., 1994; Er, 2003; Finkenauer et al., 1998). Then a comparison of fit indices across 20 data sets allows the drawing of conclusions on how appropriate the different models are to account for the data. Some specificities are also described, such as how FBMs are formed for expected events or if we need a specific model to account for FBM formation in participants who were directly involved in the event. Finally, the models of predictions are compared with respect to the structural relationships among the considered variables across 14 data sets.

CONSISTENCY AND ACCURACY

The second part of the book is related to debated issues of the consistency and accuracy of FBM. There is still no consensus on these issues and the chapters in this section of the book reflect these disagreements. However, we think that the debate is very constructive as it provides a clear agenda for future research by setting the priorities for making significant improvements in the field.

In Chapter 4, Talarico and Rubin examine if FBMs are the outcome of a special memory process. They suggest different ways to detect if special mechanisms are involved in FBMs. They claim that, in order to support the view of a special memory process, a discontinuity should be observed between ordinary memories and special FBMs. The authors start their investigation by examining the four central characteristics of FBMs (accuracy, consistency, vividness, and confidence). They also consider longevity, which has been underinvestigated by previous studies, although it is an important issue for future research in that it can help make interesting connections with the study of collective memories (see Chapters 9, 10, and 11 of this volume). Then they review both objective characteristics and subjective assessments of events thought to produce FBMs. One challenging conclusion is that the mechanism responsible for producing FBMs does not significantly differ from any ordinary autobiographical memories.

As we cannot have an objective reference for memories for personal details, direct assessments of the accuracy of FBM are not possible. Therefore, a considerable amount of research on FBM has used consistency measures as a proxy of accuracy. Chapter 5 by Julian, Bohannon, and Aue shows, with large-sample studies of public events, that the initial amount of recall could be an alternative way to assess FBM accuracy. Data on event memory indicate that when accuracy measures are available, consistency is a relatively poor predictor of accuracy. Data on memory for the reception context show that changes in consistency and amount of initial recall are equally predicted by affect and rehearsal indices. These data have important implications for future research, suggesting that the amount of initial recall for both the event and the reception context is as good a, or sometimes even better, predictor of accuracy for long-term memory as consistency.

INDIVIDUAL FACTORS: CLINICAL AND DEVELOPMENT ISSUES

In this section individual issues are explored. This has been done first by examining FBM for personal situations, rather than collective ones, then by exploring how clinical groups can vary in FBM features. Some updates are also discussed on the relation between emotionality and memory abilities. This includes a discussion of the relevance of emotions with respect to FBM, and of the effects of emotional valence and intensity on recall of auto-biographical experiences. These questions are presented within a developmental perspective.

It may seem quite surprising that only a few studies have been dedicated to FBM for first-hand experiences, in which people were active participants. Although memories for personal events are more difficult to compare, since their triggering circumstances might vary to a large extent, they could be much more relevant for people's identity and well-being than memories for public events. This can make them more likely to be rehearsed and thus more persistent and elaborated. Studies that directly compared events that were heard about second or third hand with first-hand experiences have not always found differences in consistency. But this lack of differences could be due to the methodological specificities explained in Chapter 6 by Pillemer. He provides a detailed account of the strategies used for comparing first-hand vs third-hand memories and explanations for inconsistent results. This should pave the way for more methodologically sound studies that compare predictors and characteristics of events for which people "were there" as compared to events that they only "heard about".

Chapter 7 by Budson and Gold is probably the first review chapter to summarize the formation of event memory and FBM for people having clinical disorders that are either related to memory deficits and distortions, such as Alzheimer's disease, mild cognitive impairment, and Korsakoff syndrome, or memory enhancement, such as that following a post-traumatic stress disorder. The chapter also suggests how other disorders such as social phobia or depression could provide interesting situations for the understanding of event memory and FBM. The review of the considered disorders can improve understanding of general principles governing the formation of these memories. The studies reported also provide interesting ways to differentiate the brain areas that are involved in the formation of both types of memories. One important issue is that the deficits of clinical groups do not affect the different components of the memory process in the same way. For instance, while clinical groups could generate vivid images for collective events and have similar subjective experience of the situation as non-clinical groups, they may still differ in the reported levels of consistency and accuracy.

Emotionality is considered as a key predictor of FBM. There are some uncertainties, however, about the way this variable should be investigated. In Chapter 8 Fivush, Bohanek, Marin, and McDermott Sales first provide a detailed overview on the way emotional events are remembered as compared to neutral ones. They make useful distinctions regarding the valence of the event and its nature. They also consider different aspects of recall, in addition to extent, such as the structure of narratives. Interestingly, a linear relationship was not always found between emotionality of the event and extent of recall. Then the authors examine memory for emotions. They review studies in which the number of positive and negative words used to describe events are examined as a function of age of the respondent, valence, intensity, and time (soon after vs after a few months) of the event. These data raise questions about the reasons why people recall emotions. Emotion regulation strategies are often involved, such as when people try to integrate positive meanings into negative events, thus changing the way initial emotions are recalled some months after the event. The issue of consistency of emotion recall over time is also investigated. While some consistency is found for short intervals (a few days), the issue is more complex for long intervals. Important conclusions are drawn, suggesting that not only the extent of rehearsal can strengthen consistency of memory but also the context in which rehearsal takes place, or the reappraisals that occur during rehearsal.

SOCIAL FACTORS: IDENTITY, CULTURE, AND COLLECTIVE MEMORY

We decided to dedicate a full section to social factors, as we think this has been a very promising development in recent years. The literature on FBM was initially dominated by an almost exclusive intra-individual cognitive approach. Recently, however, many papers have been published which examine social factors that explain differences in FBM formation. It is interesting to note that researchers are also more open to combining cognitive and social explanations in their account of FBM formation. Two chapters in this section illustrate this change. Both Berntsen and Hirst are cognitive psychologists who have included psychosocial theories such as social identity in their models. Their chapters convincingly show how this more integrative approach is fruitful.

In Chapter 9 Berntsen considers that the social environment is an essential issue to add to the original model of Brown and Kulik if we want to reconcile opposite findings about the key role of FBM's main predictors (surprise, emotional feelings, prior knowledge, interest, personal importance/consequences). She proposes that events that are appraised as highly relevant for a person's social identity will be highly memorable. The recent studies conducted by Berntsen and reviewed in this chapter also propose new issues regarding the investigation of long-term memories. They provide interesting designs for studying memory for events such as World War II that are already halfway between personally lived and historical. This will, hopefully, eliminate the gap between the tradition of FBM studies that investigated recent public events and studies that looked at memories for historical events. This should also increase the relevance of the work for researchers from other areas in social sciences such as sociology, political sciences, or history.

Rehearsal is a central variable for the formation of event memory and FBM. In most studies, a distinction is made between intrapersonal processes—such as thoughts and ruminations experienced by people about the event—and interpersonal processes—such as the conversations people initiate with their colleagues, friends, and relatives. When an event is public, a third component that also contributes to rehearsal is media coverage. Although there is a high consensus for including these three components in the assessment of rehearsal, hardly any studies have investigated whether each component can have a different effect on long-term forgetting curves for event memory. In Chapter 10, Hirst and Meksin argue that differences in media coverage could have an impact on the collective memory a community will form of news events. The authors provide interesting data in which they use a fine-grained analysis of changes in media coverage in relation to changes in the rate of forgetting.

In Chapter 11, Páez, Bellelli, and Rimé show through various examples the similarities in the content and processes of FBMs and collective memories (CMs), defined as shared memories of relevant public events that are related to social identity and play important psychosocial functions. Some differences are also highlighted that make the distinction between them still relevant. One important contribution of the chapter is to show that in addition to traditional sources of rehearsal investigated in FBM research (rumination, social communication, and mass media exposure), it is also important to examine other collective behaviours (such as rituals) at a macro-social level.

For example, religious rituals would be predominantly encoded into episodic or semantic memory as an outcome of their frequency and the arousal that they elicited. Interestingly, these two types of memories would be functionally related to the type of society in which they developed, having important consequences for the social organization of the society. Finally, Páez et al. used the terrorist attacks in Madrid in March 2004 to show that rituals are related to an increase in emotional reactions and social rehearsal, the two main predictors of FBM.

Chapter 12 by Wang and Aydın is a nice continuation from Berntsen. In this contribution, too, cultural issues are central in explaining the formation of FBM. The authors examine how both FBM and event memory are shaped by cultural beliefs and practices. They first emphasize that more attention needs to be dedicated to information transmission and cultural differences in the frequency and content of media coverage. These cultural differences imply a comparison not only between more or less technologically advanced countries, but also across different generations within the same society, with respect to the use of and access to the mass media. The authors analyse, for different predictors of FBM (importance, emotional reactions, rehearsal), how cultural beliefs and behaviours might have a significant impact on recall. Cultures vary in the emphasis they put on either an independent self-construal (the self as an autonomous entity) or an interdependent self-construal (a self primarily connected with others). The authors show that these different views on the self affect the content and the strength of memory.

REFERENCES

Bollen, K. A. (1989). *Structural equations with latent variables*. New York: Wiley.

Brown, R., & Kulik, J. (1977). Flashbulb memories. *Cognition, 5*, 73–99.

Conway, M. A. (1995). *Flashbulb memories*. Hove, UK: Lawrence Erlbaum Associates Ltd.

Conway, M. A., Anderson, S. J., Larsen, S. F., Donnelly, C. M., McDaniel, M. A., McClelland, A. G. R., et al. (1994). The formation of flashbulb memories. *Memory and Cognition, 22*, 326–343.

Conway, M. A., Rubin, D. C., Spinnler, H., & Wagenaar, W. A. (1992). *Theoretical perspectives on autobiographical memory*. Dordrecht, The Netherlands: Kluwer Academic.

Curci, A. (2005). Latent variable models for the measurement of flashbulb memories: A comparative approach. *Applied Cognitive Psychology, 19*, 3–22.

Er, N. (2003). A new flashbulb memory model applied to the Marmara earthquake. *Applied Cognitive Psychology, 17*, 503–517.

Finkenauer, C., Luminet, O., Gisle, L., El-Ahmadi, A., Van der Linden, M., & Philippot, P. (1998). Flashbulb memories and the underlying mechanism of their formation: Toward an emotional-integrative model. *Memory and Cognition, 26*, 516–531.

Rubin, D. C. (1995). *The construction of autobiographical memories*. Cambridge, UK: Cambridge University Press.

Rubin, D. C. (1996). *Remembering our past. Studies in autobiographical memory*. Cambridge, UK: Cambridge University Press.

Winograd, E., & Neisser, U. (1992). *Affect and accuracy in recall: Studies of "flashbulb memories"*. New York: Cambridge University Press.

Part I

Methods, statistics, and modelling issues

1 Measurement issues in the study of flashbulb memory[1]

Antonietta Curci

The problem of measuring flashbulb memory (FBM) is one of the key issues in the investigation of the phenomenon. Put in another way, it is the problem of construct validity (Carmines & Zeller, 1979) applied to the investigation of FBM. Methodologists usually recommend a careful consideration of the degree to which a given measurement model matches that which it claims to be measuring. In doing so, a clear theoretical definition of the construct under analysis needs to be provided, together with an accurate specification of the employed measurement model. In the field of FBM, researchers have differently assessed the phenomenon with respect to the different theoretical views they have adopted (see also Wright, Chapter 2 of this volume). Both explicitly and implicitly, measurement models of FBM have carried significant assumptions about its nature and inclusion in the general domain of autobiographical memory.

The present chapter first provides an overview of the different measurement models adopted in assessing FBM, by showing to what extent categorical models have increasingly appeared to offer a more satisfactory account of the phenomenon than traditional dimensional models. Subsequently, a brief outline of the peculiarities of both dimensional and categorical models will allow the reader to evaluate their appropriateness in the investigation of FBM. Finally, from both the theoretical and empirical point of view, similarities and differences between flashbulb and ordinary autobiographical memories are considered. Categorical models appear to best account for FBMs as particularly vivid and detailed memory formations, and this conclusion has significant implications for a general model of autobiographical memory.

THE MEASUREMENT OF FBM

The issue of measuring FBM dates back to the first research work on the topic. In their original paper, Brown and Kulik (1977) defined FBMs as memories for attributes of the reception context of shocking public news. In other words, people may retain for a long time not only the original event itself, but also the reception context for this event; that is, the place where they were, the time when they learned of the event, their ongoing activity, the informant, the personal reactions and reactions of others, the aftermath of the event (Bohannon, 1988; Brown & Kulik, 1977; Conway et al., 1994; Larsen, 1992). Brown and Kulik (1977) considered FBMs as particularly vivid and rich in details, and this account of the phenomenon has also been sustained by subsequent authors. As an alternative, other researchers have emphasized the special consistency and longevity of FBMs over time (for a review, see Julian, Bohannon, and Aue, Chapter 5, and also Talarico and Rubin, Chapter 4 this volume). Besides the choice of the indicators used to measure FBM (vividness, consistency, longevity, etc.) there is another issue underlying FBM investigation, which refers to the way these indicators are hypothesized to be related to the latent construct of FBM. In other words, when assessing FBM, researchers not only make assumptions concerning the specific features to be measured (vividness, consistency, longevity, etc.), but also on the mathematical model connecting these observed features with the latent construct. This in turn has noteworthy implications for the theoretical advancement of research work on FBM. The present chapter deals precisely with the latter issue, the former being the subject of other chapters of the book (see Chapters 4 and 5).

In their original study, Brown and Kulik (1977) operationalized FBM in two ways. First, individuals were scored as having a FBM if they answered "yes" to the direct question: "Do you recall the circumstances in which you first heard that . . .?" Second, a FBM is identified if people can remember at least one attribute of the reception context (Brown & Kulik, 1977; Pillemer, 1984). In assessing the phenomenon, Brown and Kulik (1977) assumed that a simple counting of attributes of the reception context would represent a good approximation to the construct of FBM. When applying such a procedure, the outcome of the assessment is an absolute scale in principle without upper boundary, since in real life the total number of members of a collection cannot be defined a priori (Luce & Suppes, 2002). It follows that the number and characteristics of attributes chosen to define FBM are completely arbitrary. Brown and Kulik (1977) selected six attributes of the context which they considered more informative of the nature of FBM, and all six attributes were given the same relevance in their model. However, the authors' choice was neither theoretically justified nor empirically grounded. Furthermore, a simple counting of attributes is completely uninformative of the intrinsic nature of the construct in analysis. In spite of this, the procedure of summing up FBM attributes (Brown & Kulik, 1977) was subsequently adopted by different authors (Bohannon, 1988; Kvavilashvili, Mirani, Schlagman, & Kornbrot, 2003; Pillemer, 1984).

Other studies have attempted to reduce the major flaw of Brown and Kulik's measurement model (1977), by attributing more prominence to some specific details of the context. Winograd and Killinger (1983) identified a FBM from the mention of ongoing activity in participants' free accounts. Wright (1993) required that participants recalled at least one attribute from location, other people present, and ongoing activity. Despite having evident limitations, these approaches introduced the idea that FBM is more than a simple collection of irrelevant attributes, since some of them are more representative of the construct than others.

Neisser and Harsch (1992), in their study on the *Challenger* disaster, employed a procedure called WAS (weighted attributes scores), which assigned different weights to different attributes of the reception context. The authors assumed that the attributes were not all equally important. Some of them were defined as "major" (i.e., location, informant, and ongoing activity), since they seemed to be essential in order to identify the situation. Some others were considered as "minor" (i.e., other people present and time), since one could be wrong on these and still essentially right about the original facts. The WAS procedure consists in assigning a score for each recalled major attribute, plus a bonus point when the participant scores above a given threshold on the set of minor attributes. More specifically, scores ranging from 0 to 2 were assigned to the individual's memories for location, informant, and ongoing activity. Furthermore, an additional score of 1 was added if the participant scored at least 3 on the indicators assessing other people present and time. As a consequence, for each individual the final WAS measure for FBM ranged from 0 to 7 (Neisser & Harsch, 1992). The WAS system was subsequently employed in more recent studies on memory for the September 11th attacks (Pezdek, 2003; Smith, Bibi, & Sheard, 2003; Tekcan, Ece, Gülgöz, & Er, 2003), and it represented a clear advancement towards a measurement model that considered FBM as a qualitatively different phenomenon from ordinary memory formations.

Recently, Curci and her colleagues (Curci & Luminet, 2006; Curci, Luminet, Finkenauer, & Gisle, 2001; Luminet et al., 2004) modelled FBM data through a statistical technique called CatPCA (categorical principal component analysis), which shares the same logic as the WAS approach (Luminet et al., 2004). CatPCA is a principal component analysis specifically aimed at scaling categorical or ordered categorical variables (van de Geer, 1993). In employing this technique, the authors aimed at getting a composite measure that combines scores of different indicator variables corresponding to the attributes of the reception context, weighted with respect to their relevance in identifying FBM. With respect to WAS, the main advantage of CatPCA is that the weights assigned to the scores are not decided a priori by the researcher, but derive from the empirical distributions of the indicator variables in the sample of respondents considered in the study (Greenacre, 1993). Luminet and his colleagues (2004) discussed the similarities and differences between the WAS and CatPCA approaches, showing that, although the scores for the two procedures were highly correlated, nevertheless CatPCA was to be preferred because it allowed the researchers to get a better and more reliable approximation of the construct of FBM.

Finally, in some recent studies the latent variable approach was applied to model FBM data (Curci, 2005; Wright, Gaskell, & O'Muircheartaigh, 1998). Following this approach, FBM is considered a latent construct which cannot be directly accessed, and all relationships within a set of indicators are accounted for by covariances between those indicators and the latent construct. Wright and his colleagues were the first to employ such a modelling in a study on the memories of Mrs Thatcher's resignation and the Hillsborough disaster (Wright et al., 1998), where FBM was considered as a continuous trait underlying a set of observed categorical indicators. Curci (2005) compared three latent variable approaches, which only differed from each other with respect to the mathematical assumptions concerning the nature of the latent construct. Two of these approaches—confirmatory factor analysis (CFA; Bollen, 1989), and latent trait analysis (LTA; Bartholomew, Steele, Moustaki, & Galbraith, 2002; Rost & Langeheine, 1997)—hypothesize that a continuous latent construct underlies a set of observed indicators. The third—latent class analysis (LCA; Bartholomew et al., 2002; McCutcheon, 1987, 2002)—assumes that the latent construct is a categorical variable. The three models were applied on data concerning memory for the reception context in both a correlational and an experimental study. The LCA approach was found to best fit FBM data, thus accounting for a categorical model for the measurement of the phenomenon.

In sum, the literature revised thus far substantiates some relevant points: (1) Traditional measurement models have increasingly appeared as inadequate to reproduce the phenomenon; (2) Assuming that the latent construct is categorical seemed to best account for FBM data; (3) Evidence concerning the measurement of FBM has implications for the theoretical understanding of the nature of the phenomenon; (4) Significant implications also ensue for a general model of autobiographical memory.

THE ASSESSMENT OF LATENT CONSTRUCTS

Dimensional vs categorical models

Before turning to a theoretical discussion on the implications of modelling FBM data, the peculiarities of both dimensional and categorical measurement models should be briefly revised, as well as their application in psychological research. Psychologists usually deal with unobservable, or latent, constructs. For instance, intelligence, introversion, mathematical ability cannot be directly measured as can height or weight, since they are concepts rather than physical entities. Nevertheless some empirical attributes can be considered as observable indicators of these underlying latent constructs (Baker, 1985). One basic assumption of latent variable models is local independence, which postulates that indicator variables are locally independent given the latent variable(s) (Lazarsfeld & Henry, 1968). In other words, after removing the variability between the latent construct and its observed indicators, the individual's responses to the items of a test are statistically independent of each other (Hambleton, Swaminathan, & Rogers, 1991; McCutcheon, 1987).

The so-called dimensional models assume that a continuous normally distributed latent construct accounts for variations among observed indicators (Moustaki, 1996). For instance, the ability to provide correct answers to a set of mathematical calculations might be conceptualized as a continuous trait—i.e., mathematical ability—which each individual holds to a different degree. Psychologists are familiar with factor analysis models, which consider observed variables as linear combinations of latent factors, plus random error terms. In other words, all pairwise associations between observed variables are accounted for by a common dependence on some latent variables. Factor analysis models preferably apply to continuous indicator variables, for which correlation coefficients can easily be computed. Fitting these models involves finding the values of the latent variable parameters that maximize the probability of reproducing a correlation matrix of indicators as close as possible to the observed product moment correlation matrix (Comrey & Lee, 1992; Kim & Mueller, 1978).

When the aim of the researcher is to reduce a set of categorical observed indicators (binary, ordered categorical, simply categorical) to a smaller set of latent factors, latent trait analysis (LTA) is one of the most accepted approaches (Bartholomew et al., 2002). Also this approach rests in the field of dimensional models. In the area of educational testing and psychological assessment, LTA is termed item response theory (IRT). A considerable overlap exists between LTA and IRT, leading authors to consider them as basically interchangeable approaches. Among psychologists the acronym IRT is more popular, and it will be preferred in the following pages. IRT rests on two basic postulates: (1) the individual's performance on a test item depends on some latent abilities called traits; (2) the relationship between the individual's item performance and latent traits can be described by a monotonically increasing function (Embretson & Reise, 2000; Hambleton et al., 1991). This function, called in IRT an item characteristic function, expresses the probability of an individual giving a correct answer to an item of a test as a function of his/her ability (trait) (Baker, 1985). IRT methods were originally unidimensional, assuming that only one latent trait accounts for variations of observed indicators, but generalizations to multidimensional models have been proposed more recently (Embretson & Reise, 2000). In the present chapter unidimensional IRT models will be discussed, since the application of IRT methods to FBM data has so far been limited to this approach (Curci, 2005; Wright et al., 1998). Only the theoretical rationale of the models and some details on the procedure will be presented here, since a technical discussion of their mathematical features is beyond the goals of the present chapter (for more details, see Bartholomew et al., 2002; Embretson & Reise, 2000; Hambleton et al., 1991).

Unidimensional IRT models differ from each other with respect to the form of the item characteristic function, and the number of parameters in the model. An example might help us to understand the logic of IRT models. In the investigation of a student's mathematical ability a starting assumption is that, in providing the correct answers to a set of mathematical computations, each individual possesses some amount of the ability under investigation. In other words, each student has a hypothetical score on the scale of the latent construct corresponding to her/his mathematical ability. This construct cannot be directly assessed but, for each student, its amount is inferred from the number of correct responses provided to the set of mathematical computations. IRT models allow the researcher to estimate the probability of an individual choosing some response categories from a set of observed indicators (i.e., correct responses to the mathematical computations) as a function of an underlying latent trait (i.e., the mathematical ability). In doing so, IRT models describe each observed indicator with respect to some properties (difficulty, discrimination, etc.) which define the position of the individual along the continuum represented by the latent trait.

If we denote the ability score as *theta*, then, at each level of *theta*, a different probability is associated with obtaining the correct answer to a given computation. This probability is denoted as P(*theta*). For each item of the set, plotting P(*theta*) as a function of *theta* will result in a smooth S-shaped curve, called an item characteristic curve (ICC). At the lowest levels of *theta*, the probability of a student providing the correct answers to the considered mathematical computation is very low, and it increases as the amount of mathematical ability possessed increases, following the shape of the ICC. The one-parameter logistic model (or Rasch model; Rasch, 1960) simply considers the location of the curve along the x-axis, by including in the equation for P(*theta*) only the so-called difficulty parameter. The higher the difficulty parameter for a given item, the higher the ability required for correctly answering that item, and the more the ICC will be located along the right side of the x-axis. In Figure 1.1, the ICC on the left has a lower difficulty parameter than the ICC on the right, and this means that less ability is required in order to provide the correct answer to the item represented by the former ICC as compared with the item represented by the latter. To illustrate, much more mathematical ability is required to take the square root of 17,498 than to perform the 12 × 24 computation. It follows that the ICC for the former operation will be located on the right side of the x-axis more than the ICC for the latter operation item. The two-parameter logistic model also includes in the equation the so-called discrimination parameter, which reflects the slope of the ICC. The steeper the ICC, the more efficiently the item discriminates respondents having high latent ability from those having low latent ability. In Figure 1.2, the ICC on the right side of the plot corresponds to an item with a higher level of discrimination than the ICC on the left side. To provide a concrete example of the discrimination parameter, the same mathematical operation of taking the square root of 17,498 will better discriminate high-school students with different levels of mathematical ability than young primary-school students or expert college students attending mathematics courses at university.

Finally, the three-parameter logistic model takes into consideration the

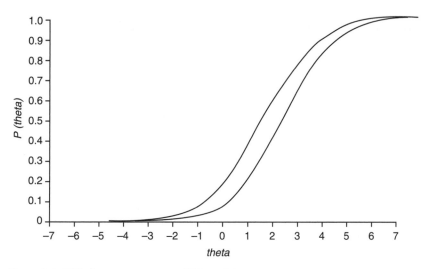

Figure 1.1 ICCs for one-parameter IRT models.

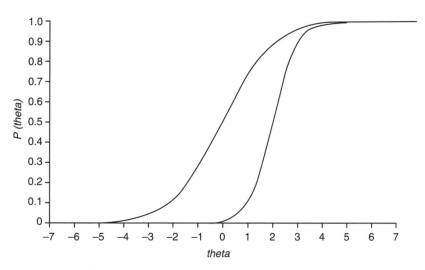

Figure 1.2 ICCs for two-parameter IRT models.

probability of getting correct answers due to simple guessing by respondents. This means that the model equation also contains a pseudo-chance para-meter, which represents the probability of an individual correctly answering the item only by guessing. To illustrate, the probability of distinguishing chemical formulas from mathematical operations is reasonably above zero for high-school students. In mathematical words, the pseudo-chance parameter corresponds to the lowest non-zero asymptote for the ICC. In Figure 1.3, the two ICCs on the right side include this pseudo-chance parameter, since the

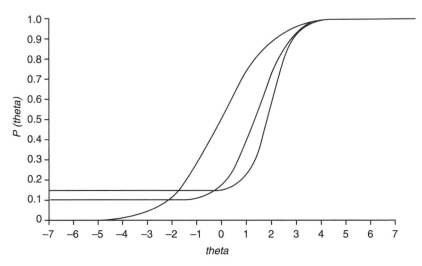

Figure 1.3 ICCs for three-parameter IRT models.

probabilities of getting correct answers to the corresponding items are never lower than some thresholds, while the ICC on the left side does not enclose this parameter. It is worth noting that IRT modelling includes both the individual's responses to a set of items, and the properties of the items that constitute the test. The item information function (IIF) and test information function (TIF) indices specify the amount of information on the latent construct provided respectively by every single item and the total set of items of the test (Baker, 1985). Finally, general fit indices can be computed to evaluate the correspondence between the whole estimated model and the data entered in the analyses (Akaike, 1974; Myung, 2003; Schwarz, 1978). IRT and LTA modelling is available in many software packages for data analysis, among others PARSCALE (Muraki & Bock, 1998), BILOG-MG (Zimowski, Muraki, Mislevy, & Bock, 1996), MULTILOG (Thissen, 1991), GENLAT (Moustaki, 2001), and R (R Development Core Team, 2006) package ltm (Rizopoulos, 2007).

A different approach in psychological assessment is represented by categorical modelling, which considers individuals to be classified into discrete classes having specific characteristics. For instance, individuals might be classified as belonging or not to a class of clinical patients based on the co-occurrence of a set of observed symptoms. In this perspective, data can be modelled following two general approaches: cluster analysis, and latent class analysis (LCA) (Meehl, 1992). Cluster analysis divides individuals on account of their similarity/dissimilarity. The procedure terminates once a division is reached, based on empirical features of the sample in analysis. Conclusions cannot be drawn regarding the latent structure of data (Meehl, 1992). For this reason, cluster methods cannot be included with latent variable models. LCA models assume that a discrete latent construct accounts for covariations among observed indicators (McCutcheon, 1987). The latent construct has different latent classes with different probabilities of occurrence. Each class of the construct corresponds to a specific response pattern of indicators of the test. This means that the probability of occurrence for each latent class of the construct is determined by the percentage of individuals in the sample exhibiting a given response pattern to the observed indicators. The meaning of a latent class is defined by the response categories of the indicators associated with that latent class of the construct (McCutcheon, 1987). This is the same as saying that the latent class t of a construct X is defined by the response category i to the item A, j to the item B, k to the item C, and so forth. To illustrate, the latent class Depression is defined by the positive answers provided by respondents to the items of a Major Depression scale (i.e., feeling depressed mood, insomnia/hypersomnia, fatigue, diminished ability to concentrate, etc.), while the non-Depression class is defined by negative answers to the listed symptoms.

Associations between latent classes and response categories of indicators are probabilistic. Indeed, for each response category, conditional probabilities are estimated, which correspond to the probability of choosing that response category of the observed indicator, given the latent construct. Also indices of fit can be computed for LCA to assess their appropriateness to account for the empirical associations among observed indicators in analysis (McCutcheon, 2002). Among the most common statistical packages to run LCA are *lEM* (Vermunt, 1997), Latent GOLD (Vermunt & Magidson, 2005), PANMARK (van der Pol, Langeheine, & de Jong, 1998), MPLUS (Muthen & Muthen, 1998), and R (R Development Core Team, 2006) package e1071 (Dimitrau, Hornik, Leisch, Meyer, & Weingessel, 2006).

Besides the mathematical specifications of the latent variable approaches so far reviewed, the main theoretical distinction between dimensional and categorical models rests in the nature of the underlying latent variable responsible for covariations among observed indicators. The application of one model instead of another implies a theoretical assumption on the nature of the construct under investigation. Furthermore, given that latent variable models are confirmative, and fit indices can generally be computed to evaluate their appropriateness to a given data set, the researcher has the opportunity to select the best-fitting model to the data in analysis, so that the theory can be submitted to scrutiny on an empirical basis (Kim & Mueller, 1978).

Beyond dimensionality: Categories as "real" entities

The traditional measurement approach in psychology has favoured dimensional models, especially in the investigation of personality characteristics (Eysenck, 1953). As specified above, factor analysis models are still the most practised methods by researchers interested in combining observed indicators into theoretically meaningful constructs, and their outcomes are currently interpreted as continuous dimensions. A categorical interpretation of latent constructs is still considered as an oversimplification of the reality or, which is worse, an arbitrary account. This is due to the fact that psychological reality is considered so complex and fluctuating that it can hardly be constrained into discrete classes (Gangestad & Snyder, 1985). This consideration—very common among personality researchers—has also influenced many areas of psychological research, including the investigation of autobiographical memory. In her work on the measurement of FBM, Curci (2005) presented dimensional models and showed that they are well suited to account for findings on ordinary autobiographical memory, although barely applicable to the investigation of FBM.

Indeed, one of the main arguments against categorical models relies on the fact that classes are usually considered *phenetically*. This means that classification mainly serves descriptive purposes, as a summarizing function. No underlying meaning is ascribed to the classes, which are completely arbitrary or quasi-arbitrary constructions (Gangestad & Snyder, 1985). On the other hand, classes might be established in *genotypic* terms, when empirical evidence suggests there is a latent entity, event, or construct that aggregates some observed characteristics. As a consequence, causal relationships might be assessed between this latent construct and the observed indicators (Gangestad & Snyder, 1985). Classes are thus meaningful, they really exist, and the goal of empirical investigation is to access the latent categorical structure of observed reality. Taxometric analysis takes for granted this point, since "taxa" are defined as natural kinds or species, not merely arbitrary categories (Ruscio, Haslam, & Ruscio, 2006; Schmidt, Kotov, & Joiner, 2004; Waller & Meehl, 1998). Three sets of reasons justify the concept of taxonicity in reality, i.e., commonsense explanations, causal interpretation of reality, and mathematical demonstrations (Meehl, 1992), and all these reasons are well suited to classification procedures in medicine, biology, or chemistry.

A commonsense validation is rather adequate when classifying animals, stones, organic diseases, and so on. In psychological research, accepting the conjecture of a discrete latent categorization is much more complicated, therefore empirical evidence might provide great support to this approach. Empirical distributions of indicators, and observed relationships among them might suggest considering the taxonicity hypothesis for a given phenomenon, which needs to be strongly supported by stringent statistical demonstrations (Meehl, 1992). In psychological research, taxonomic models have been adopted to investigate relevant constructs for the study of personality and personality disorders by Meehl (1992, 1999, 2004; Meehl & Golden, 1982). In his work on taxometrics, the author has criticized the dogmatic and a priori preference for the dimensional approach in personality assessment, and has proposed sophisticated procedures for identifying latent taxa in psychopathology. The work by Waller, Putnam, and Carlson (1996) on dissociation represents an interesting application of these procedures, to distinguish pathological from non-pathological dissociation. Evidence from this work supports the idea that non-pathological dissociation is a dimensional construct to be assessed through dimensional modelling, while pathological dissociation is a typological construct best modelled by a taxometric approach (Waller et al., 1996). Clinical research on personality disorders has applied latent class models to account for depression (Hankin, Fraley, Lahey, & Waldman, 2005), narcissism (Fossati et al., 2005), eating disorders (Gleaves, Lowe, Snow, Green, & Murphy-Eberenz, 2000; Williamson et al., 2002), and dissociation (Waller & Ross, 1997; Waller et al., 1996). In all these studies, empirical support is provided for the hypothesis of a categorical latent structure underlying covariations of a set of discrete indicators.

To sum up, in order to define a phenomenon as a real, non-arbitrary categorical formation, two requirements are needed: (1) a theoretical model concerning the categorical nature of the phenomenon; (2) evidence of a kind of discontinuity implanted in a network of empirical relationships.

FBM AND AUTOBIOGRAPHICAL MEMORY

Semantic vs episodic memories

Flashbulb memories have usually been considered as memories for the reception context of relevant public events. However, individuals' recollections of their private reception context are undoubtedly associated with a recollection of the original event itself. Empirical evidence has shown that emotional and reconstructive factors have a different impact on flashbulb and event memory. In their study on FBM for the death of President Mitterrand, Curci and her colleagues (2001) found that event memory did not significantly decrease over time, while memory for flashbulb attributes was impaired. Moreover, French respondents, who were more concerned by the death of Mitterrand than Belgian participants, appeared to be more consistent in their event memory, but no effect of provenance was found on FBM consistency (Curci et al., 2001). Pezdek (2003) compared memories for the September 11th attacks in two samples of people living in New York and in California-Hawaii respectively. New York participants reported the most accurate event memory and the least accurate memory for the reception context. The opposite pattern was found for the California-Hawaii sample (Pezdek, 2003).

From the theoretical point of view, flashbulb and event memories are considered as belonging to different memory systems (Bohannon & Symons, 1992; Curci & Luminet, 2006; Curci et al., 2001; Finkenauer et al., 1998; Pezdek, 2003; Smith et al., 2003). While FBMs are conceptualized as a form of episodic memory, event memory might be considered as a form of semantic memory (Bohannon & Symons, 1992). Bohannon and Symons (1992) showed that the degree of involvement in a public event is a better predictor of the persistence of episodic material.

The relationship between semantic and episodic forms of memory has been variously conceptualized. The so-called network models proposed that semantic nodes and their inter-relationships constitute the domain of human memory. Nodes are arranged in a hierarchical way, representing forms of knowledge varying in their degrees of generality. At the top of the hierarchy there are nodes representing general concepts (e.g., clothes). These are connected with low-level nodes which represent instances of the general concept (e.g., jacket). Episodic memories might thus be considered as allocated to nodes at the lowest level of the hierarchy (Collins & Loftus, 1975; Collins & Quillian, 1969; Tulving, 1983). In the domain of autobiographical memory this means that minimal units of autobiographical knowledge are associated to a different degree with top-level semantic nodes (Conway & Bekerian, 1987). Although a broad agreement exists in the literature on the cognitive structures involved in autobiographical memory, the debate on the organization of these structures is still open (Wright & Nunn, 2000).

The construction of autobiographical memories

One of the major criticisms of the application of network models to autobiographical memory concerns their atomistic view. In other words, network models consider human memory to be divided into general units (concepts, nouns, verbs, etc.), and specific autobiographical memories are attached to these general units in a rather arbitrary way (Anderson & Conway, 1997). In spite of the greater flexibility exhibited by these models, their application to complex autobiographical memory issues still appears inadequate. Indeed, original network models have failed to account for some distinctive characteristics of autobiographical memory. First, autobiographical memories differ across the lifespan for the same individual. A young teenager's memory of the first day at school is different when the same individual is 40 years old (Conway & Rubin, 1993). Second, autobiographical memories vary in the vividness they exhibit (Anderson & Conway, 1997). Finally, a mix of general and specific knowledge can be found in every autobiographical recollection (Conway & Pleydell-Pearce, 2000).

With respect to the first point, it should be noted that a constructivist view on autobiographical memory has put great emphasis on a process called "cyclic retrieval" (Williams & Hollan, 1981). This is a constructive process, which mediates the formation of autobiographical memories, and it is based on an iterative comparison between the outcomes of a search phase and the elaboration of memory descriptions from available cues (Conway & Rubin, 1993). As a consequence, memories are not considered as stable structures that can be accessed at any time, but they are instead transitory patterns of activation within an autobiographical knowledge base. The construction of autobiographical memory is dependent on the activation of personally relevant goals, and issues related to the self (Conway & Rubin, 1993). This means that individuals reconstruct their past with respect to the goals they are pursuing in the present, and the process of retrieval develops in conformity with the organization of the working self (Carver & Scheier, 1990; Higgins, 1987). Access to knowledge that corresponds to the goal structure of the working self is facilitated, while access to knowledge incompatible with these goals is inhibited. On the other hand, autobiographical memories ground the self, in that they provide consistency and plausibility constraints on the goals that can be held (Conway & Pleydell-Pearce, 2000). For this reason, a teen-ager's memory for the first day at school, highly concerned with the goal of being a good pupil, is fairly different from the memory retrieved by the same individual at 40 years old when other goals have become relevant.

With respect to the second and third issues, Conway and his colleagues (Anderson & Conway, 1997; Conway & Bekerian, 1987; Conway & Pleydell-Pearce, 2000; Conway & Rubin, 1993) have proposed a model that considers autobiographical memories as generated from a multilevel knowledge base through the process of activation described above. The structure of this knowledge base encompasses at least three layers. The first contains thematic knowledge about extended periods of time, the *lifetime periods* (i.e., when I was at university, when I lived at X); the second—*general events*—contains records of extended and repeated events occurring over periods of months or weeks (i.e., my holidays in France, Saturday nights at the disco); the third layer—*event-specific knowledge*—comprises highly specific and vivid details, as well as forms of images and associated feeling. FBMs can be considered as forms of event-specific knowledge in that they exhibit features of vividness and specificity which characterize this layer of autobiographical knowledge (Conway & Pleydell-Pearce, 2000). This model has the advantage of preser-ving the specificity of some forms of episodic recollections, such as FBMs, but at the same time it considers the dynamic interconnection existing between these unitary representations and the most general level of thematic knowledge.

In line with the arguments presented above, FBMs, more than ordinary autobiographical memories, correspond to recollections of event-specific sensory–perceptual details, thus they appear more vivid than any other auto-biographical memory (Conway, 1995). Unlike ordinary autobiographical memories, which convey a distributed form of knowledge representation involving the three layers of the autobiographical knowledge base, FBMs appear to arise from more densely integrated regions. What is immediately salient about FBM is the fact that people report vivid accounts of their experiences of learning important news, and rate their recollections as stable and consistent even over long periods of time. From the theoretical point of view described above the idea of a categorical nature of FBM appears to be preferable to account for these characteristics. FBMs are not simply ordinary memories with an unusual feature of vividness, but they can be considered as "whole" units or "local minima" in the space of autobiographical memory (Conway, 1995).

Evidence of discontinuity in the domain of autobiographical memory

The theoretical account of FBMs as unitary memory formations was tested by Curci (2005) in a study on the measurement of the phenomenon. The hypothesis under investigation was the following: If FBMs are triggered from more densely integrated regions of the autobiographical knowledge base (Conway, 1995), then the measurement model for FBMs should differ in its assumptions and outcome from the model used to assess ordinary autobiographical memories. While dimensional measurement models would well fit ordinary autobiographical memory data, FBMs would be better modelled through a categorical approach (Curci, 2005). Overall, findings confirmed the idea that FBMs convey an integrated form of knowledge representation (Conway, 1995), while ordinary autobiographical memories require the combination of distributed information. The latent class model appeared to be a good approximation to the clustered nature of FBMs, while the latent trait model represents more reasonably the alternative account of ordinary autobiographical memories as continuous memory formations (Curci, 2005).

In the same study, the impact of reconstructive factors was stressed with respect to the measurement of FBM (Curci, 2005). Contrary to expectations, the construct of FBM was found to be significantly associated with the mass media as a source of learning. This was probably due to the fact that the original event considered in the study (the death of President Mitterrand) was expected, and the mass media contributed considerably in spreading information about its protagonist. Furthermore, the data collection for the study took place 3 months after the original event, thus distortions could have affected individuals' memory in the meantime (Neisser & Harsch, 1992; Schmolck, Buffalo, & Squire, 2000). People certainly watched TV and read newspapers in the days immediately following the event, so that their memory for their first source of learning shifted towards the mass media script. Thus, they would have simply remembered a source of information they had encountered later, and this detail would have become strongly interconnected with the other details of the context to create a unique memory formation. As a consequence, FBM appeared vivid and consistent over time, although deeply determined by reconstructive factors. Also this point is clearly in line with the constructivist models (Conway & Pleydell-Pearce, 2000; Conway & Rubin, 1993), which emphasize the dynamic organization within the structures involved in the formation of autobiographical memories. FBMs seemed to be the outcomes of constructive processes which apply to event-specific sensory–perceptual material, thus preserving its features of specificity and vividness. In sum, the evidence reviewed so far suggests that the process of retrieving FBMs is a reconstruction based on the availability of some integrated memory units that are particularly vivid and detailed in their nature.

CONCLUSIONS

The aim of this chapter has been to provide an overview of the measurement models adopted in the investigation of FBM, as well as their implications for the theoretical consideration of the phenomenon. The revised literature has suggested that traditional linear models have progressively appeared inadequate to reproduce the object of analysis. On the other hand, categorical models have offered a promising tool for modelling FBM data. Furthermore, categorical models have allowed researchers to test hypotheses concerning the special characteristics of this class of autobiographical memories. The choice between dimensional and categorical models, far from being a simple methodological dispute, is of fundamental relevance for the general debate about the nature of FBM. From the empirical point of view, evidence of discontinuity in the domain of autobiographical memory has provided support for the theoretical account of FBM as arising from the activation of "whole" units within the autobiographical knowledge base, which integrate sensory–perceptual vivid details and general aspects of thematic knowledge into unitary representations (Conway, 1995; Curci, 2005). Finally, the so-called constructivist model of autobiographical memory (Conway & Pleydell-Pearce, 2000; Conway & Rubin, 1993) has received empirical scrutiny from the research work on FBM. The organization of the structures involved in autobiographical memory is dynamic, in that reconstructive factors determine the intrinsic nature of the phenomenon and impose some constraints on its operational measurement. The issue of assessing FBM represents a significant illustration for this general theory. Future studies should provide more empirical support to both issues of FBM as a categorical memory formation and the effects of reconstructive factors in determining the intrinsic nature of the phenomenon.

NOTE

1 The author thanks Daniel B. Wright for his helpful comments on the first draft of the manuscript of this chapter.

REFERENCES

Akaike, H. (1974). A new look at the statistical model identification. *IEEE Transactions on Automatic Control, 19*, 716–723.

Anderson, S. J., & Conway, M. A. (1997). Representations of autobiographical memories. In M. A. Conway (Ed.), *Cognitive models of memory* (pp. 217–246). Hove, UK: Psychology Press.

Baker, F. B. (1985). *The basics of item response theory*. Portsmouth, NH: Heinemann.

Bartholomew, D. J., Steele, F., Moustaki, I., & Galbraith, J. (2002). *The analysis and interpretation of multivariate data for social scientists*. Boca Raton, FL: Chapman & Hall/CRC.

Bohannon, J. N. (1988). Flashbulb memories for the space shuttle disaster: A tale of two theories. *Cognition, 29,* 179–196.

Bohannon, J. N., & Symons, V. L. (1992). Flashbulb memories: Confidence, consistency, and quantity. In E. Winograd & U. Neisser (Eds.), *Affect and accuracy in recall: Studies of "flashbulb memories"* (pp. 65–91). New York: Cambridge University Press.

Bollen, K. A. (1989). *Structural equations with latent variables.* New York: Wiley.

Brown, R., & Kulik, J. (1977). Flashbulb memories. *Cognition, 5,* 73–99.

Carmines, E. G., & Zeller, R. A. (1979). *Reliability and validity assessment.* Newbury Park, CA: Sage.

Carver, C. S., & Scheier, M. F. (1990). Origins and functions of positive and negative affect: A control-process view. *Psychological Review, 97,* 19–35.

Collins, A. M., & Loftus, E. F. (1975). A spreading activation theory of semantic processing. *Psychological Review, 82,* 407–428.

Collins, A. M., & Quillian, M. R. (1969). Retrieval time from semantic memory. *Journal of Verbal Learning and Verbal Behavior, 8,* 240–247.

Comrey, A. L., & Lee, H. B. (1992). *A first course in factor analysis.* Hillsdale, NJ: Lawrence Erlbaum Associates Inc.

Conway, M. A. (1995). *Flashbulb memories.* Hove, UK: Lawrence Erlbaum Associates Ltd.

Conway, M. A., Anderson, S. J., Larsen, S. F., Donnelly, C. M., McDaniel, M. A., McClelland, A. G. R., et al. (1994). The formation of flashbulb memories. *Memory and Cognition, 22,* 326–343.

Conway, M. A., & Bekerian, D. A. (1987). Organization in autobiographical memory. *Memory and Cognition, 15,* 119–132.

Conway, M. A., & Pleydell-Pearce, C. W. (2000). The construction of autobiographical memories in the self-memory system. *Psychological Review, 107,* 261–288.

Conway, M. A., & Rubin, D. C. (1993). The structure of autobiographical memory. In A. F. Collins, S. E. Gathercole, M. A. Conway, & P. E. Morris (Eds.), *Theories of memory* (pp. 103–137). Hove, UK: Lawrence Erlbaum Associates Ltd.

Curci, A. (2005). Latent variable models for the measurement of flashbulb memories: A comparative approach. *Applied Cognitive Psychology, 19,* 3–22.

Curci, A., & Luminet, O. (2006). Follow-up of a cross-national comparison on flashbulb and event memory for the September 11th attacks. *Memory, 14,* 329–344.

Curci, A., Luminet, O., Finkenauer, C., & Gisle, L. (2001). Flashbulb memories in social groups: A comparative study of the memory of French President Mitterrand's death in a French and a Belgian group, *Memory, 9,* 81–101.

Dimitrau, E., Hornik, K., Leisch, F., Meyer, D., & Weingessel, A. (2006). *E1071: Misc functions of the Department of Statistics (e1071), TU Wien. R package version 1.5–15.* URL http://wiki.r-project.org/rwiki/doku.php?id=packages:cran:e1071

Embretson, S. E., & Reise, S. P. (2000). *Item response theory for psychologists.* Mahwah, NJ: Lawrence Erlbaum Associates Inc.

Eysenck, H. J. (1953). *The structure of human personality.* London: Methuen.

Finkenauer, C., Luminet, O., Gisle, L., El-Ahmadi, A., Van der Linden, M., & Philippot, P. (1998). Flashbulb memories and the underlying mechanism of their formation: Toward an emotional-integrative model. *Memory and Cognition, 26,* 516–531.

Fossati, A., Beauchaine, T. P., Grazioli, F., Carretta, I., Cortinovis, F., & Maffei, C. (2005). A latent structure analysis of diagnostic and statistical manual of mental disorders, fourth edition, narcissistic personality disorder criteria. *Comprehensive Psychiatry*, *46*, 361–367.

Gangestad, S., & Snyder, M. (1985). "To carve nature at its joints": On the existence of discrete classes in personality. *Psychological Review*, *92*, 317–349.

Gleaves, D. H., Lowe, M. R., Snow, A. C., Green, B. A., & Murphy-Eberenz, K. P. (2000). Continuity and discontinuity models of bulimia nervosa: A taxometric analysis. *Journal of Abnormal Psychology*, *109*, 56–68.

Greenacre, M. J. (1993). *Correspondence analysis in practice*. London: Academic Press.

Hambleton, R. K., Swaminathan, H., & Rogers, H. J. (1991). *Fundamentals of item response theory*. Newbury Park, CA: Sage.

Hankin, B. L., Fraley, R. C., Lahey, B. B., & Waldman, I. D. (2005). Is depression best viewed as a continuum or discrete category? A taxometric analysis of childhood and adolescent depression in a population-based sample. *Journal of Abnormal Psychology*, *114*, 96–110.

Higgins, E. T. (1987). Self-discrepancy: A theory relating self and affect. *Psychological Review*, *94*, 319–340.

Kim, J-O., & Mueller, C. W. (1978). *Factor analysis: Statistical methods and practical issues*. Newbury Park, CA: Sage.

Kvavilashvili, L., Mirani, J., Schlagman, S., & Kornbrot, D. E. (2003). Comparing flashbulb memories of September 11 and death of Princess Diana: Effects of time delays and nationality. *Applied Cognitive Psychology*, *17*, 1017–1031.

Larsen, S. F. (1992). Potential flashbulb: Memories of ordinary news as the baseline. In E. Winograd & U. Neisser (Eds.), *Affect and accuracy in recall: Studies of "flashbulb memories"* (pp. 32–64). New York: Cambridge University Press.

Lazarsfeld, P. F., & Henry, N. W. (1968). *Latent structure analysis*. Boston: Houghton Mill.

Luce, D. R., & Suppes, P. (2002). Representational measurement theory. In H. Pashler & J. Wixted (Eds.), *Stevens' handbook of experimental psychology* (Vol. 4, pp. 1–41). New York: Wiley.

Luminet, O., Curci, A., Marsh, E., Wessel, I., Constantin, T., Gencoz, F., et al. (2004). The cognitive, emotional, and social impacts of the September 11 attacks: Group differences in memory for the reception context and the determinants of flashbulb memory. *Journal of General Psychology*, *131*, 197–224.

McCutcheon, A. L. (1987). *Latent class analysis*. Newbury Park, CA: Sage.

McCutcheon, A. L. (2002). Basic concepts and procedures in single and multiple group latent class analysis. In J. A. Hagenaars & A. L. McCutcheon (Eds.), *Applied latent class analysis* (pp. 56–88). New York: Cambridge University Press.

Meehl, P. E. (1992). Factors and taxa, traits and types. Differences of degree and differences of kind. *Journal of Personality*, *60*, 117–174.

Meehl, P. E. (1999). Clarifications about taxometric method. *Applied and Preventive Psychology*, *8*, 165–174.

Meehl, P. E. (2004) What's in a taxon? *Journal of Abnormal Psychology*, *113*, 39–43.

Meehl, P. E., & Golden, R. (1982). Taxometric methods. In P. Kendall & J. Butcher (Eds.), *Handbook of research methods in clinical psychology* (pp. 127–181). New York: Wiley.

Moustaki, I. (1996). A latent trait and a latent class model for mixed observed variables. *British Journal of Mathematical and Social Psychology*, *49*, 313–334.

Moustaki, I. (2001). *GENLAT: A computer program for fitting a one- or two-factor latent variable model to categorical, metric and mixed observed items with missing values.* Technical report, Statistics Department, London School of Economics and Political Science, UK.

Muraki, E., & Bock, R. D. (1998). *PARSCALE (version 3.5): Parameter scaling of rating data.* Chicago, IL: Scientific Software, Inc.

Muthen, L. K., & Muthen, B. O. (1998). *Mplus user's guide.* Los Angeles: Muthen & Muthen.

Myung, I. J. (2003). Tutorial on maximum likelihood estimation. *Journal of Mathematical Psychology, 47,* 90–100.

Neisser, U., & Harsch, N. (1992). Phantom flashbulbs: False recollections of hearing the news about Challenger. In E. Winograd & U. Neisser (Eds.), *Affect and accuracy in recall: Studies of "flashbulb memories"* (pp. 9–31). New York: Cambridge University Press.

Pezdek, K. (2003). Event memory and autobiographical memory for the events of September 11, 2001. *Applied Cognitive Psychology, 17,* 1033–1045.

Pillemer, D. B. (1984). Flashbulb memories of the assassination attempt on President Reagan. *Cognition, 16,* 63–80.

R Development Core Team. (2006). *R: A language and environment for statistical computing.* R Foundation for Statistical Computing, Vienna, Austria. ISBN 3–900051–07–0, URL http://www.R-project.org/

Rasch, G. (1960). *Probabilistic models for some intelligence and attainment tests.* Copenhagen: Danmarks Paedogogiske Institut.

Rizopoulos, D. (2007). ltm: An R package for latent variable modelling and item response theory analyses. *Journal of Statistical Software, 17,* 1–25.

Rost, J., & Langeheine, R. (Eds.). (1997). *Applications of latent trait and latent class models in the social sciences.* Münster: Waxmann.

Ruscio, J., Haslam, N., & Ruscio, A. M. (2006). *Introduction to the taxometric method: A practical guide.* Mahwah, NJ: Lawrence Erlbaum Associates Inc.

Schmidt, N. B., Kotov, R., & Joiner, T. E. (2004). *Taxometrics: Toward a new diagnostic scheme for psychopathology.* Washington, DC: American Psychological Association.

Schmolck, H., Buffalo, E. A., & Squire, L. R. (2000). Memory distortions develop over time: Recollections of the O. J. Simpson trial verdict after 15 and 32 months. *Psychological Science, 11,* 39–45.

Schwarz, G. (1978). Estimating the dimension of a model. *Annals of Statistics, 6,* 461–464.

Smith, M. C., Bibi, U., & Sheard, D. E. (2003). Evidence for the differential impact of time and emotion on personal and event memories for September 11, 2001. *Applied Cognitive Psychology, 17,* 1047–1055.

Tekcan, A., Ece, B., Gülgöz, S., & Er, N. (2003). Autobiographical and event memory for 9/11: Changes across one year. *Applied Cognitive Psychology, 17,* 1057–1066.

Thissen, D. (1991). *MULTILOG user's guide: Multiple, categorical item analysis and test scoring using item response theory.* Chicago: Scientific Software, Inc.

Tulving, E. (1983). *Elements of episodic memory.* New York: Oxford University Press.

Van de Geer, J. P. (1993). *Multivariate analysis of categorical data: Applications.* Newbury Park, CA: Sage.

Van der Pol, F., Langeheine, R., & de Jong, W. (1998). *PANMARK 3 user manual.* Voorburg: Netherlands Central Bureau of Statistics.

Vermunt, J. (1997). *Log-linear and event history analysis with missing data* (Version 1.0). Tilburg University, The Netherlands.

Vermunt, J., & Magidson, J. (2005). *Latent GOLD 4.0 user's guide*. Belmont, MA: Statistical Innovations Inc.

Waller, N. G., & Meehl, P. E. (1998). *Multivariate taxometric procedures: Distinguishing types from continua*. Thousand Oaks, CA: Sage Publications.

Waller, N. G., Putnam, F. W., & Carlson, E. B. (1996). Types of dissociation and dissociative types: A taxometric analysis of dissociative experiences. *Psychological Methods, 1*, 300–321.

Waller, N. G., & Ross, C. A. (1997). The prevalence and biometric structure of pathological dissociation in the general population: Taxometric and behaviour genetic findings. *Journal of Abnormal Psychology, 106*, 499–510.

Williams, D. M., & Hollan, J. D. (1981). The process of retrieval from very long-term memory. *Cognitive Science, 5*, 87–119.

Williamson, D. A., Womble, L. G., Smeets, M. A. M., Netemeyer, R. G., Thew, J. M., Kutlesic, V., et al. (2002). Latent structure of eating disorder symptoms: A factor analytic and taxometric investigation. *American Journal of Psychiatry, 159*, 412–418.

Winograd, E., & Killinger, W. A. (1983). Relating age at encoding in early childhood to adult recall: Development of flashbulb memories. *Journal of Experimental Psychology, 112*, 413–422.

Wright, D. B. (1993). Recall of the Hillsborough disaster over time: Systematic biases of "flashbulb" memories. *Applied Cognitive Psychology, 7*, 129–138.

Wright, D. B., Gaskell, G. D., & O'Muircheartaigh, C. (1998). Flashbulb memory assumptions: Using national surveys to explore cognitive phenomena. *British Journal of Psychology, 89*, 103–121.

Wright, D. B., & Nunn, J. A. (2000). Similarities within event clusters in autobiographical memory. *Applied Cognitive Psychology, 14*, 479–489.

Zimowski, M. F., Muraki, E., Mislevy, R. J., & Bock, R. D. (1996). *BILOG-MG. Multiple-group IRT analysis and test maintenance for binary items*. Chicago, IL: Scientific Software International.

2 Flashbulb memory methods[1]

Daniel B. Wright

The observation that some events are more memorable than others, and that some of the events on the high side of the memorability distribution are important news events, is the empirical basis of the flashbulb memory (FBM) phenomenon. As a scientific finding, it is trivial. Of course events vary in how memorable they are (and hence have a distribution), and no prizes are won for saying that some of the events that occur throughout this distribution, including the most memorable end, are news events. There are some interesting scientific questions that can be asked about FBMs, but these questions must go beyond this initial observation. Many FBM studies fail to address the more interesting questions because the way the initial FBM research (Brown & Kulik, 1977) was carried out prompted many subsequent researchers to design studies that are not appropriate to answer many of the interesting questions. Many (not all) of the scientific questions of interest to cognitive researchers about FBMs are causal, while the methods used in the prototypical FBM study are more appropriate for addressing associative questions. Further, the methods that tend to be used are well suited for differentiating among people and groups, which is arguably of more interest to sociologists, oral historians, and social psychologists than to cognitive psychologists, who are usually more interested in differences between situations and tasks (Wright & Gaskell, 1995).

Before progressing, it is worth making two things clear. First, when referring to the typical FBM study I am referring to a study where a hundred or so people from an opportunity sample are asked questions about what they were doing when they heard about a single news event. Second, the criticisms I raise are partially self-directed (for example, Wright, 1993), so the more pithy remarks are about me. I am playing devil's advocate, to some extent, but this approach highlights the difficulties.

The two basic requirements for the scientific process are measurement and theory. You must have measurement and some measurement theory (Hand, 2004) and explore some set of hypotheses that are part of a complex network of hypotheses (Wright, 2006). This chapter is divided into two sections on the basis of these two requirements. The first section examines what FBMs are and what they are not, and how researchers can decide whether a memory is a

Figure 2.1 A simplified FBM model, based on Brown and Kulik (1977) and subsequent models.

FBM. I describe various choices researchers have to make in deciding what their domain of study is and some of the methods that could be used. The second section focuses on the main scientific questions that can be asked once the conceptual issues of the first section have been addressed.

I will not discuss details of the different FBM models because there are excellent reviews in other parts of this book (for example, Luminet, Chapter 3) and also a major theme of this chapter is that there are still matters about FBM that need to be resolved before detailed discussion of the models should be made. However, it is beneficial to produce a simplified schematic of the basic model (Figure 2.1). Most FBM researchers describe how some combination of emotion, importance, and survival impact combines so that events which score high on this combination evoke some special mechanism that produces good memories. How these event characteristics combine is where the detailed discussions of FBM theorizing lie. The special mechanism hypothesis is that the qualities of FBMs cannot be accounted for by the variability in memories produced by normal processes.

CONCEPTUAL AND MEASUREMENT QUESTIONS ABOUT FLASHBULB MEMORIES

What is the population under investigation?

Figure 2.2 shows a distribution of memorability for a set of events. For now, assume that "memorability" is some variable about the quality of memories, and that beyond some value these are FBMs and if the value is less then the memory is not a FBM. People have used different ways to conceptualize this and to measure it, and these are discussed below. As with any distribution, before asking any empirical questions it is necessary to ask "What is the population of events that form this distribution?" It is unlikely that anyone believes the population of interest is just FBMs. If they did they would encounter conceptual problems categorizing FBMs and theoretical problems trying to describe what FBMs are without saying what they are not (i.e., discriminant validity). So what is the population? Is it all events experienced? All news events? All events that people recall vividly? All assassinations? Similarly, is the distribution for all people, some selected sub-population, or just an individual?

Brown and Kulik's (1977) methods provide clues to their intent. While

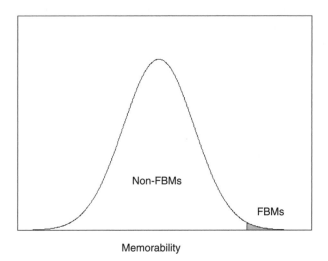

Memorability

Figure 2.2 A distribution, for some population of events, of memorability, with
events beyond some value being called FBMs.

most of the events about which they asked their sample were news events,
they also asked people to report about personal events. Thus, they were probably interested in all events that might be recalled vividly. Rather than probing
Brown and Kulik for the population of events that their catchy phrase—
flashbulb memories—was referring to, some researchers (e.g., McCloskey,
Wible, & Cohen, 1988; Neisser, 1982) attacked their assumption that FBMs
were accurate (how to differentiate the good and less good memories from
Figure 2.1), and others (e.g., Conway et al., 1994; Finkenauer et al., 1998)
went on to to develop Brown and Kulik's FBM model (how the emotion,
importance, and survival qualities from Figure 2.1 combine into memorability). Unfortunately, Brown and Kulik presented essentially no data in their
original study to support their model,[2] and it is unclear how much further
insight subsequent research has given to the concept. While memory accuracy
and models of memory are clearly important, making statements about
memories for events in some part of Figure 2.2 without considering the population being examined makes inference difficult.

It is worth thinking about some of the possible populations of events. This
is a difficult task, since there are no agreed definitions of what is an event or
what is a memory. There are questions about how microscopic or extended an
event should be, and what relationship the person needs to have with the
event. These are problems in general for memory research (Rubin, 1992). One
possibility is considering all events of which at the time somebody with a
typical adult's cognitive abilities would be able to narrate their experiences.
This set of events is what many autobiographical memory researchers might
consider their domain of interest. Another possibility is all events that can,
given the right prompt, be recalled at testing. One of the differences between

these two approaches is that many of the events that occurred will not be remembered, so the former would include events low in memorability (below some threshold for recall) and the latter would not. The latter, however, would make it easier to study false memories.

Consider two possible populations. The first is the population defined above and often assumed, though not always explicitly, for much auto-biographical memory research: all events for which a typical adult could have given a reasonable account at the time of the event. This allows the population under investigation to include events that some people would forget. This is important because forgetting events, including traumatic events, is an important area of interest (Brewin, 2003; McNally, 2003). This population has the disadvantage that it would not include events that did not happen, so this population would not be appropriate for researching false memories.[3]

The second population is one where the researchers are interested in a single event. For example, later in this chapter Judith Zur's (1998) research on La Violencia is described. Her interest was primarily aimed to document this event, not to evaluate different memory theories. Psychologists often use case studies either to illustrate a theory or to falsify one. A famous example from psychology is when Festinger, Riecken, and Schacter (1956) used the observation of a single event to illustrate cognitive dissonance. When a group of people, who believed that at a specific time aliens from the planet Clarion would save them from a great flood, realized this was not going to happen, their beliefs became stronger, in line with cognitive dissonance theory. An example from FBM research is using the incredibly vivid personal memories astronomers at the Anglo-Australian observatory had at the discovery of Supernova 1987-A (Wright & Gaskell, 1995). This illustrated that strong personal feelings can be associated with FBM memories for an event of relatively little societal importance.

What should the population of events/memories be for cognitive psychologists?

Several possibilities. One good population is all events that, if experienced, could be described by the typical adult.

What is memorability and how is it measured?

The next question is: What is the x-axis in Figure 2.2? If it is used to classify FBMs, then it must be something for which FBMs are at one extreme. Brown and Kulik (1977) and subsequent FBM researchers suggest that the prototypical FBM is an extremely long-lasting and vivid recollection. I will consider three ways of conceptualizing memorability (see also Curci, Chapter 1, this volume). The first two (categorical ratings based on Tulving's (1985) remember/know memory distinction and clarity ratings) allow the participants to define memorability, although for the first it is a discrete measure and the second a continuous measure. The final way uses the responses to memory questions and creates latent variables out of these.

Tulving (1985) differentiated two types of memories. He described "remember" memories as those that allow the person to mentally re-live the event. He described how they evoked autonoetic consciousness, a way to place oneself in the memory. He described "know" memories as those that lacked the re-living aspect of remember memories. This distinction is used in many memory studies (see also Gardiner, 1988) where participants are shown, for example, a list of words and later asked if they have seen these words before. If they say "yes" they are asked to write R if it is a remember memory and K if it is a know memory. Within autobiographical memory research there has been a move away from having participants choose between just a K (for Know) and an R (for Remember) response to choosing among K, R, and F or G (for Familiar or Guess) responses, because researchers felt that some participants were using K responses inappropriately (Gardiner, Ramponi, & Richardson-Klavehn, 2002).

The re-living self-referential description of remember memories suggests these might be similar to what researchers mean when they describe FBMs. The problem for FBM research is that in practice R responses do not capture what people usually think of as a true FBM. In a typical recognition memory study people may be shown 50 words and later asked if their memory is a K or an R memory. Many respond R, but it is questionable whether these memories are FBMs. What would be necessary is an additional category, like SRM (for super-remember-memory), to capture what it is to be a FBM. The problem with this is that Tulving's original distinction and the addition of the F category are both based on research from different areas that suggest these are qualitatively different types of memory. More research would be necessary to see if the F/K/R/SRM taxonomy was appropriate.

If four ordered categories are used, it is likely that many people would interpret the choice in a similar manner to a rating scale from "not a clear memory" to "a very clear memory". This is another alternative: ask people directly for their ratings on a clarity scale. This assumes that the scale is unidimensional and it relies on people's individual interpretations of the scale being similar. Another difficulty is that asking only a single question can be unreliable. Finally, many researchers believe that "clarity" is not the only aspect that should contribute to the flashbulb-ness dimension, but that consistency, details of memory, etc., should also be used in the measurement.

The third approach circumvents the problem of having only a single question. Brown and Kulik (1977) describe one of the defining characteristics of a FBM that people can recall the four Ws: what they were doing, how they heard, who they were with, and where they were.[4] Responses to these questions can be aggregated in some way to define the x-axis. Three ways of aggregating the data are considered here: counting the number of responses, conducting a latent trait model, and conducting a latent class model.

Moustaki (1996) provides detailed comparisons among these three methods and she does this with specific reference to FBMs so her paper is particularly valuable for FBM researchers (see also Curci, Chapter 1, this volume). Here these methods are briefly described.

The "counting the number of responses" approach involves either counting the number of times someone positively responds to each of four Ws or counting them but allowing some partial credit. The latent trait and latent class models deserve further explanation. Bartholomew and Knott (1999) described how several different latent variable models all have a similar form, and they also use FBM data to aid their explanation. Latent trait models take several categorical observed variables and try to account for covariation in responses by assuming that there are a small number (often one) of continuous latent variables underlying the responses. They are popular in education, where they are often called item response models, and are analogous to exploratory factor analysis when the observed variables are categorical. This procedure would create a dimension for the x-axis of Figure 2.2. Latent class models account for the responses by assuming that there are groups of people. People within the same group have similar probabilities for responding in certain ways, but there are large differences between people of different groups. These are popular in sociology and are becoming more popular in psychology. As discussed in the next section, it is sometimes difficult to differentiate these approaches on an empirical basis.

Are there differences between these approaches?

The choice of what the x-axis in Figure 2.2 is, and how to measure it, are important and inter-related questions. I will compare a couple of the choices for illustrative purposes. First, consider whether to use participants' responses to a clarity scale or the number of positive responses to the what, how, where, and who questions. In Wright, Gaskell, and O'Muircheartaigh (1998, Exp. 2) a large number of participants from a representative sample of the UK adult population were asked about Margaret Thatcher's resignation. They were asked how clear their memory was of the event on a 1 (Cannot remember the event) to 5 (Completely clear) rating scale, and also asked for their responses on the four W-questions. Given that presumably psychologists are astounded by people being able to recall these Ws—otherwise why would *Cognition* have published Brown and Kulik's original paper—one would expect that people who could recall all four Ws would give themselves very high ratings on the clarity scale. However, people who responded positively to all of these gave on average responses near the midpoint of the clarity scale, certainly not responses that are commensurate with the live, photographic re-living descriptions often given to FBMs. Thus, the choice of using responses to the Ws or rating scales can provide very different interpretations for what FBMs are and produce very different estimates for the number of people with FBMs for any given event.

The second comparison is between latent trait and latent class analysis. Moustaki (1996; see also Curci, 2005, and Chapter 1 of this volume) goes through the Thatcher resignation data in detail. She shows how the data can be used in these models to produce either a single latent trait along which people vary or two latent classes to which people can belong. Bartholomew and Knott (1999; for an introductory textbook on these procedures, see Bartholomew, Steele, Moustaki, & Galbraith, 2008) discuss how it is very difficult to differentiate these models empirically and that the choice often depends on the particular theory one has for FBMs. For example, there is much discussion about whether memory retrieval is based on a threshold model, where people either remember the event or not, versus whether there is some continuous memory strength dimension that predicts the probability of remembering the event. If you assume that people either have or do not have a FBM, as if some trigger either fires or does not fire, then a latent class model is probably more appropriate. However, if you assume that FBMs are simply at one end of some memorability scale, then the latent trait model is probably more appropriate. Brown and Kulik's original description of FBMs, where they adopt Livingston's (1967) "Now Print" mechanism, suggests a threshold model that is more consistent with the latent class models. Thus, the class versus trait question is of importance to the "special mechanism" debate if one believes the mechanism is like Brown and Kulik's description (and that ordinary memories vary along a continuum). However, other types of "special mechanisms" could be more continuous in nature, and therefore the choice of class versus trait does not strictly depend on the special mechanism debate unless one takes a restrictive view of the special mechanism.

There is also a statistical difficulty because it is often not possible to distinguish between class and trait models. Bartholomew and colleagues (2008) point out that often the covariance matrix of observed variables can be equally well recreated by either assuming a set of discrete latent classes or by assuming continuous latent traits. This means that the models will fit equally well. When the latent classes are very different from each other (and within the classes they are relatively homogeneous), then it is possible to differentiate classes and traits. The taxometric approach (Ruscio, Haslam, & Ruscio, 2006; Waller & Meehl, 1998; see also De Boeck, Wilson, & Acton, 2005) has become a popular method for doing this in clinical psychology and it could also be used in FBM research. Within memory research a popular approach is to assume that there are two processes, one of which is continuous and one discrete. However, even with the large number of trials from the typical recognition memory study it is often difficult to distinguish this model from others (Malmberg, 2002) and much of the data are consistent with both processes being continuous (Wixted, 2007). Because of these difficulties FBM researchers should consider both the trait and the class models of FBMs.

> *How to measure FBMs?*
>
> Use multiple measures. Consider both trait and class models (latent variable models were discussed here, but the data reduction techniques discussed by Curci in Chapter 1 can also be used).

Summary on measurement

Science requires several decisions about measurement. If FBM researchers want to advance beyond the trivial observation that some people have good memories (which have various correlated attributes) for some news events, it is necessary to be explicit about:

1   What the population under investigation is.
2   What distinguishes FBMs from other events.
3   How this variable should be measured.

Research needs to be conducted to describe the distribution that is naively shown in Figure 2.2 as a normal distribution. At present, very little can be said about this distribution, which makes any scientific statements about FBMs difficult to interpret.

TYPES OF FBM HYPOTHESES

There is some population, P, about which the researchers want to make inference. It is usually impossible to study this entire population and therefore a sample, S, is taken from it. Making inference about a population from data of a sample has a long tradition—for example, on the first page of Gossett's (1908, p. 398) classic *t* test paper: any result "is only of value in so far as it enables us to form a judgment as to the statistical constants of the population"—but requires certain rules. Depending on whether the researchers assume S is representative of P, there are two types of inference that can be made from data of S about P. If S is assumed to be representative of P, then provided that sampling and measurement error are taken into account the researchers can make positive statements about all of P.

For example, suppose you have a sample of memories that you think are representative of the population of interest, and find the correlation between the emotional reaction at the time of the event and the clarity of the subsequent memory has a 95% confidence interval of 0.3 to 0.4. This would allow you to conclude, with some confidence (although what exactly "confidence" means is another thorny issue), that the correlation in the population is within this band.

Suppose instead that you are not willing to assume that the sample is representative of the population either because the people chosen are not representative of the population of people or the memories chosen are not representative of the population of these people's memories. Instead you assume the sample is just representative of some (often unknown) subset of the population. Finding an interval of 0.3 to 0.4 only allows you to say that you are confident that the correlation is in this range for this particular subset.

This is called local inference (Lunneborg, 2000). If someone has put forward the hypothesis that "for all subsets of the population the correlation is 0.5", then the finding that this does not hold for any particular subset allows this "for all subsets" hypothesis to be rejected. Thus, the hypothesis that the motions of all bodies conform to Newton's laws can be rejected by precise observation of the orbit of the planet Mercury. This is why Popperian falsification is used in many sciences. However, while "for all subsets" hypotheses are popular in some of the sciences, it is difficult to argue for their applicability with reference to FBMs. It is likely that people would expect correlations to vary in different subsets of a population (as is usually true in the medical and social sciences; see Engels, Schmidt, Terrin, Olkin, & Lau, 2000).

Both of these are associative hypotheses, in that they are about the population joint distribution (often measured by the correlation) of emotion and clarity for either the entire population or for some subset of the population. They are not about causality, although as discussed below they can be used to inform causal theories. There are questions about the role of associative hypotheses in science (Cronbach, 1957; Fodor, 1991; Spearman, 1904; Wright, 2006), but it is clear that, particularly within FBM research, associate hypotheses are often discussed.

The sample, S, is often divided into groups. Suppose there are two groups, S1 and S2. This division could be based on something outside the control of the researcher, such as whether the participants were watching TV when some FBM event occurred, or the participants' gender. In these cases it is a "quasi-experiment" and associative inferences are usually made (i.e., emotion and clarity are associated, rather than emotion causes clarity). In some cases researchers might use the associative finding (TV is associated with a certain types of memories) to infer some causal relationship (the graphic TV images cause certain types of memories), but this requires further assumptions (such as that those watching the television are similar to those not watching the television). In other cases making causal inference from an association is not possible (for example, gender cannot cause anything; see Holland, 1986).

If the division into S1 and S2 is random, as often occurs with experiments, the researchers are able to make causal inferences more easily, albeit with some caveats (Cook & Campbell, 1979). The critical aspect of drawing causal inferences is that the two groups should differ only by sampling error (which can be estimated if random assignment is used) and whatever the researchers want to make the causal inference about. The philosophers call this the *ceteris paribus* conditional, and as Cook and Campbell (1979, p. 5) put it: "random assignment is the great ceteris paribus—that is, other things being equal—of causal inference." It is not possible to randomly allocate somebody into a condition where they think, for example, that the death of Princess Diana was an important event. Most FBM studies compare naturally occurring groups which may differ in many ways other than just what they thought about the event. In fact, it is the aim of much sociology and social psychology to document which groups of people are most affected by particular events. To make causal inference about, for example, thinking the princess's death was an important event requires some assumptions. While it would clearly be wrong for researchers to assume that, for example, people who thought Diana's death was a very important event were the same as others in all other ways, a researcher might feel that it is plausible to assume that any of the other differences are not associated with the dependent variable, memory quality. This assumption is of course testable if enough of the other possible confounding variables have been accurately measured.[5]

The purist might argue that because FBM data often cannot unequivocally lead to causal conclusions, these data are of no value in reaching causal conclusions. This narrow and short-sighted view would also send much neuropsychology and astronomy data to the dustbin. I am often asked by students if they are allowed to put forward some causal theory after collecting data from a quasi-experiment, as if the causal theory police are on the prowl. People put forward causal theories with no data—or in the case of Brown and Kulik (1977), with some of their data counter to their theory; see note 2—without fear of arrest, so having some data to help guide theory construction is an improvement!

One of most overused mantras of first-year psychology statistics is "correlation does not imply causation". Strictly speaking, finding a correlation between, say, emotion and clarity does not imply that emotion causes clarity, but finding a correlation does show that there almost certainly exists some causal relationship between various parts of the complex network of hypotheses within which these two attributes are embedded (see Meehl & Waller, 2002; Wright, 2006). If this network is viewed spatially, where the number of intervening nodes is a measure of distance, then because, all other things being equal, simpler models should be preferred to more complex models (i.e., Occam's razor), it is best to consider causal relationships between the nearest events as more likely than more distant relationships. Further, because some events are separated in time (e.g., emotion at the time of an event and clarity of a subsequent memory) and, outside of some physics hypotheses, causes precede effects, this can also help in locating possible causal relationships.

FBM research is usually correlational/quasi-experimental. The data are about associations. While specific causal statements can be made on the basis of correlational data, there are often other plausible explanations, including that some other variables cause variation in both attributes (Simon, 1954).

For example, while most FBM/autobiographical memory research shows that emotion and clarity are positively correlated, it appears this may be due to the event's importance being causally related to both (Wright & Nunn, 2000). This is supported by numerous laboratory studies which indicate that heightened emotion negatively affects memory clarity (Deffenbacher, Bornstein, Penrod, & McGorty, 2004). This is an example where the associative hypothesis (that emotion and clarity are positively related) appears in the opposite direction from the causal hypothesis (that emotion impairs memory).

While causal inference from correlational data is possible, it has numerous pitfalls, it is open to alternative interpretations, and requires caveats and assumptions. This does not mean that the data from a typical FBM study are not valuable, much of them are, but it does question whether alternative designs could address many of the causal questions in better ways.

The case study approach

Any discussion of FBM methods requires some mention of the case study approach to science. Case studies are a popular method in neuropsychology where the case is the individual person, but the phrase "case study" also applies when the case is an individual event (Wells & Windschitl, 1999). Case studies are an extreme example of the sample being representative of only a subset of the population, but they can be useful. For example, a typical method in long-term memory research with children is to show them the same event and then later test them on this event, comparing across either experimental or non-experimental groups. By using the same event, some control is provided for the study. However, it does mean that the researcher needs to be cautious about generalizing to other events. The difficulty with the single event approach with FBM research is that differences in the events are often the key variables under investigation. Therefore, controlling the event is counter-productive.

If a researcher is interested in making inferences about all events, then studying only, for example, the Hillsborough football stadium disaster limits what can be said about all events. Wright (1993) found systematic differences in people's memories of this disaster across time. He could not conclude anything in particular about events, even those of FBM calibre, only that one particular event, which was arguably of FBM calibre for many of his participants, yielded memories incompatible with the hypothesis "for all subsets of events of flashbulb calibre, there are no systematic biases in memories".

Wright (1993) does say something about the Hillsborough event. As such, it is of interest to people who actually want to know about the event. This is different from the aims of most cognitive psychologists, but in line with researchers from other disciplines. Some of the best case studies relevant to FBMs are by anthropologists studying memories for some of the bizarre and often horrific rituals in other cultures (Whitehouse, 2000). There have also been valuable studies of particular political and cultural events. In one of the best studies of FBMs, Judith Zur (1998) examined La Violencia, the violence surrounding the ethnic war in Guatemala. The authorities forbid discussion of the atrocities: "The entire history of la violencia can be read as a war against memory, an Orwellian falsification of memory, a falsification of reality" (Zur, 1998, p. 159). Zur's research provides great insight into this often forgotten war, but it also provides insight to the workings of memory in a situation that it would be immoral to mimic in a laboratory. She provides graphic illustrations that memories, some accurate and some distorted, prevail even when people are not allowed to talk about the kidnappings and murders. Zur's work provides an example, outside cognitive psychology, of using the case study approach applied to memory.

As the case study approach is relatively rare within cognitive psychology (outside neuropsychology where the individual is often the case), the question is why it became the method of choice for FBM researchers. Brown and Kulik's (1977) original study used multiple events and this allowed them to make valuable comparison across events. They used part of these data as evidence for their model. Although, as discussed in note 2, some of their data do not support this model, their design was a good approach. Most cognitive psychologists are interested in how different events elicit different types of memories. Therefore, it is surprising that the FBM literature has tended to use single events, or a small number of events, rather than asking about several events that differ by the attributes of interest.

I believe there are two reasons why cognitive psychologists have opted for the case study approach when researching FBMs. The first is the desire to examine consistency (or accuracy). In order to do this, researchers have to question participants soon after an event, and this is only practical for a single event. The second reason is that since Neisser's (1982) and McCloskey et al.'s (1988) case studies, which effectively falsified Brown and Kulik's (1977) bold "for all sets" conjecture that FBMs are very accurate, this method has gained acceptance beyond reproach as the way to study the phenomenon in general, rather than a method limited to falsifying bold conjectures. The next major news event will trigger a series of studies on FBMs. It seems that FBM studies often begin with a news event rather than a research question. The growing awareness of the FBM concept has made the study of FBMs acceptable in its own right. Figure 2.3 shows that citations of Brown and Kulik and use of the phrase "flashbulb memory" have increased dramatically in recent years. The study of FBMs has become its own area of research but, as mentioned in the first half of this paper, it has become an area of research without it being clear what FBMs are. This is an unfortunate situation.

Summary on hypotheses

There are two broad types of hypothesis: causal and associative. The design of the study should be congruent with the type of hypothesis of most

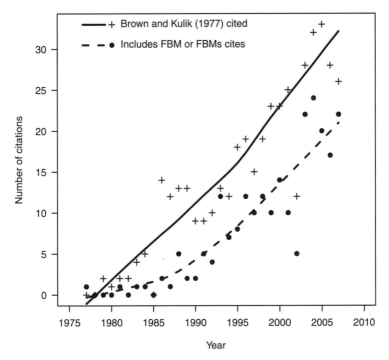

Figure 2.3 The number of times Brown and Kulik (1977) has been cited each year since publication (shown with a +) and the number of times the phrase "flashbulb memory" or "flashbulb memories" was used in titles and abstracts (shown with a •). The data are from the *ISI Web of Knowledge* collected on 13 March 2008, and go up to 2007.

importance because it is difficult to make inference of one type from a study designed to investigate the other type. Wright (2006) describes the differences between these types of hypotheses and their associated methods with reference to eyewitness testimony research, and many of the same issues apply. FBM researchers also have to decide whether they are interested in differences between people or between events. For example, Wright et al. (1998) were explicit that they were interested in group differences. Therefore they asked a large representative sample of UK adults about a couple of events, so that they could make positive statements about the associations for these events. If the interest is in group differences, then this is the right approach. If the interest is in how somebody would remember different types of events, then the better approach is to ask a relatively small number of people about a large number of events (Wright & Gaskell, 1995), as is often done in other areas of autobiographical memory research (Wright & Nunn, 2000).

CONCLUSION

As a postgraduate at the London School of Economics (LSE), I was researching what had become known as everyday memories. I would go to the library and dutifully photocopy lots of papers, some of which I would read. So that I could read without interruption, I would go off to other departments' seminar rooms. One day I found myself in the philosophy seminar room under a picture of Imre Lakatos reading Banaji and Crowder's (1989) attack on everyday memory research; I was angry. How dare somebody attack the sacrosanct topic on which I was conducting my PhD research!

The irony of my physical location only became apparent in subsequent reads. While at the LSE, Lakatos (1977) had argued that research programmes were either degenerative or progressive. Each had a core of beliefs that remained unchallenged. In the case of the everyday memory movement, Banaji and Crowder were arguing that the everyday memory movement was degenerative: "no theories that have unprecedented explanatory power have been produced; no new principles of memory have been discovered, and no methods of data collection have been developed that add sophistication or precision" (1989, p. 1185).

I now view the Banaji and Crowder (1989) paper as a very positive one for the study of everyday memories. It forces people to step back and ask questions about the methods they use, and they point people towards ways of making everyday memory research generalizable. Just because people use a particular type of stimulus does not excuse them from asking if there are better methods. It is important to make sure that FBM research avoids being in a degenerative rut. As Figure 2.3 shows, FBM research is an increasingly popular topic, but this would be problematic if its popularity protected researchers from exploring the core of what it is to be a FBM. It is necessary to develop a theory of measurement that allows FBMs to be studied in relation to other memories and to use methods that are appropriate to the research questions. The current research has shown that there exist some events that produce good memories and some events that produce bad memories. FBM researchers need to use other methods to go beyond this initial statement.

As I said at the beginning of this paper, I am playing devil's advocate to a certain degree. This book is testament that the study of FBMs has made some progress. But more progress can be made.

NOTES

1 This chapter was prepared while Dan Wright was on sabbatical at Florida International University, where he is now full-time. Much thanks to Antonietta Curci and several reviewers for useful comments on previous drafts.

2 This statement deserves further explanation. Brown and Kulik's (1977) main group comparisons, which they use to justify their model that emotion combined with consequentiality produces FBMs, were that Black people had more FBMs than White people for civil rights events, and these events were more consequential events for Black people than for White people. However, in their study Black people also rated both Robert Kennedy's assassination and Ted Kennedy's Chappaquiddick incident as more consequential than White people did, but Black people had fewer FBMs for these events. Similarly, Black people rated Martin Luther King's assassination as more consequential than John F. Kennedy's, but had fewer FBMs for King's assassination. See Wright et al. (1998) for further examples of this type. These observations do not falsify the Brown and Kulik model, but this difficulty in falsifying a causal model with correlation data is a theme of this chapter and one of the reasons why the amount written about FBMs exceeds the amount of scientific progress in understanding them.

3 There are lots of other possibilities. For example, the population in the typical memory recognition study is all the events that participants are given the opportunity to recognize.

4 Beginning with Neisser (1982) there has been much discussion about how accurate responses are to these questions. This is why researchers now usually ask people at two or more points in time. This produces a measure of consistency, rather than accuracy. Winningham, Hyman, and Dinnel (2000) discuss these issues and stress that if researchers want to use consistency as a proxy for accuracy it is important to gather initial reports very soon after the event (see also Coluccia, Bianco, & Brandimonte, 2006).

5 Another design that is sometimes used compares some event that the researchers feel is of FBM calibre with some event that they do not feel is of this calibre. These events usually vary on many variables, including presumably whatever the x-axis of Figure 2.2 is supposed to be. If the researchers wish to claim that differences on any dependent measures are due to some flashbulb-ness of the "FBM event", then they either have to claim that the events only differ on this flashbulb-ness or that no other differences are likely to relate to the dependent measures. It is unlikely that either of these is a valid assumption, thus limiting the inference that can be made from these designs.

REFERENCES

Banaji, M. R., & Crowder, R. G. (1989). The bankruptcy of everyday memory. *American Psychologist, 44*, 1185–1193.

Bartholomew, D. J., & Knott, M. (1999). *Latent variable models and factor analysis* (2nd ed). London: Arnold.

Bartholomew, D. J., Steele. F., Moustaki, I., & Galbraith, J. I. (2008). *Analysis of multivariate social science data* (2nd ed.). London: Chapman & Hall/CRC.

Brewin, C. R. (2003). *Posttraumatic stress disorder: Malady or myth?* New Haven, CT: Yale University Press.

Brown, R., & Kulik, J. (1977). Flashbulb memories. *Cognition, 5*, 73–99.

Coluccia, E., Bianco, C., & Brandimonte, M. A. (2006). Dissociating veridicality, consistency, and confidence in autobiographical and event memories for the *Columbia* shuttle disaster. *Memory, 14*, 452–470.

Conway, M. A., Anderson, S. J., Larsen, S. F., Donnelly, C. M., McDaniel, M. A., McClelland, A. G. R., et al. (1994). The formation of flashbulb memories. *Memory and Cognition, 22*, 326–343.

Cook, T. D., & Campbell, D. T. (1979). *Quasi-experimentation: Design & analysis issues for field settings.* Boston: Houghton Mifflin Company.

Cronbach, L. J. (1957). The two disciplines of scientific psychology. *American Psychologist, 12,* 671–684.

Curci, A. (2005). Latent variable models for the measurement of flashbulb memories: A comparative approach. *Applied Cognitive Psychology, 19,* 3–22.

De Boeck, P., Wilson, M., & Acton, G. S. (2005). A conceptual and psychometric framework for distinguishing categories and dimensions. *Psychological Review, 112,* 129–158.

Deffenbacher, K. A., Bornstein, B. H., Penrod, S. D., & McGorty, E. K. (2004). A meta-analytic review of the effects of high stress on eyewitness memory. *Law and Human Behavior, 28,* 687–706.

Engels, E. A., Schmidt, C. H., Terrin, N., Olkin, I., & Lau, J. (2000). Heterogeneity and statistical significance in meta-analysis: An empirical study of 125 meta-analyses. *Statistics in Medicine, 19,* 1707–1728.

Festinger, L., Riecken, H. W., & Schacter, S. (1956). When prophecy fails: A social and psychological study of a modern group that predicted the destruction of the world. [Originally published Minneapolis: University of Minnesota Press (Harper and Row). Now available from APA print-on-demand at http://books.apa.org/]

Finkenauer, C., Luminet, O., Gisle, L., El-Ahmadi, A., van der Linden, M., & Philippot, P. (1998). Flashbulb memories and the underlying mechanisms of their formation: Toward an emotional-integrative model. *Memory and Cognition, 26,* 516–531.

Fodor, J. A. (1991). You can fool some of the people all of the time, everything else being equal; Hedged laws and psychological explanations. *Mind, 100,* 19–34.

Gardiner, J. M. (1988). Functional aspects of recollective experience. *Memory and Cognition, 16,* 309–313.

Gardiner, J. M., Ramponi, C., & Richardson-Klavehn, A. (2002). Recognition memory and decision processes: A meta-analysis of remember, know, and guess responses. *Memory, 10,* 83–98.

Gossett, W., writing as "Student" (1908). The probable error of the mean. *Biometrika, 6,* 1–25.

Hand, D. J. (2004). *Measurement theory and practice: The world through quantification.* London: Edward Arnold.

Holland, P. W. (1986). Statistics and causal inference. *Journal of the American Statistical Association, 81,* 945–960.

Lakatos, I. (1977). *The methodology of scientific research programmes: Philosophical papers* (Vol. 1). Cambridge, UK: Cambridge University Press.

Livingston, R. B. (1967). Reinforcement. In G. C. Quarton, T. Melnechuck, & F. O. Schmitt (Eds.), *The neurosciences: A study program* (pp. 568–576). New York: Rockefeller University Press.

Lunneborg, C. E. (2000). *Data analysis by resampling: Concepts and applications.* Pacific Grove, CA: Duxbury Press.

Malmberg, K. J. (2002). On the form of ROCs constructed from confidence ratings. *Journal of Experimental Psychology: Learning, Memory, and Cognition, 28,* 380–387.

McCloskey, M., Wible, C. G., & Cohen, N. J. (1988). Is there a special flashbulb-memory mechanism. *Journal of Experimental Psychology: General, 117,* 171–181.

McNally, R. J. (2003). *Remembering trauma*. Cambridge, MA: Harvard University Press.

Meehl, P. E., & Waller, N. G. (2002). The path analysis controversy: A new statistical approach to strong appraisal of verisimilitude. *Psychological Methods, 7*, 283–300.

Moustaki, I. (1996). A latent trait and a latent class model for mixed observed variables. *British Journal of Mathematical and Statistical Psychology, 49*, 313–334.

Neisser, U. (1982). Snapshots or benchmarks? In U. Neisser (Ed.), *Memory observed: Remembering in natural contexts* (pp. 43–48). San Francisco: Freeman.

Rubin, D. C. (1992). Definitions of autobiographical memory. In M. A. Conway, D. C. Rubin, H. Spinnler, & W. A. Wagenaar (Eds.), *Theoretical perspectives on autobiographical memory* (pp. 495–499). The Netherlands: Kluwer Academic Publishers.

Ruscio, J., Haslam, N., & Ruscio, A. M. (2006). *Introduction to the taxometric method: A practical guide*. Mahwah, NJ: Lawrence Erlbaum Associates Inc.

Simon, H. A. (1954). Spurious correlation: A causal interpretation. *Journal of the American Statistical Association, 49*, 467–479.

Spearman, C. (1904). "General Intelligence": Objectively determined and measured. *American Journal of Psychology, 15*, 201–293.

Tulving, E. (1985). How many memory systems are there? *American Psychologist, 40*, 385–398.

Waller, N. G., & Meehl, P. E. (1998). *Multivariate taxometric procedures: Distinguishing types from continua*. Thousand Oaks, CA: Sage.

Wells, G. L., & Windschitl, P. D. (1999). Stimulus sampling in social psychological experimentation. *Personality and Social Psychology Bulletin, 25*, 1115–1125.

Whitehouse, H. (2000). *Arguments and icons: Divergent modes of religiosity*. Oxford, UK: Oxford University Press.

Winningham, R. G., Hyman, I. E., & Dinnel, D. L. (2000). Flashbulb memories? The effects of when the initial memory report was obtained. *Memory, 8*, 209–216.

Wixted, J. T. (2007). Dual-process theory and signal-detection theory of recognition memory. *Psychological Review, 114*, 152–176.

Wright, D. B. (1993). Recall of the Hillsborough disaster over time: Systematic biases of "flashbulb" memories. *Applied Cognitive Psychology, 7*, 129–138.

Wright, D. B. (2006). Causal and associative hypotheses in psychology: Examples from eyewitness testimony research. *Psychology, Public Policy, and Law, 12*, 190–213.

Wright, D. B., & Gaskell, G. D. (1995). Flashbulb memories: Conceptual and methodological issues. *Memory, 3*, 67–80.

Wright, D. B., Gaskell, G. D., & O'Muircheartaigh, C. A. (1998). Flashbulb memory assumptions: Using national surveys to explore cognitive phenomena. *British Journal of Psychology, 89*, 103–122.

Wright, D. B., & Nunn, J. A. (2000). Similarities within event clusters in autobiographical memory. *Applied Cognitive Psychology, 14*, 479–489.

Zur, J. N. (1998). *Violent memories: Mayan war widows in Guatemala*. Oxford, UK: Westview Press.

3 Models for the formation of flashbulb memories[1]

Olivier Luminet

Flashbulb memories (FBMs) are vivid, long-lasting, detailed, and consistent recollections of specific details for the reception context of shocking public events (location, time, presence of others, the informant, one's ongoing activity) (Bohannon, 1988; Brown & Kulik, 1977; Conway et al., 1994; Neisser & Harsch, 1992). Numerous studies have confirmed that a large proportion of individuals are able to report many details of their memory for the reception context, e.g., exact location, ongoing activity, type of informant, and other idiosyncratic details which often include perceptual aspects (Bohannon, 1988; Brown & Kulik, 1977; Conway et al., 1994; Larsen, 1992). There is controversy, however, on the status of FBM as a consistent memory. In some studies FBMs were described as a special class of memories, which persist almost unchanged and are consistent over time (Brown & Kulik, 1977; Conway et al., 1994; Curci & Luminet, 2006; Pillemer, 1984), even after a very long time (Berntsen & Thomsen, 2005). Other studies concluded that FBMs were neither immune to being forgotten nor uncommonly consistent as time passes (Christianson, 1989; McCloskey, Wible, & Cohen, 1988; Nachson & Zelig, 2003; Neisser & Harsch, 1992; Weaver, 1993). Although confidence scores might be persistently high over time, they were unrelated to consistency of the memories themselves (Neisser & Harsch, 1992; Talarico & Rubin, 2003).

One central argument of this chapter is that if FBM has the potential to remain consistent with time (at least in an interval of 1–2 years), it is then crucial to identify the variables that can predict its consistency. This feature needs to be distinguished from accuracy and vividness. Accuracy would be theoretically important to assess in order to test if FBM is a special class of memory. However, it would require a first data collection immediately after an event occurred for a large sample of people, which is almost impossible for public events. Vividness is a feature of memory that is more common and that would not make FBMs distinctive from other memories. Consistency could thus be viewed as the best measure available in the context of assessing FBM.

Despite the abundant literature describing FBM for public events, the majority of papers have only reported descriptives related to FBM predictors, sometimes including correlations among these predictors and the degree of vividness of FBM. Although interesting, such analyses only give partial explanations of the structure of FBM formation. For instance, they cannot account for the different paths that can occur to explain the formation of FBM. In this chapter I present models that can account for the formation of FBM.

One important asset of modelling is that although a general consensus exists about the main emotional, cognitive, and social factors affecting FBM (e.g., Conway, 1995; Finkenauer et al., 1998) strong disagreements still exist about the emphasis to place on one or the other. Modelling would thus help to determine not only which factors are most important, but also in which circumstances and how they relate to each other. It is now possible to statistically test FBM formation and maintenance using structural equation modelling (SEM). SEM is a confirmatory approach useful for testing hypotheses concerning both the measurement of latent constructs and the structural relationships between them (Bollen, 1989). The main advantage of using the SEM approach is that it provides a test of theoretical hypotheses of relationships among FBM variables. In other words, the SEM approach is designed to compare a theoretically established model with empirical evidence to assess the degree to which data do or do not fit the theory, instead of simply deriving a model based on empirical evidence.

In this chapter, I review the existing models that are proposed for the formation of FBM (Brown & Kulik, 1977; Conway et al., 1994; Er, 2003; Finkenauer et al., 1998; see also Curci & Luminet, 2006, for the particular case of expected events). I will present the basic principles of each model, the main empirical findings that were obtained using them, the strengths and limitations regarding the model itself and its theoretical background, its ability to fit the data (using the SEM approach), and the relevance of events that were analysed for the testing of models. I conclude with a systematic comparison of the fit indices and of the relationships between the variables across models and across studies.

BROWN AND KULIK (1977): THE FIRST ATTEMPT TO MODEL FBM FORMATION

In a paper that has now been cited more than 400 times (according to the Web of Science database), Brown and Kulik (1977) investigated FBM for a variety of events (public and personal). They are also known as the first to propose a model of FBM formation. This is quite paradoxical as they never tested any models themselves, but rather suggested different stages that could account for the formation of FBM. We will still present their proposals because many researchers who later statistically tested models of FBM formation referred to their assumptions as a model.

Using the prototypical event of the assassination of US President J. F. Kennedy in November 1963, the authors insisted in their definition of FBM on their "live" quality that is almost perceptual. This definition includes surprise, brevity, and "indiscriminate illumination" but Brown and Kulik added that it will be only somewhat indiscriminate (and far from complete) as some details like objects or weather would be accessible but not remembered. Their definition of FBM was restricted to the vividness criterion; no assessment of consistency was considered.

Main findings

Brown and Kulik asked 80 participants if they recalled the circumstances in which they first heard about nine different public events that were selected as highly unexpected or novel and that could differ for their level of consequentiality, depending on the ethnic background of respondents and on their personal assessment of the news. They also had to recall a personal event that involved unexpected shock. Brown and Kulik's main goal was to investigate the effect of consequentiality on the degree of elaboration of FBMs. Participants were asked to provide a free description that was later analysed by judges. The definition of FBM was quite loose, as the presence of only one canonical category in the description was enough to consider the event as a FBM, out of a list of six variables (place in which the person was when he/she heard the news, ongoing event that was interrupted by the news, informant who brought the news, affect in others upon hearing the news, own affect, and the immediate aftermath for the person on hearing the news).

Brown and Kulik compared degree of elaboration of FBM across events and groups (Caucasian vs African-Americans) based on mean comparisons. They also tested the relationship between consequentiality, rehearsal, and degree of elaboration of FBM, using Spearman rank correlations. From these results they elaborated a model that was closely related to the "Now Print!" hypothesis of Livingston (1967). They suggested that in order to initialize FBM formation, the original event has (a) to be new and unexpected and (b) to elicit surprise. If an event is routine and common it is not attended to and hence does not lead to surprise. In other words, the event's novelty determines the level of surprise. Given a sufficient level of surprise, the event is then evaluated in terms of personal consequentiality or importance, which is equated, in their perspective, with emotional arousal. Both surprise and consequentiality are considered necessary for FBM formation. Additionally, Brown and Kulik propose that overt and covert rehearsal lead to further elaboration of FBM.

In their model, mainly direct[2] relationships are suggested between predictors and FBM: surprise, consequentiality, and emotional arousal are supposed to affect the formation of FBM. However, one indirect path is suggested. Surprise is supposed to favour an appraisal of high importance that will then trigger emotional arousal. In turn, emotionality increases rehearsal that will ultimately affect FBM. The authors note that rehearsal is not a "simple reproduction of the brain events constituting the memory"

(1977, pp. 85–86). It is rather a reconstructive process particularly in the case of overt rehearsal (verbalization of feeling to others) (see Figure 3.1). An associative network between verbal narrative and retrieval cues is progressively made. In other words, more frequent rehearsal makes elaborate FBM accounts more accessible.

Strengths and limitations

The major strength of the Brown and Kulik paper was their first attempt to model knowledge from cognitive psychology and neurosciences in order to explain the formation of memory for the reception context. However, there were some strong limitations to their model. First, some predictors that were assumed to be essential (novelty, surprise) were not measured, thus precluding a valid assessment of their contribution for FBM formation. Second, the data collection was restricted to a small sample size. Third, the authors did not differentiate between consequentiality and emotional feelings but used the two concepts interchangeably. It is thus not possible to establish whether consequentiality and emotional feelings contribute independently to the formation of FBM. But the major shortcoming of the model is that it lacks a firm theoretical basis. Given the absence of underlying theory, most researchers assessed only some of the proposed variables and ignored others. This precludes an adequate test and revision of Brown and Kulik's model of FBM formation and maintenance as the findings are too scant and diverse to

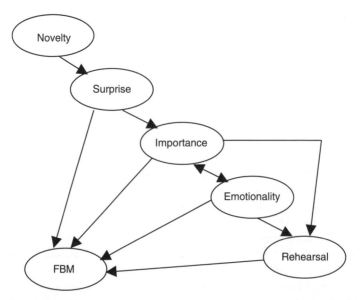

Figure 3.1 FBM formation according to Brown and Kulik's (1977) model. Double-headed arrows indicate that the two variables were considered as a single one by Brown and Kulik (1977).

provide reliable evidence (for a more detailed discussion see Conway, 1990, 1995; Conway et al. 1994).

CONWAY ET AL. (1994): THE FIRST SEM MODEL FOR FBM

Conway et al. (1994) investigated the unexpected resignation of the British Prime Minister Thatcher in 1990 in a large sample of UK and non-UK citizens. The goal of the study was to provide a causal model based on a small number of latent constructs (affect, consequentiality/importance, rehearsal, knowledge/interest) that can explain the formation of FBM. Conway et al.'s (1994) study represents the first attempt to statistically test FBM formation and maintenance using structural equation modelling (SEM). In this paper, FBMs were operationalized as those memories that were highly consistent from one data collection phase (after 2 weeks) to the other (after 11 months). Memories that did not show a high level of consistency were considered as non-FBM or ordinary autobiographical memories. A list of five attributes (memory description, people present, place, ongoing activity, and source of information) was considered, each being scored 0 (forgot the attribute or entered a different attribute at retest), 1 (basically, but not exactly, consistent answer), or 2 (perfectly consistent answer). In order to be considered as a FBM, people needed to reach a score of 9 or 10. Despite this strict criterion, 85.6% of UK citizens had a FBM. An important distinction was made in this model between encoding factors (affect, importance, and prior knowledge) and rehearsal factors. While encoding factors are supposed to predict FBM formation, rehearsal factors are predicted to influence FBM maintenance.

Main findings

The authors first separately examined the model of formation of FBM and of non-FBM (when consistency was below 90%). The FBM model showed that knowledge/interest was a central variable that had an effect on all other constructs (importance, surprise/emotionality, and rehearsal). Importance/ consequences was also a key variable that directly predicted intensity of affect and rehearsal. Importantly, no association was found between affect and rehearsal. In the non-FBM model knowledge/interest still played a central role. But this time the links of importance towards affect and rehearsal disappeared, indicating that in that case these three constructs have separate independent effects on memory. Finally, Conway et al. tested a model that involved all participants. In this combined model, FBM had two direct predictors, affect and rehearsal. Knowledge/interest and importance/consequences were two indirect predictors. Again, affect and rehearsal were found to be unrelated (see Figure 3.2). This last finding is opposite to most findings showing that intensity of affect is related to extent of rehearsal (e.g., Rimé, Finkenauer, Luminet, Zech, & Philippot, 1998).

For Conway et al. (1994), the high incidence of very detailed and consistent memory reports was an indication of FBM as a special case of memory. The fact that the same constructs were found to be relevant for both FBM and non-FBM reports would suggest that the same processes are active, but are of different strengths. The authors also insisted on the central role of the encoding constructs (affect, importance, and prior knowledge) for the formation of FBM. For them, rehearsal did not play a critical role for the formation of FBM. It would only help the elaboration of memory reports by establishing multiple access routes to FBM. They also shared the assumption of Brown and Kulik that an event must reach a threshold of significance in order to trigger a FBM. They state that "the item of news has to be judged as having consequences for self that are more significant than the consequences typically assigned to most items of news" (Conway et al., 1994, p. 339). If such a level is not reached, then an association between affect and importance is not present and FBM is not formed.

Strengths and limitations

This work had a number of strengths. The study investigated an event that involved high ratings on two key variables for the formation of FBM (importance and surprise). This was the first study (except Bohannon, 1988) that used a large sample of participants and that used group comparisons. This is

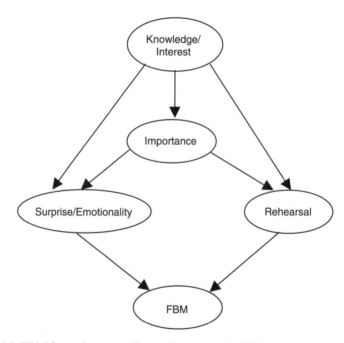

Figure 3.2 FBM formation according to Conway et al. (1994).

important as it allowed a demonstration that the structure of the relationships among variables was different for the FBM and the non-FBM groups. Conway et al. (1994) were also the first to directly investigate prior knowledge of politics and orientation to the event (attitudes). Prior knowledge is predicted to facilitate the organization and assimilation of the incoming information to existing semantic structures in memory.

However, there were several limitations to this work. First, this was a data-driven model, while it is required that a SEM model is built on theoretical assumptions (e.g., Bollen, 1989). The authors also failed to define and operationalize the appraisal of novelty and to distinguish between emotional appraisals and emotional responses. In addition, intensity of emotional feelings and surprise were considered together, while emotion models insist on their distinction (e.g., Frijda, 1986; Lazarus, 1982; Leventhal, 1984; Scherer, 1984). The event itself did not conform to the conditions for testing the FBM hypothesis (Conway, 2002): although high ratings were observed for importance and surprise, only low levels of affective reactions were recorded. However, it is assumed that a threshold for emotionality needs to be reached in order to have FBM. Additionally rehearsal, which was suggested as a key variable for FBM maintenance, was of low magnitude. Finally, the sample mainly consisted of first-year psychology students, which precludes generalizability to other populations.

FINKENAUER ET AL. (1998): A TWO-PATH MODEL

According to Finkenauer et al. (1998), the process of formation and maintenance of FBM develops through two pathways. The first connects the cognitive evaluations of novelty to FBM, through the effect of surprise and emotion. This pathway is representative of the direct effect of emotion. The second pathway represents the indirect effect of emotion. The experience of learning a relevant piece of public news induces high levels of personal importance and consequentiality, which in turn lead to intense negative emotions. This feeling state does not directly affect FBM. Rather, its impact is mediated by two consecutive processes. First, the emotional feeling state triggers rehearsal which strengthens the memory trace of the original event. This eventually enhances memory for the reception context. In this process an important role is also played by background knowledge and affective attitudes, which influence importance/consequentiality, emotional reactions, and rehearsal (Conway et al., 1994; Finkenauer et al., 1998) (see Figure 3.3).

Main findings

Finkenauer et al.'s (1998) study involved a large group of French-speaking Belgians ($N = 399$) of various age groups and backgrounds. The goal was to compare three models (Brown and Kulik, Conway, and their own model) of

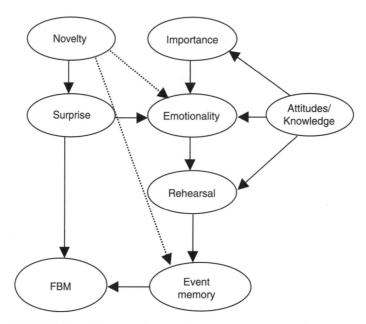

Figure 3.3 FBM formation according to Finkenauer et al. (1998). Dashed lines are
paths that were found in a subsequent test of the model (Luminet & Curci,
2008).

the formation and maintenance of FBM, using SEM. Seven to eight months
after the Belgian king's death in 1993, participants recalled the circumstances
in which they first heard the news. FBM was assessed through five items. Four
were canonical variables already investigated in previous studies (time when
respondents heard the news, place they were, people they were with, and
ongoing activity they were involved in, each scored from 0 to 1). The fifth
question was related to specific idiosyncratic details that people could
remember, scored from 0 to 5. FBM was thus operationalized as the degree of
vividness of the memory. Participants were also asked to remember specific
details about the original event (memory of the original event) and about the
following predictors of FBM: (1) personal consequentiality and importance,
(2) novelty, (3) surprise, (4) emotional feelings, (5) overt rehearsal (i.e., frequency of talking about the event and following the media), and (6) personal
attitude, which was assessed through the degree to which the person reported
having a favourable attitude towards the royal family in general.[3]

The authors compared their model with the ones developed by Brown and
Kulik (1977) and Conway et al. (1994) using the SEM approach. Results
showed that Finkenauer et al.'s model evidenced the best values of fit (CFI,
AIC) and was often the only model that had indices above standard thresholds (such as chi-square/df ratio or RMSEA).[4] Also, all—except two—causal
path linking factors were significant, while some crucial paths suggested by

the other models were not significant. For instance, FBM was not directly determined by emotional feeling states (opposite to Brown & Kulik's and to Conway et al.'s predictions) and by importance (opposite to Brown's predictions).

Strengths and limitations

One main advantage of this model over the two previous ones was a more refined analysis of the emotional process that included a distinction between appraisals and feeling states and a distinction between surprise and other emotional feelings. This allowed closer linking of certain appraisals (like novelty) and certain specific emotional feelings that are triggered, such as surprise. Finkenauer et al. (1998) also laid out a detailed analysis of the relationship between immediate emotional responses and rehearsal, including an explanation of the functions fulfilled by covert (rumination) and overt aspects (verbal communication and following the media). They suggested that overt rehearsal is more than a simple reproduction of the brain events constituting the memory. It improves the individual FBM by consolidating existing memory traces. In other words, by talking about the event and by being exposed to the media, the memory for the reception context is improved. However recall, in the form of overt rehearsal, is almost always (re)constructive, because it takes place in a social context. Overt rehearsal also contributes to creating a collective memory for what happened; that is, the political event as such. The data thereby suggest that FBM should be considered a type of memory in which both individual and social factors have a significant impact (Finkenauer, Gisle, & Luminet, 1997).

At the structural level, these data were the first to support a two-path model, in which a distinction is made between direct and indirect determinants of FBM. These results were thus in contrast with the "Now Print!" mechanism postulated by Brown and Kulik (1977), in which the information is permanently encoded in memory.

For Finkenauer et al. (1998), in addition to the direct path between surprise and FBM, there was an indirect path that explained the formation of FBM: emotional feelings had an effect on FBM through rehearsal and memory for the event. Rehearsal processes are likely to address information about the original event rather than information relative to the reception context. Hence, Finkenauer et al. (1998) proposed that the intensity of the emotional feeling state determines event rehearsal and, as a consequence, the memory of the original event, or event memory. The event memory, in turn, influences the maintenance of FBM. Theoretically, it is suggested that when learning about an original event, all currently activated information—including the reception context, sensory information, and the original event—is encoded in memory (Tulving & Kroll, 1995). Thus, both the original event and the reception context would immediately be encoded. Subsequently, during rehearsal of the original event, the reactivation of this information in memory would spread to any associated information, and thus to FBM. In this way, rehearsal strengthens the associations between the different elements constituting the memory of the entire experience (Johnson & Chalfonte, 1994). Finkenauer et al.'s model was the first to consider event memory as a variable necessary to explain the formation of FBM. It also assigned an equally central role to the direct and the indirect paths in the formation of FBM.

Finally, from a statistical viewpoint, this was the first attempt to compare different models of FBM formation at the structural level. This direct statistical comparison between different models is one important way to make progress in the field. It will allow researchers to determine the most relevant models, to suggest theoretically founded modifications to previous ones, and to specify their generalizability or the need for specificities related to the type of event that is investigated.

Despite these numerous strengths, there were also some notable limitations in this study. A major one is that FBM was not considered as a consistency measure, because memory for the reception context was assessed only once, 7–8 months after the original event. Also, only one group (Belgian citizens) was considered, while it would have been interesting to include comparison groups of people with lower involvement for the news. From this study one cannot determine the impact of specific emotional states on FBM formation, because the researchers only considered an index of global intensity of feelings. It would also be an important future goal to investigate whether such models can be applied for positive events. Finally, only attitudes were investigated, while a combined investigation of attitudes and knowledge would be preferable, as the first aspect involves mainly affective components and the second mainly cognitive ones.

A SPECIFIC APPLICATION OF FINKENAUER'S MODEL TO EXPECTED EVENTS

Although surprise is often described as a condition for eliciting FBM, some studies have found FBMs for expected news (Bellelli, 1999; Curci, 2005; Curci, Luminet, Finkenauer, & Gisle, 2001; Morse, Woodward, & Zweigenhaft, 1993; Neisser, 1982; Ruiz-Vargas, 1993; Weaver, 1993). For instance, Curci et al. (2001) compared FBM for the death of the former president of France, F. Mitterrand, in two national groups, French and Belgian citizens. The death was expected, since Mitterrand suffered from prostate cancer and he was in a terminal state. Nevertheless, the authors found that FBM developed for the event in both groups. Recently, Curci and Luminet (2008) have tested the Finkenauer et al. model on these data. Due to the nature of the event that was expected, they predicted that the direct impact of surprise and novelty appraisal on FBM would be non-significant, but that both cognitive–emotional and social factors would influence FBM through the indirect pathway. The study was based on a sample of 229 respondents, 54.1% of them French, who completed a questionnaire 1–2 months after Mitterrand's death in January 1996 and 1 year later. FBM was assessed through a consistency measure based on five attributes: exact time participants heard the news, the place they were, the other people they were with, their ongoing activity, and some other details about the reception context (to a maximum of five). The variable assessing the informant was included in the questionnaires but not considered among the FBM indicators, as a ceiling effect was found for its distribution; almost all respondents seemed to remember how they heard the news. SEM fit indices for the model were found to be acceptable for the two groups, although some indices were below the standard thresholds. The pattern of relationships among variables was almost identical in the two groups. As predicted, the direct path was not found to be significant (non-significant relationship between surprise and FBM), but all the relationships in the indirect path were significant. An additional link was found in the model, corresponding to the direct effect of emotional feeling states on FBM consistency. This link was originally considered by Finkenauer et al. (1998), in conformity with evidence of previous research (Brown & Kulik, 1977; Conway, 1995). These results suggest that an event that is expected could lead to FBM formation. One specific feature, however, is that only the indirect path from Finkenauer's model would explain the process. The unique activation of the indirect pathway accounts for the role of reconstructive processes, through rehearsal of the original news. Thus, although FBMs can be considered as consistent over time (Brown & Kulik, 1977; Conway et al., 1994; Pillemer, 1984), they are also affected by post-encoding elaborations, and are thus modifiable and prone to decay (Curci & Luminet, 2006; Curci et al., 2001).

Strengths and limitations

This study was the first to examine model formation for expected events. Other studies are thus necessary to test whether the model can hold across situations. This study also suggests some important issues for the implication of novelty and surprise in the formation of FBM and for improvements in its measurement in future studies. Novelty refers to two aspects: unexpectedness and exceptionality (Frijda, Kuipers, & ter Schure, 1989; Leventhal & Scherer, 1987; Scherer, 1988). In other words, an event might be considered novel not only because it came suddenly and unexpectedly, but also in terms of its disruptiveness with respect to one's ordinary routine. This distinction was not tested in the present study. Had it been, we could surmise that respondents would have rated the event as exceptional and out of the ordinary, particularly in the French group, but not as unexpected due to the former French president's terminal illness. New testing of a model of prediction (especially in the case of predictable events) should consider the twofold nature of the appraisal of novelty, thus taking into account the effects of both evaluations, especially for events foreseeable by public opinion.

ER (2003): A MODEL FOR PEOPLE WHO EXPERIENCE THE EVENT DIRECTLY

Er (2003) investigated models of FBM formation related to a severe earthquake that occurred in Turkey in 1999. The main goal of the study was to test if different models of FBM formation are necessary when comparing people who directly experience a major negative event (the "victim" group) with people who do not have a direct experience of the event, but simply hear about it (the "non-victim" group). For the victim group only, Er suggested a model in which personal consequences have a direct effect on the formation of FBM. Another major difference between the two groups is related to the distinction between FBM and event memory. In the victim group, the two aspects cannot be separated. If the person directly experiences a major event, he/she cannot differentiate between the memory for the event itself and the memory for recollections of specific details for the reception context. A second goal was to compare the proposed new model with existing ones (Brown & Kulik, Conway et al., Finkenauer et al.).

Main findings

For each group considered, a comparison was made between the new model (labelled "importance-driven emotional reactions") and the previous ones (Brown & Kulik, Conway et al., Finkenauer et al.) using SEM. In these analyses, FBM was operationalized by the vividness account. The five questions investigating FBM were identical to the ones considered by Finkenauer et al. (1998) (time people experienced or heard the earthquake, place they were at, people they were with, ongoing activity they were involved in, and a list of a maximum of five specific details). For the victim group (see Figure 3.4), SEM revealed that the new model had the best fit indices. Results also confirmed the assumption of a direct relationship between importance and FBM, which paralleled the hypothesis of Brown and Kulik (1977) but contradicts the findings of Conway et al. (1994) and Finkenauer et al. (1998). For the non-victim group, path diagrams were very close to Finkenauer et al.'s model, except that surprise and novelty were assessed under the same variable. The comparison of fit indices for the Er model with the other three (Brown & Kulik, Conway et al., Finkenauer et al.) revealed that indices were above standard thresholds when applying the Er and Finkenauer models, while they were below these thresholds for the two others.

One specificity of this study is related to the status of the involved group in which participants took part in the event itself rather than just hearing about it. Major natural disasters such as earthquakes are likely to leave people traumatized for a long period of time. Some will have lost close relatives, or will have relatives injured. The intense fear that was experienced would also lead some of them to develop post-traumatic stress disorder (PTSD) symptoms such as intrusive and vivid thoughts or nightmares that are often accompanied by heightened physiological reactivity. Unfortunately, the author did not provide information related to the prevalence of PTSD symptoms in the victim group. We can, however, assume that a relatively large proportion of them would experience these symptoms and thus have formed traumatic memories. Traumatic memories do not necessarily involve special memory mechanisms (Pezdek & Taylor, 2002) but it is usually found that the rate of forgetting traumatic events is less steep than the rate of forgetting non-traumatic events (e.g., Neisser et al., 1996). Also, traumatic memories are assessed as more emotional (see Fivush et al., Chapter 8, this volume). For instance, it was found that people with PTSD exhibit an inflation of the emotional aspects of their memory, (e.g., Qin et al., 2003; see Budson & Gold, Chapter 7, this volume). This means that victims may have a memory content that is different from non-victim groups. It thus seems adequate to have a distinct model when examining FBM formation for people directly exposed to a traumatic situation.

Strengths and limitations

One strength relates to the exploration of new issues in model formation. Indeed, this study provided a first proposal for models of FBM formation for events in which people were directly involved. One important implication in this case is that the event itself and the reception context co-occur in space and time (see Pillemer, Chapter 6, this volume). The better fit that was found suggests that when assessing FBM in a victim group it would be appropriate to consider this model, which involves a direct effect of importance/

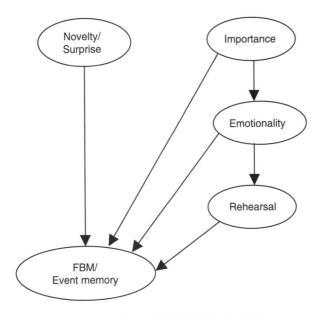

Figure 3.4 FBM formation according to Er (2003) for the victim group.

consequences on FBM. The strong link between these variables had already been suggested in previous studies. For instance, Neisser et al. (1996) found that personal involvement was the main predictor of recall in a study that compared three groups of participants concerning a major earthquake in California. Rubin and Kozin (1984) also found that an increase in personal importance is related to an increase in memory clarity. However, for non-victim groups, there is no real benefit for a new model as the results were very similar to the Finkenauer et al. model.

Three other strengths are worth mentioning. First, the selection of the event was in conformity with the FBM hypothesis that required high ratings on personal importance and consequentiality, affective reactions, and surprise (Conway, 2002). Second, a large comparison group was recruited, which allows the researcher to test separate models for more- and less-involved people. Third, this was the first time that a questionnaire measuring FBM and its predictors was closely built on another study (Finkenauer et al., 1998) that tested model formation. This allows for more direct comparisons across studies because it is always possible that differences across studies could be explained by different ways of operationalizing the variables.

Some important limitations also need to be mentioned. First, the initial data collection took place 6 months after the event. This means that the "original" memory that was investigated at that time had already been reconstructed through media exposure and social communication. Also, consistency measures were available only for a small proportion of the total sample (about 12%), with many analyses based on the single initial measure collected after 6 months. These methodological issues lead us to cautiously consider the FBM latent variable. Various concerns relate to the measurement of predictors of FBM. First, there was no direct assessment of knowledge, which was previously found as a key antecedent (Conway et al., 1994). Second, the appraisal of novelty and the emotional feeling state of surprise that follow were not conceptually distinguished. Third, there was a confound in the measure of surprise that was more conceptually related to the measure of emotionality. Finally, the author used mathematical indices (modifications indexes) that are proposed by the software in order to increase the overall fit rather than a theoretical rationale, as is required when using SEM.

TOWARDS A SYSTEMATIC COMPARISON OF THE FOUR MODELS OF FBM FORMATION

The last studies summarized above (Finkenauer et al., 1998, and Er, 2003) provided a first opportunity to compare models using the same sample set. The results suggested that the models developed by Finkenauer et al. and by Er had better fit indices as compared to Conway et al. and Brown and Kulik.

Some more systematic comparisons are necessary, however, before drawing firm conclusions on which model is to be preferred. Also, the papers by

Finkenauer et al. (1998) and by Er (2003) had some important limitations. The most notable one was that FBM was defined on a vividness basis rather than on a consistency one. The purpose of the second part of this chapter is to provide stronger bases from recent available data on the model comparison. I first present a study in which a consistency approach was adopted when comparing the four models, allowing for a more valid assessment of FBM formation. I then present results from a large set of data that allow for a more systematic comparison of fit indices and paths across models.

A MODEL COMPARISON OF THE 9/11 ATTACKS

Luminet and Curci (2008) recently conducted a study with the goal of comparing the four theoretical models accounting for FBM formation (Brown & Kulik, 1977; Conway et al., 1994; Er, 2003; Finkenauer et al., 1998) using SEM in two groups of participants (US, $N = 120$; non-US, $N = 716$) in relation to the terrorist attacks of September 11, 2001, in the US.

Main findings

FBM was considered on a consistency basis with data collected on average 21 and 524 days after the 9/11 attacks. Five items were considered to assess FBM: time of day, location of the respondents, informant, other people present, and ongoing activity, with consistency scores ranging from 0 to 2 for each item. Regarding fit indices, a model derived from Finkenauer et al. (1998) applied to the data for the 9/11 attacks provided the best indices for both the US and the non-US samples (see Table 3.1 later). The main modifications from the original model of Finkenauer et al. (1998) were related to additional effects of novelty on other predictors. While the initial model only showed a relationship between novelty and surprise, the present data also showed a relationship in both groups between novelty and emotional feeling states. This suggests that novelty has a more general impact on the emotional response than originally assumed. In addition, novelty was directly related to event memory, although only in the non-US group. This suggests a purely cognitive effect, as novelty is related to an initial orientation reaction that will then redirect attention and favour the encoding of information. Interestingly, some recent findings support the view that brain structures originally known to be involved in emotional reactions are also activated for the detection of novelty. For instance, it was shown that the amygdala is involved not only in responses to fearful stimuli but also in the detection of novel neutral faces (Schwartz et al., 2003; Wright et al., 2003). For the US group, the derived model of Finkenauer et al. was the only one for which all fit indices reached the required thresholds.

I now turn to a brief description of the model of prediction. A major difference was observed in the two groups regarding the activation of the direct and the indirect paths. In the US group strong significant relationships were found for the direct path, while the indirect path was incomplete, with no significant relationship between rehearsal and event memory. In the non-US group the direct path was not significant, while the indirect path was complete, with all the predicted relationships significant. It is important to note that in both groups of respondents FBMs were formed, suggesting that the activation of only the direct or the indirect path is sufficient for the elicitation of FBM.

An important finding to explain is that the indirect path was incomplete in the US group. The difference between the two groups is specifically related to the non-significant relationship between rehearsal and event memory. I suggest that the content of rehearsal might explain differences between the two groups. One explanation is related to large differences between the US and non-US groups in the impact of the event on people's personal lives (Luminet et al., 2004). It is likely that this impact was emphasized more in the US media. It is also likely that this difference extended to other aspects of rehearsal (rumination and social communication). Thus, the content of rehearsal was less likely to strengthen event memory as a large proportion of this information was not related to the content of the news itself. In the non-US countries there was less need to focus the content of rehearsal on the impact on people's personal lives. It is thus likely that a higher proportion of rehearsal was centred on the event itself. The more event-centred content of rehearsal in non-US countries was more likely to exert a stronger positive impact on event memory.

Another puzzling finding that requires explanation is the non-significant direct path in the non-US group. From a review of studies that tested FBM formation (see the list in Tables 3.1 and 3.2 later), I suggest that the activation of social identity (vs personal identity) could be a central component for the activation of the direct path. The idea is that, depending on circumstances, the individual's personal identity (self-definition derived from close personal relationships and idiosyncratic personality attributes) or social identity (self-definition in terms of the properties of a specific group and degree of an individual's identification with this group) will be more highly activated. For events that only triggered personal identity, no direct link between surprise and FBM was found. For more details on the effect of social identity on the formation of FBM, see Berntsen, Chapter 9, this volume, and Luminet and Curci (2008).

I will now look at the structural results when the three other models were applied to these data. Overall, the results revealed that many important predictions were not supported. For the original model of Brown and Kulik, the path from surprise to importance and the one from importance to FBM were non-significant. The failure of Conway's model to account for the present data is particularly noteworthy for the US group, as the two direct predictors of FBM (affect and rehearsal) were found to be non-significant. Moreover, prior knowledge, which was proposed as a central variable in this model, failed to predict two other latent variables (affect and importance). Only the relationship between prior knowledge and rehearsal was significant.

The application of Er's model to the present data showed that, for the US group, three paths were non-significant out of six that were predicted. For the non-US data, the model that was suggested for the non-victim group was actually very close to the Finkenauer model. The only main difference is that Er predicted a direct relationship between affect and FBM that is not predicted in Finkenauer. Results disconfirmed Er's assumptions about this relationship for the events of 9/11.

Strengths and limitations

The event that was investigated was probably the most prototypical to elicit FBM as it involved ceiling responses on the key variables of novelty/surprise, importance/consequentiality, and affective reactions. In this respect, it corresponds perfectly to the conditions for an appropriate test of the formation of FBM. This study also represents a strong improvement in modelling FBM when compared to the previous studies that used SEM. In comparison with Conway et al. (1994), the present sample is more representative for age and background. Luminet and Curci also made a distinction between intensity of affect and surprise and had high ratings on all the key variables, which was not the case for affect in Conway's model. In comparison with the data collected by Finkenauer et al. (1998), the data collection for this study took place much sooner after the event, the assessment of FBM was based on a test–retest consistency measure, and we had a group comparison.

Some future improvements need to be considered, however. It would be important in the future to have a larger sample size, particularly for the highly involved group. Also, the first data collection should have been completed more quickly in order to avoid as much as possible any reconstructive processes taking place.

COMPARISONS ACROSS MODELS

In this section, I provide a more systematic comparison of the models based on a larger set of available data. First, I compare the fit indices of the original models and their applications to different contexts. This step will allow us to draw conclusions that are theoretically grounded and supported by statistical indices. I then summarize the links between variables that were predicted in the different models and examine the extent to which these assumed links were confirmed when the models were tested with different events. For each model, we have at least two additional events to the original data collection in which the model has been tested. The data collected by Curci and Luminet (2008) on the death of President Mitterrand were not included in these comparisons, as the expected nature of the event does not allow valid comparisons with the other studies.

Comparison of the fit indices across studies

A total of 20 data sets were available for the comparison of fit indices across the four models, with at least four data sets related to each model. We only considered fit indices that were used in the majority of studies (see Table 3.1). Some other indices such as AIC, SRMR, or NNFI[5] are also very interesting but they were considered in less than half of the studies. This would thus preclude an analysis of their relevance. As mentioned in Table 3.1, five of the indices that are reported have clear statistical thresholds. This allows the reader to compare the ability of each model to take into account the different situations that were investigated. Results were the poorest for the Brown and Kulik model, particularly for AGFI[6] and RMSEA. Of a total of 20 indices that were assessed across studies for this model, only 7 (35%) were above standard thresholds. For Conway's model results were better, with a total of 14 significant indices out of 23 tested (60.9%). Actually, Conway's model was very good overall, but it completely failed to account for the data in the Turkish earthquake study by Er (2003). The proportion of significant indices was higher in Er's model, with 11 out of 16 tested (68.7%). Finally, Finkenauer's model had a total of 15 out of 20 indices that were above the thresholds (75%). It is worth noting that out of the 5 non-significant indices for Finkenauer's model, 3 were just below the threshold—0.89 instead of 0.90 for CFI in Finkenauer (4); 0.06 instead of 0.05 for RMSEA in Finkenauer (3) and (5) (see Table 3.1). Thus, Finkenauer's model had almost 90% of the indices that reached acceptable thresholds.

These results suggest that the initial model suggested by Brown and Kulik is no longer appropriate to be tested in future studies and should be abandoned. Regarding the three other models, the Finkenauer one seems better able to account for the data, but the other two are certainly interesting to use for comparison in future studies. Er's model would also be important to use for people who directly experienced the situation. One aim of future studies will be to examine how generalizable each model is as regards the type of context that is investigated (natural disaster, political event, assassination of well-known people, . . .). The number of studies that have been conducted on model formation is too small to allow for any preliminary conclusion on this issue.

Comparison of the models of predictions across studies

All four models first agree on a set of variables that need to be included in models of FBM formation. These variables are (1) the reaction of surprise when learning about the original event, (2) the appraisal of importance or consequentiality of the original event, (3) an intense emotional feeling state,

Table 3.1 Comparison of the fit indices across models and studies

	Brown and Kulik					Conway						Finkenauer					Er			
	(1)	(2)	(3)	(4)	(5)	(1)	(2)	(3)	(4)	(5)	(6)	(1)	(2)	(3)	(4)	(5)	(1)	(2)	(3)	(4)
Chi-square	230.86 (96)***	10.83 (6), ns	70.10 (6)***			27.2 (22), ns	205.91 (84)	8.54 (3)*	32.62 (3)***			305.59 (177)***	18.52 (14), ns	59.29 (16)***					18.10 (4)***	47.52 (11)***
Chi-square/df	**2.40**	**1.81**	11.68	**0.88**	**0.90**	**1.23**	**2.45**	**2.85**	10.87			**1.73**	**1.32**	3.71	**0.90**				4.53	4.32
GFI	**0.93**	**0.97**	**0.97**	0.88	0.89		**0.93**	**0.97**	**0.98**	0.88	0.82	**0.93**	**0.95**	**0.98**	0.87	**0.93**	**0.94**	**0.96**	**0.94**	**0.98**
AGFI		0.89	0.89	0.85	0.86			0.85	**0.91**	0.80	0.85		**0.91**	**0.96**	0.89	**0.93**	**0.95**	**0.96**	0.77	**0.95**
CFI	**0.96**			0.87	0.86	**0.98**	**0.96**			0.86	0.86	**0.96**				**0.94**	**0.97**	**0.98**		
RMSEA	0.06	0.07	0.12	0.06	0.09		0.06	0.13	0.12	0.07	0.06	**0.04**	**0.05**	0.06	**0.04**	0.06	**0.01**	**0.04**	0.18	0.07

Only indices in bold characters have reached the standard threshold. All other values are below the standard threshold.
*p < .05. **p < .01. ***p < .001.

Brown and Kulik model (1977). (1) = data from Finkenauer et al. (1998). (2) = data from Luminet & Curci (2008), involved group. (3) = data from Luminet & Curci (2008), non-involved group. (4) = data from Er (2003) victim group. (5) = data from Er (2003) non-victim group.

Conway et al. (1994) model. (1) = data from Conway et al. (1994). (2) = data from Finkenauer et al. (1998). (3) = data from Luminet & Curci (2008), involved group. (4) = data from Luminet & Curci (2008), non-involved group. (5) = data from Er (2003), victim group. (6) = data from Er (2003), non-victim group.

Finkenauer et al. (1998) model. (1) = data from Finkenauer et al. (1998). (2) = data from Luminet & Curci (2008), involved group. (3) = data from Luminet & Curci (2008), non-involved group. (4) = data from Er (2003), victim group. (5) = data from Er (2003), non-victim group.

Er (2003) model. (1) = data from Er (2003), victim group. (2) = data from Er (2003), non-victim group. (3) = data from Luminet & Curci (2008), involved group. (4) = data from Luminet & Curci (2008), non-involved group.

Fit indices:

- Chi-square: It is a measure of overall fit of the model to the data. It measures the distance between the sample covariance matrix and the estimated covariance matrix. A small non-significant chi-square corresponds to good fit and a large significant chi-square to bad fit (Bollen, 1989).
- Chi-square fit index divided by its degrees of freedom: It is an attempt to make the statistics less dependent on sample size. Carmines and McIver (1981) recommended that relative chi-square should be in the 2:1 or 3:1 range for an acceptable model. Kline (1998) maintained that 3 or less is acceptable.
- GFI and AGFI: The goodness of fit index (GFI) measures the amount of variance and covariance in the sample matrix that is predicted by the estimated covariance matrix. The adjusted goodness of fit index (AGFI) adjusts for the degrees of freedom in the model. Both indices range 0 to 1 and can be considered as satisfactory if they reach .90 (Bentler & Bonnet, 1980).
- A comparative fit index (CFI) is used as an incremental fit index derived from the comparison of the hypothesized model with the null model, in order to determine the amount by which the fit is improved by using the hypothesized model over the null model (Bentler, 1989). The CFI is a measure of covariation in the data reproduced by the model. Values range from 0 to 1. Values equal or greater than .90 can be considered as satisfactory (Bentler & Bonnet, 1980).
- RMSEA: The root mean square error of approximation (RMSEA) is a measure of the approximation between the model and the population covariance matrix. A perfect fit will yield an RMSEA of zero. Values equal to or equal or lower than .05 are considered good. Values exceeding .10 are indicative of a poor fit (Browne & Cudeck, 1993).

and (4) rehearsal. Second, all models suggest that FBMs are initialized by new (or unexpected) situations and that this mechanism has adaptational value (e.g., Brown & Kulik, 1977; Conway, 1995). This assumption corresponds to the "novelty-encoding" hypothesis (Tulving & Kroll, 1995), which suggests that novelty is a necessary condition for encoding information in long-term memory. Third, the models postulate that the appraisal of novelty leads to surprise. Fourth, in all models rehearsal affects FBM, although in Finkenauer et al. (1998) the effect is mediated by memory for the event.

Other aspects are shared by the majority of models. Three models (all but Er's model) predicted that rehearsal is associated with the importance of the event. Also for three models (all but Brown and Kulik's model) pre-existing personal characteristics (attitudes and/or knowledge) were included as they were thought to facilitate the assimilation of new information to long-term memory. In these models, knowledge was always supposed to be related to importance, affect, and rehearsal. Finally, the link between affect and rehearsal was always assumed except for Conway's model.

For the comparison of the statistical links between paths, 14 data sets were available, with at least 3 different data sets that tested each of the four models (Brown & Kulik, Conway et al., Finkenauer et al., Er; see Table 3.2). We first examined the direct antecedents of FBM. These results show that two of the direct predictors (emotional feelings and importance) were very rarely associated with FBM. For rehearsal and surprise the results are mixed, with more than half of the studies finding a significant relationship. It is worth noting that, for the link between surprise and FBM, four out of six non-significant relationships were found with groups with lower involvement in the news— see, in Table 3.2, Brown and Kulik (3), Conway (4), Finkenauer (3), and Er (4). It is thus possible that some level of initial involvement or the activation of social identity is required in order to trigger the surprise–FBM path (see Luminet & Curci, 2008, for a discussion). For the rehearsal–FBM direct link, four out of the five non-significant relationships were found in the group with higher involvement—see, in Table 3.2, Brown and Kulik (2), Conway (3), Finkenauer (2), and Er (2). In this case we would suggest that high involvement is likely to increase the amount of rehearsal, which, in turn, would weaken its ability to maintain consistent memories.

We then examined six links among predictors of FBM (three that predicted rehearsal: importance, emotionality, knowledge; the effect of knowedge on rehearsal and emotionality; the link between rehearsal and event memory) that were assumed by the four models. For these links, very high levels of agreement were found across studies, although the total number of studies that examined each link was quite variable (from five to nine). Although replications are called for, these initial results suggest that the links are quite strong across different contexts.

Table 3.2 Comparison of the SEM paths across models

	Brown & Kulik (1)	Brown & Kulik (2)	Brown & Kulik (3)	Conway (1)	Conway (2)	Conway (3)	Conway (4)	Finkenauer (1)	Finkenauer (2)	Finkenauer (3)	Er (1)	Er (2)	Er (3)	Er (4)	Summary (prop. YES)
Direct effect emotionality on FBM	0.02	−0.10	−0.04	0.12*[a]	0.15[a]	−0.09[a]	−0.06[a]	−0.01	n.i.	n.i.	0.61*[c]	−0.04[c]	0.58*	−0.04[c]	3/12
Direct effect rehearsal on FBM	0.32*	0.05	0.14*	0.45*	0.29*	0.07	0.13*	n.i.	n.i.	n.i.	0.54*[c]	0.11[c]	n.i.	n.i.	6/9
Direct effect surprise on FBM	0.21*	0.34*	0.05	0.12*[a]	0.15[a]	−0.09[a]	−0.06[a]	0.24*	0.32*	0.06	0.55*[c][d]	0.26*[b][d]	0.52*[d]	0.06[d]	8/14
Direct effect importance on FBM	−0.04	0.03	−0.03	n.i.	n.i.	n.i.	n.i.	n.i.	n.i.	n.i.	0.59*[c]	−0.01[c]	n.i.	n.i.	1/5
Direct effect event memory on FBM	n.i.	n.i.	n.i.	n.i.	n.i.	n.i.	n.i.	0.29*	0.20*	0.23*	n.i.[c]	n.i.[c]	0.44*	0.22*	5/5
Link importance → rehearsal	0.28*	0.34*	0.23*	0.26*	0.60*	0.37*	0.34*	n.i.	n.i.	n.i.	n.i.	n.i.	n.i.	n.i.	7/7
Link emotionality → rehearsal	0.41*	0.16	0.21*	n.i.[a]	n.i.[a]	n.i.[a]	n.i.[a]	0.62*	0.30*	0.29*	0.46*	0.30*	0.52*	0.29*	8/9
Link knowledge → rehearsal	n.i.	n.i.	n.i.	0.47*	0.18*[b]	0.26*[b]	0.28*[b]	0.14[b]	n.i.	0.08*[b]	0.51*[b]	n.i.	0.41*[b]	0.08*[b]	8/9
Link knowledge → emotionality	n.i.	n.i.	n.i.	0.37*	0.27*[a][b]	0.10*[a][b]	0.09[a][b]	0.39*[b]	n.i.	0.12*[b]	0.33*[b]	n.i.	0.42*[b]	0.12*[b]	8/9
Link knowledge → importance	n.i.	n.i.	n.i.	0.55*	0.55*[b]	0.13*[b]	−0.05[b]	0.52*[b]	n.i.	0.30*[b]	0.48*[b]	n.i.	0.37*[b]	0.30*[b]	7/9
Link rehearsal → event memory	n.i.	n.i.	n.i.	n.i.	n.i.	n.i.	n.i.	0.65*	0.15	0.24*	n.i.[c]	n.i.[c]	0.56*	0.25*	4/5

$*p < .05$.

Brown & Kulik (1) = Brown and Kulik (1977) model on Finkenauer et al. (1998) data. Brown & Kulik (2) = Brown & Kulik (1977) model on Luminet & Curci (2008), involved group. Brown & Kulik (3) = Brown & Kulik (1977) model on Luminet & Curci (2008), non-involved group. Conway (1) = Conway et al. (1994) model on original data. Conway (2) = Conway et al. (1994) model on Finkenauer et al. (1998) data. Conway (3) = Conway et al. (1994) model on Luminet & Curci (2008), involved group. Conway (4) = Conway et al. (1994) model on Luminet & Curci (2008), non-involved group. Finkenauer (1) = Finkenauer et al. (1998) model on original data. Finkenauer (2) = Finkenauer et al. (1998) model on Luminet & Curci (2008), involved group. Finkenauer (3) = Finkenauer et al. (1998) model on Luminet & Curci (2008), non-involved group. Er (1) = Er (2003) model on original data for victim group. Er (2) = Er (2003) model on Luminet & Curci (2008) data, involved group. Er (3) = Er (2003) model for non-victim group. Er (4) = Er (2003) model for non-victims on Luminet & Curci (2008), non-involved group.

n.i. = not investigated

(a) Confound between the measures of affect and surprise (considered as a single latent variable).
(b) Affective attitudes were investigated rather than prior knowledge.
(c) No distinction is made between the memory for the event latent variable and the FBM latent variable.
(d) No distinction is made between the appraisal of novelty and the emotional feeling of surprise.

CONCLUSIONS

I have shown in this chapter that the use of a SEM approach represents an important improvement for the understanding of FBM formation. It provides the opportunity to compare theoretically founded models with data from events in which FBMs were observed. The SEM approach provides information on the overall fit but also on the relationships among predictors.

The review of the events that led to the formation of FBM showed that a large number of situations can be investigated, even when they are related to low surprise (Curci & Luminet, 2008) or to low rehearsal (Conway et al., 1994). From the present data, it seems that high importance/consequences and strong emotional feelings are the only two conditions that are required for the formation of FBM. The comparison of models indicated that the Finkenauer model was the best able to fit the data and that the Brown and Kulik one evidenced the poorest fit. The comparison of the Finkenauer model across different studies revealed that, although the same structure is observed, the level of activation of the paths can change from one to another. One important conclusion is that the activation of either only the direct path or only the indirect path seems enough for the formation of FBM (Luminet & Curci, 2008). Another important conclusion is that the following seven predictors need to be considered: novelty, surprise, importance, emotional feelings, attitudes/knowledge, rehearsal, and event memory. Future studies should continue to compare models in order to identify the most relevant variables to consider. This will allow refinement of the preliminary conclusions of this chapter—for instance, that among the direct predictors of FBM, importance and emotionality were very rarely found to be significant, while event memory seems to be a more systematic significant predictor.

Finally, I would like to emphasize some recommendations for future studies that will allow the models of FBM formation to be improved. First, I believe there is a strong need for a standard questionnaire. This will provide the opportunity to make direct comparisons across studies when important events such as the 9/11 attacks happen. It will be important to collect the first data set very close to the event, using different groups that vary in their level of involvement for the news. The two components of novelty (unexpectedness and exceptionality) also need to be considered as they are assumed to have a different impact on the other predictors of FBM. The generalizability of the models that were presented in this chapter can be confirmed only when a large set of events of different natures (assassinations of public figures, natural disasters, terrorist attacks, . . .) are assessed with SEM. It will also be important to test if some particular situations (being a victim rather than being an observer) would involve some modifications in the models. A closer examination of the type of emotional feelings involved could also be an interesting avenue for future research. Until now, only the overall intensity of emotional feelings has been considered but not the type of emotions involved. It will be important to test if events related to strong positive emotions or to some particular negative states (shame, guilt, disgust) also lead to the same structure of FBM formation.

NOTES

1 This paper was written while the author was supported by grants 1.5.078.06 and 1.5.158.08 from the Belgian National Fund for Scientific Research. The author thanks Antonietta Curci who computed SEM analyses that are presented in this chapter.
2 Direct paths indicate a direct relationship between some predictors and FBM. Indirect paths indicate that the effect of a variable on FBM is mediated by one or several other variables.
3 This latter variable is not equivalent to Conway et al.'s prior knowledge about politics. It was believed that both variables reflect closely related constructs. More recent studies usually assess both attitudes and knowledge under the same latent variable.
4 The comparative fit index (CFI) is used as an incremental fit index derived from the comparison of the hypothesized model with the null model, in order to determine the amount by which the fit is improved by using the hypothesized model over the null model (Bentler, 1989). The CFI is a measure of covariation in the data repro-duced by the model. Values range from 0 to 1. Values greater than .90 can be considered as satisfactory (Bentler & Bonnet, 1980). Akaike's information criterion (AIC) (Akaike, 1987) assesses how parsimonious a model is. This criterion takes the goodness of fit as well as the number of estimated parameters into account. The model that yields the smallest value of AIC is considered best. The ratio between the model chi-square and the degrees of freedom indicates the fit of the model per degree of freedom used. A threshold value of 2 or 3 (Carmines & McIver, 1981) is usually required. The root mean square error of approximation (RMSEA) is a measure of the approximation between the model and the population covariance matrix. A perfect fit will yield a RMSEA of zero. Values equal to or lower than 0.05 are considered good. Values exceeding .10 are indicative of a poor fit (Browne & Cudeck, 1993).
5 For a definition of AIC, see note 3. SRMR: The standardized root mean square residual (SRMR) corresponds to the average difference between the predicted and observed variances and covariances in the model, based on standardized residuals. The smaller the SRMR, the better the model fit. NNFI: The non-normed fit index (NNFI) is also called the Bentler–Bonett non-normed fit index. It reflects the pro-portion by which the model fit improves as compared with the null model (random variables). It penalizes for model complexity, and it is less affected by sample size. It is not guaranteed to vary from 0 to 1, and a negative NNFI indicates that the chi-square/df ratio for the null model is less than the ratio for the given model.
6 The goodness of fit index (GFI) measures the amount of variance and covariance in the sample matrix that is predicted by the estimated covariance matrix. The adjusted goodness of fit index (AGFI) adjusts for the degrees of freedom in the model. Both indices range 0 to 1 and can be considered as satisfactory if they reach .90 (Bentler & Bonnet, 1980).

REFERENCES

Akaike, H. (1987). Factor analysis and AIC. *Psychometrika, 52*, 317–332.

Bellelli, G. (1999). *Ricordo di un giudice. Uno studio sulle flashbulb memories* [Remembering a judge: A study on flashbulb memories]. Napoli: Liguori.

Bentler, P. M. (1989). *EQS: Structural equations program manual.* Los Angeles: BMDP Statistical Software.

Bentler, P. M., & Bonnett, D. G. (1980). Significance tests and goodness-of-fit in the analysis of covariance structures. *Psychological Bulletin, 88*, 588–606.

Berntsen, D., & Thomsen, D. K. (2005). Personal memories for remote historical events: Accuracy and clarity of flashbulb memories related to World War II. *Journal of Experimental Psychology: General, 134*, 242–257.

Bohannon, J. N. (1988). Flashbulb memories for the space shuttle disaster: A tale of two theories. *Cognition, 29*, 179–196.

Bollen, K. A. (1989). *Structural equations with latent variables.* New York: Wiley.

Brown, R., & Kulik, J. (1977). Flashbulb memories. *Cognition, 5*, 73–99.

Browne, M. W., & Cudeck, R. (1993). Alternative ways of assessing model fit. In K. A. Bollen & J. S. Long (Eds.), *Testing structural equation models* (pp. 136–162). Thousand Oaks, CA: Sage.

Carmines, E. G., & McIver, S. P. (1981). Analyzing models with unobserved variables: Analysis of covariance structures. In G. W. Bohrnstedt & E. F. Borgatta (Eds.), *Social measurement: Current issues* (pp. 65–115). Beverly Hills, CA: Sage.

Christianson, S. A. (1989). Flashbulb memories: Special, but not so special. *Memory and Cognition, 17*, 433–443.

Conway, M. A. (1990). *Autobiographical memory: An introduction.* Buckingham, UK: Open University Press.

Conway, M. A. (1995). *Flashbulb memories.* Hove, UK: Lawrence Erlbaum Associates Ltd.

Conway, M. A. (2002). *Testing the flashbulb memory hypothesis.* Unpublished manuscript, University of Bristol, UK.

Conway, M. A., Anderson, S. J., Larsen, S. F., Donnelly, C. M., McDaniel, M. A., McClelland, A. G. R., et al. (1994). The formation of flashbulb memories. *Memory and Cognition, 22*, 326–343.

Curci, A. (2005). Latent variable models for the measurement of flashbulb memories: A comparative approach. *Applied Cognitive Psychology, 19*, 3–22.

Curci, A., & Luminet, O. (2006). Follow-up of a cross-national comparison on flashbulb and event memory for the September 11th attacks. *Memory, 14*, 329–344.

Curci, A., & Luminet, O. (2008, in press). Flashbulb memories for expected events: A test of the emotional-integrative model. *Applied Cognitive Psychology.* Retrieved 8 March 2008 from: doi: 10.1002/acp.1444

Curci, A., Luminet, O., Finkenauer, C., & Gisle, L. (2001). Flashbulb memories in social groups: A comparative test–retest study of the memory of French President Mitterrand's death in a French and a Belgian group. *Memory, 9*, 81–101.

Er, N. (2003). A new flashbulb memory model applied to the Marmara earthquake. *Applied Cognitive Psychology, 17*, 503–517.

Finkenauer, C., Gisle, L., & Luminet, O. (1997). When collective memories are socially shaped: Flashbulb memories of socio-political events. In J. W. Pennebaker, D. Páez, & B. Rimé (Eds.), *Collective memories of political events: Social and psychological perspectives* (pp. 191–208). Mahwah, NJ: Lawrence Erlbaum Associates Inc.

Finkenauer, C., Luminet, O., Gisle, L., El-Ahmadi, A., van der Linden, M., & Philippot, P. (1998). Flashbulb memories and the underlying mechanism of their formation: Toward an emotional-integrative model. *Memory and Cognition, 26,* 516–531.

Frijda, N. H. (1986). *The emotions.* Cambridge, UK: Cambridge University Press.

Frijda, N. H., Kuipers, P., & ter Schure, E. (1989). Relations among emotion, appraisal, and emotional action readiness. *Journal of Personality and Social Psychology, 57,* 212–228.

Johnson, M. K., & Chalfonte, B. L. (1994). Binding complex memories: The role of reactivation and the hippocampus. In D. L. Schacter & E. Tulving (Eds.), *Memory systems 1994* (pp. 311–350). Cambridge, MA: MIT Press.

Kline, R. B. (1998). *Principles and practice of structural equation modeling.* New York: Guilford Press.

Larsen, S. F. (1992). Potential flashbulbs: Memories of ordinary news as the baseline. In E. Winograd & U. Neisser (Eds.), *Affect and accuracy in recall: Studies of "flashbulb" memories* (pp. 32–63). New York: Cambridge University Press.

Lazarus, R. S. (1982). Thoughts on the relations between emotion and cognition. *American Psychologist, 37,* 1019–1024.

Leventhal, H. (1984). A perceptual-motor theory of emotion. In L. Berkowitz (Ed.), *Advances in experimental social psychology* (Vol. 17, pp. 117–182). New York: Academic Press.

Leventhal, H., & Scherer, K. (1987). The relationship of emotion to cognition: A functional approach to a semantic controversy. *Cognition and Emotion, 1,* 3–28.

Livingston, R. (1967). Reinforcement. In G. Quarton, T. Melenchunk, & F. Schmitt (Eds.), *The neurosciences: A study program* (pp. 568–576). New York: Rockfeller University Press.

Luminet, O., & Curci, A. (2008). *The 9/11 attacks inside and outside the US: Testing four models of flashbulb memory formation across groups and the specific effects of social identity.* Manuscript submitted for publication.

Luminet, O., Curci, A., Marsh, E. J., Wessel, I., Constantin, T., Gencoz, F., & Yogo, M. (2004). The cognitive, emotional and social impacts of the September 11th attacks: Group differences in memory for the reception context and the determinants of flashbulb memory. *Journal of General Psychology, 131,* 197–224.

McCloskey, M., Wible, C. G., & Cohen, N. J. (1988). Is there a special flashbulb memory mechanism? *Journal of Experimental Psychology: General, 177,* 171–181.

Morse, C. K., Woodward, E. M., & Zweigenhaft, R. (1993). Gender differences in flashbulb memories elicited by the Clarence Thomas hearings. *Journal of Social Psychology, 133,* 453–458.

Nachson, I., & Zelig, A. (2003). Flashbulb and factual memories: The case of Rabin's assassination. *Applied Cognitive Psychology, 17,* 519–531.

Neisser, U. (1982). Snapshots or benchmarks? In U. Neisser (Ed.), *Memory observed* (pp. 43–48). San Francisco: Freeman.

Neisser, U., & Harsch, N. (1992). Phantom flashbulbs: False recollections of hearing the news about Challenger. In E. Winograd & U. Neisser (Eds.), *Affect and accuracy in recall: Studies of "flashbulb memories"* (pp. 9–31). New York: Cambridge University Press.

Neisser, U., Winograd, E., Bergman, E. T., Schreiber, C. A., Palmer, S. E., & Weldon, M. S. (1996). Remembering the earthquake: Direct experience vs. hearing the news. *Memory, 4,* 337–357.

Pezdek, K., & Taylor, J. (2002). Memory for traumatic events. In M. L. Eisen, G. S. Goodman, & J. A. Quas (Eds.), *Memory and suggestibility in the forensic interview* (pp. 165–183). Mahwah, NJ: Lawrence Erlbaum Associates Inc.

Pillemer, D. B. (1984). Flashbulb memories of the assassination attempt on President Reagan. *Cognition, 16,* 63–80.

Qin, J., Mitchell, K. J., Johnson, M. K., Krystal, J. H., Southwick, S. M., Rasmusson, A. M., et al. (2003). Reactions to and memories for the September 11, 2001 terrorist attacks in adults with posttraumatic stress disorder. *Applied Cognitive Psychology, 17,* 1081–1097.

Rimé, B., Finkenauer, C., Luminet, O., Zech, E., & Philippot, P. (1998). Social sharing of emotion: New evidence and new questions. *European Review of Social Psychology, 9,* 145–189.

Rubin, D. C., & Kozin, M. (1984). Vivid memories. *Cognition, 16,* 81–95.

Ruiz-Vargas, J. M. (1993). ¿Cómo recuerda usted la noticia del 23-F? Naturaleza y mecanismos de los "recuerdos-destello" [How do you remember the 23-F news? Nature and mechanisms of "flashbulb memories"]. *Revista de Psicología Social, 8,* 17–32.

Scherer, K. R. (1984). On the nature and function of emotion: A component process approach. In K. R. Scherer & P. Ekman (Eds.), *Approaches to emotion* (pp. 293–318). Hillsdale, NJ: Lawrence Erlbaum Associates Inc.

Scherer, K. R. (1988). Criteria for emotion-antecedent appraisal: A review. In V. Hamilton, G. H. Bower, & N. H. Frijda (Eds.), *Cognitive perspectives on emotion and motivation* (pp. 82–126). Norwell, MA: Kluwer Academic.

Schwartz, C. E., Wright, C. I., Shin, L. M., Kagan, J., Whalen, P. J., McMullin, K. G., et al. (2003). Differential amygdalar response to novel versus newly familiar neutral faces: A functional MRI probe developed for studying inhibited temperament. *Biological Psychiatry, 53,* 854–862.

Talarico, J. M., & Rubin, D. C. (2003). Confidence, not consistency, characterizes flashbulb memories. *Psychological Science, 14,* 455–461.

Tulving, E., & Kroll, N. (1995). Novelty assessment in the brain and long-term memory encoding. *Psychonomic Bulletin and Review, 2,* 387–390.

Weaver, C. A. III (1993). Do you need a "flash" to form a flashbulb memory? *Journal of Experimental Psychology: General, 122,* 39–46.

Wright, C. I., Martis, B., Schwartz, C. E., Shin, L. M., Fischer, H., McMullin, K., et al. (2003). Novelty responses and differential effects of order in the amygdala, substantia innominata, and inferior temporal cortex. *Neuroimage, 18,* 660–669.

Part II
Consistency and accuracy

4 Flashbulb memories result from ordinary memory processes and extraordinary event characteristics[1]

Jennifer M. Talarico and David C. Rubin

Brown and Kulik (1977) observed a phenomenon that had captured the public's attention—seemingly indelible memory for important, emotional events. They dubbed it "flashbulb memory" (FBM) and conducted the first modern empirical study on the topic (for an earlier study, see Colegrove, 1899). The concept was equally effective in capturing the attention of memory researchers, and in the 30 years following that seminal publication the topic has been investigated almost as often as the events that lead to such memories allow. During this time, the description of the phenomenon has undergone an interesting and important transformation.

The initial hypothesis was that FBMs were the result of a unique memorial process. People had a specially designed means of automatically encoding all aspects of an important (emotional) event as it happened. This was advantageous because it enabled the individual to re-evaluate the circumstances of the event after the fact and to determine which details were important and which were inconsequential (Brown & Kulik, 1977; Gold, 1992). The prediction from this hypothesis was permanent, veridical recall of the event, though "far from complete" (Brown & Kulik, 1977, p. 75).

However, this strong hypothesis did not last long, as evidence of errors in the recall of FBMs was soon identified (Christianson, 1989; Neisser & Harsch, 1992; Neisser et al., 1996). Consequently, the FBM hypothesis underwent its first major revision. The new hypothesis argued that such a standard was unreasonable. Instead, the refined hypothesis stated that FBMs were still more consistent than one could predict with ordinary memory mechanisms (Cohen, McCloskey, & Wible, 1988, 1990; McCloskey, Wible, & Cohen, 1988; Pillemer, 1990; Schmidt & Bohannon, 1988). This new hypothesis still argued for a special, unique memorial process.

If there are special mechanisms involved in FBM then there should be three ways of detecting them: the properties of the FBMs, the conditions necessary to produce FBMs, and the way in which FBMs are processed. With regard to memory properties, the memories should be different from ordinary memories in some way; they could be more accurate, or more consistent, or more vivid, or show less loss over time than everyday memories. The second way to identify FBMs is that the conditions necessary to produce these memories should be different from ordinary events; they could require surprise, or consequentiality, or strong emotions, for example. Finally, how the individual processes the event should differ for FBMs relative to ordinary autobiographical memory. For each of these, the claim of a special mechanism requires more than just a difference that could be seen as one extreme of a continuum; there should be some discontinuity between "ordinary" memories and "special" FBMs.

In order to compare FBMs to ordinary autobiographical memories we need a description of "ordinary". Ideally we would sample all FBMs and all other autobiographical memories that an individual had, and compare them. If we are to use the literature, however, it is better to define ordinary autobiographical memories as easy-to-access memories that are brought to mind by a request for a particular kind of memory (e.g., a memory from a particular time, of a particular type of event, or in response to a particular word). The results would likely be different if FBMs were compared to trivial or noteworthy memories, but "trivial" and "noteworthy" beg the question of the dimension along which events are trivial or noteworthy: emotion, significance, importance, and so forth. Unless noted otherwise, the comparisons we report from the literature are between ordinary memories (as defined above) and FBMs.

We will proceed to review the various ways in which FBMs have been claimed to be different from other memories and the various mechanisms proposed to cause these differences. With respect to all of these we will ask if FBMs have more of some property; we will report whether there are consistent findings across studies showing that FBMs are more extreme. This is the minimal test of a special mechanism. If this test is met, we will ask if the differences are large enough to exclude a continuum on which FBMs are at one end and there is little overlap in the distributions. For the proposed mechanisms, we will also ask whether they have been shown to be necessary (i.e., can FBMs exist when these mechanisms are not invoked), and whether they have been shown to be sufficient (i.e., can FBMs occur only when these mechanisms occur). As a summary, our conclusions are indicated in Tables 4.1 and 4.2. Table 4.1 lists the ways FBMs have been claimed to be unique. Table 4.2 describes the mechanisms proposed for these differences.

CHARACTERISTICS OF FBMs

Accuracy

As is often the case in naturalistic studies of personally experienced events, objective measures of accuracy are rare. However, in the case of President George W. Bush and the events of September 11th 2001, video and photographic evidence exists in addition to published accounts of his recollections. Greenberg (2004) examined those available data and found that Bush's

Table 4.1 A summary of the differences between FBM and ordinary autobiographical memory

	FBM > AM		
Memory characteristics	No	Yes	Discontinuous
Accuracy	X		
Consistency	X		
Longevity	?		
Vividness		X	
Confidence		X	

Discontinuous implies a large difference with little overlap in the distributions; no characteristics exhibit this. We would have the same results if we replaced "discontinuous" with "as compared to noteworthy memories that were not in response to a flashbulb event".

Table 4.2 A summary of the evidence supporting the mechanisms proposed for enhancing FBM relative to ordinary autobiographical memory

	Sufficient	Necessary	Only in FBM
Event conditions			
Consequentiality	No	No	No
Distinctiveness	Yes	No	No
Emotional affect	?	?	No
Memory processes			
Significance	Yes	Yes	No
Surprise	No	No	No
Emotional intensity	?	No	No
Rehearsal	?	?	No

memory includes one prominent inaccuracy (that of seeing the first plane hit the first tower of the World Trade Center—footage that was not available until days after the attacks) and other, accurate details (his Chief of Staff Andy Card interrupting Bush's reading a story to children in a classroom and whispering in his ear that a second plane had crashed).

In another case study approach, Thompson and Cowan (1986) concluded that Neisser was most likely listening to a football game between the Giants and the Dodgers at the Polo Grounds broadcast by Red Barber when he learned of the attack on Pearl Harbor, not a baseball game as Neisser (1982) had previously recalled. Neisser (1986) argued that the particular error was important and informative, as it indicated his identification with the "American pastime" during an attack on his adopted homeland.

Berntsen and Thomsen (2005) developed a *documentary* method for evaluating factual information about individual participation in historical events (specifically the invasion and liberation of Denmark in World War II). Here, too, we see evidence of general accuracy, with specific features biased to match other elements of the narrative. Participants who experienced the events were more accurate in recalling the day of the week for each event, the exact time of the liberation announcement on the radio, and other factual questions than a younger control group who did not experience the events directly. Berntsen and Thomsen were able to evaluate the accuracy of participants' memory for the weather using archival data from various meteorological stations throughout the country. They concluded that although mostly accurate (65% overall vs < 5% for controls), when memory reports were inaccurate they were systematically biased to match the emotional tone of the event (e.g., the day of the liberation was remembered as more sunny, less cloudy, less windy, less rainy, and/or warmer than it actually was). These are not "rare recollective inconsistencies" (see Julian, Bohannon, & Aue, Chapter 5, this volume) found in anecdote, but are systematic patterns of recall found throughout this literature that cannot be ignored when convenient. Perhaps surprisingly, the issue of objective accuracy is ripe for further investigation. Identifying which event features are likely to be accurately recalled as well as the magnitude and direction of errors should be examined whenever archival data are available to confirm self-reports. However, there is a larger body of evidence that has examined consistency between memory reports as a proxy for accuracy.

Consistency

In order to obtain consistency data, two (or more) retrospective reports are collected. The report closer in time to the event is considered the standard. Later reports are then compared to that earlier report and inconsistencies are identified. Although two consistent reports are not necessarily accurate, an inconsistent report implies that at least one report is inaccurate. Contrary to the arguments of Pillemer (Chapter 6, this volume) and Julian, Bohannon, and Aue (Chapter 5, this volume), we do not consider "wrong time slices" (Neisser & Harsh, 1992) to be accurate. Recalling an event that actually occurred (e.g., a 30th birthday party) but was not the event requested (e.g., "tell me about your 40th birthday party") is inaccurate recall. Therefore, although consistency data may mistake a wrong time slice provided at time one as "accurate" and a correct time slice provided at time two as "inaccurate", the functional result will be a low consistency score correctly denoting unreliable recall over time.

The overwhelming evidence is that FBMs include inconsistencies (Christianson & Engelberg, 1999; Curci, 2005; Curci & Luminet, 2006; Curci, Luminet, Finkenauer, & Gisle, 2001; Greenberg, 2004; Larsen, 1992; Lee & Brown, 2003; McCloskey et al., 1988; Nachson & Zelig, 2003; Neisser, 1982; Neisser & Harsh, 1992; Schmolck, Buffalo, & Squire, 2000; Talarico & Rubin, 2003, 2006; Weaver, 1993; Weaver & Krug, 2004; Wright, 1993). Even those who argue for consistency allow that memory for specific details is not as good as memory for the general gist of the event (Bohannon & Symons, 1992; Pillemer, 1984; Schmidt, 2004; Schmidt & Bohannon, 1988; Thompson & Cowan, 1986) and that reports may be incomplete (Brown & Kulik, 1977). Furthermore, FBMs include no fewer inconsistencies than everyday memories (Talarico & Rubin, 2003, 2006). Therefore, in conjunction with the accuracy evidence described above, we must conclude that FBMs are not perfect copies of experienced events.

Longevity

There is a paucity of evidence in the FBM literature addressing the relative permanence of such memories due to predominant attention in the literature to claims requiring test–retest measures and the consequent difficulties in conducting such studies over lengthy delays. Anecdotally, FBMs are extremely long lasting. Empirically, studies that examine longevity typically obtain one retrospective report years after the event and evaluate it for vividness and completeness to determine whether it qualifies as a FBM. Using these criteria, 54% of Americans had a FBM for the assassination of civil rights activist Martin Luther King after 10 years (Brown & Kulik, 1977), 90% of Americans and 84% of Canadians had a FBM for President John F. Kennedy's assassination after 12 years (Yarmey & Bull, 1978), 71% of Americans had a FBM for the assassination of President Abraham Lincoln after 30 years (Colegrove, 1899), and 95% of Danes remembered the invasion and liberation of Denmark during World War II after 60 and 55 years, respectively (Berntsen & Thomsen, 2005).

Only Berntsen and Thomsen (2005) asked participants to recall another autobiographical event from the same time period (i.e., the most positive and negative personal event during the occupation period) and found that 77.1% and 85.5% were able to do so, respectively. Contrary to the claims of Brown and Kulik (1977), there are other events that one can remember from equally long ago. These data lead us to conclude that FBMs are long lasting, but they do not support the claim that FBMs are indelible nor that they are more permanent than noteworthy everyday memories. Therefore, for the two quintessential characteristics of FBMs—permanence and accuracy—there is little empirical support and yet room for more research if objective accuracy data are available from event samples of adequate age.

Vividness

However, there are characteristics of these memories that may still differentiate them from ordinary memories. Vividness has been of interest to FBM research since Brown and Kulik (1977) described the "live quality that is almost perceptual" (p. 74). Rubin and Kozin (1984) tried to reframe FBMs as "vivid memories", as they thought that enhanced vividness was the defining feature of the phenomenon. In fact, FBMs often exhibit ceiling effects in vividness ratings regardless of the delay between event and memory report (Kvavilashvili, Mirani, Schlagman, & Kornbrot, 2003; Niedzwienska, 2003; Talarico & Rubin, 2003; Weaver & Krug, 2004; Yarmey & Bull, 1978). Therefore, on average, FBMs are more vivid than ordinary memories, but some ordinary autobiographical memories are as vivid as FBMs (Talarico, LaBar, & Rubin, 2004). That is, there is an overlap in the distributions of vividness and so there is no discontinuity that would require a special mechanism.

Confidence

In contrast to objective evidence of memory inaccuracy, participants consistently report enhanced confidence in FBM accuracy. FBMs are usually recalled with a higher degree of confidence than other memories of equal age (Brown & Kulik, 1977; Paradis, Solomon, Florer, & Thompson, 2004; Talarico & Rubin, 2003, 2006; Weaver, 1993), even when individuals are confronted with evidence that the event in memory could not have occurred as it is remembered (Neisser & Harsch, 1992). Confidence is often at ceiling for FBMs (Christianson & Engelberg, 1999; Neisser et al., 1996; Niedzwienska, 2003; Talarico & Rubin, 2003, 2006; Weaver, 1993; Weaver & Krug, 2004) and often remains that high for at least months after the event (Christianson & Engelberg, 1999; Niedzwienska, 2003; Weaver & Krug, 2004). It may be that confidence ratings are based on equally reliably enhanced vividness ratings, as the two are correlated (Neisser & Harsch, 1992).

Therefore, along with vividness, the second distinctive property of FBMs is a discrepancy between meta-cognitive perception and objective reality. In fact this discrepancy may have led to the identification of the phenomenon in the first place, and may well lead to the most interesting applications of the phenomenon to ordinary memory processing. Thus, it is the secondary, phenomenological characteristics like vividness and confidence that may serve to retain the utility of the concept. If FBMs are differentiated by phenomenological experience, then the mechanisms responsible for the phenomenon must account for these differences, not explain (non-existent) encoding or retrieval differences. The question for future research must be, why are we more likely to maintain vivid, confidently held memories of these particular events? We now turn our attention away from their characteristics and to the conditions necessary to produce FBMs.

CONDITIONS NECESSARY TO PRODUCE FBMs

The vast majority of research in this field has been done in the aftermath of a public tragedy. This is because consequentiality, distinctiveness, and negative emotional affect are the primary features of the event thought to influence the formation of FBMs (i.e., a memory report that satisfies the FBM criteria for vividness and/or completeness, or a memory report that includes answers to one or more canonical questions—informant, location, ongoing activity, time/date, affect, others' reactions—in the absence of any objective accuracy or test–retest consistency data). Here, we will discuss objective characteristics of the events thought to produce FBMs. In the next section we will discuss subjective assessments of the event also thought to produce FBMs.

Consequentiality

Consequential events most often studied include disasters with loss of life (e.g., earthquakes, terrorist attacks) or events with political implications (e.g., assassinations, resignations, invasions). FBM is differentiated from traumatic memory research, as the participants in the latter are directly affected by the events being studied. In the case of FBMs, participants are rarely so personally involved. However, the events being investigated are often on such a scale that the aftermath affects the lives of participants in other, more subtle ways. For instance, all air passengers must now submit to enhanced security procedures at US airports as a direct result of the September 11th attacks (to name one of the least significant changes in everyday life as a result of a major tragic event). Is this comprehensive consequentiality responsible for FBMs? In short, no. The empirical evidence fails to support the claim that objective consequentiality is relevant for the formation (Er, 2003; Tekcan, 2001), accuracy (Berntsen & Thomsen, 2005), consistency (Niedzwienska, 2003; Weaver, 1993), or vividness (Berntsen & Thomsen, 2005; Rubin & Kozin, 1984) of FBMs. So, although these types of events may retain value as they are common to large numbers of potential participants, their consequentiality seems to be of little memorial value.

Distinctiveness

The evidence in support of distinctiveness effects is much stronger than was found for consequentiality, as it has been correlated with the formation (Edery-Halpern & Nachson, 2004; Larsen, 1992; Wright & Gaskell, 1992) and vividness (Bohn & Berntsen, 2007; Edery-Halpern & Nachson, 2004) of FBMs. Furthermore, Edery-Halpern and Nachson (2004) found that the least distinctive event in their sample was also significantly less well remembered (i.e., fewer details were recalled and more responses were left blank for this memory compared to the other events). Mahmood, Manier, and Hirst (2004) found no relationship between distinctiveness and the formation or vividness of FBMs, but distinctiveness in their study was defined as the first event in a series of similar, emotional, personally significant events (i.e., the deaths of lovers, friends, and/or family members due to AIDS). An event may be distinctive for reasons other than that it is the first of its kind, however; Brown and Kulik (1977) studied memory for a series of assassinations of political figures in a relatively brief period of time, yet each was a distinctive event. In fact, all distinctive events (using their definition of the first AIDS-related death to be experienced) fit the FBM criteria. This is not surprising given that the episodic memory literature includes ample evidence of a distinctiveness advantage (i.e., *von Restorff effect*; see Hunt & Worthen, 2006, for a review). In Brewer's (1988) study of ordinary autobiographical memories, the lower the frequency of event occurrence, the greater the likelihood of later cued recall.

Emotional affect

Another event feature known to enhance ordinary memory and thought to influence FBMs is negative emotional affect. For example, negative stimuli "pop-out" in a neutral context to a greater extent than neutral stimuli in a fearful context (Ohman, Flykt, & Esteves, 2001). As they typically involve disasters, attacks, and assassinations, most FBM studies have included only negative events. However, both positive and negative events have been found to lead to FBMs (Berntsen & Thomsen, 2005; Bohn & Berntsen, 2007; Scott & Ponsoda, 1996; Tekcan, 2001). In fact, Bohn and Berntsen (2007) showed that the same event (in this case, the fall of the Berlin Wall) was more likely to produce FBMs when it was interpreted as a positive event, consistent with pleasantness biases in autobiographical recall (Matlin & Stang, 1978; Thompson, 1985; Thompson, Skowronski, Larsen, & Betz, 1996; Walker, Skowronski, & Thompson, 2003; Walker, Vogl, & Thompson, 1997). Furthermore, there is evidence from collective memories that even profoundly negative events are more likely to persist in the culture if they evoke positive connotations. For example, Hirst and Meksin (Chapter 10, this volume) describe how the assassinations of Lincoln and Kennedy endure because each president was subsequently deified by popular culture. Similarly, there is often an emphasis on patriotism and heroism in the face of tragedy (e.g., the Pearl Harbor or September 11th attacks) in societal recollections of those events.

Other valence effects in FBMs have been neglected, with the notable exception of Berntsen and Thomsen's (2005) biased recall of whether to match the emotional tone of the invasion and liberation of Denmark during World War II (see above). Related biases have not been investigated because of the almost exclusive focus on negative, consequential events. We have already shown that consequentiality does not seem to be important for the formation of FBMs, therefore further study of positive FBMs or of valence effects in FBM in general should no longer be unnecessarily limited in this way.

Summarizing the conditions necessary to produce FBMs, what could be a unique characteristic of FBMs (consequentiality) fails to predict the memory phenomenon, and well-characterized features of ordinary autobiographical memory successfully account for FBM data (distinctiveness and emotional affect).

PROCESSING THE FLASHBULB EVENT

In addition to features of the event, characteristics of how an individual processes the event are thought to be important determinants of FBMs. Three encoding factors (significance, surprise, and emotional intensity) and one retrieval factor (rehearsal) are thought to have effects on FBMs. How these characteristics contribute to the FBM phenomenon individually and interactively is the focus of most current work in this area.

Significance

Significance, or personal importance, refers to the individual's assessment of the event, not to objective criteria concerning the influence of the event (i.e., consequentiality as described above). Participant ratings of significance are positively correlated with FBM formation (Bohannon & Symons, 1992; Conway et al., 1994; Larsen, 1992; Mahmood et al., 2004; Wright & Gaskell, 1992; but see Wright, Gaskell, & O'Muircheartaigh, 1998). Paradis et al. (2004) found that their New York City participants rated both September 11th and 12th as personally important, and their sample developed FBMs for both of those days, in terms of initial recall and later consistency. Niedzwienska (2003) also found significance to be correlated with consistency of the FBM report. Vividness has been consistently related to personal importance (Mahmood et al., 2004; Nachson & Zelig, 2003; Niedzwienska, 2003; Rubin & Kozin, 1984).

Self-report ratings are only one method of measuring personal importance, however. Cross-cultural studies are often undertaken largely to investigate differences in consequentiality and, as a corollary, significance. Event memory (i.e., memory for the factual details of an event) is consistently enhanced for those closest to the event (Curci & Luminet, 2006; Curci et al., 2001; Edery-Halpern & Nachson, 2004; Luminet et al., 2004; Pezdek, 2003; Tekcan, Ece, Gulgoz, & Er, 2003). Correspondingly, numerous investigators have found that those physically closer to an event or those more directly affected by an event are more likely to develop FBMs (Conway et al., 1994; Curci et al., 2001; Edery-Halpern & Nachson, 2004; Er, 2003; Kvavilashvili et al., 2003; Luminet et al., 2004; Neisser et al., 1996; Sharot, Martorella, Delgado, & Phelps, 2007).

In addition to cross-cultural studies, group membership has been used as a proxy for personal importance, resulting in similar conclusions. Brown and Kulik (1977) found that African-Americans were more likely to report FBMs for civil-rights-relevant events than were White participants. Berntsen and Thomsen (2005) reported enhanced vividness and accuracy for FBMs of the invasion and liberation of Denmark among those participants who had been active in the resistance movement at the time, and Wright et al. (1998) found that men (assumed to have greater knowledge of and interest in sports) were more likely to develop FBMs for the Hillsborough football stadium disaster than were women.

Otani et al. (2005) classified memory reports as FBMs or non-FBMs, yet found no difference in the significance ratings of participants in each group. Davidson and Glisky (2002) also found no differences in the significance ratings of two events, yet one event led to reliably more FBM reports than the other. Although significance contributes to FBM formation, it is not always greater in FBMs. Berntsen (Chapter 9, this volume) argues quite persuasively that it is an event's importance to our social identity specifically that determines whether an event will produce a FBM. Because FBM research has emphasized recall of public events, it is not surprising that social identity is the most salient criterion for determining significance. As irrelevant characteristics (e.g., consequentiality, negative valence) are replaced by more systematic study of relevant characteristics, the nuanced nature of such effects can be determined. It is our belief that social identity will remain a determining feature of FBM formation, but that other criteria for personal significance may also lead to vivid, confidently held FBMs as well.

We have substantial converging evidence of personal significance contributing to FBMs. As with distinctiveness, there is an abundance of data for a self-referential effect in memory performance, with personally relevant material enhancing memory (Rogers, Kuiper, & Kirker, 1977; see Symons & Johnson, 1997, for a review). Thus, the influence of significance on FBM can be predicted from more general features of autobiographical memories.

Surprise

As significance is differentiated from consequentiality, so too is surprise different from novelty. Surprise is a personal, emotional reaction to the event, not a property of the event. Note that although an event can be expected, and therefore not surprising, it can still be novel, as was seen in the case of several terrorist attacks in Israel, the sad inevitability of which does not prevent each attack from being distinct (Edery-Halpern & Nachson, 2004). Davidson and Glisky (2002) found that both initial recall and later consistency of FBMs for the death of Princess Diana were greater than for the death of Mother Theresa, which was rated as less surprising. However, equal surprise ratings were provided by those who did and those who did not develop FBMs for the Kobe earthquake (Otani et al., 2005). Berntsen and Thomsen (2005) found that participants rated the invasion of Denmark as more surprising than its liberation, but were more likely to have FBMs for the liberation than for the invasion. Therefore, each possible relationship between surprise and FBM has been identified in the literature.

What is certain is that FBMs can be found for expected events, including the moon landing or Nixon's resignation (Winograd & Killinger, 1983), the first US-led invasion of Iraq (Tekcan, 2001), and Mitterrand's death (Curci et al., 2001). Novelty effects in autobiographical memory appear more similar to the distinctiveness effects described above, but surprise per se has not been investigated in ordinary autobiographical memory. Therefore this is one of the least understood mechanisms, yet it has been one of the key determinants of event selection for FBM research and so has limited the scope of FBM research to date. The major difference between positive and negative events, for example, is that positive events tend to be expected whereas negative events are typically unexpected (Berntsen, 2002; Rubin & Berntsen, 2003; Tromp, Koss, Figueredo, & Tharan, 1995). Because surprise is thought to be important to FBMs, the vast majority of FBM research has examined negative events. However, if surprise is irrelevant to FBM, valence differences in FBM can, and should, be examined. This is especially true given that surprise tends to be a positive emotion in ordinary autobiographical memories (Talarico et al., 2004). In other words, when cued to generate memories of surprise, participants are more likely to recall pleasant events (e.g., a surprise birthday party) than unpleasant events (e.g., an unexpectedly low score on an exam).

Emotional intensity

The most contradictory findings in the FBM literature are those involving emotional intensity. There are data supporting its role in FBM formation using participant ratings (Berntsen & Thomsen, 2005; Bohannon, 1988; Bohannon & Symons, 1992; Davidson & Glisky, 2002; Paradis et al., 2004) and using culture as a proxy for emotion (Brown & Kulik, 1977; Curci et al., 2001) but almost as many that fail to find a correlation (with participant ratings: Otani et al., 2005; Smith, Bibi, & Sheard, 2003; Tekcan, 2001; with culture as a proxy: Luminet et al., 2004). The same contradictory pattern emerges for intensity and consistency, with four studies finding a positive relationship between the two (Bohannon & Symons, 1992; Conway et al., 1994; Davidson & Glisky, 2002; Schmolck et al., 2000) and five failing to find such a relationship (Christianson & Engelberg, 1999; Nachson & Zelig, 2003; Neisser & Harsch, 1992; Neisser et al., 1996; Schmidt, 2004; Talarico & Rubin, 2003). Vividness of the FBM is equally divergent. Rubin and Kozin (1984) failed to find a correlation between emotional intensity and vividness, whereas others have found the two to be related (Berntsen & Thomsen, 2005; Nachson & Zelig, 2003; Pillemer, 1984). Wright et al. (1998) found that men, who rated the Hillsborough disaster as less emotional than women, were more likely to develop FBMs.

One explanation for this variability has been to differentiate the effects of emotion on central and peripheral information individually. Brown and Kulik (1977) believed that the presence of idiosyncratic peripheral details supported the idea of an obligatory, indiscriminant encoding process resulting from emotional intensity. Other investigators have shown that emotion tends to enhance central details of an event, often to the detriment of peripheral information (Christianson & Loftus, 1991; Reisberg & Heuer, 1992). Schmidt (2004) found that although peripheral detail consistency declined over time more than did central details, moderate emotions were associated more with reliable recall of each detail type than were high emotions.

Therefore another mechanism described in the canonical memory literature, non-linear influences of emotion on memory (Yerkes & Dodson, 1908), can explain FBM formation. Furthermore, the advantage of emotionally intense experiences over neutral events is also well established in the episodic and autobiographical memory literature and is replicated in FBM. For FBMs, inconsistencies are often found for peripheral details only (as defined by some subset of the canonical questions) (Christianson, 1989; Romeu, 2006; Tekcan et al., 2003). However, how one divides the canonical questions into central vs peripheral information often coincides with whether the memory reports show consistency or inconsistency. For example, Christianson (1989) found reliable recall for "informant", "time", "location", and "others present" information and less reliable recall for "ongoing activity", "clothes worn at the time", and "first thought upon hearing the news" information. Tekcan and colleagues (2003) considered "time" and "others present" to be peripheral because those two questions were responsible for the majority of inconsistencies found in their participants' memory reports. Importantly, in none of these investigations was recall of central vs peripheral details of a non-FBM obtained.

In addition, Laney, Heuer, and Reisberg (2003) showed that the enhancement of central information is not due to emotion per se, but to the attention-capturing properties of the central information that leads to a decrease in recall of peripheral details. For FBMs, the perceptually central element is the informant and the conceptually central element is the news itself, neither of which is distinctive enough to impair peripheral recall sufficiently to generate a central detail enhancement. Because the central–peripheral distinction lacks precision in definition and consistency in application within the FBM literature as of yet, we remain unclear as to the influence of emotional intensity on FBMs.

Rehearsal

The final individual characteristic is the only non-encoding-specific mechanism discussed in this literature. Although consequentiality is often not known until after the initial news, consequentiality seems to be unimportant for FBM formation. Significance, on the other hand, is more likely to be known immediately as determined by interest in the general event domain (whether that be politics in the case of assassinations or resignations, or personal safety and national identity in the case of natural disasters or military/terrorist attacks). Although this should not imply that such evaluations are static or immune to post-event factors, rehearsal is still the only mechanism to operate exclusively post event.

Rehearsal effects seem to dissociate based on the dependent variable of interest. Increased rehearsal has been correlated with the formation of FBMs (Bohannon, 1988; Bohannon & Symons, 1992; Curci et al., 2001; Davidson & Glisky, 2002; Otani et al., 2005; Tekcan & Peynircioglu, 2002), although

Hornstein, Brown, and Mulligan (2003) found that to be true only for covert, not overt, rehearsal. For vividness, there seems to be no relationship with rehearsal (Pillemer, 1984; Rubin & Kozin, 1984).

For consistency, the pattern is quite variable. After a delay of 6 months, Pillemer (1984) found no relationship with consistency. After a 1-year delay, Davidson and Glisky (2002) found a significant correlation, as did Schmolk and colleagues (2000) at 15 months. However, at 32 months, Schmolk and colleagues (2000) found no relationship between the two. Finally, with a delay of 3 years, Bohannon and Symons (1992) again found a correlation between rehearsal and FBM. Either this relationship is completely unreliable (due to deficiencies in the measurement or due to variability in the phenomenon) or differences in other aspects of the event make such cross-experiment comparisons untenable. Bohannon and Symons (1992) report data that may support the latter explanation. They found a three-way interaction of emotion, rehearsal, and consistency for FBM probed recall data. Those who were not upset by the *Challenger* explosion displayed no differences in consistency due to rehearsal, whereas those who were upset by the accident showed decreased consistency with enhanced rehearsal. To add even greater complexity, with free recall responses there was a main effect of emotion, no effect of rehearsal, and no interaction for consistency data. Yet we know that rehearsal is a potent mechanism for sustaining memory. In fact, Hirst and Meksin (Chapter 10, this volume) describe evidence for how rehearsal via media exposure enhances long-term recall of collective memories.

Combining factors

Most events are chosen as subjects of FBM research because they exhibit many of the features we have noted here. Thus, correlations among these variables of interest are common. This has led some investigators to adopt statistical techniques such as latent variable modelling and structural equation modelling to determine the relationships among these features (see, e.g., Er, 2003; Finkenauer et al., 1998). Each of these models defined FBM as recall of some number of canonical categories or some measure of completeness and specificity, and then compared memories that satisfied the FBM criteria to those that did not. None examined vividness or confidence, the most reliable characteristics that differentiate FBMs from ordinary autobiographical memories. Their focus was to differentiate which statistical model was a better fit to the FBM data.

What we have tried to show here is that a FBM-specific model is unnecessary, as the mechanisms responsible for producing FBMs are the same as those for any other autobiographical memories. Furthermore, the data presented here suggest that significance and distinctiveness are the predominant mechanisms responsible for FBMs. This is inconsistent with the models identified above, each of which considers significance and distinctiveness to be indirect factors in FBM formation. It could still be that a unique combination of variables might substitute for a definition or description of FBMs, but the existing studies do not appear to be converging on such a combination. However, differences in measurement and definition may account for this inconsistency and the true nature of the influence of these mechanisms on the resultant characteristics of FBMs is far from understood.

SUMMARY

FBMs are distinguished from ordinary memories by their vividness and the confidence with which they are held. There is little evidence that they are reliably different from ordinary autobiographical memories in accuracy, consistency, or longevity. However, there are characteristics of the event and of the individual that can enhance each of these memory properties.

For the event conditions, consequentiality seems to be irrelevant to FBM, distinctiveness is the most predictive, and emotional affect is as yet understudied. For the individual characteristics, significance is correlated with formation, consistency, and vividness of FBMs. Of the processes discussed, significance is the most promising determinant of FBM. Surprise is one of the most common yet least understood memory process involved in FBM. Surprise has an unreliable influence on the formation and consistency of FBMs (the least reliable features of FBMs overall) and its effects on vividness and confidence (the most reliable features) have not been systematically investigated. Therefore this seems to be one of the more promising areas for future investigation. Emotional intensity is an unreliable predictor of FBM. It is likely that some of the enhanced confidence or vividness associated with FBMs is due to emotionality. However, the exact nature and scope of that influence have yet to be determined. Lastly, rehearsal is correlated with the formation of FBMs, is not correlated with vividness, and has an unreliable correlation with consistency. Because rehearsals often serve to underscore the significance of the event (e.g., increased media attention to events that affect more individuals or enhanced likelihood of retelling personally important events), disentangling the effects of rehearsal from the functions those rehearsals serve is an important goal for future investigators.

NOTE

1 The authors would like to thank Simon Tonev for helpful comments on earlier drafts. This work was supported in part by National Institute of Mental Health grant number R01 MH066079.

REFERENCES

Berntsen, D. (2002). Tunnel memories for autobiographical events: Central details are remembered more frequently from shocking than from happy experiences. *Memory and Cognition, 30,* 1010–1020.

Berntsen, D., & Thomsen, D. K. (2005). Personal memories for remote historical events: Accuracy and clarity of flashbulb memories related to World War II. *Journal of Experimental Psychology: General, 134,* 242–257.

Bohannon, J. N. (1988). Flashbulb memories for the space shuttle disaster: A tale of two theories. *Cognition, 29,* 179–196.

Bohannon, J. N., & Symons, V. L. (1992). Flashbulb memories: Confidence, consistency, and quantity. In E. Winograd & U. Neisser (Eds.), *Affect and accuracy in recall: Studies of "flashbulb" memories* (pp. 65–91). New York: Cambridge University Press.

Bohn, A., & Berntsen, D. (2007). Pleasantness bias in flashbulb memories: Positive and negative flashbulb memories of the fall of the Berlin Wall among East- and West Germans. *Memory and Cognition, 35*(3), 565–577.

Brewer, W. F. (1988). Memory for randomly sampled autobiographical events. In U. Neisser & E. Winograd (Eds.), *Remembering reconsidered: Ecological and traditional approaches to the study of memory* (pp. 21–90). New York: Cambridge University Press.

Brown, R., & Kulik, J. (1977). Flashbulb memories. *Cognition, 5,* 73–99.

Christianson, S. (1989). Flashbulb memories: Special, but not so special. *Memory and Cognition, 17,* 435–443.

Christianson, S., & Engelberg, E. (1999). Memory and emotional consistency: The MS *Estonia* ferry disaster. *Memory, 7,* 471–482.

Christianson, S., & Loftus, E. F. (1991). Remembering emotional events: The fate of detailed information. *Cognition and Emotion, 5,* 81–108.

Cohen, N. J., McCloskey, M., & Wible, C. G. (1988). There is still no case for a flashbulb-memory mechanism: Reply to Schmidt and Bohannon. *Journal of Experimental Psychology: General, 117,* 336–338.

Cohen, N. J., McCloskey, M., & Wible, C. G. (1990). Flashbulb memories and underlying cognitive mechanisms: Reply to Pillemer. *Journal of Experimental Psychology: General, 119,* 97–100.

Colegrove, F. W. (1899). Individual memories. *American Journal of Psychology, 10,* 228–255.

Conway, M. A., Anderson, S. J., Larsen, S. F., Donnelly, C. M., McDaniel, M. A., McClelland, A. G. R., et al. (1994). The formation of flashbulb memories. *Memory and Cognition, 22,* 326–343.

Curci, A. (2005). Latent variable models for the measurement of flashbulb memories: A comparative approach. *Applied Cognitive Psychology, 19,* 3–22.

Curci, A., & Luminet, O. (2006). Follow-up of a cross-national comparison on flashbulb and event memory for the September 11th attacks. *Memory, 14,* 329–344.

Curci, A., Luminet, O., Finkenauer, C., & Gisle, L. (2001). Flashbulb memories in social groups: A comparative test–retest study of the memory of French President Mitterrand's death in a French and a Belgian group. *Memory, 9,* 81–101.

Davidson, P. S. R., & Glisky, E. L. (2002). Is flashbulb memory a special instance of source memory? Evidence from older adults. *Memory, 10,* 99–111.

Edery-Halpern, G., & Nachson, I. (2004). Distinctiveness in flashbulb memory: Comparative analysis of five terrorist attacks. *Memory, 12*, 147–157.

Er, N. (2003). A new flashbulb memory model applied to the Marmara earthquake. *Applied Cognitive Psychology, 17*, 503–517.

Finkenauer, C., Luminet, O., Gisle, L., El-Ahmadi, A., van der Linden, M., & Philippot, P. (1998). Flashbulb memories and the underlying mechanisms of their formation: Toward an emotional-integrative model. *Memory and Cognition, 26*, 516–531.

Gold, P. E. (1992). A proposed neurobiological basis for regulating memory storage for significant events. In E. Winograd & U. Neisser (Eds.), *Affect and accuracy in recall studies of "flashbulb" memories* (pp. 141–161). New York: Cambridge University Press.

Greenberg, D. L. (2004). President Bush's false "flashbulb" memory of 9/11/01. *Applied Cognitive Psychology, 18*, 363–370.

Hornstein, S. L., Brown, A. S., & Mulligan, N. W. (2003). Long-term flashbulb memory for learning of Princess Diana's death. *Memory, 11*, 293–306.

Hunt, R. R., & Worthen, J. B. (Eds.). (2006). *Distinctiveness and memory*. New York: Oxford University Press.

Kvavilashvili, L., Mirani, J., Schlagman, S., & Kornbrot, D. E. (2003). Comparing flashbulb memories of September 11 and the death of Princess Diana: Effects of time delays and nationality. *Applied Cognitive Psychology, 17*, 1017–1031.

Laney, C., Heuer, F., & Reisberg, D. (2003). Thematically-induced arousal in naturally-occurring emotional memories. *Applied Cognitive Psychology, 17*, 995–1004.

Larsen, S. F. (1992). Potential flashbulbs: Memories of ordinary news as the baseline. In E. Winograd & U. Neisser (Eds.), *Affect and accuracy in recall: Studies of "flashbulb" memories* (pp. 32–64). New York: Cambridge University Press.

Lee, P. J., & Brown, N. R. (2003). Delay related changes in personal memories for September 11, 2001. *Applied Cognitive Psychology, 17*, 1007–1015.

Luminet, O., Curci, A., Marsh, E. J., Wessel, I., Constantin, T., Gencoz, F., et al. (2004). The cognitive, emotional, and social impacts of the September 11 attacks: Group differences in memory for the reception context and the determinants of flashbulb memory. *Journal of General Psychology, 131*, 197–224.

Mahmood, D., Manier, D., & Hirst, W. (2004). Memory for how one learned of multiple deaths from AIDS: Repeated exposure and distinctiveness. *Memory and Cognition, 32*, 125–134.

Matlin, M. W., & Stang, D. J. (1978). *The Pollyanna Principle: Selectivity in language, memory, and thought*. Cambridge, MA: Schenkman Publishing Company.

McCloskey, M., Wible, C. G., & Cohen, N. J. (1988). Is there a special flashbulb-memory mechanism? *Journal of Experimental Psychology: General, 117*, 171–181.

Nachson, I., & Zelig, A. (2003). Flashbulb and factual memories: The case of Rabin's assassination. *Applied Cognitive Psychology, 17*, 519–531.

Neisser, U. (1982). Snapshots or benchmarks? In U. Neisser & I. E. Hyman (Eds.), *Memory observed: Remembering in natural contexts* (pp. 68–74). San Francisco: Worth Publishers.

Neisser, U. (1986). Remembering Pearl Harbor: Reply to Thompson and Cowan. *Cognition, 23*, 285–286.

Neisser, U., & Harsch, N. (1992). Phantom flashbulbs: False recollections of hearing the news about *Challenger*. In E. Winograd & U. Neisser (Eds.), *Affect and* accuracy in recall: Studies of "flashbulb" memories (pp. 9–31). New York: Cambridge University Press.

Neisser, U., Winograd, E., Bergman, E. T., Schreiber, C. A., Palmer, S. E., & Weldon, M. S. (1996). Remembering the earthquake: Direct experience vs. hearing the news. *Memory, 4*, 337–357.

Niedzwienska, A. (2003). Misleading postevent information and flashbulb memories. *Memory, 11*, 49–558.

Ohman, A., Flykt, A., & Esteves, F. (2001). Emotion drives attention: Detecting the snake in the grass. *Journal of Experimental Psychology: General, 130*, 466–478.

Otani, H., Kusumi, T., Kato, K., Matsuda, K., Kern, R. P., Widner, R., Jr., et al. (2005). Remembering a nuclear accident in Japan: Did it trigger flashbulb memories? *Memory, 13*, 6–20.

Paradis, C., Solomon, L. Z., Florer, F., & Thompson, T. (2004). Flashbulb memories of personal events of 9/11 and the day after for a sample of New York City residents. *Psychological Reports, 95*, 304–310.

Pezdek, K. (2003). Event memory and autobiographical memory for the events of September 11, 2001. *Applied Cognitive Psychology, 17*, 1033–1045.

Pillemer, D. B. (1984). Flashbulb memories of the assassination attempt on President Reagan. *Cognition, 16*, 63–80.

Pillemer, D. B. (1990). Clarifying the flashbulb memory concept: Comment on McCloskey, Wible, and Cohen (1988). *Journal of Experimental Psychology: General, 119*, 92–96.

Reisberg, D., & Heuer, F. (1992). Remembering the details of emotional events. In E. Winograd & U. Neisser (Eds.), *Affect and accuracy in recall: Studies of "flashbulb" memories* (pp. 162–190). New York: Cambridge University Press.

Rogers, T. B., Kuiper, N. A., & Kirker, W. S. (1977). Self-reference and the encoding of personal information. *Journal of Personality and Social Psychology, 35*, 677–688.

Romeu, P. F. (2006). Memories of the terrorist attacks of September 11, 2001: A study of the consistency and phenomenal characteristics of flashbulb memories. *Spanish Journal of Psychology, 9*, 52–60.

Rubin, D. C., & Berntsen, D. (2003). Life scripts help to maintain autobiographical memories of highly positive, but not highly negative, events. *Memory and Cognition, 31*, 1–14.

Rubin, D. C., & Kozin, M. (1984). Vivid memories. *Cognition, 16*, 81–95.

Schmidt, S. R. (2004). Autobiographical memories for the September 11th attacks: Reconstructive errors and emotional impairment of memory. *Memory and Cognition, 32*, 443–454.

Schmidt, S. R., & Bohannon, J. N. (1988). In defense of the flashbulb memory hypothesis: A comment on McCloskey, Wible, and Cohen (1988). *Journal of Experimental Psychology: General, 117*, 332–335.

Schmolck, H., Buffalo, E. A., & Squire, L. R. (2000). Memory distortions develop over time: Recollections of the O. J. Simpson trial verdict after 15 and 32 months. *Psychological Science, 11*, 39–45.

Scott, D., & Ponsoda, V. (1996). The role of positive and negative affect in flashbulb memory. *Psychological Reports, 79*, 467–473.

Sharot, T., Martorella, E. A., Delgado, M. R., & Phelps, E. A. (2007). How personal experience modulates the neural circuitry of memories of September 11. *Proceedings of the National Academy of Science, 104*, 389–394.

Smith, M. C., Bibi, U., & Sheard, D. (2003). Evidence for the differential impact of time and emotion on personal and event memories for September 11, 2001. *Applied Cognitive Psychology, 17*, 1047–1055.

Symons, C. S., & Johnson, B. T. (1997). The self-reference effect in memory: A meta-analysis. *Psychological Bulletin, 121*, 371–394.

Talarico, J. M., LaBar K. S., & Rubin, D. C. (2004). Emotional intensity predicts autobiographical memory experience, *Memory and Cognition, 32*, 1118–1132.

Talarico, J. M., & Rubin, D. C. (2003). Confidence, not consistency, characterizes flashbulb memories. *Psychological Science, 14*, 455–461.

Talarico, J. M., & Rubin, D. C. (2006). Flashbulb memories are special after all; in phenomenology, not accuracy. *Applied Cognitive Psychology, 21*, 557–578.

Tekcan, A. I. (2001). Flashbulb memories for a negative and a positive event: News of Desert Storm and acceptance to college. *Psychological Reports, 88*, 323–331.

Tekcan, A. I., Ece, B., Gulgoz, S., & Er, N. (2003). Autobiographical and event memory for 9/11: Changes across one year. *Applied Cognitive Psychology, 17*, 1057–1066.

Tekcan, A. I., & Peynircioglu, Z. F. (2002). Effects of age on flashbulb memories. *Psychology and Aging, 17*, 416–422.

Thompson, C. P. (1985). Memory for unique personal events: Effects of pleasantness. *Motivation and Emotion, 9*, 277–289.

Thompson, C. P., & Cowan, T. (1986). Flashbulb memories: A nicer interpretation of a Neisser recollection. *Cognition, 22*, 199–200.

Thompson, C. P., Skowronski, J. J., Larsen, S. F., & Betz, A. L. (1996). *Autobiographical memory: Remembering what and remembering when* (pp. 67–82). Mahwah, NJ: Lawrence Erlbaum Associates Inc.

Tromp, S., Koss, M. P., Figueredo, A. J., & Tharan, M. (1995). Are rape memories different? A comparison of rape, other unpleasant, and pleasant memories among employed women. *Journal of Traumatic Stress, 8*, 607–627.

Walker, W. R., Skowronski, J. J., & Thompson, C. P. (2003). Life is pleasant—and memory helps to keep it that way! *Review of General Psychology, 7*, 203–210.

Walker, W. R., Vogl, R. J., & Thompson, C. P. (1997). Autobiographical memory: Unpleasantness fades faster than pleasantness over time. *Applied Cognitive Psychology, 11*, 399–413.

Weaver, C. A., III. (1993). Do you need a "flash" to form a flashbulb memory? *Journal of Experimental Psychology: General, 122*, 39–46.

Weaver, C. A., III, & Krug, K. S. (2004). Consolidation-like effects in flashbulb memories: Evidence from September 11, 2001. *American Journal of Psychology, 117*, 517–530.

Winograd, E., & Killinger, W. A. (1983). Relating age at encoding in early childhood to adult recall: Development of flashbulb memories. *Journal of Experimental Psychology: General, 112*, 413–422.

Wright, D. B. (1993). Recall of the Hillsborough disaster over time: Systematic biases of "flashbulb" memories. *Applied Cognitive Psychology, 7*, 129–138.

Wright, D. B., & Gaskell, G. D. (1992). The construction and function of vivid memories. In M. A. Conway, D. C. Rubin, H. Spinnler, & W. A. Wagenaar (Eds.), *Theoretical perspectives on autobiographical memory* (pp. 241–261). Dordrecht, The Netherlands: Kluwer Academic Publishers.

Wright, D. B., Gaskell, G. D., & O'Muircheartaigh, C. A. (1998). Flashbulb memory assumptions: Using national surveys to explore cognitive phenomena. *British Journal of Psychology, 89*, 103–118.

Yarmey, A., & Bull, M. P. (1978). Where were you when President Kennedy was assassinated? *Bulletin of the Psychonomic Society, 11*, 133–135.

Yerkes, R. M., & Dodson, J. D. (1908). The relation of strength of stimulus to rapidity of habit-formation. *Journal of Comparative Neurology and Psychology, 18*, 459–482

5 Measures of flashbulb memory
Are elaborate memories consistently accurate?

Megan Julian, John N. Bohannon III, and William Aue[1]

Flashbulb memories (FBMs) are vivid recollections for the circumstances of discovering surprising and consequential events such as the death of a world leader (Colegrove, 1899). FBMs can occur for both pleasant (e.g., a marriage proposal) and aversive (e.g., the World Trade Center attacks or the death of a loved one) events, and all have in common that they are remembered as if re-experiencing them (Talarico & Rubin, 2007). However, in coining the term "flashbulb memory", Brown and Kulik (1977) asserted that such memories, while vivid, are far from complete and not perfect, immutable photographs of the past experience.

INTRODUCTION TO FLASHBULB MEMORY MEASURES

In the early FBM studies, quantity of recall in narratives was the default measure of these vivid engrams. For example, Brown and Kulik (1977) asked participants, "Do you recall the circumstances in which you first heard that . . ." for 10 person–event cues (for example, the assassination of John F. Kennedy). Participants then narrated their personal circumstances of hearing the news. To classify the details reported in participants' memory stories, Brown and Kulik (1977) devised canonical narrative categories (place, ongoing event, informant, own affect, aftermath, and others' affect) to uniformly assess quantity of recall across different events (for a review of early FBM methods, see Bohannon & Symons, 1992). More elaboration per feature or the inclusion of more canonical features have commonly been equated to a stronger or better FBM.

An alternative method to estimate the strength of FBMs is through the use of memory probe questions, which directly ask participants to provide specific information. In some cases, probes addressed each of Brown and Kulik's (1977) canonical features (e.g., "Who was your informant?"; see Pillemer, 1984), whereas others used questions directed at more specific details such as "What was your informant wearing?" (e.g., Bohannon, 1988). Still others (e.g., Finkenauer et al., 1998) opted to use a combination of both types of probed questions. This discrepancy alone makes it difficult to make comparisons across studies. Some studies employed the recollective narrative (e.g., Neisser & Harsch, 1992), some used a probed recall technique (e.g., Talarico & Rubin, 2007), whereas others used both of these methods (e.g., Bohannon, 1988). Suffice to say, there was little uniformity in measuring FBM quantity during the twentieth century (Bohannon & Symons, 1992; Wright, Chapter 2, this volume).

Despite the diversity of methods, several factors have been found to relate to a participant's quantity of recall. Brown and Kulik (1977) found that participants' affect, recounts, and the perceived consequentiality of the event predicted more extensive FBM narratives. Similarly, Edery-Halpern and Nachson's (2004) study assessed Israelis' memories for five different terrorist attacks, and found that higher quantity of recall was associated with higher initial affect, higher reported overt recounts, and increased consequentiality as measured by the proximity of the attack to one's residence. However, Pillemer (1984) claimed that initial affect and not consequentiality or recounts was the main predictor of a more elaborate FBM. Likewise, in a study of memories for the 9/11 attacks in a Canadian sample, Smith, Bibi, and Sheard (2003) found that affect did not appear to influence the quantity of recall for autobiographical FBMs but seemed to enhance event memory. Bohannon, Cross, and Gratz (2007) examined the effect of discovery context on quantity of recall, and found that those who discovered the news from the media were likely to remember more about the facts of the event and those who discovered the news from another person were likely to remember more about their discovery. The occasional discrepancies between researchers on what factors influenced the quantity of recall were likely due to a combination of factors: different sample sizes, differences in the assessments (i.e., free vs probed recall), and differences in scoring methods.

Quantity of recall is certainly important, but its relation to the accuracy of such memories has been problematic. Participants tend to believe that their memory reports are accurate, but evidence suggests that people can be confident in inaccurate (or at least inconsistent) memory accounts (Neisser & Harsch, 1992; Schmolck, Buffalo, & Squire, 2000, Talarico & Rubin, 2007). Ideally one should compare memory to an array of to-be-remembered (TBR) information; recollections that match the TBR material are accurate and mismatches inaccurate. However, FBMs are based on one's idiosyncratic discovery event, making it impossible to directly assess memory accuracy. Instead, consistency across times of testing has become almost universally regarded as the only acceptable way to best estimate FBM accuracy. Researchers collect an account of a participant's discovery of an event shortly after the event and compare that to an account collected after some delay (see Bohannon & Symons, 1992; Conway, 1995; Er, 2003). The initial memory account is assumed to be veridical, so those accounts that share more features across times of testing are also assumed to be the most accurate.

The rise of consistency

Unfortunately, the assumption that consistency equals accuracy in FBM has not been empirically confirmed anywhere. Indeed, the two terms were used interchangeably (see Hornstein, Brown, & Mulligan, 2003; Neisser & Harsch, 1992; Neisser et al., 1996; Schmolck et al., 2000). FBM consistency has been used both as grounds to challenge the presence of a "special FB mechanism" and as a way to identify features that are most often associated with accurate memory accounts.

Many researchers asserted that if FBM was more consistent than every-day memory then FBM would be "special", or at least different, memory (Bohannon & Symons 1992). However, McCloskey, Wible, and Cohen (1988) used one woman's memory—a luncheon discovery of the *Challenger* disaster that was at odds with the recollections of two other people—to impeach the veridicality of all flashbulb recall. Similarly, Neisser and Harsch (1992) found that after a 2.5-year delay, some elements of some participants' original memories about their discovery of the *Challenger* disaster were irrecoverable, even after extensive cueing and showing the participants their original memory report. Both McCloskey et al. (1988) and Neisser and Harsch (1992) focused on relatively minor inconsistencies (7% after 9 months and 34% after 34 months, respectively). Neisser (1982) used his own faulty recollection of discovering the Pearl Harbor attack interrupting a radio broadcast of a New York Giants baseball game in a similar fashion. How could any part of (Neisser's) flashbulb recall be trusted if he got the sport wrong (baseball always concludes in October not December 7th)? The fact that both McCloskey et al. (1988) and Neisser (1982) used rare recollective inconsistencies to cast doubt on all autobiographical recall, and FBM in particular, was persuasive to many (see Talarico & Rubin, 2007).

Bohannon and Symons (1992), however, focused not on the rate of inconsistencies but rather on what factors were associated with more consist-ent memories. They found that FBM consistency of the *Challenger* disaster over 36 months was associated with more confidence in the memories, more extensive memories, and a stronger emotional response to the flashbulb news. Neisser et al. (1996) assessed memory consistency for memories of the 1989 Loma Prieta earthquake (in California) for participants in California and Atlanta, Georgia. They found that personal involvement in the earthquake predicted memory consistency such that Atlanta participants were less con-sistent than Californian participants. Similarly, Er (2003) assessed FBMs of the Marmara earthquake and found that memory accounts were most consistent and detailed when participants were emotionally aroused at the time of discovery. Emotional arousal was found to affect participants' mem-ory both directly and indirectly through affecting how much participants recounted their memory for discovering the event (see also Luminet, Chapter 3, this volume). Likewise, Hornstein et al. (2003) found that both emotional arousal at the time of discovery and recounts of the memory were related to consistency at a 3-month and 18-month delay. Schmolck et al. (2000) also reported higher consistency rates over 3 years for those participants who were more upset at the news of the O. J. Simpson verdict. Overall, 11% of the memory accounts had major errors and distortions after 15 months, but this number rose to over 40% after 32 months (Schmolck et al., 2000). Thus, although FBM accounts appear to be prey to distortions, heightened arousal was associated with more consistent memories.

Smith et al. (2003) found that factual memories for the 9/11 attacks were less consistent after a delay of 6 months than FBMs in a sample of Canadian participants. Similarly, Tekcan, Ece, Gülgöz, and Er (2003) found that FBMs of the 9/11 attacks were more consistent at a delay of 1 year compared to factual memories of the event. These findings were consistent with Pezdek's (2003) claim that with increasing emotional involvement, autobiographical FBM decreased and event memory increased. Because the Smith et al. sample was from Canada, and less involved in the attacks, it follows from Pezdek's (2003) theory that their factual memories will be less consistent than their FBMs. Pezdek (2003) developed this theory because she found that participants from Manhattan, presumably most involved in the 9/11 attacks, had the most consistent factual memories and the least detailed autobiographical memories when compared to participants from California and Hawaii. It is possible that a factor such as recounts could account for these findings. Those who are more personally involved in the event may have recounted the event more with others and seen more media accounts. One's factual memory is continually checked against the facts from the media, and one's auto-biographical memory can continually evolve through retelling because there is no veridical "check" on idiographic discovery memories.

An alternative method of estimating accuracy through consistency is to obtain a memory account from two people who experienced an event together. As with test–retest consistency, between-person consistency relies on the assumption that if two memory accounts are consistent they are likely to be accurate. McCloskey et al. (1988), as mentioned earlier, used anecdotal evidence of between-participant inconsistencies to suggest the fallibility of all FBMs.

Because FBM-evoking events are, by definition, consequential and high in emotionality, it is likely that these memories will be rehearsed and recounted. For events that people experience together, such as a marriage proposal, it is probable that the individuals will rehearse their memory of the event both together and with people who were not present at the time of the event. In either case, one's memory (and consistency between two people) can be affected by recounts. According to Loftus, Miller, and Burns (1978), post-event information, like that obtained through recounts, can overwrite a person's original memory, resulting in inaccuracy of recall. It is also possible that correct additional details would be incorporated into a person's memory after the event, thereby improving the memory (Yarmey & Morris, 1998). Regardless of the specific effect, however, it is clear that post-event information leads to changes in memory that can affect within- and between-person consistency independent of its accurate reflection of the initial event.

Whither consistency?

Although consistency is the currently acceptable estimate of FBM accuracy, logically there is only a weak relationship between consistency and accuracy, as shown in Figure 5.1. The only relationship between responses across time that is both consistent and accurate is when the participant responds with the same correct information at both times of testing. When a response is inconsistent, there is a chance that the response at Time 2 was also accurate. This would occur when an individual reports two distinct, but compatible, responses at Time 1 and Time 2. For example, at the time of discovery one could be talking on the phone while watching television, but report opposite activities in the two memory reports. (That is, because a participant was performing two acts simultaneously, and reports one of them at one time of test and the other at another time of test, the responses would be accurate but inconsistent.) Likewise, when a response is consistent it is possible for a participant to report the same incorrect answer at both times of testing. Assuming that in the domain of all possible answers there are more incorrect answers than correct answers, the possibility of being both accurate and consistent by chance is probabilistically small. It is more likely that after a delay an answer will be inaccurate regardless of whether or not it is consistent (see Figure 5.1). Thus, there is no reason to assume a priori that consistent answers are more likely to be veridical than any other type of answer (given that any answer occurred). Omitting an answer at either time (not shown in Figure 5.1) is also commonly scored as inconsistent when omitting an answer at Time 2 is likely to be simple forgetting and not memory mutation. We admit to this error ourselves, as the World Trade Center data reported below are so consistent (less than 5% changed answers over the 2-year course of the study) that we had to include forgetting as a nominal instance of inconsistent answers in order to have enough variance to analyse.

Lastly, as Marsh (2007) argues, narration of autobiographical experience is dependent on one's listener, with canonical features entering and exiting the account depending on factors other than faulty recall. For example, the time feature in free recall goes from rarely stated (15% of accounts) to frequently stated (65% of accounts over the 5 years of *Challenger* FBM assessment) (Bohannon et al., 2007). Rules for narration, like Grice's (1975) rules of conversation, prohibit stating the obvious (e.g., "I learned about the attacks of 9/11 on September 11"). Thus the time of the event would most likely be a shared reference that need not be stated in a narrative close to the event, whereas some years later a time-framing statement would be more likely to be offered as a required element of the story.

Because many FBM studies obtain a Time 1 measurement days after a target event occurred, it is questionable whether one can assume this memory

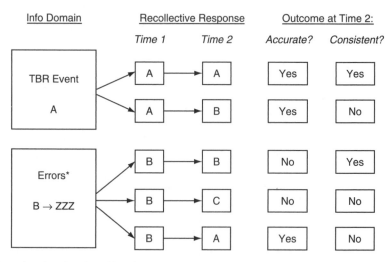

*Assuming domain of possible errors is large whereas domain of accurate TBR information is relatively small.

Figure 5.1 The relationship between accuracy and consistency across times of testing where a set of information details (A) serve as TBR material.

to be accurate. Neisser and Harsch (1992) suggested that in the days following a flashbulb event the full impact of the event becomes clear and affect is heightened (perhaps more so than at the time of the event discovery itself). Because of this heightened affect, other experiences within this time frame, specifically watching television coverage of the event, may be incorporated into one's memory for discovering the event. In this way, inaccuracies may already be a part of one's memory mere days after the event. High test–retest consistency is no guarantee that the Time 1 memory was accurate. In fact, the information changes throughout multi-hour events such as the 9/11 attacks; memory accounts obtained right after an event are unlikely to reflect accurate information that only became available (and stable) later on.

Winningham, Hyman, and Dinnel (2000) explained this with a memory consolidation model. In a study assessing memories for O. J. Simpson's acquittal, Winningham et al. (2000) compared the consistency of memories over an 8-week retention interval when the initial memory account was collected either 5 hours or 1 week after the acquittal. Results showed that the delayed group (those whose first memory account was collected at a 1-week delay) had more consistent memory accounts and reported fewer propositions in their narratives at Time 1 compared to those whose memory accounts were first collected at 5 hours after the event. Winningham et al. proposed that this was due to either simple forgetting, where the most details are lost shortly after the event, or the narrative structure of FBMs changes in the week following an event, such that some details are forgotten and other post-event information is incorporated into one's memory. Over time, a more established FBM story emerges such that memories are more consistent if the initial memory account is obtained after a delay.

Lee and Brown (2003) addressed the effect of delay on memory consistency as well, but with contradictory results. They found that test–retest consistency did not differ between participants whose initial memory accounts were obtained within 24 hours of the event or 10 days after the 9/11 attacks. However, the authors suspected that their results differed from Winningham et al.'s (2000) because of the nature of the events studied. It is possible that the arousing 9/11 attacks (compared to the less arousing O. J. Simpson acquittal) caused the memory consolidation process within mere hours after the discovery of the attacks. It is also possible that an event like 9/11 results in more FBM recounting within the first day, so that a stable memory account would emerge earlier than for events like O. J. Simpson's acquittal. It is also important to note that Lee and Brown (2003) collected the earlier initial memory account between 4 and 24 hours after the event, compared to Winningham et al. (2000) who limited the initial memory account to only 5 hours after the event. It is possible that the early initial memory accounts in Lee and Brown's (2003) study could already reflect a consolidated memory.

As with test–retest consistency, between-participant consistency logically does not relate closely to accuracy. When two people experience an event together, it is likely that they will rehearse it together as well. When two people rehearse a memory together, they are likely to have fewer memory discrepancies than if they rehearse it in isolation (Ross & Holmberg, 1990). Something about rehearsing events, possibly the effect of incorporating post-event information from a co-rehearser into one's own memory (Loftus et al., 1978), leads people to settle memory discrepancies, resulting in more congruent memories. Because it is entirely possible, even likely, that inaccurate recollections will be agreed upon and incorporated into both individuals' memories, consistency between two people's memory accounts cannot logically be equated to accuracy. Just as with test–retest consistency, two memory accounts can be consistent without being accurate, or accurate without being consistent.

Within the field of FBM, the assumption that consistency is the best measure of accuracy has run rampant. However, other fields of memory such as eyewitness testimony have found little empirical support for this assumption. This is of particular importance for eyewitness testimony because important legal decisions are made on the basis of the judge and jury's conception of the accuracy of a witness's memory. Several eyewitness testimony studies have attempted to empirically address the relationship between consistency and accuracy. Smeets, Candel, and Merckelbach (2004) had participants watch a violent video clip and report their memory of the video in narrative form both immediately after viewing the video and 3–4 weeks later. In this laboratory setting where accuracy could be determined from the TBR video, the authors found there was no reliable relationship between inconsistencies and accuracy. Participants were accurate at both times of testing (88%

accuracy rate), but the correlations between accuracy and the rate of inconsistencies were remarkably low with $r = 0.03$ and $r = -0.14$ at Time 1 and 2 respectively. Fisher and Cutler (1995) experimentally assessed the relation between accuracy and consistency by staging an event during class. Confederate intruders, visible for 30–150 seconds, interrupted the class and "stole" an item of value. Participants were given questionnaires within a few hours or days and again several days later to assess their memories for the intruders. Fisher and Cutler (1995) replicated Smeets et al.'s (2003) results, finding accuracy/consistency correlations ranging from –0.06 to 0.23. Brewer, Potter, Fisher, Bond, and Luszcz (1999) assessed consistency and accuracy by showing participants a film of a robbery. They found that only up to 17% of the variance in accuracy was explained by consistency. In experimental settings, when the TBR event is known, consistency is considered a poor predictor of accuracy. One can assume, then, that in FBM studies, when the TBR event is unknown, consistency would similarly be a poor predictor of accuracy.

Relying on consistency as the only acceptable estimate of accuracy in FBM has saddled FBM researchers with a difficult methodological burden—rush to prepare a study and get IRB approval immediately after a target event occurs, so that a memory report can be obtained with the least delay, and then wait for up to several years to assess the test–retest consistency of such a memory. Needless to say, the inconvenience of this procedure, combined with the fact that the relationship between accuracy and consistency is poor at best, suggests that alternative ways to estimate accuracy should be explored. It is possible that other factors, such as quantity of recall, may be able to predict accuracy just as well as, if not better than, consistency. If consistency, quantity of recall, and accuracy are all part of the same memory construct, it follows that how much participants say in FBM could relate the same quality of information about accuracy as consistency. If this is the case, FBM researchers will no longer be restricted to collecting data immediately after a surprising and consequential event and then waiting up to several years after the event to assess the stability of the memory over time. Instead, data could be collected at one time only, long after the event, and valid conclusions could be made about the nature and predictors of the memories. It is the goal of this study to assess whether or not FBM consistency should be abandoned as the only acceptable measure of memory accuracy.

THE CURRENT STUDY

Four data sets were employed to assess participants' FBMs: the World Trade Center (WTC) attacks, the death of Princess Diana, the capture of Saddam Hussein, and the destruction of the space shuttle *Columbia*. Sample sizes and retest samples are shown in Tables 5.1 and 5.2. A total of 1789 participants were initially tested in groups of 10 to 50 within 2 weeks of each event (see

Table 5.1 Description of flashbulb events and grouping variable

Event	Date of event	Delay to 1st test	Delay to 2nd test	Affect *		Recounts **		Exposure ***	
				T1	T2	T1	T2	T1	T2
WTC	9/11/2001	2 hours to weeks	3 months to 2 years	4.04	3.97	8.27	11.4	30.0	81.6
Columbia	2/1/2003	Next day to 2 weeks	3 months	3.18	3.13	2.29	3.03	11.5	16.5
Saddam	12/12/2003	1–2 weeks	3 months	3.11	2.95	3.72	5.75	25.7	41.2
Diana	8/31/1997	1–2 weeks	3 months	3.15	2.97	4.05	6.72	20.4	41.6
Event F-value		Total T1 Sample N = 1789	Total T2 Sample N = 1218	$F(3, 963) = 77.1$ $p < .001$		$F(3, 1022) = 41.8$ $p < .001$		$F(3, 1008) = 24.4$ $p < .001$	
Time F-value				$F(1, 963) = 11.1$ $p < .001$		$F(1, 1022) = 18.1$ $p < .001$		$F(1, 1008) = 60.7$ $p < .001$	

* Affect 1,2: $r = 0.715$, $N = 967$.
** Recounts 1,2: $r = 0.491$, $N = 1026$.
*** Exposures 1,2: $r = 0.392$, $N = 1012$.

Table 5.1). From the initial sample 1218 participants were retested after a delay of at least 3 months. The events differed as to the media coverage (exposures), affective response of the participants to the news, and how many times the participants retold their FBM stories to others (recounts).

Table 5.1 shows that all events differed from each other in media coverage, the participants' tendency to talk to others about their discoveries, and how emotional they were when getting the news. Further, all correlations between the participants' estimates at Time 1 and Time 2 were significant. The strongest prediction was in the case of emotional rating, with weaker relationships occurring in recounts and media exposures. This difference was expected. In the case of emotional response, the question directed participants to their initial reaction to the news, which should remain constant regardless of when the question was assessed. However the other two measures were expected to increase over delay as participants had more opportunities to talk to others and experience media coverage of the target events. Given that the second estimate should include both the first estimate and whatever new responses occurred between Time 1 and Time 2, it is not surprising that the correlations were positive, significant, but modest in magnitude.

All participants completed a questionnaire including a discovery narrative section, specific probe questions concerning their discoveries (e.g., What was their informant wearing?), and either a fact narrative (Columbia), fact probes (Diana), or both (WTC and Saddam). Participants also provided ratings of their emotional response ("affect"), the number of times they had recounted their discovery story to others ("recounts"), and the number of times they had been exposed to media coverage of the event ("exposures"). Participants were asked to complete the pages in order and not return to any previous sections. On average, the questionnaires were completed in 10 to 20 minutes.

Scoring

Quantity

The discovery narrative portion of the questionnaire was scored based on the presence of seven canonical features: source, activity, location, time, aftermath, others present, and others' affect. Scores ranged from 0 to 3 for each of these features. A score of 0 indicated a lack of response, a score of 1 was given for an implied response, and higher numbers were given for more elaboration. The fact narrative portion of the questionnaire was scored in a similar fashion on the basis of the following canonical features: who, what, where, when, cause, aftermath. To make both the discovery narrative and the fact narrative scores have the same range, each score was divided by the maximum possible score (scores were divided by 3 with the exception of "when", which was divided by 4). The discovery probes were scored with 0 for no response, and 1 for a response. Fact probes were scored with 0 for no response and higher numbers denoting higher degrees of accuracy. Since the questions

Table 5.2 Memory quantity and vividness by events

Event	Test N	Retest N	Discovery narrative		Fact narrative		Vividness rating (1–5)	
			T1	T2	T1	T2	T1	T2
WTC	721	546	0.410	0.537	0.523	0.527	4.23	3.54
Columbia	348	180	0.242	0.175	0.430	0.324	XX*	XX
Saddam	223	91	0.418	0.437	0.377	0.305	2.29	2.03
Diana	497	401	0.288	0.333	XX	XX	XX	3.63
Event F-value	Total T1 Sample N = 1789	Total T2 Sample N = 1218	$F(3, 1159) = 91.7$ $p < .001$		$F(2, 646) = 53.34$ $p < .001$		$F(3, 1008) = 24.4$ $p < .001$	
Time F-value			$F(1, 1159) = 7.59$ $p < .001$		$F(1, 646) = 17.96$ $p < .001$		$F(1, 1008) = 60.7$ $p < .001$	

* XX = Test not performed for that event at that time.

had varying maximum scores, the score for fact probes was divided by the maximum possible score before being analysed.

Consistency

Consistency was determined on the discovery narrative, discovery probe, fact narrative, and fact probe portions of the questionnaires. In the narratives, consistency was examined for each of the canonical features mentioned above, and for the probes consistency was found for each of the questions. For the narratives, responses were considered consistent across the two times of testing (and thus given a score of 1) if the two responses had common details and did not contradict each other. Responses were given a score of –1 for being inconsistent when there were no common details between the times of testing for a given feature or if the responses at the two times of testing blatantly contradicted each other. Consistency scores for the discovery probes were distributed in the same fashion as for the narratives. For the fact narratives, ranges for consistency were determined such that responses that were sufficiently similar were judged consistent and those that were different enough were considered inconsistent. For all of the sections, scores of 0 were only given if the participant failed to respond at one or both times of testing.

Accuracy

Accuracy scores were determined for the fact narrative section of the questionnaire only. Scores were given for each of the six canonical features listed above. A score of 0 was given only in the case of a lack of response. A score of 1 was given for a correct response with no incorrect details given. A score of –1 was given when the participant included incorrect details. To determine the accuracy of responses, sources such as online news databases were consulted.

RESULTS AND DISCUSSION

FBM vs factual event recall

Source of discovery

Data were collapsed across events for all analyses. For the critical narrative recall measures in both discovery and fact, the recollection narratives were scored identically and all measures were taken initially within 2 weeks of the respective events. In the probed recall data (excluding the Columbia data because no fact probes were used in that study), the single largest effect was the information type by source interaction, $F(1, 813) = 35.5$, $p < .001$ (see Figure 5.2). The participants who discovered the events from another person

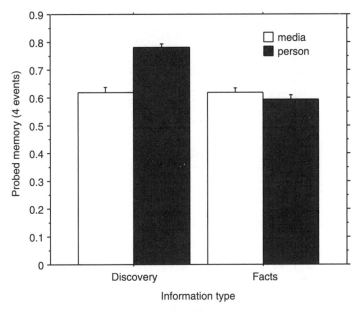

Figure 5.2 The source by information interaction, $F(1, 813) = 35.5$, $p < .001$. Participants getting the news from another had more extensive discovery memories than the media group.

had significantly more probed discovery details than those who got the news from the media. Memory for the facts of the events was quite similar between those who discovered the events from another person vs from the media. In other words, one's source of discovery affected memory for discovery details, but not fact details (see Bohannon et al., 2007).

Media exposures

Exposures (participant-estimated number) were divided into five levels such that a rough quintile split occurred with the number of exposures reported for each group shown in the name of the group (i.e., e0-3 means that participants who reported no exposures to three media story exposures were in the lowest exposure group). A 5 (Exposure Group) × 2 (Test Type: Narrative, Probe) × 2 (Information Type: Discovery, Facts) repeated measures ANOVA was performed on Memory Quantity data for Time 2. Results revealed no main effect for Exposure Group, $F(4, 761) = 0.955$, $p = .43$. Media exposures, in and of themselves, do not affect overall Memory Quantity at Time 2. There was an interaction between Information Type and Exposure Group, $F(4, 761) = 3.029$, $p < .02$ (see Figure 5.3). Media exposures only had an effect on memory for the facts of the event but not for discovery memory. Participants who had more media exposures had a more extensive factual event memory. When participants are exposed to media accounts of the facts of an event,

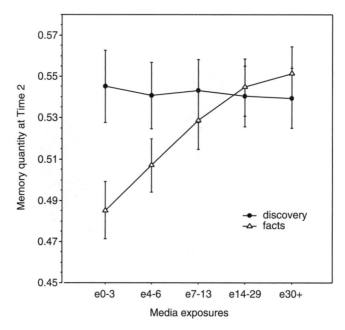

Figure 5.3 The interaction between information type and exposure group, $F(4, 761) =$ 3.029, $p < .02$.

only the facts are likely to be rehearsed, not one's personal discovery circumstances, so more media exposures only improve one's memory for the facts, not one's discovery memory.

Conclusions

Although discovery and fact recall tap into qualitatively different types of memory, they showed similar patterns across most independent variables. While the specific results were not reported here, for both recounts and affect higher levels were associated with enhanced discovery and fact recall. While recounts would be expected to solely affect discovery recall, it is likely that facts are included when one recounts a discovery event, so fact recall may benefit through recounts as well. Media exposures, on the other hand, affect fact but not discovery recall because the media relates uniquely to the facts of an event. Source of discovery also affected fact and discovery memory differently. Discovery memory was stronger for those whose source was another person, whereas fact recall was similar regardless of source of discovery. Fact and discovery recall seem to behave the same except in regard to independent variables (like media exposures and source of discovery) that would logically affect fact and discovery recall differently.

Quantity vs consistency in FBM

To determine whether quantity of recall and consistency across times of testing are fundamentally different measures, the variables below were assessed within the discovery memory data at Time 2. Data were collapsed across events for all analyses.

Affect and recounts

Affect rating and recounts were each divided into four levels. Affect levels were grouped by rating into individual rating groups (5, 4, and 3), with the lowest ratings (1 and 2) combined for the lowest affect group, and a 4 (Affect) × 4 (Recounts) × 2 (Memory Estimates: Quantity and Consistency) repeated measures ANOVA was performed on the narrative data. The results indicated that the main predictors of affect and rehearsal worked on both estimates of narrative memory in a similar fashion. Higher levels of affect were associated with increased quantity of recall and consistency, $F(3, 1102) = 3.604$, $p < .01$ (see Figure 5.4). Higher levels of recounts were also associated with increased quantity of recall and consistency in discovery memory, $F(3, 1102) = 9.46$, $p < .001$ (see Figure 5.5).

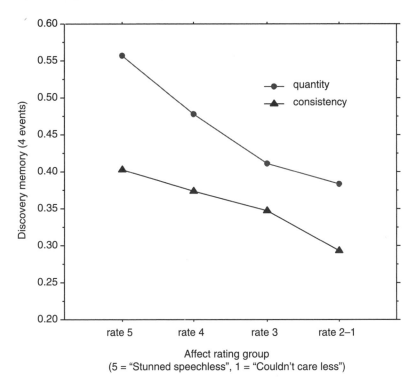

Figure 5.4 The main effects of affect, $F(3, 1102) = 3.604$, $p < .01$, and memory estimate, $F(1, 1102) = 64.2$, $p < .001$. There was no interaction.

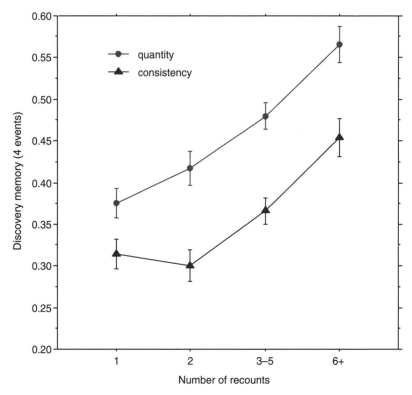

Figure 5.5 The effect of recounts, $F(3, 1102) = 9.46$, $p < .001$, was similar for both estimates of memory quantity and consistency.

Conclusions

Whereas consistency across times of testing has commonly been assumed to be the best and only estimate of accuracy in FBM, our analyses show that quantity and consistency had remarkably similar patterns with respect to affect and recounts. The fact that quantity and consistency behaved identically suggests that both measures may provide equivalent information. Further analyses are necessary within the fact memory data to determine how accuracy measures relate to both quantity and consistency.

Quantity vs consistency vs accuracy in factual event memory

The previous analyses showed that quantity of recall and consistency across times of testing show similar patterns across a variety of independent variables, but this does not tell the whole story. The ultimate goal is to show that quantity and consistency estimate *accuracy* equally well. There is a particular set of comparisons that might shed light on the relationship between FBM narratives and their accuracy. In laboratory experiments, known TBR information is compared to participants' recollections to determine accuracy. In FBM the idiosyncratic discovery event is inestimable by the investigator so a direct measure of accuracy is impossible. However, Figure 5.6 shows a distinct similarity between assessments of flashbulb event fact narratives and more traditional discovery narratives. Both assessments use unstructured free recall and canonical narrative features (see Nachson & Zelig, 2003).

Both the WTC and Columbia data sets (see Table 5.2) have fact narratives that were scored for accuracy as well as quantity of recall for each fact feature and consistency over time. Both data sets have a 3-month delay for specified participants. Memory accuracy can then be estimated by a comparison of known TBR facts about each event and the participants' reporting of those facts, as well as how extensive and consistent over time their answers were. Although accuracy can only be determined from the fact data, the similarity in measurement methods between fact and discovery memory allows the inference that if accuracy could be known for discovery memory, it would function in much the same way for discovery memory as it does for fact memory.

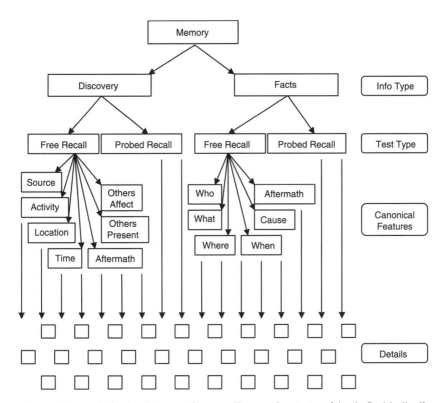

Figure 5.6 The similarity between free recall narrative tests of both flashbulb discovery information and facts about the event itself.

Affect

A 4 (Affect Level) × 3 (Memory Estimates: Quantity, Consistency, and Accuracy) repeated measures ANOVA was performed. The effect of affect interacted with memory estimate, $F(6, 858) = 6.45, p < .001$ (see Figure 5.7). Quantity of reported features, the number of accurate features, and the number of consistent features all increased with increasing emotional response. However, consistency seems to top out at an affect rating of 4 whereas quantity and accuracy continue to rise at the highest levels of affect. This result agreed with Metcalf and Jacobs' (1998) prediction that very high rates of arousal would eventually degrade declarative memory for events. In this case, it appeared that only consistency, not accuracy or quantity of recall, was adversely affected by very high rates of arousal.

It is possible that participants who were wordier or had a lower threshold of reporting particular features could have reported more features and been both more accurate and consistent. In other words, it is possible that the number of features reported artificially inflated the relationship between the estimates. Therefore, a separate calculation was performed, removing the number of features reported from each estimate. Because each feature's elaborate nature was scored 0 (absent) to 3 (elaborate), dividing the total score by the number of features (6) and the total possible score (3) yielded a quantity/

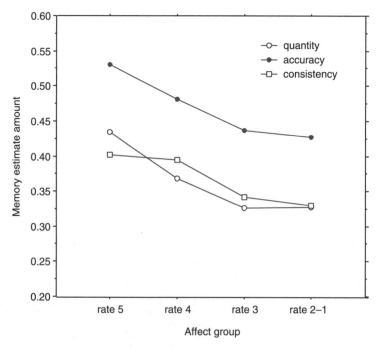

Figure 5.7 The main effect of affect, $F(6, 858) = 6.45, p < .001$. There was no interaction with estimate of memory.

elaboration score that was independent of the number of features in the narrative. Similarly, the number of accurate features was divided by the number of reported features, and an estimate of accuracy independent of memory extent was obtained. Lastly, an identical procedure was performed on the number of consistent features reported at Time 2.

A 4 (Affect Level) × 3 (Memory Estimates) repeated measure ANOVA was performed on the residual memory estimates. There was a significant affect by memory estimate interaction, $F(6, 820) = 2.41, p < .01$, that was almost identical in form to that of the comparison dependent on memory quantity. Across one known variable of affect, memory quantity and accuracy behaved similarly, even when controlling for participants' wordiness.

Recounts

Recounts were also examined through a 2 (Recounts) × 3 (Memory Estimate: Quantity, Consistency, Accuracy) repeated measures ANOVA. There was a main effect of recounts, $F(1, 282) = 5.023, p < .05$, such that those who recounted their discovery story to others many times had enhanced memory accounts. There was also a memory estimate by recount group interaction, $F(2, 564) = 5.21, p < .01$. This interaction was the result of both quantity and accuracy showing increases with increasing recounts, whereas consistency was relatively stable across recount levels. This suggests that quantity of recall may provide a better estimate of accuracy than consistency.

Delay to initial test

An additional perspective can be gained by examining the participants' delay to initial testing (Winningham et al., 2000). Neisser and Harsch (1992) argued that shortly after a flashbulb event, participants' memory accounts of their discoveries consolidate, enhancing consistency but reducing accuracy. Participants in the WTC and Columbia data sets were tested within 2 hours of the event and up to 2 weeks after the event. A 4 (Initial Delay: Same Day, Next Day, 1 Week, and 2 Week) × 3 (Memory Estimates) repeated measures ANOVA was performed. Results revealed a main effect of initial delay on factual narrative recall, $F(3, 444) = 22.9, p < .001$; there was no significant interaction with memory estimates. An initial rise in memory the day after the event and subsequent fall in memory measures after a delay of at least a week was almost identical across memory estimates.

Conclusions

When measures of quantity, consistency, and accuracy were compared within the fact recall data, all three measures responded similarly to several different variables. Higher affect was associated with enhanced quantity, consistency, and accuracy, although consistency was somewhat compromised at the highest levels of affect. When controlling for wordiness, the three memory estimates still showed largely parallel patterns. More recounts were also associated with memory benefits. However, whereas quantity and accuracy measures showed this increase, consistency remained relatively stable across recount groups. For delay to initial test, quantity, consistency, and accuracy all showed an equivalent pattern with the most extensive, accurate, and consistent memories being those for which Time 1 was the day after the event. Quantity, consistency, and accuracy varied similarly for affect, recounts, and delay to initial test. However, in the cases where there was a discrepancy between measures, quantity of recall appeared to approximate accuracy better than consistency; quantity of recall seems to be a better estimate of accuracy than consistency.

Relationship between quantity, consistency, and accuracy

Lastly, despite similarities in patterns of results comparing means, it is possible that each estimate of memory is only minimally related to the others. Participants who were most accurate at Time 2 may not be those who report the greatest number of features at Time 2 or are the most consistent between their Time 1 and Time 2 reports. Therefore, correlations between pairs of memory estimates were calculated. Significance was determined conservatively. A correlation was deemed significant if it attained an alpha of .001 within the WTC data alone, the Columbia data alone, and in the overall data set. In other words, the relationship had to be present for both events and not interact with events so that the slope of the regression line would be similar across events. Both estimates influenced by amount of recall and independent of amount of recall were included. The results are shown in Table 5.3.

There is a strong positive correlation between the number of accurate features and number of features reported, number of consistent features, and elaboration per feature. When amount of features reported is removed then neither elaboration of features nor consistency of reported features predicted

Table 5.3 Correlations across longitudinal (3-month delay only) samples of WTC and Columbia*

Criterion	No. of features reported	No. of consistent features	No. of accurate features	Elaboration per feature	[p] of consistency
No. of accurate features	0.759	0.596	1.00	0.284	−0.059 ns
[p] of accuracy per feature	−.017 ns	0.284 ns	0.405	0.035 ns	0.289 ns

* Correlations had to be significant ($p < .001$) in both events and in the combined data set to be judged significant. $N = 426$.

accuracy. Consistency should no longer be considered the best and only predictor of accuracy in FBMs. Memory consistency predicted accuracy as well as the elaborate quantity of recall. Because both consistency and quantity were significantly correlated with accuracy, it is probable that they are fundamentally the same measure.

SUMMARY, IMPLICATIONS, AND LIMITATIONS

Consistency across times of testing should be abandoned as the only acceptable estimate of accuracy in FBMs. When consistency and quantity of recall were compared in FBM with respect to affect, recounts, and media exposures, the two memory estimates showed extremely similar patterns. However, because accuracy cannot be determined for FBM, it is not possible to determine within discovery recall how quantity and consistency relate to accuracy. Because memories of the facts of the event were collected at the same time as the discovery memories and were assessed in an identical narrative fashion, fact recall (for which accuracy measures were obtained) was used to determine their relation to accuracy. Quantity, consistency, and accuracy all showed similar patterns across affect, recounts, and delay to initial test. In the cases where there was a difference between the quantity and consistency measures, it was always the case that quantity and accuracy appeared to be more similar than consistency and accuracy. Participants who reported more features in factual event narratives were also likely to be more accurate.

When reading anecdotal failures of flashbulb-like recall, please note there is no evidence that any single inconsistent/inaccurate memory element impeaches an entire array of related elements. When the overall number of factual canonical features was partialled out from our data, no consistent correlation occurred between the probability of consistent elements and accurate elements, nor was there a significant correlation between the elaborate nature of a canonical fact account and its accuracy (see Table 5.3). For example, Thompson and Cowan (1986) re-examined Neisser's Pearl Harbor discovery memory after hearing a memory from Red Barber, the famous sports announcer from New York. The comparison is offered in Table 5.4. In contrast to Neisser's personal horror over the "wild" inaccuracy of his own recall, the total memory is spot-on and likely accurate, with eight out of nine features standing up to verification.

If accuracy of FBMs can be approximated by measuring quantity of recall instead of consistency across times of testing, FBM researchers are no longer bound to collecting "rushed" data immediately after an event and waiting months, or even years, to obtain a Time 2 memory account for the sake of measuring consistency. Instead, researchers can collect data at one time, long after an event, and estimate accuracy by examining participants' quantity of recall. Those who report the most features in their memory account will

Table 5.4 Ulric Neisser's FBM for discovering the Pearl Harbor attack

Feature	Neisser's memory	What really happened
Source	Radio broadcast interruption	Radio broadcast interruption
Location	Home in NYC	Probably correct
Activity	Listening to sports on radio	Probably correct
When	7 December 1941, Sunday 12:30–1:30 pm	7 December 1941, Sunday 12:30–1:30 pm
Sport	*Baseball*	*Football*
Announcer	Red Barber	Red Barber
Where played	NY Polo Grounds	NY Polo Grounds
Team playing	NY Giants	NY Giants
Opponent team	Brooklyn Dodgers	Brooklyn Dodgers
Source	(Neisser, 1982)	(Thompson & Cowan, 1986)

likely be the most consistent and accurate. There is no reason to assume that consistency provides a better estimate of accuracy than can be obtained through quantity of recall alone.

Our study relied on the assumption that the accuracy of FBM will function in the same way as the accuracy of fact memory in terms of its relationship to consistency and quantity of recall (see Wright, Chapter 2, this volume). Discovery and fact recall are differentially affected by post-event information. Often with flashbulb events like September 11th, the hours after the event are filled with confusion and the veridical facts of the event are only revealed later. Thus, when memory accounts are collected shortly after the event and then again after a significant delay, inconsistencies could be the result of people correcting their memories. In other words, the Time 1 fact account would be inaccurate and the Time 2 account accurate. For discovery memories, the TBR information is only at the time of discovery, so any changes are more likely to be inaccurate. Therefore, the FBM Time 1 account would tend to be more accurate.

However, in the above example it is consistency's relationship with accuracy that is uncertain. It is possible that quantity of recall overcomes the differences between fact and discovery recall. Our results suggest that simply reporting a feature in a recollective narrative means it is likely to be accurate and consistent. Additionally, we showed that quantity of recall might actually be more closely related to accuracy than consistency.

To conclude, FBM research has often relied on the assumption that consistency is the best and only available predictor of FBM accuracy. A comparison of quantity, consistency, and accuracy shows that this is not the case. Quantity and consistency responded similarly to affect and recounts in discovery recall. In fact recall, quantity, consistency, and accuracy all behaved similarly with delay to initial test. As all three memory estimates showed the same patterns, it follows that consistency is not the only acceptable estimate of accuracy in FBM; quantity of recall may provide equivalent, if not better, information with regard to the accuracy of FBM.

NOTE

1 The authors would like to thank all the undergraduate scientists who participated in the Butler University Autobiographical Memory lab over the years and whose dedication made this chapter possible. Parts of this chapter have been previously reported at the meetings of the Southeastern Psychological Association, Association for Psychological Science, and the International Society for Research on Emotions.

REFERENCES

Bohannon, J. N. (1988). Flashbulb memories for the space shuttle disaster: A tale of two theories. *Cognition, 29*, 179–196.

Bohannon, J. N., Cross, V., & Gratz, S. (2007). The effects of affect and source on flashbulb memory. *Applied Cognitive Psychology, 21*, 1–14.

Bohannon, J. N., & Symons, V. L. (1992). Flashbulb memories: Confidence, consistency and quantity. In U. Neisser & E. Winograd (Eds.), *Affect and accuracy in recall* (pp. 19–67). New York: Cambridge University Press.

Brewer, N., Potter, R., Fisher, R. P., Bond, N., & Luszcz, M. A. (1999). Beliefs and data on the relationship between consistency and accuracy of eyewitness testimony. *Applied Cognitive Psychology, 13*, 297–313.

Brown, R., & Kulik, J. (1977). Flashbulb memories. *Cognition, 5*, 73–99.

Colegrove, F. (1899). Individual memories. *American Psychologist, 10*, 228–255.

Conway, M. A. (1995). *Flashbulb memories.* Hillsdale, NJ: Lawrence Erlbaum Associates Inc.

Edery-Halpern, G., & Nachson, I. (2004). Distinctiveness in flashbulb memory: Comparative analysis of five terrorist attacks. *Memory, 12*, 147–157.

Er, N. (2003). A new flashbulb memory model applied to the Marmara earthquake. *Applied Cognitive Psychology, 17*, 503–517.

Finkenauer, C., Luminet, O., Gisle, L., El-Ahmadi, A., Van der Linden, M., & Philippot, P. (1998). Flashbulb memories and the underlying mechanisms of their formation: Toward an emotional-integrative model. *Memory and Cognition, 26*, 516–531.

Fisher, R. P., & Cutler, B. L. (1995). The relation between consistency and accuracy of eyewitness testimony. In G. Davies, S. Lloyd-Bostock, M. McMurran, & C. Wilson (Eds.), *Psychology, law, and criminal justice: International developments in research and practice* (pp. 21–28). Oxford, UK: Walter De Gruyter.

Grice, H. P. (1975). Logic and conversation. In P. Cole & J. Morgan (Eds.), *Syntax and semantics* (Vol. 3). New York: Academic Press.

Hornstein, S. L., Brown, A. S., & Mulligan, N. W. (2003). Long-term flashbulb memory for learning of Princess Diana's death. *Memory, 11*, 293–306.

Lee, P. J., & Brown, N. R. (2003). Delay related changes in personal memories for September 11, 2001. *Applied Cognitive Psychology, 17*, 1007–1015.

Loftus, E. F., Miller, D. G., & Burns, H. J. (1978). Semantic integration of verbal information into a visual memory. *Journal of Experimental Psychology: Human Learning and Memory, 4*, 19–31.

Marsh, E. J. (2007). Retelling is not the same as recalling: Implications for memory. *Current Directions in Psychological Science, 16*, 16–20

McCloskey, M., Wible, C. G., & Cohen, N. J. (1988). Is there a special flashbulb mechanism? *Journal of Experimental Psychology: General, 117*, 171–181.

Metcalfe, J., & Jacobs, W. J. (1998). Emotional memory: The effects of stress on "cool" and "hot" memory systems. In D. Medin (Ed.), *The psychology of learning and motivation: Advances in research and theory* (pp. 187–222). San Diego, CA: Academic Press.

Nachson, I., & Zelig, A. (2003). Flashbulb and factual memories: The case of Rabin's assassination. *Applied Cognitive Psychology, 17*, 519–531.

Neisser, U. (1982). Snapshots or benchmarks? In U. Neisser (Ed.), *Memory observed* (pp. 68–74). San Francisco: Worth Publishers.

Neisser, U., & Harsch, N. (1992). Phantom flashbulbs: False recollections of hearing the news about Challenger. In E. Winograd & U. Neisser (Eds.), *Affect and accuracy in recall* (pp. 9–32). New York: Cambridge University Press.

Neisser, U., Winograd, E., Bergman, E. T., Schreiber, C. A., Palmer, S. E., & Weldon, M. S. (1996). Remembering the earthquake: Direct experience vs. hearing the news. *Memory, 4*, 337–357.

Pezdek, K. (2003). Event memory and autobiographical memory for the events of September 11, 2001. *Applied Cognitive Psychology, 17*, 1033–1045.

Pillemer, D. B. (1984). Flashbulb memories of the assassination attempt on President Reagan. *Cognition, 16*, 63–80.

Ross, M., & Holmberg, D. (1990). Recounting the past: Gender differences in the recall of events in the history of a close relationship. In J. M. Olson & M. P. Zanna (Eds.), *The Ontario Symposium, Vol. 6* (pp. 135–152). Hillsdale, NJ: Lawrence Erlbaum Associates Inc.

Schmolck, H., Buffalo, E. A., & Squire, L. R. (2000). Memory distortions develop over time: Recollections of the O.J. Simpson trial verdict after 15 and 32 months. *Psychological Science, 11*, 39–45.

Smeets, T., Candel, I., & Merckelbach, H. (2004). Accuracy, completeness, and consistency of emotional memories. *American Journal of Psychology, 117*, 595–609.

Smith, M. C., Bibi, U., & Sheard, D. E. (2003). Evidence for the differential impact of time and emotion on personal and event memories for September 11, 2001. *Applied Cognitive Psychology, 17*, 1047–1055.

Talarico, J. M., & Rubin, D. C. (2007). Flashbulb memories are special after all: In phenomenology, not accuracy. *Applied Cognitive Psychology, 21*, 557–578.

Tekcan, A. I., Ece, B., Gülgöz, S., & Er, N. (2003). Autobiographical and event memory for 9/11: Changes across one year. *Applied Cognitive Psychology, 17*, 1057–1066.

Thompson, C., & Cowan, T. (1986). Flashbulb memories: A nicer interpretation of a Neisser recollection. *Cognition, 22*, 199–200.

Winningham, R. G., Hyman, I. E., & Dinnel, D. L. (2000). Flashbulb memories? The effects of when the initial memory report was obtained. *Memory, 8*, 209–216.

Yarmey, A. D., & Morris, S. (1998). The effects of discussion on eyewitness memory. *Journal of Applied Social Psychology, 28*, 1637–1648.

Part III

Individual factors: Clinical and development issues

6 "Hearing the news" versus "being there"

Comparing flashbulb memories and recall of first-hand experiences

David B. Pillemer

I first learned about the 2001 World Trade Center disaster during a short break in the middle of a research methods class I was teaching at Wellesley College. A television was on display in the department secretary's office and I saw the initial news coverage, still unsure about the cause or motive.

As a young child I was told by my mother that my father had died unexpectedly. She delivered the news to me and my three brothers as we walked slowly up the driveway to our house, in the dark, our lives forever changed.

As a college student I was behind the wheel of my old convertible, sun shining at eye level, when a young child darted out into a busy Chicago intersection. A powerful slam on the brakes was not enough to keep the car from hitting the child, sending her airborne. I experienced a wave of relief upon seeing her lying in the street, fully conscious, active and crying.

All three episodes were highly emotional, distinctive, thought about, and talked about, so it is not surprising that they are vividly remembered many years later. All three memories fit comfortably into the general categories of autobiographical memory and personal event memory (Pillemer, 1998). Yet the events differ in ways that may have important consequences for long-term memory. The recollection of September 11, 2001 is a classic flashbulb memory, containing a description of personal circumstances when first learning about a surprising and consequential public event. The memory of my father's death also records a salient news reception event, although in this case the episode is personal rather than public, newsworthy only to a select few. In contrast, the memory of the car accident records a first-hand experience in which I was a principal actor. The accident could be a source of hearing-the-news memories for other people, including the child's father who was not at the scene. But for me there was no separate news reception event; my personal circumstances behind the wheel helped to define the critical episode.

Brown and Kulik (1977) first defined flashbulb memories (FBMs) as "memories for the circumstances in which one first learned of a very surprising and consequential (or emotionally arousing) event", and offered the assassination of President John Kennedy as the "prototype case" (p. 73).

Following Brown and Kulik, scores of researchers have examined *FBMs of public events*, including attacks on, deaths of, or resignations of world leaders (e.g., Christianson, 1989; Conway et al., 1994; Curci, Luminet, Finkenauer, & Gisle, 2001; Finkenauer, Luminet, Gisle, El-Ahmadi, van der Linden, & Philippot, 1998; Pillemer, 1984), World War II events (Berntsen & Thomsen, 2005), the 1986 explosion of the space shuttle *Challenger* (Bohannon, 1988; McCloskey, Wible, & Cohen, 1988; Neisser & Harsch, 1992), the 1989 California earthquake (Neisser, Winograd, Bergman, Schreiber, Palmer, & Weldon, 1996), and the September 11 attacks on the World Trade Center in 2001 (e.g., Curci & Luminet, 2006; Talarico & Rubin, 2003). This list represents only a fraction of the total number of studies on similar topics.

Brown and Kulik (1977) also examined memories of first learning of a "personal, unexpected shock" (p. 79), what could be termed *FBMs of personal events*. Brown and Kulik's instructions to participants guided recall to moments when significant personal news was received, and by far the most common memory theme was learning about the death of a parent. Studies of remembering one's own life circumstances when receiving important private news are rare. With only a few exceptions (e.g., receiving notification of college admission; Tekcan, 2001), the FBM literature is dominated by large-scale surveys of newsworthy public events.

Memories that represent circumstances in which one is an active participant rather than a passive recipient could be termed *memories of first-hand experience*. My memory of the car accident described earlier defines the episode and gives it meaning. Slamming on the brakes is not simply an idiosyncratic personal detail, unrelated to the substance of the memory. Rather, this action was timely enough to soften the blow to the young child, thereby averting disaster. Similarly, the bright sun shining in my eyes is much more than an indication of the weather that day; it contributed to the dangerous situation. Because first-hand experiences are so diverse and ubiquitous—including car accidents, trauma, birthday celebrations, the first kiss, and scoring the winning goal—there appears to be little added value in using the targeted term "FBM" to describe them.

Brown and Kulik (1977, p. 99) speculated that properties of FBMs also characterize recall when the target event is personal: "Probably the same 'Now Print!' mechanism accounts both for the enduring significant memories in which one has played the role of protagonist and those in which one has only been a member of an interested audience of millions." Their speculation about similar underlying memory processes deserves more close and careful scrutiny. Brown and Kulik's original study of FBMs has inspired books (Conway, 1995; Winograd & Neisser, 1992) and dozens of journal articles. The goal of this work is not simply to examine memories of hearing about the occasional public tragedy. Rather, the purpose is to enrich our understanding of personal event memory, including highly emotional and tragic events that happen to us directly. For example, studies of FBMs have contributed to the debate about the accuracy of eyewitness testimony (e.g., Ceci

& Bruck, 1993). Do FBMs of public events provide a useful and valid model of memories of events that happen to us directly, when we are central players?

In this chapter I first identify reasons why FBMs of public events, which occur so rarely over the course of one's life, generate such intense scientific interest. Second, I outline potential dissimilarities between FBMs and memories of first-hand experience. Third, I question the validity of global comparisons between these two memory types. Fourth, I describe and evaluate a small set of carefully designed research studies that directly compare memories of news reception events and first-hand experiences.

WHY ARE FBM STUDIES SO POPULAR?

Brown and Kulik's (1977) original presentation of FBM was engaging and provocative. They presented a phenomenon that all readers could readily identify in their own personal experience, yet they emphasized its unusual nature: "It is not the memory of the tragic news that invites inquiry, but the memory of one's own circumstances of first hearing the news. There is no obvious utility in such memories" (p. 74). Brown remembered being on the phone with the dean's secretary at Harvard University when he learned that Kennedy had been shot, but his personal circumstances were unrelated to the public news event. Brown and Kulik noted that "there is something strange about this recall" (p. 74), and described their research endeavour as being "on the trail of a mystery" (p. 98).

Although FBMs may be unusual, they are universally recognized. Academic psychologists know that introducing this topic to students, colleagues, or friends invariably triggers a stream of personal testimonials. The concept is so ubiquitous that Gary Larson parodied it in a cartoon with the caption "More facts of nature: All forest animals, to this very day, remember exactly where they were and what they were doing when they heard that Bambi's mother had been shot." In the cartoon, a possum was "just getting ready to cross the interstate". In short, Brown and Kulik identified a phenomenon that was at the same time common knowledge, compellingly curious, and lacking any scientific explanation—favourable conditions for inspiring empirical study.

FBMs are an especially attractive research topic for several reasons. Almost everyone is familiar with the concept and is able to produce a memory on demand, so that potential research participants are plentiful. Following an event like the 2001 attack on the World Trade Center, there is a ready pool of people who have received news of the same public trauma at about the same time. The methodology is straightforward—all that is required is a well-constructed questionnaire and a willing group of respondents. The set of target events is always expanding—every new public shock or tragedy provides a unique opportunity to test existing hypotheses. In contrast, it is more challenging to conduct large-scale surveys of the "sundry private shocks in each person's life", because of the "absence of a very large population of like-minded people" (Brown & Kulik, 1977, p. 75).

An additional reason why FBM studies are so popular is the intense, almost single-minded scientific interest in the issue of recall accuracy as opposed to other memory functions. Brown and Kulik's provocative title *Flashbulb Memories* and flowery rhetoric suggested the existence of an extraordinarily powerful and unique memory mechanism. They described circumstances under which the "central nervous system will 'take a picture'" (p. 84), and referred to the underlying FBM as "unchanging as the slumbering Rhinegold" (p. 86). If one looks beyond the rhetoric, Brown and Kulik's theoretical model clearly predicts variations in narrative memory elaboration, partly as a result of constructive processes accompanying retellings (Pillemer, 1990). Nevertheless, the strongest possible claims about FBMs—that they are unfailingly accurate, complete, and resistant to forgetting (e.g., McCloskey, Wible, & Cohen, 1988)—generated considerable controversy and strong motivation to conduct empirical tests as new public events presented themselves.

"HEARING THE NEWS" IS NOT THE SAME AS "BEING THERE"

Brown and Kulik (1977) proposed that FBMs of first learning about shocking public events reveal a general cognitive mechanism. The mechanism would have survival value because emotional and important events are frequently experienced directly. For first-hand experiences, the surrounding circumstances define the target event and provide important clues about how to respond to similar episodes in the future. Brown and Kulik speculated that for our distant ancestors the appearance of a new and dangerous carnivore would trigger a vivid memory because the concomitant information—the precise location where the intruder was spotted, the ongoing activities that could have provoked an attack, and so on—has protective value. In contrast, present-day FBMs of first hearing about distant public events provide no such survival benefits, because the surrounding circumstances—where you were and what you were doing—are unrelated to the substance of the newsworthy occurrence. FBMs of public events simply reflect the automatic activation of a memory mechanism that evolved earlier, for different purposes.

Although Brown and Kulik speculated that both hearing the news and first-hand experience are recorded by the same underlying memory mechanism, several dissimilarities are apparent. Consequentiality (personal importance or life impact) of these two types of memory certainly differs in fundamental ways. People who experienced from a distance the resignation of Margaret Thatcher (Conway et al., 1994), the explosion of the space shuttle *Challenger* (Neisser & Harsch, 1992), or the attack on the World Trade Center (Talarico & Rubin, 2003) may rate these events as highly important on a seven-point scale presented in a memory questionnaire, but the perceived *personal* life impact must be of a different order than the shock of an unexpected death of a parent or spouse, a serious accident, or a crime victim-ization. As a citizen of the US it would be difficult to rate the *Challenger* explosion, the death of a president, or a terrorist attack as anything other than consequential, but its day-to-day life impact may pale in comparison to first-hand trauma. Shocking public news and traumatic first-hand experience are likely to be rated differently on Berntsen and Rubin's (2006) new Central-ity of Event Scale, which includes items such as "I feel that this event has become a central part of my life story" and "This event permanently changed my life".

A key difference between first-hand experience and hearing the news is that memories of personal circumstances are related thematically to the tar-get event in the former case only: "Although the fact that an assassination or resignation has occurred may have real consequences for citizens of a given country . . . the *occasion on which they heard about it* surely does not" (Neisser et al., 1996, p. 353). When thinking or talking about the World Trade Center attacks, memories frequently centre on the newsworthy event itself; personal details come up only when attention is directed specifically to "hearing the news" stories. When thinking or talking about a life-threatening car accident, the personal details *are* the story (see Curci & Luminet, 2006; Curci, Chapter 1, this volume; and Hirst & Meksin, Chapter 10, this volume, for discussions of the distinction between event memories and FBMs).

Because details of first-hand experience are connected in meaningful ways to the target event, the likelihood of gross memory errors or major distor-tions may be reduced. Brewer (1992) and Neisser and Harsch (1992) attrib-uted some FBM errors to "wrong time slice", in which a reported memory represents a real occurrence but does not capture the very first time a person heard the news. For example, a person who heard fleetingly from a passer-by that an attack on the World Trade Center had occurred, but later on wit-nessed the full terror on the television news, might retain the memory of the brief and indefinite first telling for a short time only, and later identify the visually shocking television episode as the "first time". In research studies, wrong time-slice errors weaken the test–retest consistency of FBMs because the transient memory of the unremarkable original event is displaced by a completely different but also accurate memory. These substitution errors are less likely to occur for first-hand experiences because personal circumstances help to define the target event: "A person hit by a car may misremember its color, or the day of the week, but will rarely confuse being hit by a car with, say, falling down a mountain" (Schwarz & Gilligan, 1995, p. 22).

Differences between recollections of hearing the news and first-hand experience may result in part from differences in rehearsal that occur in the days, months, and years after initial encoding. Memories of shocking first-hand experiences may be thought about and talked about more frequently and with greater intensity than memories of learning about distant public events. Episodes experienced directly may come to mind readily because they contain information that promotes current well-being. For example, memories of first-hand experiences can serve a directive function (Pillemer, 1992, 1998, 2003). As described by Brown and Kulik (1977), vivid and long-lasting memories of dangerous and unsettling events would have survival value because they guide present activities away from similar sources of trouble. A contemporary example involves a recent jog on a sunny day, when a large tree limb unexpectedly fell several yards behind me, triggering a detailed memory of the location and ongoing activity. Months later, whenever I near the same spot on the running path, the memory comes to mind and I approach with caution. Examples of memory directives are plentiful in personal life histories (Pillemer, 1998), and the directive function has been shown empirically to be a prominent component of autobiographical memory (Bluck, Alea, Habermas, & Rubin, 2005). Frequent and focused rehearsal, both overt and covert, should enhance the likelihood that a first-hand memory will be highly elaborated and long lasting, although by no means does it guarantee that the memory will be fully accurate.

In contrast to memories of first-hand experiences, news reception memories would not serve a primarily directive or protective function because their content is unrelated to the distant danger or trauma. Instead, memories of news reception events appear to enhance interpersonal connection and personal identity, what have been called the social and self functions of autobiographical memory (Bluck, 2003; Bluck, Alea, Habermas, & Rubin, 2005). Neisser (1982) was the first to emphasize the social motivation to create and preserve elaborate FBMs: "We discuss 'how we heard the news' with our friends and listen eagerly to how *they* heard. We rehearse the occasion often in our minds and our conversations, seeking some meaning in it" (p. 48). According to Neisser's account, the self and social functions are intertwined. Memories of hearing the news become an integral part of a person's autobiographical narrative, marking critical intersections between an individual's life and the rest of humanity: "we remember the details of a FBoccasion because those details are the links between our own histories and 'History'. We are aware of this link at the time and aware that others are forging similar links" (p. 48).

The social and self functions of FBMs would appear to be especially salient when the public event is truly momentous and consequential, such as the Kennedy assassination or the terrorist attacks of September 11, 2001. For newsworthy but less important events, the motivation to incorporate a "hearing the news" memory into the life narrative and to share the memory with others is minimal. For example, FBMs of the assassination attempt on President Reagan, an event that did not have devastating consequences, were rarely rehearsed overtly: most respondents in Pillemer's (1984) study described a FBM 1 month after the shooting but reported never recounting the memory previously. Five years later, McCloskey et al. (1988) found that about 50% of their respondents had memories of the Reagan shooting. The absence of a motive to remember and to share may contribute to FBM decay.

Memories of hearing the news and first-hand experience may differ with respect to the adaptive functions that they serve, but considerable overlap also exists. Memories of first-hand experience not only inform future behaviours and decisions, they also contribute strongly to personal identity and are shared with others to achieve important interpersonal goals. For example, a child's memory of being kidnapped (Terr, 1990) not only contains information about potential dangers to be avoided, it also contributes to his or her evolving sense of self, and sharing memories of the event with others may elicit empathic responses (Pillemer, 2003). Alternatively, a FBM of hearing about a public tragedy provides some guidance about how to respond personally to such episodes in the future. Many adults who provided memories of learning about the assassination attempt on President Reagan reported first thinking about previous assassinations or attempts (Pillemer, 1984). These memories may have offered some reassurance that shocking public events had happened before and that people were able to cope quickly and move forward. Nevertheless, in most cases connections between specific memory content and personal well-being will be stronger for first-hand events, and this may increase the frequency and purposefulness of rehearsal, and thus the elaborateness and persistence of memories.

This brief comparison of memory types is intended to highlight potential contrasts between hearing the news and first-hand experience. New research, including systematic comparisons of memory functions and rehearsal processes, is necessary to evaluate the speculative conceptual analysis presented here. In the following sections I examine whether existing empirical studies can bring the contrasts into clearer focus.

HOW VALID ARE GLOBAL ASSESSMENTS OF MEMORY ATTRIBUTES?

Two basic strategies exist for comparing memories of hearing the news and first-hand experience. The first involves comparing these two categories of memory with respect to indices of quality, including consistency, elaboration, and persistence. For example, one could assess whether memories of first-hand experiences tend to be more consistent over time than memories of hearing the news. A second strategy involves identifying relationships between memory qualities and predictor variables (including emotion, surprise, consequentiality, and rehearsal) and then comparing these relationships across episodes of hearing the news and first-hand experience. For example, one could determine if rehearsal is a good predictor of memory consistency for both news reception events and first-hand episodes.

The validity and usefulness of global comparisons of memory types based on existing data are questionable for several reasons. First, memories of first-hand experience make up an extremely broad and diverse analytical category. Conway (1995) referred to memories of first-hand experiences as "real"

FBMs, presumably because they are far more common than memories of hearing the news. "Real" FBMs included "personal" FBMs, such as highly accessible episodes from the first year in college (e.g., Pillemer, Goldsmith, Panter, & White, 1988), and "traumatic" FBMs, such as eyewitness accounts of a crime (e.g., Yuille & Cutshall, 1986). Other researchers have used the term "FBM" to describe topics as diverse as the first menstrual period (Pillemer, Koff, Rhinehart, & Rierdan, 1987) and memories reported by patients in group psychotherapy (Thomsen & Berntsen, 2003). Pillemer (1998) and Rubin and Kozin (1984) identified a wide variety of life events that can give rise to vivid and detailed memories of personal circumstances, including major life turning points, personal injury or accidents, sports triumphs and disappointments, special romantic encounters, and moments of personal insight that have special meaning only for the individual. The task of finding consistent patterns of results within this expansive data set, which can then be compared directly to FBMs of hearing the news, is daunting.

Drawing firm overall conclusions about the more circumscribed body of research on FBMs of public events also poses a considerable challenge. Newsworthy events vary widely in their personal, national, and global influence; for example, the assassination attempt on President Reagan in 1981 or the California earthquake of 1989 would appear to be far more limited in scope of impact than the terrorist attacks of September 11, 2001. Outcomes may differ across studies because the target events are not equally newsworthy or life altering. Although some tentative data patterns are discernible across studies, there is no one agreed upon set of conclusions, or an agreed upon methodology for study design, or an agreed upon standard for evaluating study outcomes. (See Wright, Chapter 2, this volume, and Berntsen, Chapter 9, this volume, for extended discussions of methodological issues in FBM research.)

Research examining the consistency of FBMs of the space shuttle disaster provides a good illustration of the challenges posed by between-study differences. McCloskey et al. (1988) examined consistency of FBMs at 1 week and 9 months after the event, using a "relatively lax criterion" (p. 174). Responses given at 9 months to four direct questions involving location, activity, source, and reaction were compared to initial responses and coded as same, more specific, more general, inconsistent, or don't remember. Neisser and Harsch (1992) elicited open-ended and cued memories of the space shuttle disaster within 1 day and again about 2½ years later. Overall consistency was scored on a seven-point scale. Time 2 responses to the categories of location, activity, and informant were given a score of 2 for "essentially correct", a score of 0 for "obviously wrong", and a score of 1 for "intermediate cases" (p. 17). A "bonus point" was awarded depending on the quality of descriptions of two "minor" attributes: time of day and others present. Bohannon and Symons (1992) examined consistency using yet another questionnaire design, coding scheme, and time delay. The delay was 3 years and only the category of location was used to evaluate consistency. It is difficult to come up with a precise estimate of FBM consistency for the space shuttle disaster, let alone for the more expansive FBM literature, in part because methods and time delays differ widely across studies.

Researchers also measure predictors of FBM consistency, such as intensity of emotional reactions to the event, in different ways. For example, Neisser and Harsch's (1992) participants answered the open-ended question, "How did you feel about it?" The researchers then converted qualitative responses to scores: respondents who used at least two "strong and negatively toned terms" were assigned a score of 3, those who used one such term were assigned a 2, and those who gave a more neutral or qualified response were assigned a 1. Using this scheme, no effect of emotion on memory was apparent. Bohannon and Symons (1992) directly obtained quantitative emotion ratings on a five-point scale—as the authors predicted, higher affect ratings were strongly associated with more consistent reports. Substantial between-study differences exist even among researchers who employ quantitative ratings: some use three-point scales (e.g., Conway et al., 1994), five-point scales (e.g., Bohannon & Symons, 1992; Pillemer, 1984), seven-point scales (e.g., Curci & Luminet, 2006; Neisser et al., 1996; Talarico & Rubin, 2003), and eleven-point scales (Christianson, 1989). The scales have a variety of verbal anchors. Using different measurement metrics could contribute to between-study differences in outcomes. (See Curci, Chapter 1, this volume, for a detailed discussion of measurement issues in FBM research.)

It is hard to determine the precise effect of methodological differences between studies, but it would be a mistake to discount their importance and base comparisons primarily on researchers' summary conclusions (e.g., whether the data are interpreted as supporting a claim of memory consistency or inconsistency). The burgeoning scientific literature on FBMs seems ripe for a systematic quantitative research review or meta-analysis (e.g., Cooper & Hedges, 1994; Light & Pillemer, 1984). In the case of memory consistency, for example, all studies that have assessed this quality would be included in the analysis. Consistency rates would be entered with key study characteristics to determine if consistency scores vary systematically as a function of coding strategy, time delay (e.g., Schmolck, Buffalo, & Squire, 2000), age of participants (e.g., Conway et al., 1994), and other possible sources of outcome differences.

DIRECT COMPARISONS OF HEARING THE NEWS AND FIRST-HAND EXPERIENCE

One way to avoid ambiguities associated with between-study differences in methodology is to conduct direct comparisons within studies. In this way, researchers can ensure that methods are consistent across event types. A handful of studies have included memories of both hearing the news and direct experience (Christianson, 1989; Er, 2003; Neisser et al., 1996; Rubin & Kozin, 1984; Talarico & Rubin, 2003; Weaver, 1993).

Early in the history of FBM research, Rubin and Kozin (1984) recognized the need for comparative analyses. They elicited college students' three "clearest memories". Participants were given a definition of FBMs to guide their recall. The open-ended probes produced a variety of event types, such as accidents, sports events, encounters with members of the opposite sex, and deaths. Vivid memories overwhelmingly described first-hand experiences; spontaneous descriptions of news reception events were rare (4 of 174 memories). The extremely low incidence of memories of hearing the news could be attributable in part to the immediate historical context of the data collection in 1982; college students would not have been exposed recently to a major public tragedy.

Rubin and Kozin (1984) also provided specific memory cues for 20 events. Probes for first-hand experiences included receiving an admissions letter to college, a car accident, the seventeenth birthday, and the first date. Probes for hearing the news events included the shootings of President Reagan, the Pope, and President Sadat of Egypt, as well as President Nixon's resignation. Several of the first-hand experiences were identified by most students as producing flashbulb-quality memories: a car accident that they were in or witnessed, the night of the senior prom, meeting your college roommate for the first time, and speaking in front of an audience, among others. The public event that produced the highest incidence of exceptionally vivid memories was the assassination attempt on President Reagan (50%); proportions of other memories of hearing the news that were rated as flashbulb quality were well below 50%. The relatively low percentage of people reporting FBMs of newsworthy events may be attributable in part to the absence of recent public tragedies that were perceived as truly momentous.

Following Rubin and Kozin (1984), researchers have employed two principal strategies to compare FBMs of newsworthy events and memories of first-hand experiences: (1) comparing memories representing direct versus indirect exposure to the same momentous event (Er, 2003; Neisser et al., 1996) and (2) comparing memories of hearing about newsworthy events to memories of unrelated mundane personal events that had occurred at about the same time (Christianson, 1989; Talarico & Rubin, 2003; Weaver, 1993).

Using the first research strategy, Neisser et al. (1996) obtained memories of personal circumstances when learning about the Loma Prieta or "San Francisco" earthquake of 1989, famous for its postponement of the baseball World Series. Direct versus indirect participation was a critical variable. Some college student respondents were Californians who felt the tremors themselves and therefore could provide a memory of first-hand experience. Other students lived in Atlanta and provided a memory of hearing the news. Memories were obtained days after the event and again 1½ years later. Consistency was scored using a modified version of Neisser and Harsch's (1992) three-point scale (consistent, partly consistent, inconsistent). Comparisons between samples focused on a score composed of three central informational categories: location, activity, and others present.

Between-sample differences in memory consistency were dramatic and revealing. Californian students' responses were almost perfectly consistent over the 1½ year time interval, with performance "essentially at ceiling" (Neisser et al., 1996, p. 345). In contrast, Atlanta students' memories of hearing the news showed substantial evidence of inconsistencies. In Atlanta, memories of students who had relatives and friends in the affected area were far more consistent than memories of students who did not. Other studies also have found high FBM consistency among respondents who had strong interest and personal investment in the target event (e.g., Conway et al., 1994). Neisser et al. (1996) concluded that "recall can be accurate, even if it takes an earthquake to make it so" (p. 356).

Neisser et al. (1996) provided strong evidence for the idea that first-hand experiences may be remembered vividly and consistently for months and years. The authors speculated that rehearsal may play a key role in memory preservation. Narratives that portray a "how I didn't die story" illustrate the directive and social functions of recalling first-hand experiences: "Nearness to real danger gives such stories a distinctiveness that few accounts of 'hearing the news' can match" (p. 356). In contrast, the Atlanta students were a continent away from danger, and would not be strongly motivated to think about and share their personal memories, with the exception of respondents who had Californian friends and relatives.

Er (2003) conducted a study similar in design to the study by Neisser et al. (1996). Turkish participants who directly experienced the 1999 Marmara earthquake were compared to participants who only heard the news. Memory was assessed by a questionnaire administered 6 to 9 months after the earthquake and again 6 months later. Victims of the earthquake were more likely than people who heard the news indirectly to have detailed and vivid memories. Memories reported by on-site victims were more consistent than memories reported by participants who experienced the event indirectly; consistency scores for victims were virtually at ceiling. The authors concluded that FBM inconsistencies observed in prior studies may be attributable to the fact that participants "were not directly affected by the events" (p. 515).

Talarico and Rubin (2003) used a different strategy to examine FBM consistency. They compared FBMs of the September 11 terrorist attacks to memories of an ordinary personal event; both memories were obtained 1 day after September 11 and again 1, 6, or 32 weeks later. College students were asked direct questions about September 11, including the categories of informant, time, location, others present, and activity. A second set of questions involved "an everyday event from the participant's life in the days prior to the attacks" (p. 455). Everyday events reported by college students were "typical for the life of an average college student", and included parties, sporting events, and studying (p. 456). As such, they qualify as first-hand experiences. Direct questions included type of event, time of occurrence, location, others present, and activity. Students listed several words that could be used to cue the particular everyday memory in a future testing. They also completed the Autobiographical Memory Questionnaire for both the September 11 memory and the everyday memory; the questionnaire asks participants to provide ratings of a variety of memory features.

Memory consistency was assessed using relatively lenient criteria. For example, when describing others who were present, the Time 1 response "friend" and Time 2 response "Sue" were scored as consistent (p. 456). Everyday memories and FBMs showed similar levels of consistency across time periods. FBMs were rated as more emotional and were rehearsed more frequently than were everyday memories, but these qualities did not lead to greater consistency.

Talarico and Rubin's (2003) main finding—that memories of unremarkable everyday events appear to be as consistent as memories of a shocking public disaster—is so striking that it deserves careful scrutiny. One issue concerns the uniqueness of self-selected events. Everyday events singled out by participants appear to represent particular instances of recurrent activities of a typical college student. A memory of studying in the dorm, for example, may have several scripted components (location—dorm room; activity— studying; time—after dinner) that would remain consistent using lenient scoring criteria, even if the original event is not remembered vividly.

A second issue involves the classification of the self-nominated events as "everyday". Participants singled out an event to be included in a formal psychological study. Then they answered a series of questions about it and completed the Autobiographical Memory Questionnaire with this particular event in mind. The event may have been ordinary to begin with, but after this focused rehearsal it would appear to have lost its casual, everyday status. In addition, the request for words to "serve as a cue for that unique event in the future" (p. 456), although necessary for follow-up testing, seems to suggest to the participant that the memory could or would be requested again at a later date.

An earlier study conducted by Weaver (1993) produced a pattern of findings similar to those reported by Talarico and Rubin (2003). As part of a classroom exercise in cognitive psychology, college students were told that "the next time they saw a roommate (or a friend, if they lived alone), they should do their best to remember all the circumstances surrounding that event" (p. 41). By chance, the 1991 bombing of Iraq began at about the time that the classroom exercise was conducted, and memory questionnaires were completed for both the roommate interaction and hearing the news of the bombing. Follow-up questionnaires were administered 3 months and 11 months later. Memory consistency over time for the two events was similar, with only scattered differences favouring memories of hearing about the public event. The author provided a motivational explanation for the persistence of ordinary memories involving a roommate: "What does appear to be necessary is having the instructions (or intentions) to remember the event" (p. 45).

Christianson's (1989) earlier comparison of a FBM and a personal memory suggests that, in the absence of elaborative rehearsal, special cueing, or a request to remember, everyday memories are susceptible to rapid decay. Christianson obtained memories of hearing about the assassination of Swedish Prime Minister Olof Palme 6 weeks after the shooting and again 1 year later, and compared them to respondents' most vivid memory from the Saturday before the first interview. Participants were unaware at Time 1 that they would be contacted again in the future. The personal memory was elicited at Time 2 with a request for a memory of "the event you described from the last Saturday before we called you the first time" (p. 437). The average memory consistency rate for personal circumstances (informant, time of day, location, activity, others present, clothes worn, first thoughts) when learning about the Palme assassination was .80 using lenient scoring criteria. Memories of the personal event were scored as consistent if the second memory "included a general description of the same event, regardless of what specific details were mentioned" (p. 439); the consistency rate was only .22. The authors concluded that "the Palme-related circumstances were much better retained than the personal event" (p. 439). Part of the very large difference in consistency rates for memories of the newsworthy event and the personal event could be due to differences in directed rehearsal during the Time 1 interview; participants responded to specific questions and provided ratings only for their memories of the Palme assassination.

Rather than demonstrating the ordinariness of FBMs, Talarico and Rubin's (2003) and Weaver's (1993) findings may illustrate the power of event distinctiveness, rehearsal, and motivated remembering. When an everyday event is singled out for special attention and detailed analysis as part of a research study, it is likely to persist for months with a good degree of consistency. Distinctiveness and rehearsal were identified early on by Rubin and Kozin (1984) as likely contributors to memory vividness, and the recent data further underscore their potential importance. In contrast, FBM processes are more automatic; momentous events are distinctive, talked about, thought about, and vividly remembered in the absence of an intervention by a researcher. Although FBMs of hearing about public tragedies may well be less robust than memories of momentous first-hand experiences (Er, 2003; Neisser et al., 1996), it would be premature to equate them with memories of the multitude of mundane and recurring events in our lives.

CONCLUSIONS

The distinction between memories of learning about newsworthy public events and memories of first-hand experience appears to be meaningful on both conceptual and empirical grounds. Conceptual analysis suggests that memories of first-hand experience are more likely than memories of hearing the news to serve a directive function, because personal circumstances contain useful information related to future well-being. Direct experiences also contribute strongly to a sense of personal identity. As a result, memories of salient and important first-hand experiences may receive more frequent and purposeful rehearsal, which could enhance persistence and consistency.

Global comparisons between memories of hearing the news and first-hand experiences are problematic. Studies representing each category are so diverse, and the research methods so variable, that it is difficult to draw summary conclusions with a high degree of confidence. One way to achieve a synthesis would be to conduct meta-analytic reviews, in an effort to identify general and interpretable patterns. In future studies, efforts could be made to standardize test procedures and protocols to enable more valid between-study comparisons. For example, the recently developed Centrality of Event Scale (Berntsen & Rubin, 2006) could be used to assess life impact.

A promising but difficult to implement research strategy involves comparing memories of first-hand experiences and hearing the news that involve the same momentous event. Neisser et al.'s (1996) within-study comparison suggested that these two memory types differ in important ways: Memories of experiencing the California earthquake first hand were more consistent over time than memories of hearing the news, and memories of hearing the news that involved family and friends were more consistent than such memories with little personal involvement. Er (2003) produced a similar pattern of findings for the Marmara earthquake.

Talarico and Rubin (2003) and Weaver (1993) adopted a different research strategy to evaluate the robustness of FBMs. They compared memories of momentous newsworthy events to memories of unrelated everyday events. Although the results seem to indicate that FBMs of shocking public events are no more consistent over time than memories of ordinary personal experiences, this conclusion seems premature. When everyday memories are singled out for extensive analysis or when participants are encouraged to remember them, their status is changed from mundane to distinctive. FBMs are distinctive, rehearsed, and memorable on their own. All researchers agree that FBMs are not infallible, and data presented by Neisser et al. (1996) and Er (2003) show that memories of hearing the news can be more vulnerable to distortion and decay than memories of momentous first-hand encounters. But the strong possibility remains that FBMs of public events are more robust than memories of most ordinary life experiences, and that factors such as emotion and rehearsal contribute to their longevity and consistency.

REFERENCES

Berntsen, D., & Rubin, D. C. (2006). The centrality of event scale: A measure of integrating trauma into one's identity and its relation to post-traumatic stress disorder symptoms. *Behaviour Research and Therapy, 44,* 219–231.

Berntsen, D., & Thomsen, D. K. (2005). Personal memories for remote historical events: Accuracy and clarity of FBMs related to World War II. *Journal of Experimental Psychology: General, 134,* 242–257.

Bluck, S. (2003). Autobiographical memory: Exploring its functions in everyday life. *Memory*, *11*, 113–123.

Bluck, S., Alea, N., Habermas, T., & Rubin, D. C. (2005). A tale of three functions: The self-reported uses of autobiographical memory. *Social Cognition*, *23*, 91–117.

Bohannon, J. N. III. (1988). Flashbulb memories for the space shuttle disaster: A tale of two theories. *Cognition*, *29*, 179–196.

Bohannon, J. N. III., & Symons, V. L. (1992). Flashbulb memories: Confidence, consistency, and quantity. In E. Winograd & U. Neisser (Eds.), *Affect and accuracy in recall: Studies of "flashbulb" memories* (pp. 65–91). New York: Cambridge University Press.

Brewer, W. F. (1992). The theoretical and empirical status of the flashbulb memory hypothesis. In E. Winograd & U. Neisser (Eds.), *Affect and accuracy in recall: Studies of "flashbulb" memories* (pp. 274–305). New York: Cambridge University Press.

Brown, R., & Kulik, J. (1977). Flashbulb memories. *Cognition*, *5*, 73–79.

Ceci, S. J., & Bruck, M. (1993). Suggestibility of the child witness: A historical review and synthesis. *Psychological Bulletin*, *113*, 403–439.

Christianson, S. A. (1989). Flashbulb memories: Special, but not so special. *Memory and Cognition*, *17*, 435–443.

Conway, M. A. (1995). *Flashbulb memories*. Hillsdale, NJ: Lawrence Erlbaum Associates Inc.

Conway, M. A., Anderson, S. J., Larsen, S. F., Donnelly, C. M., McDaniel, M. A., McClelland, A. G. R., et al. (1994). The formation of flashbulb memories. *Memory and Cognition*, *22*, 326–343.

Cooper, H., & Hedges, L. V. (Eds.). (1994). *The handbook of research synthesis*. New York: Russell Sage Foundation.

Curci, A., & Luminet, O. (2006). Follow-up of a cross-national comparison on flashbulb and event memory for the September 11th attacks. *Memory*, *14*, 329–344.

Curci, A., Luminet, O., Finkenauer, C., & Gisle, L. (2001). Flashbulb memories in social groups: A comparative test–retest study of the memory of French President Mitterrand's death in a French and a Belgian group. *Memory*, *9*, 81–101.

Er, N. (2003). A new flashbulb memory model applied to the Marmara earthquake. *Applied Cognitive Psychology*, *17*, 503–517.

Finkenauer, C., Luminet, O., Gisle, L., El-Ahmadi, A., van der Linden, M., & Philippot, P. (1998). Flashbulb memories and the underlying mechanisms of their formation: Toward an emotional-integrative model. *Memory and Cognition*, *26*, 516–531.

Light, R. J., & Pillemer, D. B. (1984). *Summing up: The science of reviewing research*. Cambridge, MA: Harvard University Press.

McCloskey, M., Wible, C. G., & Cohen, N. J. (1988). Is there a special flashbulb-memory mechanism? *Journal of Experimental Psychology: General*, *117*, 171–181.

Neisser, U. (1982). Snapshots or benchmarks? In U. Neisser (Ed.), *Memory observed: Remembering in natural contexts* (pp. 43–48). San Francisco: W. H. Freeman.

Neisser, U., & Harsch, N. (1992). Phantom flashbulbs: False recollections of hearing the news about Challenger. In E. Winograd & U. Neisser (Eds.), *Affect and accuracy in recall: Studies of "flashbulb" memories* (pp. 9–31). New York: Cambridge University Press.

Neisser, U., Winograd, E., Bergman, E. T., Schreiber, C. A., Palmer, S. E., & Weldon, M. S. (1996). Remembering the earthquake: Direct experience vs. hearing the news. *Memory*, *4*, 337–357.

Pillemer, D. B. (1984). Flashbulb memories of the assassination attempt on President Reagan. *Cognition, 16,* 63–80.

Pillemer, D. B. (1990). Clarifying the flashbulb memory concept: Comment on McCloskey, Wible, and Cohen (1998). *Journal of Experimental Psychology: General, 119,* 92–96.

Pillemer, D. B. (1992). Remembering personal circumstances: A functional analysis. In E. Winograd & U. Neisser (Eds.), *Affect and accuracy in recall: Studies of "flashbulb" memories* (pp. 236–264). New York: Cambridge University Press.

Pillemer, D. B. (1998). *Momentous events, vivid memories: How unforgettable moments help us to understand the meaning of our lives.* Cambridge, MA: Harvard University Press.

Pillemer, D. B. (2003). Directive functions of autobiographical memory: The guiding power of the specific episode. *Memory, 11,* 193–202.

Pillemer, D. B., Goldsmith, L. R., Panter, A. T., & White, S. H. (1988). Very long-term memories of the first year in college. *Journal of Experimental Psychology: Learning, Memory, and Cognition, 14,* 709–715.

Pillemer, D. B., Koff, E., Rhinehart, E. D., & Rierdan, J. (1987). Flashbulb memories of menarche and adult menstrual distress. *Journal of Adolescence, 10,* 187–199.

Rubin, D. C., & Kozin, M. (1984). Vivid memories. *Cognition, 16,* 81–95.

Schmolck, H., Buffalo, E. A., & Squire, L. R. (2000). Memory distortions develop over time: Recollections of the O.J. Simpson trial verdict after 15 and 32 months. *Psychological Science, 11,* 39–45.

Schwarz, R., & Gilligan, S. (1995). The devil is in the details. *The Family Therapy Networker, 19,* 21–23.

Talarico, J. M., & Rubin, D. C. (2003). Confidence, not consistency, characterizes flashbulb memories. *Psychological Science, 14,* 455–461.

Tekcan, A. I. (2001). Flashbulb memories for a negative and a positive event: News of Desert Storm and acceptance to college. *Psychological Reports, 88,* 323–331.

Terr, L. (1990). *Too scared to cry.* New York: Basic Books.

Thomsen, D. K., & Berntsen, D. (2003). Snapshots from therapy: Exploring operationalisations and ways of studying flashbulb memories for private events. *Memory, 11,* 559–570.

Weaver, C. A. III (1993). Do you need a "flash" to form a flashbulb memory? *Journal of Experimental Psychology: General, 122,* 39–46.

Winograd, E., & Neisser, U. (1992). *Affect and accuracy in recall: Studies of "flashbulb" memories.* New York: Cambridge University Press.

Yuille, J. C., & Cutshall, J. L. (1986). A case study of eyewitness memory of a crime. *Journal of Applied Psychology, 71,* 291–301.

7 Flashbulb, personal, and event memories in clinical populations[1]

Andrew E. Budson and Carl A. Gold

Throughout this book investigations are described into how and why personal memories associated with national traumatic events seem more vivid and somehow frozen in time compared to memories of ordinary events. However, not all individuals show the same reaction to traumatic events. Some individuals, such as those afflicted with Alzheimer's disease, exhibit problems of impaired memory. Other individuals, such as those suffering from post-traumatic stress disorder, experience memories that are too vivid or recurrent. In this chapter we will discuss how memory for national traumatic events relates to these and other disorders. It should be noted that very few studies have evaluated memory for national traumatic events in clinical populations. This chapter will focus on those important studies.

Following Brown and Kulik (1977), many of the studies reviewed in this chapter have made the distinction between memory for the personal reception context surrounding an event (memory of place, time, activity, and so on when individuals first learned of the event)—the "FBM"—versus memory for the event itself. For shorthand, we will refer to memory for the personal reception context as *personal* memory (or memory for personal information), and memory for the event itself as *event* memory (or memory for event information). As detailed in Chapters 1 (Curci), 3 (Luminet), and 4 (Talarico & Rubin), the specific criteria necessary for a personal memory to reach the status of a FBM is controversial. Most agree that important core factors include importance, novelty, surprise, and emotionality. As will become clear in the studies reviewed below, few if any studies in clinical populations have assessed for all of these factors. Thus, we will mainly use the term "personal memory" rather than "FBM" when discussing these studies.

ALZHEIMER'S DISEASE AND MILD COGNITIVE IMPAIRMENT

The most common cause of memory problems is Alzheimer's disease (AD), a degenerative disease of the brain caused by the accumulation of beta-amyloid plaques and neurofibrillary tangles. This pathology has a predilection for specific brain regions, including the hippocampus, amygdala, entorhinal cortex, parietal cortex, inferolateral temporal cortex, and (somewhat less) frontal cortex (Solomon & Budson, 2003). As disease-modifying treatments for AD are being developed, there has recently been an intense focus to try to determine which older adults will eventually develop Alzheimer's disease. Petersen and colleagues have investigated patients with what they have termed mild cognitive impairment (MCI), who develop Alzheimer's disease at a higher rate than usual. Patients with MCI, amnestic type (the most common type), show impairment on tests of memory but are not demented and perform normally on tests of other neuropsychological domains (Petersen et al., 2001). About 70% of patients with MCI ultimately develop AD, at a rate of about 15% per year.

Studies in healthy individuals have demonstrated that emotional stimuli are better remembered than neutral stimuli (Phelps, LaBar, & Spencer, 1997). Studies using functional neuroimaging and patients with brain lesions have provided evidence that whereas the hippocampal region may play a general role in episodic remembering, recruitment of the amygdala is specifically associated with emotional memories (Alkire, Haier, Fallon, & Cahill, 1998; Canli, Zhao, Brewer, Gabrieli, & Cahill, 2000; Hamann, Cahill, McGaugh, & Squire, 1997; Kensinger & Schacter, 2006; Packard & Cahill, 2001). Although patients with AD and MCI show primary deficits in episodic memory attributable to pathology in hippocampus and entorhinal cortex, because of their amygdala pathology (Chu, Tranel, Damasio, & Van Hoesen, 1997) researchers have hypothesized that these patients would also show impairment in both processing of, and memory for, emotional stimuli (Albert, Cohen, & Koff, 1991; Allender & Kaszniak, 1989; Brosgole, Kurucz, Plahovinsak, & Gumiela, 1981; Cadieux & Greve, 1997).

A number of laboratory studies have investigated emotional memory in patients with AD. Several investigators have suggested that the emotional memory effect is impaired in patients with AD. Hamann, Monarch, and Goldstein (2000) studied emotional responses and emotional memory in patients with AD compared to older adult controls. Patients with AD demonstrated normal emotional responses to picture stimuli as measured by arousal ratings and skin-conductance responses. On a recognition test, however, patients with AD did not show the emotional memory effect for negative pictures observed in healthy older adults. Several studies have also found impairment in emotional memory in patients with AD when the effect was examined using pictures (Abrisqueta-Gomez, Bueno, Oliveira, & Bertolucci, 2001), unrelated words (Kensinger, Brierley, Medford, Growdon, & Corkin, 2002), semantically related words (Budson et al., 2006), and brief narratives (Kensinger, Anderson, Growdon, & Corkin, 2004).

Other studies, however, found that patients with AD exhibited a normal emotional memory effect. Kazui et al. (2000) found that patients with AD remembered an emotionally arousing story better than a neutral one, and that the extent of the memory improvement was similar to that of healthy older adult controls. Moayeri, Cahill, Jin, and Plotkin (2000) found that patients with AD remembered emotionally negative parts of an audio-visual story compared with the emotionally neutral parts. Also, Boller et al. (2002) found that patients with AD remembered emotional stories better than neutral stories.

Budson et al. (2006) speculated that the discrepancy between those studies that found an emotional memory effect in AD and those that did not might be attributable to the differences between examining emotional items as isolated stimuli versus emotional items as part of a story. Although patients with AD did not show an emotional memory effect in the studies that examined isolated stimuli, they did show an emotional memory effect in the studies that examined emotional items as part of a story. If this analysis is correct, then we would expect that patients with AD would show enhanced memories for emotionally charged real-life stories such as national traumatic events, the type of events that may generate FBMs.

In the first of such studies, Ikeda et al. (1998) examined the extent to which patients with AD could remember a natural disaster they survived (the Kobe earthquake) compared with the memory for an MRI scan they underwent. Using a 12-item questionnaire, these authors found that 86% of the patients remembered the earthquake, whereas only 31% remembered the MRI scan. In a follow-up study, Mori et al. (1999) correlated the volume of the amygdala and hippocampus with the amount of information that patients could recall about the earthquake. Although hippocampus and amygdala both showed an initial positive correlation, only the correlation with the amygdala remained significant after effects of age, sex, education, whole brain volume, and disease severity were accounted for. Mori et al. (1999) suggested that these findings indicate that the amount of amygdalar damage in AD patients may determine their deficits in emotional memory. More generally, the findings suggest that the amydala may be more central to emotional memory than the hippocampus. See Chapter 8 (Fivush) for a further discussion of physiological measurements of emotional memory.

Several recent studies examined the memory of patients with AD for the September 11, 2001 terrorist attacks. In a brief study, Thompson et al. (2004) evaluated 13 patients with AD living in the United Kingdom for their memories of the September 11th attacks. Records were reviewed for clinic visits from September 11 to October 11, 2001, for patients with AD whose assessment included the question "What has been in the news the past week or two?" Four patients recalled some details about the September 11th attacks, while nine did not. The four who recalled information were asked again about the attacks 1 year later. All still recalled some factual information about the attacks, although they were unable to recall the personal information regarding where they were, what they were doing, and who they were with when they first heard the news of the attacks. The authors concluded that these patients had FBMs, although because of the lack of personal details they were qualitatively different from those reported by healthy older adults. They also concluded that the primary episodic memory deficit in patients with AD is attributable to poor encoding and not faulty consolidations, as those patients who initially remembered the attacks still remembered them.

Using a detailed questionnaire administered during telephone interviews, Budson et al. (2004) investigated emotional responses to, and memory for, the September 11th attacks in 22 patients with AD, 21 patients with MCI, and 23 healthy older adult controls in the initial weeks following the event and again 3 to 4 months later. The questionnaire was loosely based on one previously used by Schmolck, Buffalo, and Squire (2000), and was developed by the 9/11 Memory Consortium (Randy L. Buckner, Andrew E. Budson, John Gabrielli, William Hirst, Marcia K. Johnson, Cindy Lustig, Keith Lyle, Mara Mather, Kevin Ochsner, Elizabeth A. Phelps, Daniel L. Schacter, Jon S. Simons, and Chandan Vaidya). Of the 44 questions administered, Budson et al. presented an analysis of 13 personal information questions concerning where the person was and what they were doing when they heard the news of the attacks, 6 factual information questions concerning the factual details of the attacks, 14 questions regarding their present and predicted future emotional states, 3 questions regarding the extent to which they reviewed the events of September 11th, and 2 questions regarding how well they expected to remember the answers to the personal information questions in the future. For these latter 2 questions, how well participants expected to remember their personal information in 3 months and 1 year, responses were based on a 1 (low) to 5 (high) scale. Recall and recognition performance was recorded for the personal and factual information questions. Participants were interviewed by telephone initially from 19 September to 2 October 2001 (initial time point), and then again 3 to 4 months later from 11 December 2001 to 17 January 2002 (3-month time point).

There were several notable findings from the study of Budson et al. (2004). First, patients with AD and older adults reported very similar intensity of all emotions measured (sadness, anger, fear, frustration, confusion, and shock). However, patients with MCI reported less intensity of the emotions anger, fear, and confusion compared to the other groups (Figure 7.1). Second, distortions of memory for personal information were very common among all participants at the 3-month time point, but were most common in patients with AD. Memory distortions were, in fact, considerably higher than "I don't know" responses (response failures) for personal information for all groups. The authors suggested that distortions of memory were likely attributable to participants' overly high level of confidence that they would remember the information. Lastly, Budson et al. (2004) performed an analysis similar to Cohen, Conway, and Maylor (1994) to ascertain if their participants formed FBMs. Five personal information questions were analysed: time they heard the news of the attacks, the people they were with, where they were, what they were doing, and the source of the news. Figure 7.2 shows the percentage of participants who answered one, two, three, four, or all five of these personal information questions correctly at the 3-month interview relative to the initial

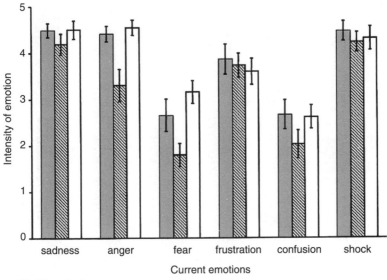

Figure 7.1 Intensity of emotional reaction on a 1 (low) to 5 (high) scale for patients
with Alzheimer's disease (AD), mild cognitive impairment (MCI), and
older adults as a function of emotion (sadness, anger, fear, frustration,
confusion, shock). Error bars show the standard error of the mean. From
Budson et al. (2004).

one for each group. As can be seen, using the strict criterion for FBMs that all
five questions were answered correctly, approximately half of the participants
in both the older adult and MCI groups were able to form FBMs, whereas
almost no participants in the AD group were able to do so. (The reader can
see from Figure 7.2 how the percentage of participants who formed FBMs
increases as the criterion is relaxed to allow fewer correctly answered questions.) The fact that, compared with healthy older adults, patients with AD
reported very similar intensity of emotions but significantly less memory
demonstrates that even a normal emotional reaction cannot overcome the
memory dysfunction of AD.

In a follow-up study, Budson et al. (2007) examined the participants from
the study of Budson et al. (2004) with another telephone questionnaire
approximately 1 year after the attacks. Adding this 1-year time point allowed
the authors to examine the change over time in correct memories from the
initial to the 3-month to the 1-year time points, in addition to the change over
time in distorted and failed memories from the 3-month to the 1-year time
points. ("Correct" memories are both stable over time from the initial interview and, for factual information, accurate.) In this study, Budson et al.

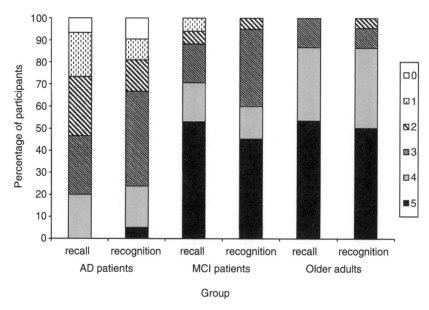

Figure 7.2 Percentage of participants who answered one, two, three, four, or five personal information questions (time, people, place, activity, and source) correctly at the follow-up interview relative to the initial one as a function of group (patients with Alzheimer's disease [AD], mild cognitive impairment [MCI], and older adults) and response type (recall vs recognition). From Budson et al. (2004).

(2007) found that, compared to healthy older adults, patients with AD (and MCI) showed (1) lower levels of personal and factual information at the initial time point, (2) a greater decline in their recognition of personal and factual information from the initial to the 3-month time point, (3) a similar stability of their personal information from the 3-month to the 1-year time point, and (4) a similar decline in factual information from the 3-month to the 1-year time point (Figure 7.3). It is particularly interesting to note how the patterns of decline of correct personal (Figure 7.3a) versus correct factual (Figure 7.3d) recognition differ regarding the effects of both time and group. The authors speculated that these results were consistent with the idea that patients with AD and MCI show impaired encoding of information and a more rapid rate of forgetting until the information has been consolidated; once the information has been consolidated its decay rate becomes the same as that of healthy older adults. Lastly, it is worth noting in Figure 7.3 how correct personal information—reflecting the core qualitative experience that characterizes FBMs—is quite stable for all groups from the 3-month to the 1-year time points, in contrast to the steady decline of correct factual information.

Can patients with AD and MCI form FBMs? The answer is unequivocally

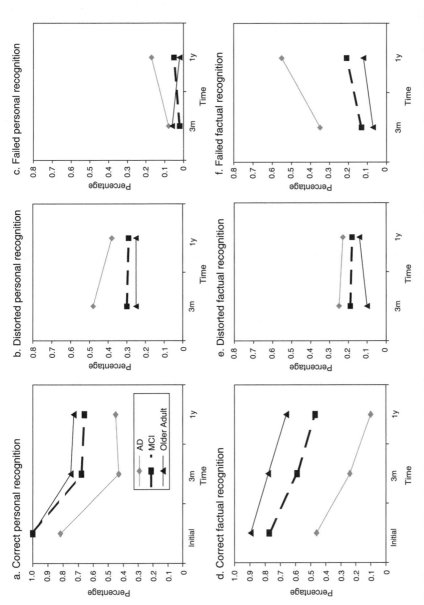

Figure 7.3 Adjusted recognition data for personal and factual information in patients with AD (AD), patients with MCI (MCI), and older adult controls (Older Adult) showing correct, distorted, and failed responses. From Budson et al. (2007).

"yes" for patients with MCI (see Figure 7.2). The answer is more complicated for patients with AD. When we examine all the studies reviewed above, several conclusions can be drawn. First, patients with AD exhibit impaired personal and factual memory for national traumatic events. It is likely that few patients with AD are able to form FBMs, at least using strict criteria (Figure 7.2). It is possible that the "special mechanism" that some researchers (e.g., Brown & Kulik, 1977) believe occurs at encoding of especially emotional events may not occur in AD patients. However, the majority of patients with mild to moderate AD reported in these studies were able to remember some personal and factual details related to a national traumatic event. Furthermore, the memories formed by these patients related to a national traumatic event appear relatively stable over time once they have been consolidated (Budson et al., 2004, 2007; Thompson et al., 2004) (Figure 7.3).

KORSAKOFF SYNDROME, OTHER CAUSES OF AMNESIA, AND FOCAL BRAIN LESIONS

Caused by a thiamine deficiency usually associated with alcoholism, Korsakoff syndrome is marked by dense amnesia and a tendency to confabulate. Patients with Korsakoff syndrome have lesions of the mammillary bodies and several thalamic nuclei including the anterior, mediodorsal, and dorsolateral nuclei (Mesulam, 2000).

Working in The Netherlands, Candel, Jelicic, Merckelbach, and Wester (2003) investigated memory for the September 11, 2001 attacks in inpatients with pre-existing Korsakoff syndrome. Fifteen middle-aged individuals with Korsakoff syndrome and an equal number of age-matched controls were first interviewed 7 months after the terrorist attacks and then again 2 months later. Because of the long delay (7 months) between the event and initial interview, caution should be taken in drawing conclusions from this study. The same 13 questions were asked at both interviews and were divided into three sections: event recall, personal memory for learning of the attacks, and semantic or factual knowledge about the attacks. Five participants with Korsakoff syndrome were excluded from the experiment at the initial interview when they could not recall the disaster that occurred on September 11, even after cues were provided by the interviewer. Of the eight participants with Korsakoff syndrome who completed the follow-up interview (besides the five who were excluded, two of the original fifteen were discharged from the unit), three remembered the attacks without cueing and four others recalled the attacks after cues were offered. All control participants recalled the attacks at 7 and 9 months after September 11. To quantify personal memory for the attacks, "FBM scores" were created by scoring responses to six questions about the circumstances of learning of the attacks (e.g., where they were, what they were doing beforehand, what they did afterwards, who they were with, the source of the news, and the emotional impact on a five-point scale). Candel et al. (2003) reported that several of the individuals with Korsakoff syndrome were able to form detailed FBMs. Still, participants with Korsakoff syndrome had significantly lower FBM scores than healthy controls and were far less consistent between interviews. The factual knowledge section of the interviews consisted of six questions about the factual details of the attacks. At the initial interview, Candel et al. (2003) did not find a statistically significant difference between the factual memory scores of the participants with Korsakoff syndrome and the controls. At the follow-up interview, Candel et al. (2003) found a significant difference between the factual memory scores of the two groups that reflected an increase in the scores by controls and a decrease in the scores by Korsakoff patients. The authors concluded that amnesic patients are able to remember some aspects of a highly emotional event, including some factual details, 7 and 9 months later. However, the inconsistency in their personal information reports suggests that their ability to form FBMs is poor at best. It should also be mentioned that because the initial interview occurred 7 months after the event, even consistent reports between the initial and follow-up interviews in these patients might be inaccurate.

Davidson, Cook, Glisky, Verfaellie, and Rapcsak (2005) evaluated memory for the attacks of September 11, 2001 in three groups: 12 patients with medial temporal lobe/diencephalon amnesia, 13 patients with frontal lobe lesions, and 18 healthy controls. In addition to four patients with Korsakoff syndrome, the amnesic group also included individuals with focal damage due to anoxia, encephalitis, and stroke. The frontal lobe lesion group was composed of individuals who had suffered damage due to anterior communicating artery aneurysm, head trauma, stroke, and tumour. (The specific locus of each lesion was reported for the majority of participants in the patient groups.)

Davidson et al. (2005) asked participants to answer questions similar to those used in Candel et al. (2003) to test personal memory (reception event or source) and factual memory (target event) for the attacks. Participants were first interviewed within 1 month of the attacks and again 6 months later. Four members of the medial temporal lobe/diencephalon group, including two with Korsakoff syndrome, were excluded from the study when they could not recall the events of September 11 even after explicit cueing. For participants with medial temporal lobe/diencephalic lesions, Davidson et al. (2005) found major impairments in both personal and factual memory for the attacks. These participants were particularly impaired in their long-term memory for the factual details of the attacks. Participants with frontal lobe lesions displayed memory for the factual details that was nearly as accurate as that of the controls. In contrast, these participants were impaired in long-term source memory; that is, in their recall of personal details of how and when they learned of the attacks. In summary, Davidson et al. (2005) found that patients with medial temporal lobe/diencephalic lesions had global memory deficits for personal and factual memory of the attacks, while frontal lobe patients were selectively impaired in personal memory for a highly emotional event. These findings suggest that frontal lobe structures are not involved in the formation of factual memories, but may be necessary for the formation or retrieval of personal memories.

The studies of Candel et al. (2003) and Davidson et al. (2005) suggest that patients with amnesia attributable to Korsakoff syndrome or lesions of the medial temporal lobe/diencephalon are unable to form FBMs because they are greatly impaired for both the factual details and personal memories related to a national traumatic event. Patients with frontal lobe lesions, on the other hand, show normal memory for the factual details of the event itself, but show impairment in their memory for the personal details regarding how and when they learned of the event (Davidson et al., 2005). Thus, FBMs are also impaired in patients with frontal lobe lesions. These studies also highlight the important roles that the medial temporal and frontal lobes play in the formation of FBMs.

POST-TRAUMATIC STRESS DISORDER

Following a life threatening or other terrifying event, a person may develop a constellation of signs and symptoms known as post-traumatic stress disorder (PTSD) (DSM-IV, 1994). The most striking of these is the involuntary and often emotional recollection of the initial trauma or the moments immediately preceding the trauma. This troubling symptom may occur in the form of intrusive thoughts, nightmares, or flashbacks, and may be triggered by even weak environmental cues. Individuals with PTSD are known to have disorganized memories for the trauma that caused the disorder, as well as difficulty in recalling autobiographical memories unrelated to the trauma and generalized emotional numbing (Halligan, Michael, Clark, & Ehlers, 2003; McNally, Litz, Prassas, Shin, & Weathers, 1994). For a thorough review of the impact of PTSD on cognitive abilities, see McNally (2006).

Studying memory for national traumatic events in PTSD seems natural, as some researchers have suggested that FBMs and PTSD are related psychological reactions to trauma (Sierra & Berrios, 1999). Despite this, only one study has examined FBM formation for a national event in individuals with pre-existing PTSD. Using written surveys, Qin et al. (2003) evaluated memory and emotions for the September 11, 2001 terrorist attacks on the United States in clients, staff, and visitors of a Veterans Administration Hospital in Connecticut. Of the 428 surveys handed out 1 month after the attacks, 131 were returned. Of the participants, 24 reported that they had been diagnosed with PTSD; 20 of these reported that they were currently taking medication for PTSD symptoms. All 24 of these PTSD patients had been diagnosed prior to the September 11 attacks and their symptoms were not causally related to the attacks. Qin and colleagues (2003) did not gather data on how long the patients had been diagnosed with PTSD or on the events that caused PTSD.

The participants with PTSD were matched to 24 other participants who had experienced life-threatening traumas, but had not developed PTSD. Nine months later, 75 of the 115 respondents to the first survey returned a second survey. A total of 12 of the original 24 PTSD sufferers and 13 of the 24 original matched trauma controls returned this follow-up questionnaire. For both the initial and follow-up surveys, the matched trauma control participants did not differ from the PTSD participants on a number of important characteristics related to memory and emotion, including age, gender, level of education, other psychiatric illnesses, and veteran status.

The two surveys used in the Qin and colleagues (2003) study were modified versions of the questionnaires written by the 9/11 Memory Consortium, described above. Qin et al. (2003) nominally divided these questions into 10 categories, including current emotion towards the attacks and memory of emotion at the time of the attacks, predictions of memory accuracy, factual memory about the attacks, and autobiographical memory. The results of the survey conducted 1 month after the attacks revealed that the PTSD and matched trauma control groups significantly differed in their current emotions about the attacks: PTSD participants were angrier about the attacks and more fearful of a future attack. The PTSD participants also recalled having a greater behavioural disturbance in the days immediately following September 11 than did the controls, and had fewer intrusions in their factual event memory—an unexpected result without clear explanation. Overall, however, 1 month after the attacks differences between the PTSD and matched trauma controls groups were few. The two groups did not significantly differ on the frequency or vividness of intrusive thoughts about the attacks, on how often they thought about or discussed the attacks, or on the quality of their autobiographical memory for first learning of the attacks.

Results of the 10-month survey conducted by Qin and colleagues (2003) revealed more meaningful differences between the PTSD participants and the matched trauma controls on measures of post-trauma symptoms, memory, and emotion. PTSD sufferers experienced significantly more intrusive thoughts about the attacks than did the controls. In fact, the PTSD participants reported the same frequency of intrusive thoughts at 10 months as they did at 1 month after the attacks, while the control group had fewer intrusive thoughts over time. In terms of memory, neither group showed decrements in autobiographical memory for learning of the attacks in terms of proportion of questions answered, amount of detail in the answers, subjective vividness of the memory, and consistency between the initial and follow-up reports. The PTSD group did forget factual details about the attacks. The PTSD participants remembered experiencing higher levels of personal worry immediately after attacks than they did at 1 month after the attacks. PTSD participants also provided answers to a significantly greater proportion of the autobiographical memory questions at 10 months than they did at 1 month, with no change in the level of detail of these answers or subjective vividness. Finally, PTSD participants, but not controls, remembered their initial prediction of the short-term likelihood of a future attack as higher than it had actually been.

Overall, the findings of Qin and colleagues (2003) suggest that 1 month after a national traumatic event, individuals with pre-existing PTSD have memories and emotions related to the trauma that are very similar to those of individuals who have also experienced previous trauma, but who have not developed PTSD. However, 10 months after the national traumatic event, individuals with PTSD reported more frequent intrusive thoughts about the attacks, fewer remembered factual details of the attacks, and they inflated personal and emotional components of their memories for learning of the attacks compared to controls. Qin et al. (2003) concluded that the survey findings are in accordance with the PTSD literature, noting that intrusive memories of trauma are a hallmark of PTSD. Although the attacks of September 11 did not cause the PTSD in the participants studied in Qin and colleagues (2003), individuals with pre-existing PTSD are known to be more emotionally affected by subsequent traumas than healthy individuals, so the lack of decline in intrusive thoughts 10 months after the attacks is perhaps not surprising. Ehlers, Hackmann, and Michael (2004) found that intentional recall of trauma in PTSD is marked by poor memory for temporal order and major deficits in remembering key subsequent details that would correct impressions or predictions made at the time of the trauma. Ehlers et al. (2004) theorized that many of these details, if remembered, would likely reduce the emotion associated with the individuals' appraisal of the trauma. The PTSD participants in Qin and colleagues (2003) forgot factual details of the trauma of September 11 (suggesting impaired event memory) and inflated the emotional and personal aspects of their memory for learning of the attacks (suggesting distorted personal memory). In their summary, Qin et al. (2003) stress that these results do not necessarily implicate a causal relationship between any particular aspects of PTSD and decreased event memory or inflated personal memory, and note that many differences exist between healthy older adults and individuals with PTSD (e.g., prescription drugs being taken, co-morbid psychiatric illnesses, etc.). Nonetheless, because the results of Qin and colleagues (2003) found that individuals with PTSD showed impaired event memory and distorted personal memory, it is reasonable to hypothesize that individuals with PTSD may generate vivid memories for national traumatic events that may be similar in their subjective experience to FBMs, but are inaccurate and distorted.

SUMMARY OF FINDINGS

This chapter has presented recent findings of memory for national traumatic events in individuals with a variety of neurologic and psychiatric disorders. The studies reviewed suggest that memory for personal and factual information related to national traumatic events can be greatly modulated by these different disorders: memories are sometimes impaired, sometimes enhanced, and sometimes distorted. Table 7.1 summarizes the findings presented earlier in the chapter. The results of these studies also suggest that research into memory for national traumatic events in clinical populations can enhance our understanding of FBMs in healthy individuals as well as improving our understanding of memory in these clinical populations.

FUTURE STUDIES

In this section, methodological improvements and future areas of study will be presented for the clinical conditions already considered (AD/MCI, Korsakoff syndrome, and PTSD) and then for two other disorders (depression, social phobia) that have not yet been studied using a FBM paradigm. Particular attention will be paid to methodological improvements, as this is a major area of concern in FBM studies; see also Chapter 2 (Wright).

AD and MCI

Several features of Budson et al. (2004, 2007) could be improved in future observational studies of this type. First, Budson et al. (2004) did not verify the responses of the AD and MCI participants at the time of their initial interview. Second, that study did not directly measure surprise and personal consequentiality, which are critical for making the results comparable with those of studies of FBMs. Third, Budson et al. (2004) did not include memory for a non-emotional control event to compare with the memory of the attacks of September 11. The absence of a control event prevents direct comparisons with laboratory studies in addition to constraining the conclusions. One simple possibility would be to use the phone call of the experimenter to the participant as the non-emotional event. Using this phone call has numerous advantages. All participants will have experienced a similar event and the personal and factual information reported regarding this event is likely to be accurate and relatively easy to verify. Fourth, an increased sample size at the initial time point would allow for greater power to detect differences at the 1-year time point, given the high attrition rate of the patients with AD. It is possible that some interactions from the 3-month to the 1-year time point may not have been detected because of a lack of power due to the small sample size. Fifth, interviewing the participants at more frequent intervals would help to ensure that floor effects were absent in the patients with AD. Sixth, patients with MCI are heterogeneous in aetiology. Studies suggest that only about 70% of such patients eventually convert to AD (Petersen et al., 2001). Follow-up is essential to determining which patients truly had incipient AD.

One limitation of Budson et al. (2004, 2007) deserves special emphasis.

Table 7.1 Selected studies of national traumatic events in different patient populations

Study	Population(s) and no.	Experimental design	Methods	Main findings
Budson et al. (2004)	Alzheimer's disease (n = 22), mild cognitive impairment (n = 21), & older adult controls (n = 23)	Case-control, 44-item questionnaire	Identical interviews completed less than 1 month and about 3 months after the 9/11 attacks	Patients with AD and controls reported very similar intensity of all emotions measured (sadness, anger, fear, frustration, confusion, and shock). Patients with MCI, however, reported less intensity of the emotions anger, fear, and confusion compared to the other groups. Distortions of memory for personal information were very common among all participants at the 3-month time point, but were most common in patients with AD. Using the strict criteria for FBMs that five personal information questions were answered correctly, approximately half of the participants in both the older adult and MCI groups were able to form FBMs, whereas almost no participants in the AD group were able to do so.
Budson et al. (2007)	Alzheimer's disease (n = 14), mild cognitive impairment (n = 19), & older adult controls (n = 22). (Follow-up of Budson et al., 2004)	Case-control, 44-item questionnaire	Same interview as Budson et al. (2004) completed 1 year after the 9/11 attacks	Compared to healthy older adults, patients with AD and MCI showed lower levels of personal and factual information at the initial time point, a greater decline in their recognition of personal and factual information from the initial to the 3-month time point, a similar stability of their personal information from the 3-month to the 1-year time point, and a similar decline in factual information from the 3-month to the 1-year time point.
Candel et al. (2003)	Korsakoff syndrome (n = 15) & controls (n = 15)	Case-control, 13-item questionnaire	Identical interviews completed 7 and 9 months after the 9/11 attacks	Most of the Korsakoff patients remembered the 9/11 attacks 7 months after the event. Of those patients who remembered the attacks, most displayed "FBM scores" based on memory for personal details of the attacks similar to controls at 7 months. However, these memories were not consistent between the 7- and 9-month interviews. Korsakoff patients had less semantic knowledge of the attacks than controls at both time points, and their semantic knowledge decreased between interviews.

Study	Population	Design	Procedure	Results
Davidson et al. (2005)	Frontal lobe ($n = 13$) & medial temporal lobe lesions ($n = 14$), & controls ($n = 18$)	Case-control, 10-item questionnaire	Identical interviews completed less than 1 month and about 6 months after the 9/11 attacks	Patients with medial temporal lobe/diencephalic lesions showed major impairments in both personal and factual memory for the attacks and were particularly impaired in their long-term memory for the factual details of the attacks. Patients with frontal lobe lesions displayed memory for the factual details that was nearly as accurate as that of the controls. However these frontal lobe patients were impaired in long-term source memory.
Qin et al. (2003)	Pre-existing PTSD (initial $n = 24$, follow-up $n = 12$) & controls (initial $n = 24$, follow-up $n = 13$)	Case-control, questionnaire	Identical surveys completed 1 month and 10 months after the 9/11 attacks	The PTSD patients and controls displayed few differences in memory or subjective ratings of personal impact and emotion at the 1-month time point. However, relative to control participants, PTSD patients had a deficit in factual memory and a tendency to inflate the personal and emotional aspects of the attacks at the 10-month follow-up.

Compared to AD patients, healthy older adults reported that they both followed the media coverage more closely and talked more about the attacks. Therefore, it is not possible to definitively attribute the differences observed between the groups to memory differences, and not to differences in the review and re-encoding of information. Although undesirable from a theoretical vantage point, the differences reported in this study may be generalizable to other memories outside the laboratory. That patients with AD review information less frequently than healthy older adults may be attributable to a number of factors, including a diminished social network and reduced access to certain types of media (e.g., the Internet), in addition to changes in cognition and memory. Further investigation of such differences may be an important area of future research in our understanding of memory in AD and other cognitively impaired patients outside the laboratory.

Korsakoff syndrome

Some design limitations exist in Candel et al. (2003), the study of memory for a national traumatic event in Korsakoff syndrome patients. As mentioned earlier, the findings of this study are difficult to interpret in terms of FBM, as the initial interview occurred some 7 months after the September 11 attacks. Future studies of patients that conduct the initial interview in closer proximity to the traumatic event (in fitting with the methodology of FBM research in general) would be able to validate the findings of Candel et al. (2003) while also further investigating the role of the mammillary bodies and related structures in emotional, personal, and event memory.

PTSD

To better understand PTSD, future studies of memories for a national traumatic event might be conducted using a cohort design that combines several forms of testing. Traditionally, PTSD was thought to develop only after exposure to a personally experienced trauma such as rape, motor vehicle accident, animal attack, or military combat. However, many clinicians now diagnose the disorder in individuals who are responding to traumatic events that did not explicitly threaten life or limb, such as watching the attacks of September 11th on television (McNally, 2006). Using a cohort design, researchers could follow healthy individuals after a national traumatic event that did not directly threaten the lives of any of the individuals. Participants would periodically return surveys assessing their memory and emotions for the event, similar to those used in Qin et al. (2003). At similar intervals they would also visit a clinician for neuropsychological testing and assessment of the presence of PTSD, the onset of which may range from 1 week to 30 years post trauma (Kaplan & Sadock, 1996). Brain imaging, such as magnetic resonance imaging and event-related potentials, can be combined with behavioural surveys and questionnaires in an integrated approach over time to better understand the cognitive, emotional, and neural mechanisms that related to the development of PTSD.

One outcome of future studies may be the identification of additional demographic, neuropsychological, and neurological risk factors that can lead to the development of PTSD. Such risk factors have been assessed for Americans following the September 11, 2001 attacks (Adams & Boscarino, 2006; Laugharne, Janca, & Widiger, 2007; Silver, Holman, McIntosh, Poulin, & Gil-Rivas, 2002) and for Spanish citizens after the Madrid train bombings of 11 March 2004 (Vazquez, Perez-Sales, & Matt, 2006). Additional questions could also be addressed, such as whether individuals who subsequently develop PTSD are initially different in terms of their memory, emotion, cognitive ability, demographics, or some biological measure from those who experience the same trauma but do not develop PTSD. If not, do individuals who develop PTSD eventually diverge in some way from the individuals who do not? While partial answers to these questions have been provided by other studies using cohort and other designs (for a thorough review of predictors of pathological response to terrorism, see Yehuda, Bryant, Marmar, & Zohar, 2005), integrative cohort studies with memorial, emotional, neuropsychological, and biological foci would be invaluable to furthering our understanding of PTSD and, by extension, FBMs.

Depression

Major depression is a very common mood disorder that affects individuals of all ages. Depression has been shown to impair several facets of memory. While no studies have evaluated memory for a national traumatic event in depressed individuals, several studies of autobiographical memory have been conducted. Many of these studies have focused on findings of "overgeneral autobiographical memory" in depressed individuals (for a review see Williams et al., 2007). For example, when asked to describe a single happy memory in detail, a depressed individual might answer by naming a period of her life during which she was happy, or by describing a category of experiences. Some researchers have argued that overgeneral memory is a defence against retrieving painful or emotional memories (Burnside, Startup, Byatt, Rollinson, & Hill, 2004). However, other findings of overgeneral memory do not support this behavioural account. Overgeneral memory has been found in euthymic individuals who had previously been depressed and who had little reason to avoid distressing memories (Spinhoven et al., 2006). Also, depressed teenagers who had a history of trauma displayed less overgeneral memory than depressed teenagers without a history of trauma (Kuyken, Howell, & Dalgleish, 2006). Thus, it is possible that overgeneral memory is a cognitive change produced by neural changes associated with depression. Regardless of its mechanism, overgeneral memory has implications for memories of national traumatic events in depression. Because depression is common after a national trauma, and because depression has been correlated with poor memory specificity following a stressful life event (van Minnen, Wessel, Verhaak, & Smeenk, 2005), better understanding of overgeneral memory in depression may aid our understanding of FBMs in healthy individuals.

Social phobia

Social phobia is a disorder in which individuals become anxious in social situations that would not be considered stressful to healthy people. For example, while walking down the sidewalk of a city street, an individual with social phobia might believe that all of the other people on the street are watching her or him and passing judgement. This may lead to feelings of anxiety, shame, and fear. After arriving home, she or he may mentally replay the scene from the street again and again. It is this inflation of the personal and emotional aspects of social situations—both at the time of the initial situation and in remembering it—that makes social phobia an interesting disorder to evaluate in terms of FBM.

No studies to date have measured memory for a national traumatic event in individuals with social phobia. However, a handful of studies have examined autobiographical memory in social phobia. D'Argembeau, Van der Linden, d'Acremont, and Mayers (2006) compared individuals with social phobia to healthy controls on their recall for personally experienced social and non-social events. The participants also provided ratings of the phenomenal characteristics of their memories. D'Argembeau et al. (2006) found that for non-social events the two groups did not differ in the number of details or the amount of self-referential information. However, for social events the memories of the individuals with social phobia contained fewer details related to the event and more self-referential information and such individuals often remembered these situations from an out-of-body, observer perspective. Because Qin et al. (2003) found inflated emotional and personal aspects of memory for the attacks of September 11 in patients with PTSD, and because social phobia is also an anxiety disorder, it might be useful to conduct a single study comparing the two conditions to one another and to healthy controls. Such a study would further our understanding of anxiety disorder and the role of emotion in memory formation and retrieval.

NOTE

1 This chapter was supported by National Institute on Aging grants R01 AG025815 and P30 AG13846.

REFERENCES

Abrisqueta-Gomez, J., Bueno, O. F., Oliveira, M. G., & Bertolucci, P. H. (2002). Recognition memory for emotional pictures in Alzheimer's patients. *Acta Neurologica Scandinavica*, *105*, 51–54.

Adams, R. E., & Boscarino, J. A. (2006). Predictors of PTSD and delayed PTSD after disaster: The impact of exposure and psychosocial resources. *Journal of Nervous and Mental Disease*, *194*, 485–493.

Albert, M. S., Cohen, C., & Koff, E. (1991). Perception of affect in patients with dementia of the Alzheimer type. *Archives of Neurology*, *48*, 791–795.

Alkire, M. T., Haier, R. J., Fallon, J. H., & Cahill, L. (1998). Hippocampal, but not amygdala, activity at encoding correlates with long-term, free recall of non-emotional information. *Proceedings of the National Academy of Science*, *95*, 14506–14510.

Allender, J., & Kaszniak, A. W. (1989). Processing of emotional cues in patients with dementia of the Alzheimer's type. *International Journal of Neuroscience*, *46*, 147–155.

Boller, F., El Massioui, F., Devouche, E., Traykov, L., Pomati, S., & Starkstein, S. E. (2002). Processing emotional information in Alzheimer's disease: Effects on memory performance and neurophysiological correlates. *Dementia and Geriatric Cognitive Disorders*, *14*, 104–112.

Brosgole, L., Kurucz, J., Plahovinsak, T. J., & Gumiela, E. (1981). On the mechanism underlying facial-affective agnosia in senile demented patients. *International Journal of Neuroscience*, *15*, 207–215.

Brown, R., & Kulik, J. (1977). Flashbulb memories. *Cognition*, *5*, 73–99.

Budson, A. E., Simons, J. S., Sullivan, A. L., Beier, J. S., Solomon, P. R., Scinto, L. F., et al. (2004). Memory and emotions for the September 11, 2001, terrorist attacks in patients with Alzheimer's disease, patients with mild cognitive impairment, and healthy older adults. *Neuropsychology*, *18*, 315–327.

Budson, A. E., Simons, J. S., Waring, J. D., Sullivan, A. L., Hussoin, T., & Schacter, D. L. (2007). Memory for the September 11, 2001, terrorist attacks one year later in patients with Alzheimer's disease, patients with mild cognitive impairment, and healthy older adults. *Cortex*, *43*, 875–888.

Budson, A. E., Todman, R. W., Chong, H., Adams, E. H., Kensinger, E. A., Krangel, T. S., et al. (2006). False recognition of emotional word lists in aging and Alzheimer disease. *Cognitive Behavioral Neurology*, *19*, 71–78.

Burnside, E., Startup, M., Byatt, M., Rollinson, L., & Hill, J. (2004). The role of overgeneral autobiographical memory in the development of adult depression following childhood trauma. *British Journal of Clinical Psychology*, *43*, 365–376.

Cadieux, N. L., & Greve, K. W. (1997). Emotion processing in Alzheimer's disease. *Journal of the International Neuropsychological Society*, *3*, 411–419.

Candel, I., Jelicic, M., Merckelbach, H., & Wester, A. (2003). Korsakoff patients' memories of September 11, 2001. *Journal of Nervous and Mental Disease*, *191*, 262–265.

Canli, T., Zhao, Z., Brewer, J., Gabrieli, J. D. E., & Cahill, L. (2000). Event-related activation in the human amygdala associates with later memory for individual emotional experience. *Journal of Neuroscience*, *20*, RC99.

Chu, C. C., Tranel, D., Damasio, A. R., & Van Hoesen, G. W. (1997). The autonomic-related cortex: Pathology in Alzheimer's disease. *Cerebral Cortex, 7,* 86–95.

Cohen, G., Conway, M. A., & Maylor, E. A. (1994). Flashbulb memories in older adults. *Psychology and Aging, 9,* 454–463.

D'Argembeau, A., Van der Linden, M., d'Acremont, M., & Mayers, I. (2006). Phenomenal characteristics of autobiographical memories for social and non-social events in social phobia. *Memory, 14,* 637–647.

Davidson, P. S. R., Cook, S. P., Glisky, E. L., Verfaellie, M., & Rapcsak, S. P. (2005). Source memory in the real world: A neuropsychological study of flashbulb memory. *Journal of Clinical and Experimental Neuropsychology, 27,* 915–929.

Ehlers, A., Hackmann, A., & Michael, T. (2004). Intrusive re-experiencing in posttraumatic stress disorder: Phenomenology, theory, and therapy. *Memory, 12,* 403–415.

Halligan, S. L., Michael, T., Clark, D. M., & Ehlers, A. (2003). Posttraumatic stress disorder following assault: The role of cognitive processing, trauma memory, and appraisals. *Journal of Consulting and Clinical Psychology, 71,* 419–431.

Hamann, S. B., Cahill, L., McGaugh, J. L., & Squire, L. R. (1997). Intact enhancement of declarative memory for emotional material in amnesia. *Learning and Memory, 4,* 301–309.

Hamann, S. B., Monarch, E. S., & Goldstein, F. C. (2000). Memory enhancement for emotional stimuli is impaired in early Alzheimer's disease. *Neuropsychology, 14,* 82–92.

Ikeda, M., Mori, E., Hirono, N., Imamura, T., Shimomura, T., Ikejiri, Y., et al. (1998). Amnestic people with Alzheimer's disease who remembered the Kobe earthquake. *British Journal of Psychiatry, 172,* 425–428.

Kaplan, H. I., & Sadock, B. J. (1996). *Concise textbook of clinical psychiatry.* Baltimore, MD: Williams & Wilkins.

Kazui, H., Mori, E., Hashimoto, M., Hirono, N., Imamura, T., Tanimukai, S., et al. (2000). Impact of emotion on memory. Controlled study of the influence of emotionally charged material on declarative memory in Alzheimer's disease. *British Journal of Psychiatry, 177,* 343–347.

Kensinger, E. A., Anderson, A., Growdon, J. H., & Corkin, S. (2004). Effects of Alzheimer disease on memory for verbal emotional information. *Neuropsychologia, 42,* 791–800.

Kensinger, E. A., Brierley, B., Medford, N., Growdon, J. H., & Corkin, S. (2002). Effects of normal aging and Alzheimer's disease on emotional memory. *Emotion, 2,* 118–134.

Kensinger, E. A., & Schacter, D. L. (2006). Amygdala activity is associated with the successful encoding of item, but not source, information for positive and negative stimuli. *Journal of Neuroscience, 26,* 2564–2570.

Kuyken, W., Howell, R., & Dalgleish, T. (2006). Overgeneral autobiographical memory in depressed adolescents with, versus without, a reported history of trauma. *Journal of Abnormal Psychology, 115,* 387–396.

Laugharne, J. A., Janca, A. A., & Widiger, T. B. (2007). Posttraumatic stress disorder and terrorism: 5 years after 9/11. *Current Opinion in Psychiatry, 20,* 36–41.

McNally, R. J. (2006). Cognitive abnormalities in post-traumatic stress disorder. *Trends in Cognitive Sciences, 10,* 271–277.

McNally, R. J., Litz, B. T., Prassas, A., Shin, L. M., & Weathers, F. W. (1994).

Emotional priming of autobiographical memory in post-traumatic stress disorder. *Cognition and Emotion, 8,* 351–367.

Mesulam, M. M (2000). *Principles of behavioral and cognitive neurology (2nd ed.).* New York: Oxford University Press.

Moayeri, S. E., Cahill, L., Jin, Y., & Plotkin, S. G. (2000). Relative sparing of emotionally influenced memory in Alzheimer's disease. *NeuroReport, 11,* 653–655.

Mori, E., Ikeda, M., Hirono, N., Kitagaki, H., Imamura, T., & Shimomura, T. (1999). Amygdalar volume and emotional memory in Alzheimer's disease. *American Journal of Psychiatry, 156,* 216–222.

Packard, M. G., & Cahill, L. (2001). Affective modulation of multiple memory systems. *Current Opinion in Neurobiology, 11,* 752–756.

Petersen, R. C., Doody, R., Kurz, A., Mohs, R. C., Morris, J. C., Rabins, P. V., et al. (2001). Current concepts in mild cognitive impairment. *Archives of Neurology, 58,* 1985–1992.

Phelps, E. A., LaBar, K. S., & Spencer, D. D. (1997). Memory for emotional words following unilateral temporal lobectomy. *Brain and Cognition, 35,* 85–109.

Qin, J., Mitchell, K. J., Johnson, M. K., Krystal, J. H., Southwick, S. M., Rasmusson, A. M., et al. (2003). Reactions to and memories for the September 11, 2001 terrorist attacks in adults with posttraumatic stress disorder. *Applied Cognitive Psychology, 17,* 1081–1097.

Schmolck, H., Buffalo, E. A., & Squire, L. R. (2000). Memory distortions develop over time: Recollections of the O.J. Simpson trial verdict after 15 and 32 months. *Psychological Science, 11,* 39–45.

Sierra, M., & Berrios, G. E. (1999). Flashbulb memories and other repetitive images: A psychiatric perspective. *Comprehensive Psychiatry, 40,* 115–125.

Silver, R. C., Holman, E. A., McIntosh, D. N., Poulin, M., & Gil-Rivas, V. (2002). Nationwide longitudinal study of psychological responses to September 11. *Journal of the American Medical Association, 288,* 1235–1244.

Solomon, P. R., & Budson, A. E. (2003). Alzheimer's disease. *Clinical Symposia, 54,* 1–44.

Spinhoven, P., Bockting, C. L., Schene, A. H., Koeter, M. W., Wekking, E. M., & Williams, J. M. (2006). Autobiographical memory in the euthymic phase of recurrent depression. *Journal of Abnormal Psychology, 115,* 590–600.

Thompson, R. G., Moulin, C. J., Ridel, G. L., Hayre, S., Conway, M. A., & Jones, R. W. (2004). Recall of 9.11 in Alzheimer's disease: Further evidence for intact flashbulb memory. *International Journal of Geriatric Psychiatry, 19,* 495–496.

Van Minnen, A., Wessel, I., Verhaak, C., & Smeenk, J. (2005). The relationship between autobiographical memory specificity and depressed mood following a stressful life event: A prospective study. *British Journal of Clinical Psychology, 44,* 405–415.

Vazquez, C., Perez-Sales, P., & Matt, G. (2006). Post-traumatic stress reactions following the March 11, 2004 terrorist attacks in a Madrid community sample: A cautionary note about the measurement of psychological trauma. *Spanish Journal of Psychology, 9,* 61–74.

Williams, J. M. G., Barnhofer, T., Crane, C., Hermans, D., Raes, F., & Watkins, E. (2007). Autobiographical memory specificity and emotional disorder. *Psychological Bulletin, 133,* 122–148.

Yehuda, R., Bryant, R., Marmar, C., & Zohar, J. (2005). Pathological responses to terrorism. *Neuropsychopharmacology, 30,* 1793–1805.

8 Emotional memory and memory for emotions[1]

Robyn Fivush, Jennifer G. Bohanek, Kelly Marin, and Jessica McDermott Sales

When Brown and Kulik (1977) first introduced the concept of "flashbulb memory" it resonated with commonsense views. We all have the subjective sense that we have vivid and accurate memories for highly consequential events in our lives. Whether these events are in the public media, such as political assassinations, celebrity deaths or national catastrophes, or more personal experiences, such as the death of a loved one, a tragic accident or an act of interpersonal violence, the sense is that these kinds of memories are clear and detailed almost as if they were burned into the brain. Indeed, William James (1890) called memories of traumatic events "cerebral scars".

Research over the ensuing decades has refined Brown and Kulik's original conceptualization, and, as the chapters in this book indicate, there is both growing consensus over some aspects of flashbulb memories, as well as ongoing debates. More specifically, memories of highly consequential events do not seem to be forgotten as quickly as other types of events, yet at the same time flashbulb memories seem to be subject to the same kinds of reconstruction and error over time as other memories (see Conway, 1995; Luminet, Chapter 3, this volume; Talarico & Rubin, Chapter 4, this volume; and Winograd & Neisser, 1992, for overviews). Moreover, research has established specific dimensions that predict the clarity and consistency of flashbulb memories over time, including level of emotional reaction, personal significance, prior knowledge about the event, and subsequent rehearsal (Bohannon, 1988; Bohannon & Symons, 1992; Conway et al., 1994; Finkenauer et al., 1998). Ongoing concerns continue to focus on how flashbulb memories are defined and measured (see especially Curci, Chapter 1, and Wright, Chapter 2, in this volume), and how best to understand the phenomenon of flashbulb memories in larger social and cultural contexts (see Berntsen, Chapter 9, Hirst & Meksin, Chapter 10, Pillemer, Chapter 6, Páez, Bellelli, & Rimé, Chapter 11, and Wang Aydın, Chapter 12, in this volume).

In this chapter we place the research on flashbulb memories in the context of memory for highly emotional events. More specifically, we argue that memory of *emotional events* depends in part on memory of *emotion*. How individuals integrate memory of emotional reactions and states into their memories of what occurred is a critical part of how and what will be remembered over time (Payne et al., 2006). Emotions provide the interpretative and evaluative framework for understanding what the events in our lives mean for us and our place in the world (Fivush & Baker-Ward, 2005). In essence, memory of emotion provides evidence of how individuals create meaning out of their experience (Bartlett, 1932).

In order to place this argument in context, we first describe research on both flashbulb memories and on memories of emotional events more broadly. We then turn to a discussion of why memory of emotion is critical in this process and present research describing how emotion is recalled both as a function of the valence and the intensity of the event. Throughout, we take a developmental perspective in two senses. First, we examine how memory of emotion changes over time, as a measure of how individuals continue to engage in the meaning-making process even as time since the event increases. Second, we examine memory of emotion in both children and adults in order to explore how the meaning-making process may change with increasing age and emotional and cognitive skills.

PERSONAL SIGNIFICANCE AND EMOTIONAL IMPACT

By definition, flashbulb memories are memories of events that are assumed to have high emotional impact and personal significance (see Luminet, Chapter 3, this volume, for an overview). However, unlike many other events studied in the psychology laboratory, these are events that occur in the real world and that thousands, if not millions, of individuals experience at the same time. The great advantages of studying events such as these is that researchers can compare the amount and accuracy of information recalled about the event itself (e.g., an assassination, a natural disaster) when everyone has experienced the same event. Moreover, these events are of high significance in that they are culturally canonical events that define a point in history. Within this literature, a distinction is made between recall of the event and the reception context, often studied as the amount of information that can be recalled about a specific number of predefined categories (e.g., how, where, and when one heard the news). In addition to examining the amount of information that is recalled, researchers have been particularly concerned with the consistency of recall over time, both for details about the event itself and the reception context (see Conway, 1995; Julian, Bohannan, & Aue, Chapter 5, this volume; and Winograd & Neisser, 1992, for reviews).

Although this body of research has provided important information about the human memory system, there are several problems of interpretation. First, although large numbers of participants are being asked to recall ostensibly the same event, thus providing some measure of experimental control, this is only the case for the event itself and not the reception context. Individuals hear the news in very different contexts and circumstances, and these memories are highly idiosyncratic. Thus we cannot determine accuracy in memories of the reception context over time, only consistency. Moreover, because these events are culturally canonical, they are discussed in ongoing individual conversations and in the media within the first few days of the event, and again and again to commemorate anniversaries, when related events occur, and so on. Thus memory for the facts of the event may or may not represent information acquired at the time of hearing the news. Finally, just because these events are culturally important, it does not mean that they have personal significance for any given individual (see Berntsen, Chapter 9, this volume; and Pillemer, 1992, & Chapter 6 of this volume, for related arguments).

Whereas Brown and Kulik originally focused on personal significance of the event, arguing for an evolutionarily adaptive response to events that will likely have consequences for the individual, more recently theorists have argued that it may be the emotional arousal inherent in these kinds of events that leads to better memory, rather than personal significance per se. Brown and Kulik equated emotional arousal with personal significance, but they are theoretically distinct constructs; one can encounter an event that has high emotional arousal that may have little or no personal significance (although the reverse may not occur). Both Conway et al. (1994) and Finkenauer et al. (1998) have examined personal significance and emotional arousal as two independent factors in the formation of a flashbulb memory. Both found that the initial appraisal of the personal significance of the event led to the intensity of the emotional reaction; if the event was appraised as more personally significant, the individual reported higher levels of emotional arousal. Most important, it was the emotional arousal that directly affected the formation of a flashbulb memory, not the assessment of personal significance. This research demonstrates both that personal significance and emotional arousal are separable components and that each may affect memory differently, with emotional arousal having the most direct impact on memory.

This interpretation is in accord with a large body of literature demonstrating that highly emotional events are generally better recalled than neutral events (see Christianson, 1992; Christianson & Lindholm, 1998; Reisberg & Hertel, 2003, for reviews of research with adults; and Fivush, 1998; Fivush & Sales, 2003; Pezdek & Taylor, 2001, for reviews of research with children). Two basic methodologies have been used to examine possible differences in memories of highly emotional and mundane events. One methodology focuses on individuals' memories of real-world events, and the second relies on experimental studies of memory for emotional stimuli.

Memories of real-world emotional events

In order to assess memories of real-world emotional events, researchers have relied on both questionnaires and narrative methodologies. For example, using questionnaire assessments, witnesses to real-word crimes display accurate recall over several months (Christianson & Huebinette, 1993; Yuille &

Cutshall, 1986). However, there may be differences in recall for different kinds of negative events. Tromp, Koss, Figueredo, and Tharan (1995) asked women to rate their memories of rape, as well as other unpleasant and pleasant experiences, and responses were subcategorized to address the notion of flashbulb memories, including a high level of surprise, important consequences, intense feelings at the time of the event, a clear and detailed memory, and frequent rehearsal. Importantly, rape memories were less "flashbulb"-like than other unpleasant memories, and even less well recalled than highly pleasant memories, suggesting that, although stressful events may be well recalled in general, extremely high levels of stress may disrupt memory.

Children also recall most highly emotional experiences well (see Fivush, 1998; Pezdak & Taylor, 2001, for reviews). Clinical case studies describing children's memories of truly horrendous experiences, such as being kidnapped or witnessing the murder of a parent (Malmquist, 1986; Terr, 1988), find that children older than 3 years at the time of experience continue to recall vivid details about the event even years later. More systematic research on memories of medical emergencies and procedures also finds that children aged 3 and older retain accurate and vivid memories of stressful medical events over a period of years (Goodman, Quas, Batterman-Faunce, Riddlesberger, & Kuhn, 1994; Peterson, 1999; Peterson & Bell, 1996; Peterson & Whalen, 2001). However, as with adults, extreme levels of stress may impair memory when compared to moderate stress levels. Children more highly stressed by a painful medical procedure recalled less about the event than less-stressed children (Merrit, Orstein, & Spicker, 1994), and Bahrick and colleagues found that children more highly stressed by the experience of Hurricane Andrew, a devastating natural disaster, recalled less information initially, and less information in free recall 6 years later, than children experiencing more moderate levels of stress (Bahrick, Parker, Fivush, & Levitt, 1998; Fivush, Sales, Goldberg, Bahrick, & Parker, 2004).

Whereas most research focuses on amount and accuracy of recall, a growing body of research centres on differences in narrative content and coherence of positive versus negative events. Stemming from trauma theory (McNally, 2003), it is argued that highly stressful events may lead to fragmented and incoherent memories. However, in general, adults' narratives of negative events tend to be longer, more vivid, and more consistent over time than narratives of positive events, whereas narratives of positive events are more structurally complex (Bohanek, Fivush, & Walker, 2005; Peace & Porter, 2004; see Talarico & Rubin, Chapter 4, this volume for a review). Emotional intensity also plays a role. Narratives of intensely negative events are longer, more vivid, and more detailed than narratives of moderately negative events (Bohanek et al., 2005; Gray & Lombardo, 2001; Porter & Birt, 2001). Research with children suggests that narratives of negative events are more coherent and focus more on causes and explanations than narratives of positive events (Ackil, Van Abbema, & Bauer, 2003; Bauer et al., 2005; Burch, Austin, & Bauer, 2004; Fivush, Hazzard, Sales, Sarfati, & Brown, 2003).

Summing across research on memories of real-world emotional events, using different methodologies and different age groups, it is clear that negative events are recalled more accurately than mundane or, possibly, positive events, although at high levels of stress, memory may become compromised. Narratives of negative events are also longer and more detailed than narratives of mundane or positive events. Findings on narrative coherence are mixed, but most studies find that negative events are more coherent (but see Bohanek et al., 2005) and focus more on causes and explanations than do narratives of positive or mundane events.

Experimental studies of emotional memory

The second methodology used in comparing memories of negative and positive events includes laboratory experiments that manipulate the emotional valence and intensity of what participants view, either in slides or videos, and then assess amount and accuracy of recall. Results are remarkably consistent across studies. Participants recall and recognize emotional material better than neutral material (Bradley, Greenwald, Petry, & Lang, 1992; Christianson, 1992). More specifically, participants show enhanced recall of the emotionally arousing stimuli but decreased recall of the surrounding neutral material, indicating that emotional arousal enhances memory specifically for emotion (Payne et al., 2006). Several studies have established that physiological responses, such as heart rate and galvanic skin response, increase during presentation of emotional material (Bradley et al., 1992; Buchanan, Etzel, Adolphs, & Tranel, 2006), and that there is more activation in the amygdala when viewing emotional compared to neutral material (Bradley et al., 1992; Buchanan et al., 2006; Canli, Zhao, Desmond, Glover, & Gabrieli, 1999; Hamann, Ely, Grafton, & Kilts, 1999). Moreover, these physiological and neurological responses are linked to better memory, indicating that emotional material creates a cascade of biological responses that enhance memory (Buchanan et al., 2006; Canli et al., 1999; Hamann et al., 1999). Thus studies of memory in the real world and in the laboratory similarly find that highly emotional events are better recalled than mundane events, suggesting that emotion enhances memory. It might be noted as well that whereas high levels of emotion have consistently been related to better memory, other factors, such as distinctiveness of the event and retention interval, have shown more inconsistent results with some studies finding that highly distinctive and more recently experienced events are recalled better than less distinct and more remote events, and other studies not finding these effects (see Reisberg & Hertel, 2003, for a review)

One way in which emotions may facilitate memory is through a focusing of attention (Easterbrook, 1959). Emotional responses may activate responding such that individuals are more alert and pay more attention, but only to those aspects of the event that are central to the emotional response. Both adults (Reisberg, Heuer, McLean, & O'Shaughnessy, 1988) and children (Peterson

& Bell, 1996) show better recall of central aspects of emotional events than of peripheral aspects of those same events. Critically, what is central and what is peripheral is controversial. In the flashbulb memory literature, it is argued that the news event itself is central (e.g., the details of President Kennedy's assassination), and the reception context (e.g., where one heard the news, who one was with), including one's emotional reaction, is peripheral. But clearly, given the impact of emotional arousal on recall, one central component of emotional events must be the emotion itself. How do individuals recall their emotional reactions and responses to events? Memory of one's emotional reaction to the important events in one's life is part of the fabric of weaving together autobiographical memory into a coherent life narrative.

MEMORY FOR EMOTIONS

Emotions provide the interpretative, evaluative structure to our memories (Fivush & Haden, 2006; Fivush & Nelson, 2005). Even everyday events are emotionally valenced and the ways in which the events of our lives are remembered are clearly dependent on the emotional tone (Levine, 2004; Stein & Liwag, 1997). Moreover, there is some suggestion that when highly stressful experiences occur, attention is not just focused on external events, but also turns inward, to assess and evaluate one's emotional reactions (McNally, 2003).

In fact, traumatic memories are rated as more emotional than are other types of memories (Berntsen, 2001; Porter & Birt, 2001; van der Kolk & Fisler, 1995; but see Byrne, Hyman, & Scott, 2001, for an exception). Further, findings from the trauma literature suggest that, over time, trauma narratives may contain less information about the actions and dialogue related to the event but more information about thoughts and emotions, particularly those reflecting attempts to organize the trauma memory (Foa, Molnar, & Cashman, 1995). Interestingly, the focus on emotional aspects of the event is related to well-being. When asked to narrate traumatic experiences, those people who are able to express some negative emotion and increase their use of positive emotion in their narratives over time report doing better psychologically and physically (see Frattaroli, 2006; Pennebaker, 1997, for reviews).

In the remainder of this chapter we explore how both children and adults recall the emotional aspects of highly arousing events. This body of research takes a semi-naturalistic approach in that, across studies, children and adults are asked to freely narrate a variety of emotional experiences that vary by valence (positive versus negative experiences), intensity (highly versus moderately arousing), and time (both soon after the event occurred and after time has passed). From these narratives, the number of both positive and negative emotion words used to describe the event are examined. It should be noted at the outset that we operationalized emotional recall as the number of emotion words included in the narrative. This is obviously a relatively constrained measure of emotion recall. Certainly, the use of emotion words indicates that emotion is an integrated part of the memory, but high emotional arousal can be expressed in several other ways as well, including narrative devices that express emphasis and urgency, and tone of voice. Here we were specifically interested in how memory of emotional reactions to an event is explicitly expressed in verbal recall.

Three basic questions are addressed: How does recall of emotions differ when narrating negative versus positive experiences? How does recall of emotions change over the short term (i.e., a period of days or weeks)? How does recall of emotion change over the long term (i.e., a period of months or years)? By examining these patterns, we are able to provide a developmental framework for understanding how the emotional aspects of highly emotional experiences are recalled over time.

Positive versus negative emotion

Whereas previous research has demonstrated that negative events are better recalled than mundane events, few studies have specifically examined memory for the emotion associated with the event. Exactly what kind of emotion do individuals recall about emotional events, and how does recall of emotion vary as a function of valence and intensity of the experience?

Most research examining recall of emotion has emerged from the expressive writing technique developed by Pennebaker (1997) in which participants are asked to write about their deepest thoughts and feelings concerning stressful events, compared to participants asked to write about mundane daily activities. In a recent meta-analysis of 146 experimentally controlled expressive writing studies, Frattaroli (2006) found that disclosure of thoughts and feelings during expressive writing has significant positive effects on psychological and physical health. More relevant for our arguments here, and not surprising, when individuals write about stressful events they recall more emotion than when writing about mundane activities, and, perhaps more surprising, participants recall both negative and positive emotion when narrating stressful events (Pennebaker, 1997; Pennebaker & Francis, 1996), suggesting that emotion recall is multidimensional, and that individuals are able to integrate both negative and positive emotions within their recall of negative events. However, this research does not examine narratives of positive events. Moreover, the focus is on group differences between writing groups, and therefore only mean amounts of emotion expressed across all days of writing are reported. Because participants often write about different stressful events across the days of writing, it is not possible from these data to determine the amount of emotion recalled about a specific event, or how consistently emotion is recalled over time.

The few studies that have directly compared individuals' recall of both positive and negative emotion within both positive and negative event narratives are listed in Table 8.1. The top panel presents results from two studies with adult females. Bohanek, Fivush, and Walker (2005) directly compared event narratives varying by both valence and intensity; they asked participants to narrate an intensely negative event from their life, a moderately negative event, an intensely positive event, and a moderately positive event. While individuals recalled both positive and negative emotion associated with all four event types, they recalled more negative emotion about negative events and more positive emotion about positive events. Although the means suggest that individuals recalled more negative emotion about moderately negative experiences than about intensely negative experiences, this was not a statistically reliable difference. In contrast, in mothers' narratives about experiences associated with their child's asthma, Fivush, Sales, and Bohanek (in press) found that events associated with fear included more negative emotion recall than events associated with frustration, an arguably less emotionally intense experience, suggesting that as emotional intensity increases, recall of emotion increases as well.

The second panel in Table 8.1 displays the results of studies with children. Children with asthma narrating positive and negative events mirror the findings with their mothers (Fivush et al., in press). These results suggest that even children recall emotion in a multidimensional fashion, at least by age 9, reporting both positive and negative emotions associated with both positive and negative events. However, again, there is more recall of positive emotion when narrating positive events, and more recall of negative emotion when narrating negative events. And again, similar to their mothers, these children recall more negative emotion about a scary event associated with their asthma than about a frustrating event. Bohanek (2006) also found that children recall more positive emotion when narrating positive events and more negative emotion when recalling negative events, although overall level of recall of emotion did not differ between the positive and negative events. Finally, Brown (in progress) examined narratives of positive and negative events in both typically developing children and children with Asperger's syndrome. Both groups of children showed a similar pattern of emotion recall, but surprisingly both groups recalled more positive emotion than negative emotion associated with the negative event.

The third panel in Table 8.1 displays the results of studies with co-constructed emotional events. In these studies, parents and their children are asked to discuss together events that they have experienced in the past. Not surprisingly, we see many of the same patterns of emotion use within these narratives. The co-constructed narratives contain more positive emotion in the positive narratives and more negative emotion in the negative narratives. Further, we see that parents and children also incorporate negative emotion into their positive narratives and positive emotion into negative narratives, and also integrated more positive emotion into the negative narratives than negative emotion into the positive narratives.

However, co-constructed narratives also provide the opportunity to explore

Table 8.1 Mean number of positive and negative emotion words recalled in narratives of positive and negative events

Study	Participants	Specifics	Positive/neutral events		Negative events	
			Positive emotion	Negative emotion	Positive emotion	Negative emotion
Adult/Independent						
Bohanek et al. (2005) Written narratives of events varying by valence	College students N = 44	Intense events	4.49	1.01	2.10	2.69
		Moderate events	4.93	0.86	1.92	3.25
Fivush et al. (in press) Oral narratives of scary, frustrating, and happy events by mothers of children with asthma	Adult females N = 51	Happy	3.86	0.25		
		Scary			0.88	5.55
		Frustrating			0.86	4.15
Children/Independent						
Fivush et al. (in press) Oral narratives of scary, frustrating, and happy events by asthmatic children	Children (9–12 yrs) N = 56	Happy	1.98	0.18		
		Scary			0.34	2.61
		Frustrating			0.21	2.04
Bohanek (2006) Oral narratives of positive and negative events	Children (11–14 yrs) N = 24	N/A	5.52	1.61	1.63	4.54
Brown (in progress) Oral narratives of positive and negative events by typically developing and children with Asperger's syndrome	Children (8–12 yrs) Typical (N = 78) Children w/ Asperger's (N = 46)	Typical	3.20	0.50	2.58	1.29
		w/ Asperger's	3.87	0.32	3.43	1.30
Parent–child co-constructed						
Bauer et al. (2005) Mothers and children verbally co-construct narratives of a tornado and a positive event post tornado	Mothers and children (2.6–11.8 years) N = 28	Mothers	0.93	0.44	1.54	2.14
		Children	1.19	0.33	1.32	3.21
Fivush & Wang (2005) American and Chinese mothers and children verbally co-construct narratives of positive and negative events	Mothers and children (4 yrs) N = 31	Euro-American Mothers	4.54	0.35	1.74	2.87
		Children	0.62	0.26	0.39	1.29
		Chinese Mothers	4.40	0.54	0.93	6.24
		Children	2.07	0.24	0.30	2.07
Bohanek (2006) Families co-construct oral narratives of positive and negative events	Mothers, fathers, and all siblings (focal child 9–12 yrs) N = 40	Mothers	7.95	1.68	2.9	7.53
		Fathers	4.98	1.08	2.6	4.18
		Children	4.78	1.38	1.55	3.28

possible socialization mechanisms that may be especially important for children's interpretation and understanding of emotional events. For instance, all but one of the co-constructed narrative studies presented in Table 8.1 demonstrate the differential emotional contributions of parents and children during the co-construction task. Specifically, Fivush and Wang (2005) found that in general, mothers are contributing more emotion talk to these conversations than are the children. Similarly, the data from Bohanek (2006), in which families as a whole were asked to reminisce about past emotional experiences, suggest that, overall, mothers are recalling more emotion than fathers or children (most families had more than one child and children ranged from preschool to teenagers). Further, mothers recalled more negative emotion about the negative event and more positive emotion about the positive event, whereas fathers and children did not recall positive and negative emotion differentially between the two events. Although Bauer et al. (2005) did not observe similar results in the co-constructed narratives provided by dyads who had experienced a tornado, importantly all three studies indicate that parents and children show similar patterns of emotion use during both positive and negative event conversations.

These patterns suggest that recalling specific emotions is an integral part of recall of both positive and negative experiences for both children and adults. Moreover, although the type of emotion recalled overall matches the emotional tone of the event, it also seems to be the case that more positive emotion is integrated into negative event narratives than negative emotion is integrated into positive event narratives. This raises the question of the functions of recalling emotion. Obviously some emotion is recalled automatically as the memory is retrieved (Brewin, 2003). But emotion is also deliberately integrated into emotional memory in the service of emotional regulation and coping (Lazarus & Folkman, 1984; Pennebaker, 1997). A critical component of coping is to re-appraise a negative situation in order to find some positive outcome (Lazarus & Folkman, 1984; McAdams, 2004). Thus, in considering emotion recall, it is not simply the emotion experienced at the time that will be recalled, but efforts towards coping and meaning-making that will lead to the integration of positive emotions into negative events, and may likely lead to inconsistent recall of emotional experience over time.

The influence of intensity of emotion is more difficult to determine. Only two studies directly compared narratives of negative events differing in intensity and the results are mixed. Bohanek et al. (2005) found no reliable effect of intensity, although the means suggest that more emotion is recalled about more moderate as compared to more intense emotional events, whereas Fivush et al. (in press) found that more intensely emotional events were recalled in more emotional detail than moderately emotional events by both adults and children. One challenge in this research is obviously how to capture intensity of emotion, especially when individuals are recalling different events. One way to address this problem is to compare individuals who have all experienced the same event but under different levels of emotional intensity.

In a study examining narratives of the 9/11 disaster, in which terrorists flew planes into the World Trade Center buildings and the Pentagon killing thousands of people, those participants who knew someone killed in the attacks, and therefore were presumably more stressed than individuals who did not know someone killed, recalled less positive and negative emotion in their narratives of the event than individuals who were not personally connected to the disaster (Fivush, Edwards, & Mennuti-Washburn, 2003). Similarly, preschool children who experienced Hurricane Andrew under conditions of high stress, where windows blew in and roofs collapsed as the family withstood the storm, recalled fewer positive and negative emotions in their narratives of the storm than children who experienced more moderate stress of trees falling outside the house and water leaks (Sales, Fivush, Parker, & Bahrick, 2005). Mothers of these children showed a similar pattern (Parker, Bahrick, Fivush, & Johnson, 2006). Mothers who experienced moderate stress during the storm recalled more internal states (which includes emotion) than mothers who experienced low stress, but mothers who experienced high levels of stress recalled fewer internal states than did moderately stressed mothers. These results, together with the Fivush et al. (in press) findings, suggest that recall of emotion may increase with emotional intensity of the event to a point, but when the event becomes emotionally overwhelming, recall of emotion may decrease. It is possible that memory for emotional aspects of events follows an inverted-U shaped function (see also Easterbrook, 1959), such that moderate levels of emotional arousal lead to increased recall of emotion, but at extremely high levels of emotional arousal recall of emotions falls off.

Clearly we need more research to sort out these relations. We need to consider multiple factors, including how to conceptualize intensity, as well as issues regarding how emotion recall may change over time. Given the robust research findings on the fading of negative affect (Walker, Skowronski, & Thompson, 2003), it seems quite likely that individuals will recall less negative emotion even about highly intense negative experiences over time. Indeed, narratives of 9/11 included less negative emotion 6 months later than they did 1 month after the attacks. In contrast, the narratives at 6 months included more positive emotion than narratives from 1 month after the attacks, suggesting ongoing event reappraisal (Fivush et al., 2003).

On the other hand, children recalling Hurricane Andrew as preschoolers and then again as 9- to 10-year-olds actually reported more negative emotion over time, as well as more positive emotion, but this may be due to increased ability to express memory in language over this developmental age period (Sales et al., 2005). Thus we need to consider how developing language and memory abilities interact with time since the event in assessing emotion recall over time. Both efforts after meaning-making and active coping may lead to less negative emotion and more positive emotion being recalled about highly negative experiences over time, but this may only be apparent in older children and adults who already have the language skills to express their memories.

Moreover, in addition to assessing the amount of emotion recalled over time, it is also important to consider how consistent individuals are in their recall of emotion associated with specific experiences. The research in Table 8.1 focuses on narratives given at one time point. The flashbulb memory literature is concerned with consistency of recall over time, and whether highly emotional events are more consistently recalled than mundane events. Within this literature, consistency is conceptualized as recall of the same information, both about the news event and the reception context. Although consistency can be operationalized in different ways (e.g., strong versus weak criteria), the main question has focused on whether individuals recall basically the same information over time. Here, we take a more restricted look at whether individuals are consistent in their recall of the emotions associated with stressful events.

Short-term consistency in recall of emotions

In the aftermath of a highly stressful event, especially public events as studied in the flashbulb memory literature, individuals engage in multiple tellings and retellings of their experience. Indeed, rehearsal of the event has been found to be a strong predictor of consistency in flashbulb memories over time (Bohannon, 1988; Conway et al., 1994; but see Shapiro, 2006, for somewhat different findings). In this chapter we review research that explicitly examines whether individuals are consistent in their recall of their emotional reactions over a series of retellings within a short period of time, by examining correlations between recall of positive emotion words over time and recall of negative emotion words over time.

In order to address this issue we examined recall of positive and negative emotions in both children and adults during an expressive writing intervention. In expressive writing, individuals are asked to write in a diary for about 15 minutes a day for a series of days about highly stressful events in their lives. In the majority of this research, data are presented as means across days of writing for the experimental versus the control group, so individual consistency in recall of emotion is not reported in these studies. However, as shown in the top panel of Table 8.2, we have examined individual consistency in two expressive writing studies, one with adults and one with children.

In a diary study of the 9/11 attacks, college students were asked to write for 5 consecutive days about their deepest thoughts and feelings concerning the event (Fivush et al., 2003). Diaries were begun 4 to 6 weeks after the attacks. As already mentioned, those who knew someone killed in the attacks recalled less emotion than those who did not know someone killed. These patterns remained stable over the 5 days of writing. In addition, correlations computed on individuals' recall of emotion indicated that those participants who recalled more negative emotion on the first day of writing continued to recall more negative emotion on subsequent days of writing than individuals who recalled less negative emotion on the first day of writing, as shown in Table 8.2. Similar patterns were obtained for recall of positive emotions. Thus, adults

Table 8.2 Consistency of emotion recall over time

Study	Retention interval	Participants	Positive emotion	Negative emotion
Short-term consistency				
Fivush et al. (2004) Written narratives of 9/11	Across 5 consecutive days[a]	College students N = 57	.52*	.56*
Fivush et al. (2008) Written narratives of highly stressful events	Across 3 consecutive days	Children (9–13 years) N = 29	.35*	.51*
Long-term consistency				
Fivush et al. (2003) Written narratives of 9/11	6 months	College students N = 57	.03	.31*
Bohanek et al. (2005) Oral narratives of sexual assault	2 years	Female adults (18–57 years at first interview) N = 22	.18	.73*
Bohanek & Fivush (2008) Written narratives of intensely positive and moderately negative events	2 years	College students N = 27		
		Intensely negative events N = 20	.30	.57**
		Moderately negative events N = 10	.32	.04
		Intensely positive events N = 18	.20	.44+
		Moderately positive events N = 16	.10	−.02
Sales et al. (2005) Oral narratives of Hurricane Andrew	6 years	Children (3–4 years at first interview) N = 35	−.03	.12

a Correlation coefficient computed across all days as α.
+ p < .10.
* p < .05.
** p < .01.

are consistent over a brief period of time in the extent to which they focus on their emotions in their recall of a highly stressful event.

Children show this same pattern (see Table 8.2). Fivush, Marin, Crawford, Reynolds, and Brewin (2008) asked 9- to 13-year-old children to write about highly stressful events for 15 minutes a day for 3 consecutive days. Because children were free to write about any event they chose, some children chose to write about different events on each day of writing. In order to ascertain consistency of emotion recall, here we only examined those children who wrote about the same event across all 3 days of writing. Within this group, those children who recalled more negative emotion on the first day of writing continued to do so across all 3 days of writing, and patterns were similar for recall of positive emotions. Although limited, the research suggests high consistency in emotion recall over short periods of time, indicating somewhat stable individual differences in focus on emotion when recalling stressful events. Would we see the same patterns across longer delays?

Long-term consistency in recall of emotions

Although there is a good deal of evidence that negative affect generally fades over time (Walker, et al., 2003), the question addressed here is whether those individuals who recall a great deal about their emotions associated with a stressful event shortly after its occurrence continue to recall more about their emotions than do others as time passes. As displayed in the bottom half of Table 8.2, the answer is complicated. Fivush et al. (2004) and Bohanek, Mennuti-Washburn, Fivush, and Koss (2005) found that adults show long-term consistency in recall of negative emotion when recalling intensely negative events (9/11 and sexual assault experiences). Bohanek et al. (2005) further showed long-term consistency in recall of negative emotion in intensely positive events, but not in recall of negative emotions associated with moderately negative or positive experiences. On the other hand, across all three studies, adults show no long-term consistency in recall of positive emotion when recalling either positive or negative events. In contrast to adults, Sales et al. (2005) found no long-term consistency in children's recall of negative or positive emotion associated with Hurricane Andrew, but this study examined recall from preschool to preteen years, which is an extremely long delay across a critical developmental period.

This pattern suggests, first, that although negative affect may generally fade over time, individuals are consistent in the extent to which they recall negative emotion associated with highly aversive experiences even years after the event occurred. But the limited evidence on moderately negative events suggests that this pattern may be limited to highly emotional events. Adults are not consistent in recalling negative emotion associated with only moderately stressful experiences. And, interestingly, children show a very different pattern, suggesting that consistency of recall of emotions associated with intensely emotional events emerges later in development.

SUMMARY AND IMPLICATIONS FOR
FLASHBULB MEMORIES

Overall, the research indicates that recall of emotion is multidimensional, with recall of both negative and positive emotion integrated into recall of both negative and positive events. More emotion, and more negative emotion, is recalled about highly negative events than moderately emotional events, and recall of negative emotions about highly aversive events is consistent over time, at least for adults. In the flashbulb memory literature, consistency of memory is taken as evidence of a vivid enduring memory that can be characterized as flashbulb-like, whereas the emotional reaction to the event is most often assessed as a response to a direct question (see Julian, Bohannan, & Aue, Chapter 5, and Luminet, Chapter 3, in this volume). The research reviewed here also suggests that emotion is a critical aspect of recall of emotional events, and may influence the way in which other aspects of the event are recalled.

Similar to findings in the flashbulb memory literature, recall of emotion associated with intensely emotional events is more consistent than recall of emotion associated with moderately emotional events. However, the flashbulb memory literature almost exclusively studies events that are publicly experienced and shared. These types of events take on historical and cultural significance and there is effort after collective meaning-making, individually with family and friends, and societally through media and commemorations (Hirst & Meksin, Chapter 10, and Páez, Bellelli, & Rimé, Chapter 11, this volume). This is similar to narrative studies of 9/11 and Hurricane Andrew; these are events that reshaped our cultural landscape. In contrast, many of the other events studied in the narrative memory literature are not public; in fact, just the opposite. Trauma, and perhaps especially sexual violence, is not simply private; it is silenced and rarely, if ever, shared with others even in personal conversation (Brewin, 2003). Yet we see very similar patterns in adults' recall of emotion associated with both public and private highly aversive events. This pattern has interesting implications for issues of consistency and coherence, both within the flashbulb memory literature and in the larger literature on memory of emotional events.

First and foremost, this pattern suggests that consistency of recall may not be a simple function of talking with others and developing a "good story" about what happened. Obviously, rehearsal is a critical factor in the retention of memories, and it has been argued that flashbulb memories are consistent over time exactly because they are of events that are most likely to be discussed and rehearsed with others. Through these discussions individuals come to form a more canonical story of the event, leading to both coherence and consistency (Neisser, 1982). Yet the patterns here suggest that consistency, at least for the emotional aspects of an event, may be just as great for events that are not canonical or shared, either in public forums or in private discussions. This suggests that we need a more complex model of consistency and coherence. In particular, we need to distinguish between consistency for the emotional and the non-emotional aspects of event memories.

One speculative possibility is that memories of highly stressful events are anchored by the negative affect. However, this does not necessarily lead to consistency for recalling other aspects of the event. Extrapolating from the expressive writing research discussed earlier, perhaps it is in the process of sharing these events with others that they become more coherently organized, and through this process, recall becomes more consistent. Indeed, there is some research to suggest that attentive listeners elicit more coherent narratives than inattentive listeners (Pasupathi, Stallworth, & Murdoch, 1998). Thus it may be in the context of talking about stressful experiences with others, particularly sympathetic others, that a more coherent narrative and therefore more consistent account of the event is formed. Events that are narrated more coherently are subsequently better recalled (Pasupathi, 2001), suggesting that, in the process of organizing a coherent narrative, individuals are simultaneously creating a more enduring memory representation.

It may also be possible that, in the process of discussing events with others, the positive affect associated with the event increases. This could be the case for at least two reasons. First, Taylor's (1991) mobilization–minimization hypothesis suggests that individuals deal with stressful situations through mobilizing cognitive, emotional, and social resources, leading to seeking out opportunities to talk about the event with others, and to share affect. In this process, individuals minimize the negative affect and begin to increase the positive affect associated with stressful situations. Second, there is growing evidence from the expressive writing research that disclosing stressful experiences may lead to an increase in positive affect through coping strategies that reframe the event in more positive ways (Pennebaker, 1997).

If this interpretation is correct then there are at least two implications for coherence and consistency. First, we would expect less consistency in overall recall just after a stressful event has occurred, perhaps over the course of the first few days. Although there may be consistency in recall of the negative affect, recall of other aspects of the event should be more variable, as the individual tries to process the experience. In the course of discussing the experience with others, a more coherent narrative should evolve, leading to higher consistency of all aspects of the story. Thus consistency should show a non-linear function over time, with low consistency in the immediate aftermath of a stressful event and increasing consistency as the story becomes more coherent and stabilizes. This might also mean that consistency for the non-emotional aspects of an event would be higher for publicly shared events than for private events, especially those that are never discussed. Some support for this interpretation comes from the trauma literature, which demonstrates relatively incoherent and inconsistent recall of highly traumatic events that are not shared with others, such as sexual violence and battle experiences (Brewin, 2003; McNally, 2003).

This interpretation also highlights the developmental nature of memory, both across age and across time since the experience occurred. In terms of age differences, in the only study to examine consistency of emotion recall over time, children who experienced a devastating natural disaster as preschoolers were not consistent in their recall of emotion over time. But this study only examined one very lengthy retention interval (6 years), and this retention interval stretched from the early beginnings of narrative ability in the preschool years to the mastery of basic narrative skills in childhood (Hudson & Shapiro, 1991). This is also the period during which autobiographical narratives emerge as culturally canonical forms for recalling the personal past (Nelson & Fivush, 2004) and there is increasing sophistication of understanding of emotions and emotional language (Denham, 1998), and therefore we may see a different pattern over this developmental period. More research on changes in memory across wide developmental age spans is needed.

In terms of time since the event occurred, this interpretation emphasizes changes in memory over time. In contrast to memory models that focus on rehearsal as a buffer against forgetting, this interpretation stresses reconstructive efforts after meaning as time goes by. It is as individuals try to understand the stressful events of their lives that the story evolves and emerges. Thus flashbulb memories may become "flashbulbs" as individuals process, discuss, and create meaning from stressful and emotionally difficult events, rather than being formed at the moment of experience. This interpretation is consistent with arguments about the collective nature of flashbulb memories and the role they play in social identity and cultural definition (Berntsen, Chapter 9, this volume; Hirst & Meksin, Chapter 10, this volume; Páez, Bellelli, & Rimé, Chapter 11, this volume). However, these arguments focus on the social and cultural reasons for sharing the event with others; here we argue that it may also be the individual's high emotional arousal that creates the need to work towards meaning and coherence.

The research reviewed indicates that recall of emotion is central to memory for emotional events. In examining recall of emotion, we have shown that emotional memories are complex and integrative, yet intriguingly only negative emotion associated with highly aversive events is recalled consistently over time. These findings confirm and extend current conceptualizations of flashbulb memories being formed through emotional arousal, and provide new directions for exploring how efforts after meaning-making over time may be facilitated or hindered through the recall of highly aversive emotional reactions.

NOTE

1 This paper was written while the first author was a senior fellow in the Center for the Interdisciplinary Study of Law and Religion at Emory University, sponsored by a grant from The Pew Charitable Trusts. The opinions expressed here are those of the authors and do not necessarily reflect the views of The Pew Charitable trusts.

REFERENCES

Ackil, J. K., Van Abbema, D. L., & Bauer, P. J. (2003). After the storm: Enduring differences in mother–child recollections of traumatic and nontraumatic events. *Journal of Experimental Child Psychology, 84*, 286–309.

Bahrick, L. E., Parker, J. F., Fivush, R., & Levitt, M. (1998). The effects of stress on young children's memory for a natural disaster. *Journal of Experimental Psychology: Applied, 4*, 308–331.

Bartlett, F. C. (1932). *Remembering: A study in experimental and social psychology.* New York: Cambridge University Press.

Bauer, P., Stark, E., Lukowski, A., Rademacher, J., Van Abbema, D., & Ackil, J. (2005). Working together to make sense of the past: Mothers' and children's use of internal states language in conversations about traumatic and nontraumatic events. *Journal of Cognition and Development, 6*, 463–488.

Berntsen, D. (2001). Involuntary memories of emotional events: Do memories of traumas and extremely happy events differ? *Applied Cognitive Psychology, 15*, 135–158.

Bohanek, J. G. (2006). *Family narratives of shared emotional experiences and relations to child outcome.* Unpublished doctoral dissertation, Emory University, Atlanta, GA.

Bohanek, J. G., & Fivush, R. (2008). *Change in the content and structure of women's narratives of emotional events over time predicts psychological outcomes.* Manuscript in preparation.

Bohanek, J. G., Fivush, R., & Walker, E. (2005). Memories of positive and negative emotional events. *Applied Cognitive Psychology, 19*, 51–66.

Bohanek, J. G., Mennuti-Washburn, J., Fivush, R., & Koss, M. (2005). *Affect and coherence in women's narratives of sexual assault: Relations to psychological well-being.* Poster presented at the meetings of the International Society for Traumatic Stress Studies, April.

Bohannon, J. N. (1988). Flashbulb memories for the space shuttle disaster: A tale of two theories. *Cognition, 29*, 179–196.

Bohannon, J. N., & Symons, L. V. (1992). Flashbulb memories: Confidence, consistency and quantity. In E. Winograd & U. Neisser (Eds.), *Affect and accuracy in recall: Studies of "flashbulb" memories* (pp. 65–91). New York: Cambridge University Press.

Bradley, M. M., Greenwald, M. K., Petry, M. C., & Lang, P. J. (1992). Remembering pictures: Pleasure, and arousal in memory. *Journal of Experimental Psychology of Learning, Memory, and Cognition, 18*, 379–390.

Brewin, C. (2003). *Posttraumatic stress disorder: Malady or myth?* New Haven, CT: Yale University Press.

Brown, B. (dissertation in progress). *The content and structure of autobiographical memories in children with and without Asperger syndrome.* North Carolina State University, Raleigh, NC.

Brown, R., & Kulik, J. (1977). Flashbulb memories. *Cognition, 5*, 73–99.

Buchanan, T. W., Etzal, J. A., Adolphs, R., & Tranel, D. (2006). The influence of autonomic arousal and semantic relatedness on memory for emotional words. *International Journal of Psychophysiology, 61*, 26–33.

Burch, M., Austin, J., & Bauer, P. (2004). Understanding the emotional past:

Relations between parent and child contributions in emotionally negative and nonnegative events. *Journal of Experimental Child Psychology, 89*, 276–297.

Byrne, C. A., Hyman, I. E., & Scott, K. L. (2001). Comparisons of memories for traumatic events and other experiences. *Applied Cognitive Psychology, 15*, 119–133.

Canli, T., Zhao, Z., Desmond, J. E., Glover, G., & Gabrieli, J. D. E. (1999). fMRI indentifies a network of structures correlated with retention of positive and negative emotional memory. *Psychobiology, 27*, 441–452.

Christianson, S. A. (1992). Emotional stress and eyewitness memory: A critical review. *Psychological Bulletin, 112*, 284–309.

Christianson, S. A., & Huebinette, B. (1993). Hands up: A study of witnesses' emotional reactions and memories associated with bank robberies. *Applied Cognitive Psychology, 7*, 365–379.

Christianson, S. A., & Lindholm, T. (1998). The fate of traumatic memories in childhood and adulthood. *Development and Psychopathology, 10*, 761–780.

Conway, M. (1995). *Flashbulb memories.* Mahwah, NJ: Lawrence Erlbaum Associates Inc.

Conway, M., Anderson, S. J., Larsen, S. F., Donnely, C. M., McDaniel, M. A., McClelland, A. G. R., et al. (1994). The formation of flashbulb memories. *Memory and Cognition, 22*, 326–343.

Denham, S. A. (1998). *Emotional development in young children.* New York: Guilford Press.

Easterbrook, J. A. (1959). The effect of emotion on cue utilization and the organization of behavior. *Psychological Review, 66*, 183–201.

Finkenauer, C., Luminet, O., Gisle, L., El-Ahmadi, A., Van der Linden, M., & Philippot, P. (1998). Flashbulb memories and the underlying mechanisms of their formation: Toward an emotional-integrative model. *Memory and Cognition, 26*, 516–531.

Fivush, R. (1998). Children's recollections of traumatic and non-traumatic experiences. *Development and Psychopathology, 10*, 699–716.

Fivush, R., & Baker-Ward, L. (2005). The search for meaning: Developmental perspectives on internal state language in autobiographical memory. *Journal of Cognition and Development, 6*, 455–462.

Fivush, R., Edwards, V. J., & Mennuti-Washburn, J. (2003). Narratives of 9/11: Relations among personal involvement, narrative content and memory of the emotional impact over time. *Applied Cognitive Psychology, 17*, 1099–1111.

Fivush, R., & Haden, C. A. (2005). Parent–child reminiscing and the development of a subjective self. In B. Homer & C. Tamis-LaMonda (Eds.), *The development of social cognition and communication.* Mahwah: NJ: Lawrence Erlbaum Associates Inc.

Fivush, R., Hazzard, A., Sales, J. M., Sarfati, D., & Brown, T. (2003). Creating coherence out of chaos? Children's narratives of emotionally negative and positive events. *Applied Cognitive Psychology, 17*, 1–19.

Fivush, R., Marin, K., Crawford, M., Reynolds, M., & Brewin, C. (2008). Children's narratives and well-being. *Cognition and Emotion, 21*, 1414–1434.

Fivush, R., & Nelson, K. (2006). Parent–child reminiscing locates the self in the past. *British Journal of Developmental Psychology, 24*, 235–251.

Fivush, R., & Sales, J. M. (2003). Children's memories of emotional events. In D. Reisberg & P. Hertel (Eds.), *Memory and emotion* (pp. 242–271). New York, Oxford University Press.

Fivush, R., Sales, J. M., & Bohanek, J. G. (in press). Mothers' and children's narratives of asthma-related stressful events. *Memory*.

Fivush, R., Sales, J. M., Goldberg, A., Bahrick, L., & Parker, J. (2004). Weathering the storm: Children's long-term recall of Hurricane Andrew. *Memory*, *12*, 104–118.

Fivush, R., & Wang, Q. (2005). Emotion talk in mother–child conversations of the shared past: The effects of culture, gender, and event valence. *Journal of Cognition and Development*, *6*, 489–506.

Foa, E. B., Molnar, C., & Cashman, L. (1995). Change in rape narratives during exposure therapy for posttraumatic stress disorder. *Journal of Traumatic Stress*, *8*, 675–690.

Frattaroli, J. (2006). Experimental disclosure and its moderators: A meta-analysis. *Psychological Bulletin*, *132*, 823–865.

Goodman, G. S., Quas, J. A., Batterman-Faunce, J. M., Riddlesberger, M. M., & Kuhn, J. (1994). Predictors of accurate and inaccurate memories of traumatic events experienced in childhood. *Consciousness and Cognition*, *3*, 269–294.

Gray, M. J., & Lombardo, T. W. (2001). Complexity of trauma narratives as an index of fragmented memory in PTSD: A critical analysis. *Applied Cognitive Psychology*, *15*, 171–186.

Hamann, S. B., Ely, T., Grafton, S., & Kilts, C. (1999). Amygdala activity related to enhanced memory for pleasant and aversive stimuli. *Nature Neuroscience*, *2*, 289–293.

Hudson, J. A., & Shapiro, L. (1991). Effects of task and topic on children's narratives. In A. McCabe & C. Peterson (Eds.), *New directions in developing narrative structure* (pp. 89–136). Hillsdale, NJ: Lawrence Erlbaum Associates Inc.

James, W. (1890). *The principles of psychology*. New York: Dover.

Lazarus, R. S., & Folkman, S. (1984). *Stress, appraisal, and coping*. New York: Springer Publishing Co.

Levine, L. (2004). Emotion and memory research: A grumpy overview. *Social Cognition*, *22*, 530–554.

Malmquist, C. P. (1986). Children who witness parental murder: Post-traumatic aspects. *Journal of the American Academy of Child Psychiatry*, *25*, 320–325.

McAdams, D. (2004). The redemptive self: Narrative identity in America today. In D. R. Beike, J. M. Lampinen, & D. A. Behrend (Eds.), *The self and memory* (pp. 95–116). New York: Psychology Press.

McNally, R. (2003). *Remembering trauma*. Cambridge, MA: Belknap Press/Harvard University Press.

Merritt, K. A., Ornstein, P. A., & Spicker, B. (1994). Children's memory for a salient medical procedure: Implications for testimony. *Pediatrics*, *94*, 17–23.

Neisser, U. (1982). Snapshots or benchmarks? In U. Neisser (Ed.), *Memory observed* (pp. 43–48). San Francisco: Freeman.

Nelson, K., & Fivush, R. (2004). The emergence of autobiographical memory: A social cultural developmental theory. *Psychological Review*, *111*, 486–511.

Parker, J. P., Bahrick, L., Fivush, R., & Johnson, P. (2006). The impact of stress on mother's memory of a natural disaster. *Journal of Experimental Psychology: Applied*, *12*, 142–154.

Pasupathi, M. (2001). The social construction of the personal past and its implications for adult development. *Psychological Bulletin*, *127*, 651–672.

Pasupathi, M., Stallworth, L. M., & Murdoch, K. (1998). How what we tell becomes what we know: Listener effects on speakers' long-term memory for events. *Discourse Processes*, *26*, 1–25.

Payne, J. D., Jackson, E. D., Ryan, L., Hoscheidt, S., Jacobs, W. J., & Nadel, L. (2006). The impact of stress on neutral and emotional aspects of episodic memory. *Memory*, *14*, 1–16.

Peace, K. A., & Porter, S. (2004). A longitudinal investigation of the reliability of memories for trauma and other emotional experiences. *Applied Cognitive Psychology*, *18*, 1143–1159.

Pennebaker, J. W. (1997). *Opening up*. New York: Guilford Press.

Pennebaker, J. W., & Francis, M. E. (1996). Cognitive, emotional, and language processes in disclosure. *Cognition and Emotion*, *10*, 601–626.

Peterson, C. (1999). Children's memories for medical emergencies: 2 years later. *Developmental Psychology*, *35*, 1493–1506.

Peterson, C., & Bell, M. (1996). Children's memory for traumatic injury. *Child Development*, *67*, 3045–3070.

Peterson, C., & Whalen, N. (2001). Five years later: Children's memories for medical emergencies. *Applied Cognitive Psychology*, *15*, 1–18.

Pezdek, K., & Taylor, J. (2001). Memories of traumatic events. In M. Eisen, G. S. Goodman, & J. S. Quas (Eds.), *Memory and suggestibility in the forensic interview* (pp. 165–184) Hillsdale, NJ: Lawrence Erlbaum Associates Inc.

Pillemer, D. (1992). Remembering personal circumstances: A functional analysis. In E. Winograd & U. Neisser (Eds.), *Affect and accuracy in recall: Studies of "flashbulb" memories* (pp. 236–264). New York: Cambridge University Press.

Porter, S., & Birt, A. R. (2001). Is traumatic memory *special*? A comparison of traumatic memory characteristics with memory for other emotional life experiences. *Applied Cognitive Psychology*, *15*, 101–117.

Reisberg, D., & Hertel, P. (Eds.). (2003). *Memory and emotion*. New York: Oxford University Press.

Reisberg, D., Heuer, F., McLean, J., & O'Shaughnessy, M. (1988). The quantity, not the quality, of affect predicts memory variables. *Bulletin of the Psychonomic Society*, *26*, 100–103.

Sales, J. M., Fivush, R., Parker, J., & Bahrick, L. (2005). Stressing memory: Relations of children's memory of Hurricane Andrew, stress and psychological well-being over time. *Journal of Cognition and Development*, *6*, 529–546.

Shapiro, L. R. (2006). Remembering September 11th: The role of retention interval and rehearsal on flashbulb and event memory. *Memory*, *14*, 129–147.

Stein, N. L., & Liwag, M. D. (1997). Children's understanding, evaluation and memory for emotional events. In P. W. van der Broek, P. J. Bauer, & T. Bourg (Eds.), *Developmental spans in event comprehension and representations: Bridging fictional and actual events*. (pp. 199–235). Mahwah, NJ: Lawrence Erlbaum Associates Inc.

Taylor, S. E. (1991). Asymmetrical effects of positive and negative events: The mobilization–minimization hypothesis. *Psychological Bulletin*, *110*, 67–85.

Terr, L. C. (1988). What happens to early memories of trauma? A study of twenty children under age five at the time of documented traumatic events. *Journal of the American Academy of Child and Adolescent Psychiatry*, *27*, 96–104.

Tromp, S., Koss, M. P., Figueredo, A. J., & Tharan, M. (1995). Are rape memories different? A comparison of rape, other unpleasant, and pleasant memories among employed women. *Journal of Traumatic Stress*, *8*, 607–627.

Van der Kolk, B. A., & Fisler, R. (1995). Dissociation and the fragmentary nature of traumatic memories: Overview and exploratory study. *Journal of Traumatic Stress, 8*, 505–525.

Walker, W. R., Skowronski, J. T., & Thompson, C. P. (2003). Life is pleasant—and memory helps keep it that way! *Review of General Psychology, 7*, 203–210.

Winograd, E., & Neisser, U. (1992) (Eds.). *Affect and accuracy in recall: Studies of "flashbulb" memories.* New York: Cambridge University Press.

Yuille, J. C., & Cutshall, J. L. (1986). A case study of eyewitness memory of a crime. *Journal of Applied Psychology, 71*, 291–301.

Part IV

Social factors:
Identity, culture,
and collective memory

9 Flashbulb memories and social identity[1]

Dorthe Berntsen

In January 1972 my parents had recently bought their first television set. At that time in Denmark it was not unusual for programmes to be cancelled with a "Technical problems, we apologize" statement appearing on the black and white television screen. However, on Friday 14 January the normal evening entertainments were for no obvious reason replaced by three people playing chamber music. The chamber music went on and on with no explanation. It was a nuisance for a child at my age, I had been looking forward to the usual Friday night entertainments. After a while, the chamber music was finally interrupted by the announcement that the Danish King Frederik the 9th had died, after which the music resumed. I remember that even after this clarification, my brothers and I were still grumpy: How could the death of the king be so important that chamber music had to replace *The Persuaders* with Tony Curtis and Roger Moore? The next day Crown Princess Margrethe officially took over the throne in a television-transmitted ceremony. She appeared on the balcony at Amalienborg Palace in Copenhagen to receive the greetings from the thousands of people who had gathered. She entered the balcony immediately after the Prime Minister had yelled from the same balcony the news of the king's death in all four directions of the compass, as the tradition prescribed. I remember watching this on TV together with my mother while we were having our afternoon coffee and sharing our sympathy for this young princess, now queen, who came out on the balcony, pale and moved, to take up her new duties less than 24 hours after her father had passed away.

A few years ago, on 26 December 2003, roughly 50,000 people died in an earthquake in Iran. I have no memory of where I was and what I was doing when I first heard this horrible news. Does this mean that the latter, to me personally, was less emotional, less surprising, less important, and less consequential than the news of the king's death when I was 9 years old? Following the literature on FBMs, this seems to be what we should assume. However, I think this assumption is wrong. To me personally, both events were quite insignificant. Neither of them in any direct way affected me or people close to me. At a personal level, I knew the king and his family no more than I knew the thousands of victims of the earthquake in Iran. While personally irrelevant, the death of the king was nonetheless central to my social identity as a Dane. In contrast, Iran was geographically and culturally too distant to me for the tragic news of the devastating earthquake to have similar effects. Social identity, rather than personal relevance, is central for the formation and maintenance of FBMs for public events. I will develop and pursue this view in the present chapter. I first review some of the inconsistent findings that have characterized FBM research. I then suggest that many of these inconsistencies may be solved by basing our understanding of FBMs on mechanisms related to social identity.

CONFLICTING FINDINGS IN RESEARCH ON FBMs

The notion of FBMs was introduced by Brown and Kulik (1977). They defined this phenomenon as ". . . memories for the circumstances in which one first learned about a very surprising and consequential (or emotionally arousing) event" (p. 73). Hearing the news of the assassination of John F. Kennedy was described as "the prototypical case" (p. 73). Thus, even though Brown and Kulik (1977) mentioned FBMs in relation to personal events, their descriptions and prototypical example of FBMs suggest that vivid memories for *personal* events are non-essential for this phenomenon.

The key issue related to FBMs, according to Brown and Kulik, is not memory for the news event itself, but why we remember our personal circumstances on receiving this news, since "there is no obvious utility in such memories" (p. 74). In addition to dealing with personal circumstances for the reception of public news, FBMs had three outstanding characteristics, according to Brown and Kulik (1977). They were characterized by "an almost perceptual clarity" (p. 73). They were assumed to be relatively accurate, though at the same time "very far from complete" (p. 75). And, finally, they were assumed to be highly durable, indeed indelible. As Brown and Kulik wrote: "It is our assumption that the FB memory is always there, unchanging as the slumbering Rhinegold" (p. 86).

Operationalizations of FBMs vary greatly across different studies (see Talarico & Rubin, Chapter 4, this volume; Thomsen & Berntsen, 2003, for a review). One reason seems to be that Brown and Kulik's (1977) anecdotal description of the phenomenon allows several possible operationalizations (e.g., focusing on subjective clarity versus objective accuracy). In their original work, a FBM was present if a person confirmed that he or she remembered the personal circumstances for receiving the news and was able to provide at least one canonical category (such as information on ongoing activity). Other studies have found these operational criteria too lenient and alternatively tested the claims of accuracy and stability by measuring how well a memory report given immediately after the event agrees with a memory report given at a later time (e.g., Conway et al., 1994; Neisser & Harsch, 1992). Yet another class of studies has measured only the phenomenological qualities of the memories, such as vividness and details at the time of recall (e.g., Kvavilashvili, Mirani, Schlagman, & Kornbrot, 2003). A few studies have examined claims of long-term durability by measuring memories after very long delays (e.g., Berntsen & Rubin, 2006; Berntsen & Thomsen, 2005; Tekcan & Peynircioglu, 2002; Winograd & Killinger, 1983).

These approaches tap different memory aspects that need not be parallel. For example, people can have vivid FBMs that may be highly inaccurate (e.g., Neisser & Harsch, 1992). Talarico and Rubin (2003) demonstrated that FBMs differ from memories for a mundane control event only with regard to confidence, not with regard to consistency. Bohn and Berntsen (2007) found that people with a positive versus negative emotional attitude to the same event showed a different pattern with regard to accuracy and subjective clarity. The positive group scored higher on clarity, the negative group scored higher on accuracy, consistent with what has been found in laboratory studies using other emotional material (more detail on this study is offered later in this chapter). Such inconsistencies regarding operationalizations question whether FBMs are a unified and distinct phenomenon. It further questions the validity of the FBM notion that not only do researchers use different operationalizations, they also present conflicting findings regarding causal mechanisms for the formation of FBMs even when the same operationalization has been used (see Talarico and Rubin, Chapter 4, this volume, for a review). As illustrated by Figure 9.1, in Brown and Kulik's (1977) account certain (non-specified) critical levels of surprise and consequentiality triggered the formation of FBMs through the activation of a special neural mechanism, labelled Now Print!—a purported biological mechanism, ensuring an extraordinarily detailed encoding of the surrounding circumstances. A narrative (and measurable) correlate of the memory representation is further developed through repeated rehearsal of the event. However, a prerequisite for this rehearsal to take place is the immediate formation of the memory through the Now Print mechanism. Thus, the emotional reaction that triggers the Now Print mechanism cannot be bypassed. As argued by Brown and Kulik (1977) ". . . the registration of surprise and unexpectedness in the central nervous system is the first step and the sine qua non of all else" (p. 84). Brown and Kulik (1977) presented only indirect evidence in support of their purported biological mechanisms. Their main evidence was observations of group differences, which is in complete agreement with a central point

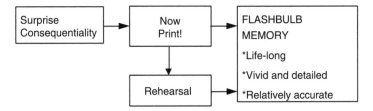

Figure 9.1 The original model of FBM formation introduced by Brown and Kulik (1977).

to be developed in this chapter. Brown and Kulik showed markedly higher frequencies of FBMs among African-Americans as compared to White Americans for the news of the assassination of four political leaders engaged with questions of civil rights. These differences were matched by generally higher ratings of consequentiality among African-Americans for the same four events. Surprise was not measured, but nevertheless claimed to be decisive.

Brown and Kulik's (1977) original model has been the target of much criticism. One of the strongest and earliest critics was Neisser (1982) who argued against the idea of a special brain mechanism forming enduring, accurate memories at the time of encoding. Alternatively, he suggested that flashbulb-like memories were formed through frequent rehearsal in thoughts and conversations. This rehearsal was motivated by a need of the individual to experience him or herself as part of history: "We remember the details of a flashbulb occasion because those details are the links between our own histories and 'History'" (p. 48). It is not clear from Neisser's (1982) account how some events get to become 'History' in a particular culture and others not. Neisser (1982) did not present empirical evidence for this alternative view, but other studies have shown that rehearsal can be more decisive for the formation of FBMs than emotional involvement at the time of the event (Otani et al., 2005) and also that FBM may evolve in response to expected, non-surprising events (Berntsen & Thomsen, 2005) and/or events rated low on measures of emotion and consequentiality (Neisser et al., 1996). Because other studies have shown strong effects of emotion and little importance of rehearsal (e.g., Pillemer, 1984), one may assume that the relative importance of emotion versus rehearsal varies as a function of characteristics of the target event.

Several alternatives to Brown and Kulik's (1977) original model have been presented (e.g., Conway et al., 1994; Er, 2003; Finkenauer et al., 1998; see also Luminet, Chapter 3, this volume). Even though these models are all generated from studies in which FBMs have been operationalized in terms of a certain level of consistency, the models do not agree with one another with regard to causal mechanisms. For Conway et al. (1994) prior interest and knowledge is the critical variable that instigates the relevant emotional reactions, which eventually lead to FBM formation. In contrast, Finkenauer et al. (1998) found that novelty and surprise formed a direct pathway to explain FBMs. These factors were able to lead directly to the formation of FBMs, whereas importance and emotional feeling state supported the formation of FBMs indirectly through recurrent rehearsal. Er (2003) presented an alternative to both of these models by arguing that the initial appraisal of importance or consequentiality is crucial for prompting the emotional reactions that participate in the formation of FBMs.

The divergences between these three models may reflect that they are based on FBM data for three different events (the resignation of the British prime minister Margaret Thatcher, the unexpected death of Belgian King Baudouin, and a devastating earthquake in Turkey, respectively). The relative importance of prior knowledge/interest, surprise, and appraisal of consequences may simply vary as a function of differences between these three events and how they each affected the population under study. When analyses are based on data related to each of these specific events considered in isolation, such differences may lead to different FBM models.

Does this mean that we need a new FBM model for each distinct FBM event? This does not seem to be a very satisfactory solution. Faced with such conceptual and empirical inconsistencies, some researchers have argued that FBMs are not different from other autobiographical memories of emotional events (Mahmood, Manier, & Hirst, 2004; Sierra & Berrios, 1999) or from other vivid autobiographical memories (Rubin & Kozin, 1984; see also Talarico and Rubin, Chapter 4, this volume). I do not disagree with the analyses that have led these researchers to draw such conclusions. On the other hand, I do not think that their analyses reflect the only possible perspective from which the phenomenon of FBMs can be viewed. In the following I will introduce an alternative understanding that may be able to unify different approaches to the study of FBMs and resolve some of the conflicting findings.

RECONCEPTUALIZING FBMs

Following theories of categorization (e.g., Rosch, 1978), I suggest that a reconceptualization of FBMs should begin with Brown and Kulik's (1977) prototypical FBM case rather than their debatable attempts at developing a formal definition. The prototypical case is remembering the personal circumstances for receiving the news of the Kennedy assassination. This case helps to identify some important differences between FBMs and other emotional memories. First, a FBM is related to the reception of a public event—thus, an event that is shared within a given community. Second, instead of focusing on the central details (that is, the news event itself) a FBM maintains the surrounding irrelevant details related to the personal context for the reception of this news. Several studies have found that the personal reception context is remembered better over time than information about the news event itself (Bohannon, 1988; Shapiro, 2006; Smith, Bibi, & Sheard, 2003; Tekcan, Ece, Gülgöz & Nurham, 2003; but see Nachson & Zelig, 2003). Such focus is the opposite of the tunnel memory effect that is often found for autobiographical memories of intensely negative events (e.g., Berntsen, 2002; see Christianson, 1992, for a review). The notion of tunnel memory refers to a tendency to focus exclusively on the most central, emotion-related details, which clearly would be information about the news event itself in the case of FBMs. The tunnel memory phenomenon has been found to apply to personal memories for emotional events, thus an increased focus on peripheral details relative to the central information seems to distinguish FBMs from other emotional autobiographical memories.

Consistent with Brown and Kulik's (1977) prototypical case, I suggest that the presence of FBMs varies as a function of the social and cultural relevance of the public news event, whereas personal relevance plays a minor role. More specifically, I suggest that the activation of a person's social identity is a crucial causal factor for the development of a FBM of a given news event. The person has to appreciate that the news has relevance for a social group that he or she identifies with (see Hirst & Meksin, Chapter 10, and Páez, Bellelli, & Rimé, Chapter 11 in this volume for related perspectives).

According to social identity theory (Tajfel, 1982), our self-concepts consist of two subsystems. One is our personal identity dealing with our personal achievements, bodily attributes, competences, and so forth. The other is our social identity, consisting of each individual's identifications with the social groups of which he or she perceives him- or herself as a member (e.g., Turner, 1982). Perceptions of group membership are shaped by such factors as similarity, common fate, proximity, and shared threat (Turner, 1982, p. 27), for which reason social groups are often segmented in terms of nationality, political affiliation, religion, gender, and the like. According to social identity theory, the relative dominance of these two components of the self-system will vary as a function of characteristics of the situation. Thus, at times, our personal identity may be almost completely dominant in determining our behaviour, whereas at other times our social identity determines our behaviour, such as when a person is jeopardizing personal interests to support central values of his or her group, or—less favourably—when a sense of personal responsibility is overshadowed by group behaviour, such as when fans of opposing sport teams get involved in brutal fights. I base what follows on this standard version of social identity theory, although alternative views can be found (e.g., see Worchel, Morales, Páez, & Deschamps 1998).

It is possible to classify oneself as belonging to a certain social class (e.g., the group of Europeans) without a strong sense of identification with that group for the moment. This means that the strength of our identification with a certain group may vary from situation to situation depending on characteristics of the context (Deschamps & Devos, 1998). One possibility that I will pursue here based on social identity theory is that public events that are perceived to strongly affect a social group in which the individual perceives him- or herself as a member will make identification with this group particularly salient. As a result of this process, the person may develop a detailed and vivid memory of his or her personal circumstances for hearing the news. This memory serves as an illustration of how the news of this event was able to interrupt his or her ordinary (and usually self-serving) activities, and is therefore an expression of group commitment or "belongingness" (Maslow, 1943). Because groups like individuals are striving to maintain a positive self-image (Baumeister & Hastings, 1997), long-term durability of FBMs to some extent depends on whether the target event is seen to support or to challenge positive values of the group.

A graphic description of this model is shown in Figure 9.2. The activation of social identity may lead to an emotional reaction formed by either the

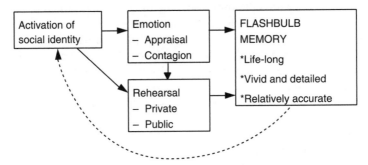

Figure 9.2 An alternative model of FBM formation taking activation of social identity as a causal mechanism.

individual's subjective appraisal of the relevance of the event or by contagion when observing the reaction of others (such as children observing the reaction of adults). The emotional salience as well as the social relevance of the FBM may lead to increased rehearsal, both individually and in public. However, the rehearsal and commemoration processes may also bypass subjective emotional reactions, as illustrated by the direct arrow from the social identity box to the rehearsal/commemoration box in Figure 9.2. This is because some rehearsal and commemoration processes are likely to be instigated at the level of the community—such as television programmes of the event whose frequency will be independent of the initial emotional reaction of the individual (Fridja, 1997). The outcome may be memories with the three main characteristics assumed by Brown and Kulik (1977)—that is, memories that are life-long, subjectively vivid, and relatively accurate ("though very far from complete", p. 75).

Such memories are important for supporting and maintaining the individual's identification with the social group concerned, as illustrated by the dotted arrow from the FBM box to the social identity box in Figure 9.2. It should also be emphasized that while accurately maintained details are a possible property of FBMs in the current model, they are not necessary. Vividness and expressiveness as symbolic representations of group identification are more central characteristics. Details with such symbolic connotations are therefore better maintained than less telling parts of the personal circumstances, which may lead to errors and biases in the memory reports—a point I will illustrate later.

CONSISTENCIES IN FBM RESEARCH: GROUP DIFFERENCES

The model presented in Figure 9.2 is not necessarily in conflict with previously suggested FBM models (e.g., Conway et al., 1994; Er, 2003; Finkenauer et al., 1998). It does not defy important cognitive and emotional processes at the level of the individual. But it brings these processes into a social and cultural context that helps to resolve some of the inconsistencies that previous theoretical and empirical work has left unresolved. The main evidence in support of the alternative model is the fact that in spite of the inconsistencies that generally muddle FBM research, one variable has consistently been shown to have an effect across a variety of studies, involving different populations and different public events and using different operationalizations and measures of FBMs (such as subjective clarity and consistency). That variable is membership in social groups.

Table 9.1 shows studies that have compared measures of FBMs for the same event between social groups that would be most likely to differ regarding their attitude and level of involvement in the target event. The table includes only studies that have clearly measured effects of social groups. It therefore does not include studies that have varied mere geographical proximity towards an event on a relatively small scale (e.g., Edery-Halpern & Nachson, 2004; Sharot, Martorella, Delgado, & Phelps, 2007) because it is doubtful that such variation corresponds to differences in group membership. All of the studies in Table 9.1 have found differences consistent with what one would expect based on the assumption that social identity plays a central role for the formation of FBMs. Although a few measures failed to show significant differences (as indicated by "No" in Table 9.1), numerical differences in the expected direction were observed in almost all cases. These group differences do not show uniform associations with measures of cognitive and/ or emotional mechanisms (such as self-reported measures of rehearsal and emotion), for which reason they cannot simply be reduced to such standard purported FBM mechanisms. The following is a brief review of the studies in Table 9.1.

Brown and Kulik (1977) found substantially more FBMs among African-Americans as compared to White Americans for the news of the assassination of four political leaders engaged with questions of civil rights. These group differences on FBM prevalence were matched by higher ratings of consequentiality among African-Americans for the same four events. Even though surprise was claimed to be decisive for the formation of FBMs, it was not measured, nor was emotional arousal or amount of rehearsal.

Morse, Woodward, and Zweigenhaft (1993) found that twice as many female as male participants reported FBMs for the US Senate hearings for confirmation of Clarence Thomas as a Supreme Court Justice. These hearings involved an examination of allegations of sexual harassment, for which reason the event was expected to instigate more FBMs among women than men, consistent with the findings. The female participants also showed more knowledge of and experience with sexual abuse, but the relation between such knowledge and the presence of a FBM was not analysed. Wright, Gaskell, and O'Muircheartaigh (1998) found gender differences in relation to the Hillsborough football stadium disaster. Male participants had more vivid

Table 9.1 Studies examining group differences in relation to the formation of FBM

First author	Year	Event	Groups	Central dep. var.	Expected effect?
Brown	1977	Death of civil rights leaders	Black vs White	Self-reported FBM	Yes
Yarmey	1978	Kennedy assassination	US vs Canadians	Self-reported FBM	Yes for young
				Details and clarity	No
Morse	1993	Clarence Thomas hearings	Female vs male	Self-reported FBM	Yes
Conway	1994	Thatcher's resignation	UK vs non-UK	Consistency	Yes
Neisser	1996	Earthquake, California	Resid. vs fam. vs others	Consistency	Yes
Gaskell	1997	Hillsborough stadium disaster	Female vs male	Subjective clarity	Yes
Curci	2001	President Mitterrand's death	French vs Belgian	Consistency	Yes
Er	2003	Earthquake, Turkey	Residents vs others	Consistency	Yes
Kvavilashvili	2003	Princess Diana's death	UK vs Italian	Subjective clarity	Yes
				Details and clarity	Yes
Pezdek	2003	September 11, 2001	New York vs others	Accuracy for event	Yes
				Details and clarity	No
Luminet	2004	September 11, 2001	US vs non-US	Accuracy for event	Yes
				Details and clarity	Yes
Berntsen	2005	WWII invasion, liberation	Resistance vs others	Accuracy for event	Yes
				Subjective clarity	Yes
Otani	2005	Nuclear accident, Japan	Residents vs others	Consistency	Yes
Curci	2006	September 11, 2001	US vs non-US	Accuracy for event	Yes
				Consistency	No

memories for the event, in spite of the fact that females rated it as more emotional and important. The fact that these two studies show differential effects of gender depending on the nature of the FBM event, combined with the fact that most other FBM studies report no gender differences (e.g., see Edery-Halpern & Nachson, 2004), suggests that the findings reported by Morse et al. (1993) and Wright et al. (1998) may have been mediated by the activation of a social identity as females and males, respectively.

Three studies in Table 9.1 examined FBMs for disasters among people who lived in the disaster area, versus others (Er, 2003; Neisser et al., 1996; Otani et al., 2005). All three studies found more FBMs (operationalized in terms of consistency) among residents as compared to others. In addition, Neisser et al. (1996) found no differences regarding frequency of FBMs among residents vs non-residents with relatives and friends in the affected area, whereas both groups had more consistent memories than non-residents with no relatives or friends in the disaster area. This suggests that factors other than geographical proximity were decisive for these effects. The three disaster studies reported different findings with regard to cognitive and emotion variables mediating the group effects. Pezdek (2003) compared memory for the September 11 terrorist attack between participants from New York versus California and Hawaii. She found that the sample from New York had better memory for facts related to the event, but gave slightly less detailed descriptions of the reception context as compared to the other two groups. Consistency over time was not measured.

A number of studies in Table 9.1 have compared FBMs for the same event among different nationalities. Yarmey and Bull (1978) found that US partici- pants tended to have more FBMs than Canadian participants for the assas- sination of President Kennedy measured via self-reports at 12 years delay, but this difference was only significant for the younger participants (18–22 years) in the two nationalities. No differences between the nationalities were observed on self-reported vividness and details. Using a consistency criterion for FBMs, Conway et al. (1994) found substantially more FBMs among their UK parti- cipants than non-UK participants for the British prime minister Margaret Thatcher's resignation. Curci, Luminet, Finkenauer, and Gisle (2001) found more FBMs for the French president Mitterrand's death among French versus Belgian participants. Kvavilashvili et al. (2003) found that UK partici- pants had more vivid and detailed FBMs for the death of Princess Diana as compared to an Italian group. Luminet et al. (2004) examined immediate memory for facts and ratings of subjective reactions in response to the news of the September 11 terrorist attack among participants from the US and seven other nationalities. The US sample showed better memory for fact, more background knowledge, and higher ratings of emotions as compared to the non-US participants. Within the non-US nationalities, the Turkish sample scored particularly low on these measures. In a follow-up study, Curci and Luminet (2006) examined memory consistency among the US partici- pants versus five of the other nationalities (the Turkish sample was not included). Very high consistency scores were observed in all groups. The US participants had more accurate memories with regard to facts related to the news event itself and they had more specific memories of the personal context for receiving the news. A non-significant difference regarding consistency was observed in the same direction.

Berntsen and Thomsen (2005) studied FBMs in relation to the World War II German occupation of Denmark. They found that participants who had reported ties to the Danish resistance had more accurate memories and rated their memories higher on measures of subjective clarity. Their memories were also more rehearsed and associated with stronger affect.

In summary, most if not all FBM studies that have systematically examined memory characteristics as a function of membership in social groups have found effects in the expected direction. These group effects do not seem to be paralleled by the same emotion and cognitive variables (e.g., rehearsal and affect) measured at the level of the individual. Taken together, the group differences reviewed here therefore support the claim that social identity interacts with the formation of FBMs in ways that extend beyond the individualistic mechanisms with which FBM research has been mostly concerned. My point is not that cognitive and emotional processes at the level of the individual are irrelevant. Clearly, knowledge of group membership is a cognitive representational structure in the mind of the individual (Turner, 1982). My point is merely that the kind of cognitive processing that is decisive for the formation and maintenance of FBMs derives from the social identity subsystem of the person's self-knowledge and that this knowledge is shared among individuals who consider themselves as members of the same social groups.

SOCIAL IDENTITY AND LONG-TERM MAINTENANCE OF FBMs

The effects of social identity on FBMs are likely to be more pronounced with the passage of time due to the selection and biases that are imposed on the individual memories via processes of rehearsal (such as media coverage) within the social group. It is likely that events that support central values of the group get more media attention and are more commemorated than events that challenge the positive self-image of the group. A couple of studies of FBMs for remote events can be seen to support this view.

Bohn and Berntsen (2007) compared FBMs between participants with a positive versus negative emotional attitude towards the fall of the Berlin Wall in 1989. The negative group consisted of former East German communists (who were still members of the socialist party when the study was conducted in 2002) whereas the positive group was a mixture of former West German liberals and East and West Germans with no party affiliations. Despite the fact that the fall of the Berlin Wall was found to have substantially more serious consequences for the socialist group both according to their subject-ive ratings and according to historical facts (many lost their jobs and were socially degraded; see Bohn & Berntsen, 2007), and in spite of the fact that they answered a number of factual questions more correctly, their personal memories for the reception of the news were rated significantly less subject-ively clear and involved less reliving than memories in the liberal/positive group. One likely explanation for these lower ratings of clarity was that the former East German communists had also talked less about the event and considered the event as less central to their personal and national identity as compared to the liberal/positive group. Consistent with this assumption, measures of personal and national identity were highly correlated with sub-jective memory clarity. Because the fall of the Berlin Wall clearly challenged central values of the socialist group by demonstrating that many of their values were not shared by the majority of East Germans, there may have been a need to downplay the importance of this event in memory in order to maintain the group. This need should have been especially pronounced among individuals who did not give up their group membership but chose to stay in the party under these unfavourable circumstances (Ellemers, Spears, & Doosje, 2002). Thus, the findings make sense under the assumption that the fall of the wall questioned central values of the socialist group, for which reason FBMs for this event were reduced through reduced rehearsal, and vice versa in the liberal/positive group (Baumeister & Hastings, 1997).

In a related study, Berntsen and Thomsen (2005) asked 145 older Danes if they remembered their personal context for receiving the news of the German occupation of Denmark in April 1940 and the announcement of the German capitulation in May 1945. In addition, we asked them for their memory of their most positive and most negative personal event from the time of the occupa-tion (Berntsen & Thomsen, 2005). They were asked to offer written descrip-tions of these four categories of memories as well as to rate their characteristics on a number of scales. When we read through these memory descriptions, it soon became obvious that a number of them dealt with the importance of group membership (Danes versus Germans) and national identity (Berntsen, 2005). For example, many memory reports illustrated that apparent trivial situations could be remembered for decades, if the situation in question had addressed dilemmas of group commitment (e.g., showing the appropriate Danish attitude) versus kindness to all fellow human beings (including German soldiers). A 73-year-old woman reported the following situation as her most negative memory from the period of the war (my translation):

> I was on the train from Hellerup together with my father some time in 1940–1941. A German soldier was sitting opposite to us, and with all my childish attitude I looked at him rather grumpily. He bent forward and said: "Can't you smile at all?" I could not, but the episode remains so clear in my memory, contemplated through the years—he presumably had children at home in Germany?

Almost all of our participants reported that they had a FBM for both the news of the German invasion on 9 April 1940 and the announcement of the liberation on 4 May 1945. And indeed most of the participants were able to provide rather detailed descriptions of their personal contexts for the reception of these news events. Memory descriptions for the invasion suggested that, in many cases, the news of the invasion did not immediately cause an emotional reaction, consistent with the view presented in Figure 9.2. The appropriate reaction in many cases had to be learned through the observation of others, often authority figures such as school teachers or parents. Frequently, the emotional reaction was described as being delayed as an effect of such social learning processes. In such cases, the emotional reaction might be classified as contagion (see Figure 9.2). Consider a few examples to make the point (my translations):

I was a student at the agriculture school . . . We saw the planes and later the ships from the windows. All the students were brought together in the lecture hall and a highly moved vice-chancellor announced that Denmark had become occupied. Then we all sang the national hymns with a sincerity that probably surprised us all. What made the strongest impression on me was that the vice-chancellor cried. This was the first time in my life that I saw an adult man crying . . .

(Male, 81 years old)

I had had my confirmation on 7 April and I was supposed to have my communion in the cathedral in Aarhus on 9 April [the day of the invasion]. I do not remember my parents' reaction [to the news of the invasion] but my own was a worry that now I might not be able to go to Aarhus (we lived far out in the countryside). Juvenile egoism! Later the same day I realized how horrible the news in fact was, when I was in the cathedral, listening to the grave speech of the priest.

(Female, 77 years old)

Compared to memories for the invasion, memories for the liberation were scored significantly higher on almost all measures of subjective clarity. They were also rated as more rehearsed and associated with stronger emotion at the time of the event (see Berntsen & Thomsen, 2005). Because various analyses ruled out that this advantage was due to the liberation taking place 5 years later in the participants' lives, and because both of the events could be considered as highly important for this particular historical period (of which they represented the beginning and end, respectively), there was no obvious explanation for the advantage of the liberation memory. One possible, although speculative, explanation is that this advantage was due to the fact that according to historical analyses the liberation had been much more commemorated over the years than the invasion, and the related fact that this event has played (and still plays) a much more positive role for the Danish national identity than the invasion. As summarized by Kirchhoff, Lauridsen, and Trommer (2002, p. 251; my translation):

> Of all the events [from 1940 to 1945] the liberation day became clearly the most important. In comparison, the day of the invasion . . . was associated with greater potential for conflict. For the liberation day, the happy ending of the war, the national reconciliation between politicians and the resistance and the international recognition of Denmark as an allied nation could be used as a perspective for the interpretation of all the years of the occupation and point forward towards a postwar society . . .

Thus, the liberation day agrees with central values of the Danish national identity, such as democracy and freedom, whereas the day of the invasion challenges such positive self-perception, because the Danish army gave in after only 3 hours of resistance and because the Danish government stayed in power and collaborated with the Wehrmacht for the following 3 years (e.g., Kirchhoff et al., 2002).

In addition to being associated with more subjective clarity, many memory reports of the liberation appeared to be scripted in a way that seemed motivated by the positive historical value of this event in relation to the Danish national identity. Roughly half of the memory reports included one or more of the following details: the Danish flag, removing (and often burning) the dark shades that the Wehrmacht had demanded should cover the windows at night, lighting candles in the windows, finding "goodies" (e.g., tobacco, chocolate, coffee, wine) saved from the time before the war. The symbolic value of the Danish flag in relation to national identity is obvious. Replacing dark shades with burning candles is easily seen as a symbolic victory of light over darkness. Finding goodies saved from the time before the occupation can be seen as a symbolic restoration of a temporarily lost world. Such symbolic meaning may explain why exactly these details were salient in many of our participants' liberation memories, as illustrated by this report from an 83-year-old female (my translation):

> I was at home, because we knew that something might happen soon. But even though we were prepared for it [the capitulation], we did not fully understand it right away. We were like paralysed. But then it came. We shouted and cried. Shortly after my father came in with a wrinkled flag, which he nailed to a broomstick, and then with my father in front we— my mother and I—went out on our balcony and raised the Danish flag. I will never forget that moment. . . . Then we ran into the streets and celebrated with all the others. Around ten o'clock there was some shooting, and we went home. At home my mother had roasted, grinded and made *real* coffee. In all our windows, she had lit candles. Soon my home was filled with people, known as well as unknown—and then we were singing, while my brother was playing the piano, and we continued till 3 o'clock at

night. May 4th and 5th [the liberation dates] are among the greatest memories from my life.

Such symbolic meaning of details may help to explain distortions in FBM reports. Even though most participants were able to provide accurate reports of the weather on the days of the invasion and liberations, systematic biases were also found. For the invasion such biases presented the weather as worse than it had actually been (worse operationalized as less sun, lower temperature, more wind, more precipitation than the objective weather data) whereas the opposite was true for the day of the liberation (see Berntsen & Thomsen, 2005, for details). Rather than simply viewing such distortions as reflecting emotions at the level of the individual (light and warmth being standard metaphors for positive emotion, darkness and cold for negative emotions), the effects may reflect the role of the invasion and liberation in the national discourse. The years of the German occupation are often described as "the five dark years" and the day of the invasion was the beginning of the dark years, thus itself a dark day (although it was bright and sunny according to the objective weather data). The liberation, on the other hand, has been celebrated as the victory of light over darkness.

SUMMARY AND CONCLUDING COMMENTS

Ironically, a very nice summary of social identity theory is found in Roger Brown's (1986) social psychology book. It is surprising that he and James Kulik ignored this theory when developing their model of FBMs. In Brown and Kulik's (1977) original model of FBMs, the causal mechanisms are found at the level of the individual, in terms of individual experiences of surprise and consequentiality. The same is true for the subsequent revisions of this model. FBM research has thus shared that emphasis on cognitive and emotional processes at the level of the individual that is generally found in psychology (e.g., see Berntsen & Rubin, 2004; Ellemers et al., 2002, for discussions). At the same time, research into FBMs is characterized by a number of inconsistencies that may be resolved by reference to social factors that extend beyond cognitive and emotional variables at the level of the individual. Here I have suggested that the activation of a person's social identity is a crucial factor for the development and maintenance of FBMs. The main evidence for this claim is that membership in social groups shows consistent effect in almost all FBM studies that have examined this issue. Factors related to social identity and group maintenance may also be able to account for some biases and distortions in FBMs.

One advantage of basing a FBM model on the notion of social identity is that it resolves some of the contradictions that are left unresolved by previous models. As illustrated in Figure 9.2, social identity may enhance memory consolidation and maintenance via three different paths: (1) by enhancing the initial emotional reaction to the new event, (2) by enhancing initial emotional reaction as well as subsequent rehearsal, and (3) by enhancing rehearsal through public means without any remarkable initial emotional reaction by the person at the time of the event. Invoking the notion of social identity as a cognitive and social construct therefore allows us to explain why FBMs sometimes occur in response to strong emotion without identifiable effects of rehearsal (Pillemer, 1984), why they sometimes appear to be an effect of both strong emotion and rehearsal (e.g., Finkenauer et al., 1998), and why they sometimes appear to be primarily a rehearsal effect (Otani et al., 2005). The main point is that such traditional FBM factors correlate with the activation of social identity in ways that are partly dependent on the nature of the target event and its cultural and social context. They are not the key mechanisms. FBMs develop as a result of a public event bringing to the foreground a person's identification with a social group affected by the event. Having a FBM testifies to "belongingness" and identification with the group.

NOTE

1   The work reported here was supported by a grant from the Danish Research Council for the Humanities.

REFERENCES

Baumeister, R. F., & Hastings, S. (1997). Distortions of collective memory: How groups flatter and deceive themselves. In J. W. Pennebaker, D. Páez, & B. Rimé (Eds.), *Collective memory for political events. Social psychological perspectives* (pp. 277–293). Mahwah, NJ: Lawrence Erlbaum Associates Inc.

Berntsen, D. (2002). Tunnel memories for autobiographical events: Central details are remembered more frequently from shocking than from happy experiences. *Memory and Cognition, 30*, 1010–1020.

Berntsen, D. (2005). *Lidt skydning i gaderne tog vi ret roligt . . . En psykologisk tematisering af erindringsbilleder fra Danmarks besættelse 1940–45 [A little shooting in the streets didn't bother us much . . . Autobiographical memories from the German occupation of Denmark 1940–45 from a psychological perspective]*. Aarhus: Klim.

Berntsen, D., & Rubin, D. C. (2004). Cultural life scripts structure recall from autobiographical memory. *Memory and Cognition, 32*, 427–442.

Berntsen, D., & Rubin, D. C. (2006). Flashbulb memories and posttraumatic stress reactions across the life-span: Age-related effects of the German occupation of Denmark during WWII. *Psychology and Aging, 21*, 127–139.

Berntsen, D., & Thomsen, D. K. (2005). Personal memories for remote historical events. Accuracy and clarity for flashbulb memories related to WWII. *Journal of Experimental Psychology: General, 134*, 242–257.

Bohannon, J. N. III (1988). Flashbulb memories for the space shuttle disaster: A tale of two stories. *Cognition, 29*, 179–196.

Bohn, A., & Berntsen, D. (2007). Pleasantness bias in flashbulb memories: Positive and negative flashbulb memories of the fall of the Berlin wall. *Memory and Cognition, 35,* 565–577.

Brown, R. (1986). *Social psychology* (2nd ed.). New York: The Free Press.

Brown, R., & Kulik, J. (1977). Flashbulb memories. *Cognition, 5,* 73–99.

Christianson, S-Å. (1992). Emotional stress and eyewitness memory: A critical review. *Psychological Bulletin, 112,* 284–309.

Conway, M. A., Anderson, S. J., Larsen, S. F., Donnelly, C. M., McDaniel, M. A., McClelland, A. G. R., et al. (1994). The formation of flashbulb memories. *Memory and Cognition, 22,* 326–343.

Curci, A., & Luminet, O. (2006). Follow-up of a cross national comparison on flashbulb and event memory for the September 11th attacks. *Memory, 14,* 329–344.

Curci, A., Luminet, O., Finkenauer, C., & Gisle, L. (2001). Flashbulb memories in social groups: A comparative test-retest study of the memory of the French President Mitterrand's death in a French and a Belgian group. *Memory, 9,* 81–101.

Deschamps, J.-C., & Devos, T. (1998). Regarding the relationship between social identity and personal identity. In S. Worchel, J. F. Morales, D. Páez, & J-C. Deschamps (Eds.), *Social identity, international perspectives* (pp. 1–12). London: Sage.

Edery-Halpern, G., & Nachson, I. (2004). Distinctiveness in flashbulb memory: Comparative analysis of five terrorist attacks, *Memory, 12,* 147–157.

Ellemers, N., Spears, R., & Doosje, B. (2002). Self and social identity. *Annual Review of Psychology, 53,* 161–186.

Er, N. (2003). A new flashbulb memory model applied to the Marmara earthquake. *Applied Cognitive Psychology, 17,* 503–517.

Finkenauer, C., Luminet, O., Gisle, L., El-Ahmadi, A., Van der Linden, M., & Philippot, P. (1998). Flashbulb memories and the underlying mechanisms of their formation: Toward an emotional-integrative model. *Memory and Cognition, 26,* 516–531.

Frijda, N. H. (1997). Commemorating. In J. W. Pennebaker, D. Páez, & B. Rimé (Eds.), *Collective memory for political events. Social psychological perspectives* (pp. 103–127). Mahwah, NJ: Lawrence Erlbaum Associates Inc.

Gaskell, G. D., & Wright, D. B. (1997). Group differences in memory for a political event. In J. W. Pennebaker, D. Páez, & B. Rimé (Eds.), *Collective memory for political events. Social psychological perspectives* (pp. 175–189). Mahwah, NJ: Lawrence Erlbaum Associates Inc.

Kirchhoff, H., Lauridsen, J. T., & Trommer, A. (2002). *Gads leksikon om dansk besættelsestid 1940–1945 [Gad's encyclopaedia about the occupation of Denmark, 1940–45].* Copenhagen: Gad's Forlag.

Kvavilashvili, L., Mirani, J., Schlagman, S., & Kornbrot, D. E. (2003). Comparing flashbulb memories of September 11 and the death of Princess Diana: Effects of time delay and nationality. *Applied Cognitive Psychology, 17,* 1017–1031.

Luminet, O., Curci, A., Marsh, E. J., Wessel, I., Constantin, T., Gencoz, F., et al. (2004). The cognitive, emotional, and social impacts of the September 11 attacks: Group differences in memory for the reception context and the determinants of flashbulb memory. *Journal of General Psychology, 131,* 197–224.

Mahmood, D., Manier, D., & Hirst, W. (2004). Memory for how one learned of multiple deaths from AIDS: Repeated exposure and distinctiveness. *Memory and Cognition, 32,* 125–133.

Maslow, A. H. (1943). A theory of human motivation. *Psychological Review, 50,* 370–396.

Morse, C. K., Woodward, E. K., & Zweigenhaft, R. L. (1993). Gender differences in flashbulb memories elicited by the Clarence Thomas hearings. *Journal of Social Psychology*, *133*, 453–458.

Nachson, I., & Zelig, A. (2003). Flashbulb and factual memories: The case of Rabin's assassination. *Applied Cognitive Psychology*, *17*, 519–531.

Neisser, U. (1982). Snapshots or benchmarks? In U. Neisser (Ed.), *Memory observed. Remembering in natural contexts* (pp. 43–49). San Francisco: Freeman.

Neisser, U., & Harsch, N. (1992). Phantom flashbulbs: False recollections of hearing the news about *Challenger*. In E. Winograd & U. Neisser (Eds.), *Affect and accuracy in recall: Studies of "flashbulb memories"* (pp. 9–32). Cambridge, UK: Cambridge University Press.

Neisser, U., Winograd, E., Bergman, E. T., Schreiber, C. A., Palmer, S. E., & Weldon, M. S. (1996). Remembering the earthquake: Direct experience vs hearing the news. *Memory*, *4*, 337–357.

Otani, H., Kusumi, T., Kato., K., Matsuda, K., Kern. R. P., Widner, R., et al. (2005). Remembering a nuclear accident in Japan: Did it trigger flashbulb memories? *Memory*, *13*, 6–20.

Pezdek, K. (2003). Event memory and autobiographical memory for the events of September 11, 2001. *Applied Cognitive Psychology*, *17*, 1033–1045.

Pillemer, D. B. (1984). Flashbulb memories of the assassination attempt on President Reagan. *Cognition*, *16*, 63–80.

Rosch, E. (1978). Principles of categorization. In E. Rosch & B. Lloyd (Eds.), *Cognition and categorization* (pp. 27–46). Hillsdale, NJ: Lawrence Erlbaum Associates Inc.

Rubin, D. C., & Kozin, M. (1984). Vivid memories. *Cognition*, *16*, 81–95.

Shapiro, L. (2006). Remember September 11th: The role of retention interval and rehearsal on flashbulb and event memory. *Memory*, *14*, 129–147.

Sharot, T., Martorella, E. A., Delgado, M. R., & Phelps, E. A. (2007). How personal experience modulates the neural circuitry of memories of September 11. *Proceedings of the National Academy of Sciences*, *104*, 389–394.

Sierra, M., & Berrios, G. E. (1999). Flashbulb memories and other repetitive images: A psychiatric perspective. *Comprehensive Psychiatry*, *40*, 115–125.

Smith, M. C., Bibi, U., & Sheard, D. E. (2003). Evidence for the differential impact of time and emotion on personal and event memories from September 11, 2001. *Applied Cognitive Psychology*, *17*, 1047–1055.

Tajfel, H. (Ed.). (1982). *Social identity and intergroup relations*. Cambridge, UK: Cambridge University Press.

Talarico, J. M., & Rubin, D. C. (2003). Confidence, not consistency, characterizes flashbulb memories. *Psychological Science*, *14*, 455–461.

Tekcan, A. I., Ece, B., Gülgöz, S., Nurham, E. (2003). Autobiographical and event memory for 9/11: Changes across one year. *Applied Cognitive Psychology*, *17*, 1057–1066.

Tekcan, A. I., & Peynircioglu, Z. F. (2002). Effects of age on flashbulb memories. *Psychology and Aging*, *17*, 416–422.

Thomsen, D., & Berntsen, D. (2003). Snapshots from therapy: Exploring operationalizations and ways of studying flashbulb memories for private events. *Memory*, *11*, 559–570.

Turner, J. (1982). Toward a cognitive redefinition of the social group. In H. Tajfel (Ed.), *Social identity and intergroup relations* (pp. 15–40). Cambridge, UK: Cambridge University Press.

Winograd, E., & Killinger, W. A. Jr. (1983). Relating age at encoding in early childhood to adult recall: Development of flashbulb memories. *Journal of Experimental Psychology: General, 112*, 413–422.

Worchel, S., Morales, J. F., Páez, D., & Deschamps, J.-C. (Eds). (1998). *Social identity, international perspectives*. London: Sage.

Wright, D. B., Gaskell, G. D., & O'Muircheartaigh, C. A. (1998). Flashbulb memory assumptions: Using national surveys to explore cognitive phenomena. *British Journal of Psychology, 89*, 103–121.

Yarmey, A. D., & Bull, M.P. (1978). Where were you when president Kennedy was assassinated? *Bulletin of the Psychonomic Society, 11*, 133–135.

10 A social-interactional approach to the retention of collective memories of flashbulb events[1]

William Hirst and Robert Meksin

Flashbulb memories (FBMs) are memories of the circumstances in which a person learned about a newsworthy public event. In this chapter we want to depart from the usual practice in studies of FBMs and concentrate not on the FBM itself, but the memory of the event that gave rise to the FBM. One reason why scholars have been so fascinated by FBMs is that they point to the rare instances in which the autobiographical intersects with the collective (Neisser, 1982). Most historically important events may find themselves incorporated into the collective memory a community has of its past, but people rarely remember where and when they learned about them (Larsen, 1992). The appointment of Judge Alito to the Supreme Court may figure in the American collective memory, but only a few Americans possess a clear FBM of the circumstances in which they learned of the final confirmation of his appointment. What is extraordinary about flashbulb-memory-inducing events (henceforth, FB events) is that they become incorporated into both a community's collective memory and community members' individual autobiographies. Americans remember both the events of 9/11 and the circumstances in which they learned about them.

When viewed this way, it seems as important to know something about the memories people form of FB events (which we will refer to simply as *event memories*) as the memories they form of the circumstances in which they learn of the event (FBMs). How well retained are event memories? Does their retention differ from FBMs? And how do memories for FB events differ from memories of non-flashbulb, but nevertheless newsworthy, public events?

We employ the term *collective memory* here because FBMs and memories for FB events are associated with communities, not groups of unrelated individuals. In particular, members of one community, and not another, are more likely to form FBMs and event memories than are members of another community, in part because the FB event is consequential for only one of the communities (see Berntsen, Chapter 10, and Wang & Aydın, Chapter 12, this volume). As Brown and Kulik (1977) uncovered, African-Americans were more likely to form FBMs of the assassination of Malcolm X than were European-Americans. Similarly, in a study by Kvavilashvili, Mirani, Schlagman, and Kornbrot (2003), British participants were more likely to report, after a delay of 51 months, FBMs for the death of Princess Diana than were Italians. As for memory for the event itself, Curci and Luminet (2006; see also Luminet et al., 2004) found that Americans had better event memory for the terrorist attack of September 11, 2001 than did non-Americans (see also Curci, Luminet, Finkenauer, & Gisle, 2001).

There are at least two approaches one could use to study the collective memories a community forms of a FB event. One could adopt what we will call an interpretative approach. What meaning does the collective memory have for the community? Does the meaning usually assigned to collective memories for FB events differ from the meaning usually assigned to other types of collective memories? However, we are concerned here with the second approach, which focuses on mechanisms or processes, not interpretations. That is, we want to uncover the underlying mechanisms or processes that lead to the formation of a collective memory of a FB event, and to discover whether these mechanisms or processes differ from those involved in the formation of a FBM or the formation of other types of collective memory. In the end, like autobiographical memory, the mechanisms are reconstructive in nature (Anderson & Conway, 1997; Conway & Pleydell-Pearce, 2000; Conway & Rubin, 1993). The question here is: What is the nature of these mechanisms?

These mechanisms could be intrapsychic—such as those involved in the impact of emotional change on memory—or social-interactional. Social-interactional explanations are particularly important when discussing the formation of collective memories because memories probably become shared across a community due to what happens outside the individual, not within the individual. In examining social-interactional explanations, we want to focus on the memory practices of the community—that is, how the community deals mnemonically with a newsworthy event. A community will often make a commitment to discuss and explore a news event, with some events eliciting a high level of commitment, others a lesser level. Moreover, the practices in which a community engages, in order to fulfil their commitment, will differ from event to event. In examining his memory for news events, Larsen (1992) noted that some news events received extended media coverage, whereas others were merely commented on in the media for one or, at most, two days. Thus, the importance of the Alito confirmation was marked by live television coverage of confirmation hearings, but this level of commitment fell short of the extensive, all-day-long media coverage of the terrorist attack of 9/11.

These considerations lead us to the basic question that we will address in this paper: How do the memory practices associated with FB events, in particular the pattern of media coverage, influence the character of the collective memory formed of the FB event? And how can the media practices associated with other "non-flashbulb" events also shape their character as collective memories? Media coverage might also affect the formation of the FBM itself—in that it reminds people of the circumstances in which they learned of the event (Curci & Luminet, 2006). Our interest here is in its effect on memory for the FB event itself.

Media coverage is mainly thought of as a means of informing the public, but it is also widely recognized as a memory practice undertaken by the community, or at least by authorities in the community, to shape the community's memory (Hoskins, 2007; Iyengar & Kinder, 1987). At a minimum, the media can shape a community's memory because it serves as an externally driven initiator of rehearsal. People, of course, can rehearse an item privately, at their own discretion. The media essentially tells people what to rehearse and establishes at least a minimum level of rehearsal. Each repeated presentation of the news event on television reinforces the observer's memory of the event. Moreover, as a public conveyance, the media does not initiate rehearsal merely in one individual, but in a large segment of a community. In other words, it offers a good means of shaping and reinforcing not just individual memory but also collective memory.

Of course, there are other ways in which the memory of a community can be reinforced though the memory practices of a community. Indeed, most scholars treat commemoration and memorialization as the main means by which a community remembers (see, for instance, Gillis, 1994). However, we want to focus on media coverage—broadly conceived here to include not just television, but radio, newspaper, movies, books, Internet, and so on—because it seems to play such a critical role in FB events.

We want to examine the consequences of different patterns of media coverage on the collective memory a community forms of news events, both FB events and other newsworthy events. Our interest is not on short-term, but long-term effects, inasmuch as collective memories are important because of their lasting influence on collective identity (see Berntsen, Chapter 9, Páez, Bellelli, & Rimé, Chapter 11 and Wang & Aydın, Chapter 12, in this volume).

MEMORY FOR FBM-INDUCING EVENTS

In studying the effects of media on event memory, we will mainly be focusing on the issue of rate of forgetting, specifically whether the pattern of the rate of forgetting of collective memories of FB events differs from the pattern of the rate of forgetting of FBMs and other types of collective memories. Moreover, we will explore the relation of these patterns of forgetting to the media coverage that surrounds the event.

A dilemma: Different patterns for forgetting found for memories of FB events

We might begin to explore the pattern of forgetting observed for FB events by comparing them with the pattern of forgetting observed for FBMs, confining ourselves to the few studies that probe both FBMs and event memories.

Among these studies there seems to be agreement that consistency for FBMs in some cases remains stable over time, and in other cases declines the first year, but whatever the rate of forgetting in the first year, forgetting appears to level off at some point, often around a year or so, with some aspects of the memory still preserved for years, if not decades (Berntsen & Thomsen, 2005; Bohannon, 1988; Bohannon & Symons, 1992; Kvavilashvili et al., 2003; Neisser & Harsh, 1992; Shapiro, 2006; Smith, Bibi, & Sheard, 2003; Tekcan, Berivan, Gülgöz, & Er, 2003; Weaver & Krug, 2004; also see Talarico & Rubin, 2003).[2] In most of these studies, consistency is measured by comparing not simply whether two memories were similar across testing sessions, but also the level of detail and completeness of the memory.

There is less agreement about the pattern of forgetting observed for event memory. In most of the relevant studies the investigator often posed three or more questions about the FB event and then coded the responses as to their accuracy, but also in many cases, as with FBMs, the level of detail and completeness. In one of the earliest studies examining event memory, which probed memories for the *Challenger* explosion, Bohannon and Symons (1992) found that, whereas forgetting essentially stopped at the 8-month interval for FBMs, event memories continued to decline, for instance, 20% between the 15-month and 36-month intervals. Other studies are consistent with Bohannon and Symons' claim of continual forgetting, although they do not examine memory over a long enough period to justify a strong conclusion. Tekcan et al. (2003), for instance, examined Turkish citizens' memory for 9/11, probing 3 days, 6 months, and 1 year after the attack. The consistency in the autobiographical FBMs remained unchanged across the three time intervals, with no more than 3% variation from one time interval to the next. On the other hand, there was a 28% decline in accuracy between the first and second testing period for event memory. The decline was not as drastic between the second and third testing periods, but it was still perceptible (9%). Smith et al. (2003) reported similar findings, exploring Canadians' memory of the 9/11 attack. They found that accuracy for event memory continued to decline over a 6-month period, whereas the number of remembered personal information details actually increased.

In a large study for memory for the attacks of September 11, Hirst, Phelps, and colleagues (2008) found a different pattern. They probed for FBMs and event memories 2 weeks, 11 months, and 35 months after the attack. Unlike many other studies, they assessed FBMs and event memories in an all-or-nothing fashion: A memory was consistent or accurate or it was not. Their measure was significantly correlated with the more traditional graded measures. Hirst, Phelps, and colleagues found the same pattern of forgetting for FB and event memory. In assessing event memory, they asked questions such as "How many planes were involved?", "Where was President Bush when he heard about the attack?", and "What time did the first plane hit the World Trade Tower?" For FBMs there was a consistency score of .63 for their participants' FBM at 11 months, whereas the match between the initial report at Week 2 and the third-year report was a slightly lower .57. ("1" would be the highest; "0" the lowest.) The pattern was the same for event memory: Participants got an average of .88 of the five questions they were asked about details of the terrorist attack correct 2 weeks after the attack, whereas they got an average of .77 and .78 of them correct after 11 month and 35 months, respectively. The size of the sample (overall, more than 3000) and the diversity of the sample (from across the United States) make it difficult to discount the findings.

It would appear, then, that unlike FBMs the pattern of forgetting observed with event memory differs from study to study: Some studies observed asymptotic levelling of forgetting after about a year, other studies observed continuous forgetting over the long term. Of course, these differences might be traced to different methodologies across studies, but we suspect that more theoretical explanations are possible.

Explaining the dilemma: An intrapsychic explanation

Pezdek (2003) has offered what might be viewed as a possible intrapsychic explanation of the differences just noted. She hypothesized that members of different communities assign different levels of emotional attachment to the event. For Pezdek, what she called emotional attachment varies with the extent to which individuals participated in the event. By that we assume she means the degree to which an individual feels a strong emotional response to the event. Pezdek examined the 9/11 attack, collecting responses 7 weeks after the attack from individuals who resided in New York City, California, and Hawaii. Although this single-probe methodology did not allow Pezdek to study the consistency of FBMs over time (indeed, Pezdek classified a memory as "flashbulb" solely on the basis of its vividness), she could contrast the amount of detail in these memories with the accuracy of event memories. Of interest here is her finding that the New Yorkers in her sample generally evidenced better event memory than the Californians or the Hawaiians. This superior event memory occurred despite the inferior FBM that New Yorkers showed when compared to the Californians and Hawaiians. Pezdek speculated that because they were more involved with the unfolding events of September 11, New Yorkers responded emotionally to the event more than the Californians or the Hawaiians did. Consequently, they remembered the details of the events better than Californians or Hawaiians. On the other hand, the chief emotional response of the Californians and the Hawaiians was to the circumstance in which they learned of the event, hence their superior FBMs. This line of reasoning could also account for Nachson and Zelig's (2003) finding that event memory for the assassination of Prime Minister Rabin 11 months after the event was better than the corresponding FBM in that, given the size and history of Israel, Israelis are likely to have a strong emotional response to the assassination, especially since one Jew killed another.

Following a similar line of reasoning, we might expect a more rapid rate of forgetting for event memory over FBM as emotional response to the event declines. Thus Tekcan et al. (2003) and Smith et al. (2003) found a faster decay rate for event memories than for FBMs because they were looking at people who had not been "living through" the events of 9/11, respectively Turks and Canadians. Similarly, Curci and Luminet (2006) showed that whereas FBMs were well preserved over time in their global sample, event memories declined over time, with the rate of decline greater for the European and Asian subsamples than the American subsample. On the other hand, in the Hirst et al. (2008) data there were no substantial differences in their sample between those who resided in New York City and those who resided in Californian cities (specifically, San Francisco, Los Angeles, Palo Alto, and Santa Cruz). The consistency measure for FBMs 11 months after the attack was .59 for New York City residents and .61 for the Californian cities. The measure for accuracy for facts at an 11-month retention interval was .81 and .80, respectively.

A social-interactional explanation

As we stated in the introduction, whereas intrapsychic explanations can no doubt account to a significant degree for the rate of forgetting observed for both FBMs and event memories, our interest is mainly in social-interactional explanations, in that social-interactional explanations are more likely to bear on issues of collective memory than intrapsychic ones. Specifically, we build on our assertion that media coverage might be important.

FB events involve both an explosion of media coverage in the first few weeks after the initiating event and, in many cases, continued media coverage for years to come (Bouvier, 2005; Dayan & Katz, 1992). Several studies of FBM and event memory have specifically asked about the extent to which participants rehearsed, thought about, and talked about either the circumstance in which they learned of the FB event or the event itself, or probed for the extent to which participants attended to the media (e.g., Bohannon & Symons, 1992; Christianson, 1989, 1992; Finkenauer et al., 1998; Mahmood, Manier, & Hirst, 2004; McCloskey, Wible, & Cohen, 1988; Neisser et al., 1996; Otani et al., 2005; Wright, 1993). These studies generally find a positive correlation between the self-report of extent of rehearsal and the accuracy of event memory. Most models of FBMs reflect this correlation by positing a direct connection between rehearsal and event memory (Brown & Kulik, 1977; Conway et al., 1994; Er, 2003; Finkenauer et al., 1998).

Many of these studies, and the extant models, do not distinguish between the effects of internally driven acts of rehearsal (e.g., thinking about it) and externally driven acts of rehearsal (e.g., media coverage). The former would more accurately be characterized as a memory practice of an individual, not a community, and could properly be viewed as intrapsychic. Our interest, however, is in a community's intentional or unintentional efforts to remember an event. That is, we are interested in externally driven acts of rehearsal, not internally driven ones. Media coverage is the quintessential externally driven act of rehearsal.

Only a few studies have explicitly focused on the role of media in the maintenance of FBMs and event memories. They generally find that media coverage affects event memories, but not FBMs (Curci & Luminet, 2006; Er, 2003; Shapiro, 2006). The results usually examine whether media coverage, or attention to the media, affects consistency or accuracy overall. For example, Curci and Luminet (2006) found in their study of 9/11 that attention to the media varied across the multi-nation sample and that this difference could provide a partial account of why there were national variations in the accuracy of event memory. However, no study provides a fine-grained analysis of changes, in which they track changes in media coverage and changes in the rate of forgetting. Consequently, the extant work does not address straightforwardly the dilemma that partially motivates this chapter—that some studies find a continual decline in memories for FB events, whereas others find an asymptote forming after about a year.

As already hinted at, we suspect that this difference between studies can be traced, at least in part, to a difference in the pattern of media coverage. At least in the first few weeks, perhaps months, we suspect that media coverage is similar across FB events. There is intense media coverage in almost all the examples of FB events we can think of. It is around the first anniversary when differences emerge. For some events, there is a new burst of coverage with each new anniversary, as well as sporadic media attention between anniversaries. For other events, the initial interest cannot be sustained. So 9/11 receives immense media coverage as each anniversary approaches; the anniversaries of the verdict in the O. J. Simpson trial go substantially unobserved, even though interest in O. J. Simpson (though not necessarily his trial) continues.

It seems reasonable to assume that the initial burst of media coverage may play a critical role in eliciting a strong memory for the event per se and facilitating the formation of the FBM itself (Bohannon & Symons, 1992; Christianson, 1989; Finkenauer et al., 1998; Mahmood et al., 2004; McCloskey et al., 1988; Neisser et al., 1996; Otani et al., 2005; Wright, 1993). But what happens after this initial burst? The extant work suggests that the memory for the event itself will, at least initially, begin to decay (Bohannon & Symons, 1992; Finkenauer et al., 1998; Nachson & Zelig, 2003; Smith et al., 2003; Tekcan et al., 2003; Wolters & Goudsmit, 2005). Most of these studies rarely involve retention interval of more than a year or so. In other words, they do not examine a period of time long enough to capture the difference in media coverage we are positing. With the burst of media coverage that occurs around anniversaries, forgetting might be arrested, with even the possibility of an asymptotic levelling of forgetting emerging around the first-year anniversary. Of course, the coverage over years may probably occur in spurts, for instance at anniversaries. A fine-grained analysis might find not asymptotic forgetting after the first year, but initial improvement that subsides over time until the memory is once again refreshed by anniversary coverage. However, a gross analysis would suggest that performance has levelled off.

It is possible, then, that memories for FB events might asymptote after a year when the media observes anniversaries, but would continue to decay after a year when it does not. We can test this hypothesis by looking at the two FBM studies that have examined event memory over a 3-year period— Bohannon and Symons' (1992) study of the *Challenger* explosion and Hirst and colleagues' (2008) study of 9/11. Although it would be better if we could compare results across a number of studies instead of just two, we firmly believe that the two available studies investigated typical FB events, in that both events were public and extremely shocking.

Figure 10.1 plots the drop in accuracy of the event memory over a 3-year period and a rough estimate of the drop in the amount of media coverage of the events between each memory probe. In order to make the time period comparable, we divide the time line into three periods of 1 month in length: the first month after the event, month 11 after the event, and month 35 after the event.[3] We estimate the 9/11 media coverage by using the *New York Times* index service to determine the number of articles in the *Times* in which the phrase "September 11" appeared. We then calculate the proportion of mentions over the number of days in the targeted period. Finally, using these three proportions, we calculate z-scores for each period. Other probes might

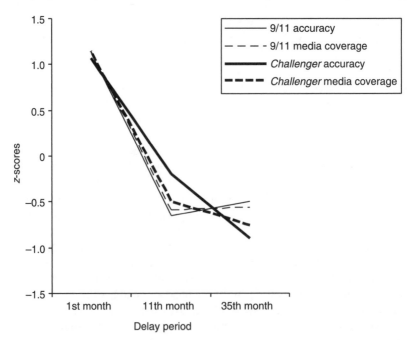

Figure 10.1 Relation between media coverage and memory accuracy for facts about a FB event: the *Challenger* explosion and the terrorist attack of September 11, 2001.

have produced different absolute numbers, but they probably would not have affected the pattern of the z-scores for 9/11. In the first 2 weeks, there was extensive coverage. This coverage dropped off dramatically over the next 11 months. The level of coverage did not decline after the 11-month period, remaining fairly consistent up to the third anniversary. As Figure 10.1 indicates, this pattern nicely mirrors the pattern of forgetting that Hirst et al. (2008) observed for event memory. In order to facilitate comparison, we recalibrate Hirst et al.'s accuracy scores to z-scores calculated across the three time periods. We found a similar pattern when we used *The Boston Globe* and *U.S. News and World Report* as reference texts.

As we noted, Bohannon and Symons (1992) found a different pattern of forgetting, with forgetting continuing throughout the 3-year period. We once again tabulated the extent of media coverage over the three time periods in Figure 10.1, now using the disjunction of "Challenger" and "Explosion" as our probe in our *New York Times* survey. We also recalibrated Bohannon and Symons' accuracy scores to obtain z-scores. As Figure 10.1 indicates, unlike the pattern observed for the terrorist attack of September 11, media coverage continued to decline after the 11-month marker, paralleling the continued decline in memory. Again, the pattern was similar for *U.S. News and World Report*. *The Boston Globe* does not provide an indexing system back to 1986.

These findings would suggest that the asymptotic forgetting that Hirst et al. (2008) found and the continuous forgetting Bohannon and Symons discovered can be traced at least in part to the different patterns of media coverage for 9/11 and the *Challenger* explosion.

Could media coverage also explain why the event memory for 9/11 evidenced continuous forgetting in Smith et al. (2003) and Tekcan et al. (2003)? It is more difficult to obtain comparable data on media coverage for Turkish and Canadian newspapers. We can, however, examine the amount of coverage on the third anniversary of these tragedies on major television channels with a commitment to news in each of these countries. Specifically, we contrast the level of coverage on CBS in the US, the CBC in Canada, and TRT-2 in Turkey. On September 11, 2004, during these television channels' prime time hours, CBS devoted the entire time to 9/11-related material, and the CBC 50% of the time. TRT-2 did not have any programme devoted solely to 9/11. Although there may be several routes to the more rapid forgetting of event information observed in the Tekcan and Smith study, in contrast to the Hirst et al. study these television and newspaper statistics suggest that media coverage may play a role. It is worth reiterating in this context that Curci and Luminet (2006) found in their 9/11 study that attention to the media varied across nations. Moreover, those participants from countries associated with limited media attention evidenced worse event memory than those from countries with good media attention.

One might trace these observations not to the effect of rehearsal, but to interest. People who are interested in the tragedy pay more attention to the media, presumably making interest as likely a candidate for driving accuracy as the rehearsal itself. Although interest no doubt has a direct bearing on accuracy, the rehearsal benefit of media probably does as well. Whereas interest might explain why a memory might decay more slowly over time, it is unlikely to account for an improvement after an extended decay.

Hirst et al. (2008) found just such improvement by examining the effect of Michael Moore's film *Fahrenheit 911* on memory for President Bush's location when he heard of the attack. After Andrew Card whispered to Bush that there was a second plane crash and "The nation was under attack", Bush sat listening to the schoolchildren read *The Pet Goat* for a full 6 minutes before getting up and leaving. Moore included this 6 minutes in his film, a long segment that clearly attracted the audience's attention. When Hirst et al. contrasted the overall event memories of those who had seen the Moore film with those who had not, they found no difference between the two groups in the first survey at Week 2 in their memory for Bush's location (.87 and .86, respectively) and a marked but uniform decay in performance between Survey 1 and Survey 2. (Performance on Survey 2 was .60 and .54, respectively.) On Survey 3, however, which was given approximately a month after the film's release, those who saw the film showed a dramatic improvement (.91 of the participants correctly remembered Bush's location), whereas those who did not see the movie showed a much smaller improvement (.71). This enhanced improvement in the Moore watchers is most likely traced to the enduring effect the movie had on its viewers' memories. We suspect that the improvement for the non-moviegoers reflected the media coverage that surrounded the film.

Thus, the asymptotic levelling of forgetting one observes for at least some FB events may reflect, at least in part, the continued media coverage that occurs over long periods of time. If media coverage is not present over several years, forgetting is more likely to continue.

A further exploration into the effects of media: Is intense initial media coverage enough to produce asymptotic forgetting after a year?

We are suggesting, then, that the initial spurt of media coverage is not the cause for the 1-year asymptote in forgetting that we observe for some, but not all, FB events. Although this initial explosion accompanies all FB events, what seems to create the early asymptote is whether there is sustained coverage of the events, not just for a few months but periodically for years. The media attention presumably increases the level of rehearsal, and an increase in rehearsal arrests the rate of forgetting. Thus, an event might induce a FBM, but the rate at which the event itself is forgotten will depend not on whether a FBM is formed, not on the extent of the initial rehearsal, but at least in part on the level of continual media coverage.

One way to examine this proposal is to look at initially highly practised material that is not subject to continual rehearsal. Particularly relevant here are the studies of Bahrick and colleagues on the long-term retention of material learned in college, e.g., Spanish vocabulary, college-town street names, and names of fellow students (Bahrick, 1983, 1984; Bahrick, Bahrick, & Whittlinger, 1975). Although this material does not have the emotional charge of FB events, it can serve as a useful comparison to Bohannon and Symons (1992) and Hirst et al. (2008) in that it is initially intensively rehearsed, like FB events, but like the *Challenger* explosion and unlike 9/11 it is then neglected.

The findings of Bahrick and colleagues were similar to those of Bohannon and Symons and Hirst et al. for the first year of retention. Here all three found an exponential rate of forgetting. The difference among the studies is the time frame at which asymptotic levelling occurred. Bahrick and colleagues found forgetting continued for 3 to 5 years after the initial learning and then ceased. Bohannon and Symons do not look beyond a retention interval of 3 years, so it is impossible to tell if they also would have observed a levelling off similar to Bahrick and colleagues. Hirst et al.'s (2008) results clearly differ from those of Bahrick and colleagues because the former found no further forgetting after the first year.

For us, the most straightforward explanation of why the asymptotes differ is the nature of the continual practice. According to Bahrick and colleagues, extensive initial rehearsal ensures the forgetting will level off at some point. The levelling off will occur even if an item is not practised after initial learning, but substantial initial practice is necessary if information is to become represented in "permastore", which according to Bahrick and colleagues is the memory system responsible for the very-long-term retention of semantic information. Although we do not doubt that how well something is initially learned may be an important factor in creating an asymptote in a forgetting curve, we also see a critical role for rehearsal. For us, the differences in onset of the asymptote across studies may rest mainly not in the material participants studied, nor in the level of initial rehearsal, but in differences in the pattern of rehearsal after the initial burst. So 9/11 was extensively rehearsed after the first few months, whereas the school material Bahrick and colleagues studied and the *Challenger* explosion studied by Bohannon and Symons suffered neglect after initial bouts of rehearsal.

Do all collective memories exhibit the pattern of forgetting observed for memories of FBM-inducing events?

Unlike FB events, many newsworthy events become less accessible over time. Many collective memories are from a distant past, not, if you like, "lived through". The war of 1812 is no doubt part of the American collective memory, but no one alive "lived through" it. Present-day Americans did, however, live through the terrorist attack of September 11. In employing the term "lived through" we do not mean to imply that the "lived through" collective memories are autobiographical or episodic. Most Americans did not directly experience the collapse of the World Trade Center towers or the crash of

United Flight 93. They experienced learning about the events from others or on TV; they did not experience the event itself. In this sense, both "The war of 1812" and "The terrorist attack of 9/11" are semantic memories for most Americans. The former, however, is distant; the latter is "lived through".

Belli, Schuman, and Jackson (1997) have looked at the degree to which people forget important public events that are not necessarily FB events. Confining their discussion to non-FB collective memories, they showed that "lived through" collective memories are more memorable than "distant" collective memories. They went on to establish that "lived through" collective memories occurring during what has been called the transition period in a person's life—between the 15th and 30th year of most individuals' lives—are more readily accessible than all but the most recent collective memories (see also Schuman, Rieger, & Gaidys, 1994; Schuman & Scott, 1989). That is, non-FB collective memories are generationally specific. This generation effect is similar to the reminiscence bump Rubin and his colleagues found for autobiographical memories (e.g., Rubin & Schulkind, 1997). Rubin and his colleagues supplied a "cue" word to participants, such as "industry", and asked them to report the first autobiographical memory that came to mind. Except for their most recent autobiographical events, people were much more likely to recount memories from their transition period than from other periods in their life.

Belli et al. (1997) conjectured that the generation effect for collective memories they studied emerged because events from the transition period were better encoded at the time of their occurrence than were events from other periods in a person's life. They based their proposal on their participants' memory for the events many years after they occurred. Under these circumstances, memories for events that occurred during the transition period were more detailed than memories for events that occurred at other points in an individual's life. We could ask whether the same "initial-better-encoding" conjecture applies to FB collective memories as well.

Building on the data of Hirst et al. (2008), Meksin, Koppel, and Hirst (2004) focused on the memories reported about 9/11 after a few days and after 11 months. They assumed that 9/11 will figure in the American collective memory, even when it is assessed several decades from now. Past work on collective memory has shown that people are more likely to include as part of their collective memory FB events that occurred during their transition period than FB events that occurred at other points in their lives (Schuman & Scott, 1989). Moreover, some sociologists now write of the 9/11 generation as they previously wrote about Generation X or Y, suggesting that 9/11 will loom large in the collective memory of those in their transition period in 2001 (Wild et al., 2006). If the "better-initial-encoding" hypothesis is correct, then Meksin et al. should find better memories for the 9/11 generation than for older individuals. However, they found that when it comes to facts about the attack of 9/11, participants from 18 to 30 years of age actually remembered less than participants from 40 to 65 years of age, not just initially after the attack but also after a year. The reason for this poorer memory seems straightforward: As Meksin et al. reported, the younger group attended less to the media (not just radio and television, but also relevant Internet material) and reported less social sharing than the middle-aged group, even over a 3-year period. Such an explanation once again underscores the importance of media in shaping our collective memories. However, it does not explain why 9/11 might in the end figure as an "important" historical memory for the "9/11 generation".

There are several possible ways to address this issue of why 9/11 might figure as a generationally important event. First, contrary to our expectation, it will not figure as an important historical memory for the "9/11 generation" after all. Belli et al. (1997) may be right—if the memories are not well encoded initially, it will not figure as a significant historical memory. This explanation goes against the grain of most discussions of 9/11, however, which describe it as a critical juncture in American history (Meyerowitz, 2003). Second, 9/11 may be a distinctive sort of collective memory, in that it will figure critically in every generation's ranking of historical events. Other events, such as World War II, seem to have the same level of import-ance. Almost everyone, independent of when they were born, lists War World II as one of the important events from the last century (Schuman & Scott, 1989). Third, the significance of an historical event may not simply rest on how well it is encoded initially, but also on the importance assigned to it after the fact. The "9/11 generation" might treat the terrorist attack as significant only because they have been told it is and, over time, have come to believe it is. Another account would suggest that, over time, the younger generation may read more about September 11 and this subsequent rehearsal may make the event more prominent and memorable.

One explanation that intrigues us comes directly out of the data Meksin et al. (2004) collected. It is, if you like, an intrapsychic rather than social-interactional explanation. The "9/11 generation" may have spent more time trying to make sense of the event, over a longer period of time, than did the older group. Younger people may have more difficulty understanding how the tragedy could have happened and hence may have had to think more about it than the middle-aged group. They may have initially possessed a relatively impoverished system of relations for the attack but, with time and further reflection, as well as delayed attention to the media, they might have built a more complex system of relations. They might watch less media about 9/11 initially, but they might think more about it in an attempt to make sense of it. And as a result, as noted above, they might attend to more media in the future. In this way, for the younger group, then, the memory might become important and memorable in the long term, even if it is poorly remembered initially and in the short term. Middle-aged adults, on the other hand, might view even a national tragedy as nothing particularly new. They have lived through past tragedies and, as far as they are concerned, they will live through this tragedy as well. As a result, the representations of the middle-aged group may remain more static over time, reflecting the minimal needs the middle-aged group has to modify their initial representation.

In support of these conjectures, Meksin et al. found that the younger group was more confused, according to their self-reports, than the middle-aged group. They also tended to use terms that indicated more cognitive processing when describing what the event meant to them—that is, terms like *believed*, *thought*, *wondered*. Media attention that follows the year after an event may affect event memory, but it may not play a significant role in marking an event as generation defining.

What happens when media attention is non-existent: The case of memory for personal, emotionally charged events?

A critical defining feature of FB events is that they are public, not personal. Does this make a difference when it comes to long-term retention? We think it does. Personal tragedies are much less likely to receive media coverage than public tragedies. As a consequence, given the large role we have assigned to media attention in the long-term retention of FB events, personal, emotionally charged events should be more susceptible to forgetting than public ones. Thus it is not surprising that we know of no study reporting a complete failure to remember a lived-through, publicly experienced, emotionally charged event across a population. There is probably too much media coverage immediately following a public trauma for consolidation to fail. On the other hand, there are numerous reports of complete forgetting of personal traumas, such as an incident of sexual abuse (e.g., Schooler, Ambadar, & Bendikese, 1997). People can exhibit traumatic amnesia for personal events, but rarely for public ones. It would be interesting to know what the effect of media attention has on cases of sexual abuse that have garnered substantial publicity.

Of course, even for public traumas, media coverage is not guaranteed. There may be attempts to silence the public and the media. Mention of the Hungarian Revolution did not appear in the Communist era textbooks, and the disappearance of many Argentineans in the 1970s could not be talked about publicly for many years. Such officially sanctioned silencing may be quite effective, at least when it comes to transgenerational collective memories. When the successors to the Pharaoh Akhenaten decided to obliterate him from history, their sculpture and hieroglyphic defacements wiped out the memory of this pharaoh not only for a generation, but for centuries (Assmann, 1997). His historical existence only surfaced when Napoleon's archeologists began digging through Egypt.

On the other hand, we doubt that these attempts at silencing would be effective for those who lived through the event. There are many social practices other than media attention that can lead to long-term retention. While governments and other authorities can effectively control the media, it is more difficult for them to reign in private conversations. A collective memory can be preserved through conversations, even if it is not afforded media coverage. For instance, for many Estonians, Russia did not "liberate" Estonia from "bourgeois tyranny" after World War II, as is portrayed by the Russian authorities in Estonian textbooks, on Estonian television, and through Estonian films. Rather they remember the event as an "invasion". We suspect that this Estonian vernacular collective memory is preserved through informal conversations among friends, relatives, even acquaintances (Wertsch, 2002; see also Schuman, Belli, & Bischoping, 1997). Of course, such private conversations about an alternative rendering of the past can burst into the public, as was the case for *Las Madres de Plaza de Mayo* in Buenos Aires, when the women protested at the disappearance of their children. In the main, however, they remain underground, yet still effective.

Conversations may then supply a means of preserving lived-through public tragedies when media coverage is absent. They may also supply a means of preserving private tragedies. People frequently talk to each other about family mishaps, for instance, horrifying traffic accidents. But, again, unlike public events, personal tragedies may be just that—personal affairs. In instances of personal tragedy, people often have the option to be silent, in a way that might be impossible for publicly experienced traumas. For many reasons, an individual may exercise this option. It is unlikely for a whole community to do so. People are inclined to talk about emotionally distressing material (Luminet, Bouts, Delie, Manstead, & Rimé, 2000). One individual may, for personal reasons, resist this urge, but rarely will groups of 10, let alone communities of millions.

CONCLUDING REMARKS

In this chapter we have concentrated on the memory practices that a society undertakes in response to a FB event and their impact on collective memory, specifically examining the role of media coverage. We found that the pattern of forgetting associated with a FB event was not predicted by its FBM quality, but by the pattern of media coverage. In particular, we were interested in the 1-year asymptotic forgetting observed with some collective memories of FB events. This pattern of forgetting is, if not unique, at least distinctive. It is not found for all collective memories of FB events, only those with continual media coverage lasting not just days or weeks, but for years. It is also not found for historically important, but distant collective memories. Moreover, personal but emotionally charged events, such as sexual abuse, do not necessarily evidence the same pattern of forgetting as we observed for collective memories of FB events.

One might wonder why FB events are likely to initiate extensive media coverage. Many of the characteristics associated with FB events are those that might be thought to interest the public and the media: that they concern the general public, not just one or a few individuals, that they are consequential for the community, and that they are emotionally evocative for most members of the community. The latter may be particularly relevant in as much as people are much more likely to transmit information about an emotionally disturbing event than a neutral one (Luminet et al., 2000).

Of course, media coverage is just one form of social sharing that can initiate externally driven rehearsal. Conversation can do so as well. Indeed, the pattern of forgetting we have reported here for memories of FB events may have arisen not simply because of the media coverage that follows the event, but also because of the conversations that follow. The available evidence suggests that when public tragedies such as 9/11 occur, people devote much of their conversation to the topic. When Mehl and Pennebaker (2003) monitored the conversations of University of Texas students immediately after the 9/11 attack, they found that the monitored students spent more time talking in dyads than in groups, but that the topic of discussion for these intimate pairings was 9/11.

In the end, one wants to understand the retention of FBMs and memories for FB events not only because of the role they play for autobiographical and collective memory, but also for their contribution to individual and collective identity (Manier & Hirst, 2008). We have argued that the varying effort a community makes to "cover" an event in the media has a profound effect on the way the community subsequently remembers the event. With a continuing commitment by its media to cover the event over the long term, the community may forget many details in the first year, but not thereafter. In effect, with the right media coverage, a permanent site for the FB event will quickly be found in the collective memory of the community. In such an instance not only will members of a community possess a long-lasting and vivid memory of the circumstances in which they learned of an event, they will also possess an equally vivid and long-lasting memory of the event itself. What intrigues us is that these overlapping narratives could provide a means of understanding the bonds between individual and community that some FB events seem to promote.

NOTES

1 The authors gratefully acknowledge the support of NIHM grant #0066972.
2 Even in studies that only examine FBMs, this pattern of forgetting seems present. The one exception is Schmolck, Buffalo, and Squire's (2000) study of FBMs for the verdict from the O. J. Simpson trial. They found increased forgetting when they assessed consistency 2 and 3 years after the trial. The nature of this FB event eliciting the FBM and its peripheral concern to many Americans suggests that the O. J. Simpson trial may not be the best case for establishing a pattern of forgetting for public, emotionally charged events.
3 Bohannon and Symons and Hirst et al. tested their participants at different delays. Hence the need to discuss testing periods rather than specific testing delays.

REFERENCES

Anderson, S. J., & Conway, M. A. (1997). Representations of autobiographical memories. In M. A. Conway (Ed.), *Cognitive models of memory. Studies in cognition* (pp. 217–246). Cambridge, MA: MIT Press.

Assmann, J. (1997). *Moses the Egyptian: The memory of Egypt in Western monotheism*. Cambridge, MA: Harvard University Press.

Bahrick, H. P. (1983). The cognitive map of a city—50 years of learning and memory. In G. Bower (Ed.), *The psychology of learning and motivation: Advances in research and theory*. (Vol. 17, pp. 125–163). New York: Academic Press.

Bahrick, H. P. (1984). Semantic memory content in permastore: Fifty years of memory for Spanish learned in school. *Journal of Experimental Psychology: General, 113*, 1–29.

Bahrick, H. P., Bahrick, P. O., & Wittlinger, R. P. (1975). Fifty years of memory for names and faces: A cross-sectional study. *Journal of Experimental Psychology: General, 104*, 54–75.

Belli, R. F., Schuman, H., & Jackson, B. (1997). Autobiographical misremembering: John Dean is not alone. *Applied Cognitive Psychology, 11*, 187–209.

Berntsen, D., & Thomsen, D. K. (2005). Personal memories for remote historical events: Accuracy and clarity of flashbulb memories related to World War II. *Journal of Experimental Psychology: General, 134*, 242–257.

Bohannon, J. N. III (1988). Flashbulb memories for the space shuttle disaster: A tale of two theories. *Cognition, 29*, 179–196.

Bohannon, J. N. III, & Symons, V. L. (1992). Flashbulb memories: Confidence, consistency, and quantity. In E. Winograd & U. Neisser (Eds.), *Affect and accuracy in recall* (pp. 65–90). Cambridge, UK: Cambridge University Press.

Bouvier, G. (2005). "Breaking" news: The first hours of the BBC coverage of 9/11 as a media event. *Journal for Crime, Conflict, and the Media, 1*, 19–43.

Brown, R., & Kulik, J. (1977). Flashbulb memories. *Cognition, 5*, 73–79.

Christianson, S-Å. (1989). Flashbulb memories: Special, but not so special. *Memory and Cognition, 17*, 435–443.

Christianson, S-Å. (1992). Do flashbulb memories differ from other types of emotional memories? In E. Winograd & U. Neisser (Eds.), *Affect and accuracy in recall* (pp. 191–211). Cambridge, UK: Cambridge University Press.

Conway, M. A., Anderson, S. J., Larsen, S. F., Donnelly, C. M., McDaniel, M. A., McClelland, A. G. R., et al., (1994). The formation of flashbulb memories. *Memory and Cognition, 22*, 326–343.

Conway, M. A., & Pleydell-Pearce, C. W. (2000). The construction of autobiographical memories in the self-memory system. *Psychological Review, 107*, 261–288.

Conway, M. A., & Rubin, D. C. (1993). The structure of autobiographical memory. In A. F. Collins, S. E. Gathercole, M. A. Conway, & P. E. Morris (Eds.), *Theories of memory* (pp. 103–137). Hillsdale, NJ: Lawrence Erlbaum Associates Inc.

Curci, A., & Luminet, O. (2006). Follow-up of a cross-national comparison of flashbulb and event memory for the September 11th attacks. *Memory, 14*, 329–344.

Curci, A., Luminet, O., Finkenauer, C., & Gisle, L. (2001). Flashbulb memories in social groups: A comparative test–retest study of the memory of French President Mitterrand's death in a French and a Belgian group. *Memory, 9*, 81–101.

Dayan, D., & Katz, E. (1992). *Media events: The live broadcasting history*. Cambridge, MA: Harvard University Press.

Er, N. (2003). A new flashbulb memory model applied to the Maramara earthquake. *Applied Cognitive Psychology, 17*, 503–517.

Finkenauer, C., Luminet, O., Gisle, L., El-Ahmadi, A., van der Linden, M., & Philippot, P. (1998). Flashbulb memories and the underlying mechanisms of their formation: Toward an emotional-integrative model. *Memory and Cognition, 26*, 516–531.

Gillis, J. R. (Ed.). (1994). *Commemoration: The politics of national identity*. Princeton, NJ: Princeton University Press.

Hirst, W., Phelps, E., & the 9/11 Memory Consortium (2008). *The long-term retention of flashbulb memories and memories for flashbulb events*. Manuscript submitted for publication.

Hoskins, A. (2007). *Media and memory*. New York: Routledge.

Iyengar, S., & Kinder, D. R. (1987). *News that matters*. Chicago: Chicago University Press.

Kvavilashvili, L., Mirani, J., Schlagman, S., & Kornbrot, D. E. (2003). Comparing flashbulb memories of September 11 and the death of Princess Diana: Effect of time delays and nationality. *Applied Cognitive Psychology, 17*, 1017–1031.

Larsen, S. F. (1992). Potential flashbulb memories: Memories of ordinary news as the baseline. In E. Winograd & U. Neisser (Eds.), *Affect and accuracy in recall* (pp. 65–90). Cambridge, UK: Cambridge University Press.

Luminet, O., Bouts, P., Delie, F., Manstead, A. S. R., & Rimé, B. (2000). Social sharing of emotion following exposure to a negatively valenced situation. *Cognition and Emotion, 14*, 661–668.

Luminet, O., Curci, A., Marsh, E., Wessel, I., Constantin, T., Gencoz, F., et al. (2004). The cognitive, emotional, and social impacts of the September 11 attacks: Group differences in memory for the reception context and the determinants of flashbulb memory. *Journal of General Psychology, 17*, 171–181.

Mahmood. D., Manier, D., & Hirst, W. (2005). Flashbulb memories for repeated experiences of death. *Memory and Cognition, 32*, 125–134.

Manier, D., & Hirst, W. (2008). A cognitive taxonomy of collective memories. In A. Nuenning & A. Erll (Eds.), *Cultural memory studies: An international and interdisciplinary handbook*. New York: De Gruyter.

McCloskey, M., Wible, C. G., & Cohen, N. J. (1988). Is there a special flashbulb-memory mechanism? *Journal of Experimental Psychology: General, 117*, 171–181.

Mehl, M., & Pennebaker, J. W. (2003). The social dynamics of a cultural upheaval: Social interactions surrounding September 11, 2001. *Psychological Science, 14*, 579–585.

Meksin, R., Koppel, J., & Hirst, W. (2004, January). *Generation distinctions in memories for September 11, 2001*. Paper presented at the meeting of the Society for Applied Research in Memory and Cognition, Wellington, New Zealand.

Meyerowitz, J. (Ed.). (2003). *History and September 11*. Philadelphia: Temple University Press.

Nachson, I., & Zelig, A. (2003). Flashbulb and factual memories: The case of Rabin's assassination. *Applied Cognitive Psychology, 17*, 519–531.

Neisser, U. (1982). Snapshots or benchmarks? In U. Neisser (Ed.), Memory observed: Remembering in natural contexts (pp. 43–48). San Francisco: W. H. Freeman.

Neisser, U., & Harsh, N. (1992). Phantom flashbulbs: False recollections of hearing the news about *Challenger*. In E. Winograd & U. Neisser (Eds.), *Affect and accuracy in recall* (pp. 9–31). Cambridge, UK: Cambridge University Press.

Neisser, U., Winograd, E., Bergman, E. T., Schreiber, C. A., Palmer, S. E., & Weldon,

M. S. (1996). Remembering the earthquake: Direct experience vs. hearing the news. *Memory, 4*, 337–357.

Otani, H., Kusumi, T., Kata, K. Matsuda, K., Kern, R. P., Widner, R., et al. (2005). Remembering a nuclear accident in Japan: Did it trigger flashbulb memories? *Memory, 13*, 6–20.

Pezdek, K. (2003). Event memory and autobiographical memory for events of September 11, 2001. *Applied Cognitive Psychology, 17*, 1033–1045.

Rubin, D., & Schulkind, M. D. (1997). The distribution of autobiographical memories across the lifespan. *Memory and Cognition, 25*, 859–866.

Schmolck, H., Buffalo, E. A., & Squire, L. R. (2000). Memory distortions develop over time: Recollections of the O.J. Simpson trial verdict after 15 and 32 months. *Psychological Science, 11*, 39–45.

Schooler, J. W., Ambadar, Z., & Bendikese, M. (1997). A collaborative case study approach for investigating discovered memories of sexual abuse. In M. A. Conway (Ed.), *Recovered memories and false memories* (pp. 251–292). New York: Oxford University Press.

Schuman, H., Belli, R. F., & Bischoping. K. (1997). The generational bias of historical knowledge. In J. W. Pennebaker, D. Páez, & B. Rimé (Eds.), *Collective memory of political events: Social psychological perspectives*. Mahwah, NJ: Lawrence Erlbaum Associates Inc.

Schuman, H., Rieger, C., & Gaidys, V. (1994). Collective memories in the United States and Lithuania. In N. Schwartz & S. Sudman (Eds.), *Autobiographical memories and the validity of retrospective reports* (pp. 313–333). New York: Springer Verlag.

Schuman, H., & Scott, J. (1989). Generations and collective memories. *American Sociological Review, 54*, 359–381.

Schwartz, B. (2000). *Abraham Lincoln and the forge of national identity*. Chicago: University of Chicago Press.

Shapiro, L. R. (2006). Remembering September 11th: The role of retention interval and rehearsal on flashbulb and event memory. *Memory, 14*, 129–147.

Smith, M. C., Bibi, U., & Sheard, D. E. (2003). Evidence for the differential impact of time and emotion on personal and event memories for September 11, 2001. *Applied Cognitive Psychology, 17*, 1047–1055.

Talarico, J. M., & Rubin. D. C. (2003). Confidence, not consistency, characterizes flashbulb memories. *Psychological Science, 14*, 455–461.

Tekcan, A., Berivan, E., Gülgöz, S., & Er, N. (2003). Autobiographical and event memory for 9/11: Changes across one year. *Applied Cognitive Psychology, 17*, 1057–1066.

Weaver, C. A. III, & Krug, K. S. (2004). Consolidation-like effects in flashbulb memories: Evidence from September 11, 2001. *American Journal of Psychology, 117*, 517–530.

Wertsch, J. (2002). *Voices of collective remembering*. New York: Cambridge University Press.

Wild, R., Somers, P., Biddix, P., Wetstein, K., Deloach-Packnett, G., & Hofer, J. (2006). *In search of generation 9/11*. Retrieved 21 December 2006 from http://www.edb.utexas.edu/faculty/somers/911/gen_%20911_ver3.htm

Wolters, G., & Goudsmit, J. (2005). Flashbulb and event memory of September 11, 2001: Consistency, confidence and age effects. *Psychological Reports, 96*, 605–619.

Wright, D. B. (1993). Recall of the Hillsborough disaster over time: Systematic biases of "flashbulb" memories. *Applied Cognitive Psychology, 7*, 129–138.

11 Flashbulb memories, culture, and collective memories

Psychosocial processes related to rituals, emotions, and memories

Dario Páez, Guglielmo Bellelli, and Bernard Rimé

This chapter examines the parallels existing between flashbulb memories (FBMs) and collective memories (CMs) with a special accent on the impact of social processes on memory. In this context we will also discuss Whitehouse's (2000, 2004) model of emotionally loaded rituals with regard to the current state of FBM studies and in relation to neo-Durkheimian models of rituals.

FBMs AND COLLECTIVE MEMORIES: SIMILARITIES IN CONTENT AND PROCESSES

FBMs are distinctly vivid, precise, concrete, and long-lasting memories of the personal circumstances surrounding people's discovery of shocking public events. Even though FBMs are not as accurate or permanent as is suggested by the photographic flashbulb metaphor (Neisser & Harsh, 1992), their forgetting curve is far less affected by time than is the case for other types of memories investigated in basic memory research (e.g., Bohannon & Symons, 1992).

In general, FBM studies have focused on one single major emotional event. In line with Brown and Kulik's (1977) inaugural research, subsequent studies dealt predominantly with events involving public violence. We categorize FBM studies available until 2006 in PsycList by the types of events studied (see Bellelli, Curci, & Leone, 2000). As shown in Table 11.1, episodes of *collective violence* such as the 9/11 2001 terrorist attacks ranked first in frequency ($N = 19$) among types of events considered in FBM studies. Next, almost the same number of studies ($N = 17$) examined events of *political violence*, such as the assassination of political leaders (e.g., US presidents Abraham Lincoln and John F. Kennedy, Swedish prime minister Olof Palme), or attempted assassinations (e.g., of US president Ronald Reagan). *Collective catastrophes* and *death of famous people* ranked respectively third and fourth. Thus, 15 studies dealt with episodes such as the *Challenger* disaster (1986), the Hillsborough disaster (1989), the San Francisco earthquake (1989), and the Chernobyl disaster (1986), and 12 studies focused on the non-violent death of important political figures (e.g., Spanish dictator Francisco Franco,

Table 11.1 Frequency distribution of types of events considered in FBM studies

	Events		Studies	
Types of events	*Number*	*Per cent of total*	*Number*	*Per cent of total*
Collective violence	3	7.9	19	25.3
Political violence	11	28.9	17	22.7
Collective catastrophes	8	21.1	15	20.0
Death of famous people	8	21.1	12	16.0
Political crises	3	7.9	5	6.7
Other	5	13.2	7	9.3
	38	100.0	75	100.0

Events were categorized by two independent scholars based on the abstracts of the studies.

Belgian King Baudouin). A smaller number of studies regarded *political crises*, such as the resignation of the UK prime minister Margaret Thatcher.

Each of the events reviewed elicited in some 40–100% of investigated persons a clear and vivid remembering of what happened (e.g., the scene of the shooting of President Kennedy). In addition, however, these persons usually also recalled with high perceptual clarity the personal circumstances in which they learned about the event or the context of reception.

It can be remarked that these events, which were demonstrated as generating FBM, shared most of the characteristics of events representing typical instances of CM. CMs are shared memories of relevant public events that are related to social identity and play important psychosocial functions (Neal, 2005). First, as is the case for CMs, FBMs result from traumatic or markedly negative events which are usually unexpected, painful, and extraordinary. Feelings of novelty and surprise among exposed persons indeed count among the best predictive variables for FBM. Second, as is the case for CMs, FBMs evolve from events that affect collectively a large number of people, either as members of a national community or as members of a political group. Thus, both centrality of the event to one's own self and event-related previous knowledge predict FBM formation. Third, as is the case for CMs, FBMs relate to important changes in society or to important threats to social cohesion and values, which is supported by the fact that appraisals of consequentiality and of importance of an event predict FBM formation. To illustrate, the assassination of John F. Kennedy marked the end of a "political innocence" in America, as was also the case in Sweden with the assassination of O. Palme. Along similar lines, Franco's death symbolized the end of a political era (Pennebaker & Banasik, 1997). American casualties in the Korean war were similar to those suffered in Vietnam. However, because American objectives had been achieved in the Korean war, and because the military engagement in Korea was perceived as consensual, this war did not form a part of American collective memories (Neal, 2005).

Fourth, as is the case for CM, FBM events are largely socially shared both through viewing mass media and through interpersonal rehearsal. Overt rehearsal is indeed another predictor of FBM formation. A large majority of people learned about FBM events from the mass media, and then kept following news about these events in subsequent hours and days. In addition, most people shared the event with others, as was the case for some 55% of respondents in the study that focused on the Belgian King Baudouin's unexpected death (Finkenauer et al., 1998) and in the study on Judge Di Pietro's resignation in Italy (Bellelli et al., 2000). The case of JFK's assassination offered a paradigmatic example of such collective sharing and rehearsal. According to Neal, indeed, "The nation was engrossed in television coverage of the funeral ceremony . . . and the subsequent funeral procession to Arlington" (Neal, 2005, p. 108). Sixth, CM and FBM events such as attacks, disasters, political assassinations, and crises all provoke shared emotions such as surprise and interest, as well as anger, sadness, fear, and anxiety. Reported emotionality also counts among the predictors of FBM. Finally, CM and FBM events *both involve participation in collective behaviours and rituals* in the forms of political demonstrations, of worship, of funerary rituals and so forth (Páez, Rimé & Basabe, 2005). To illustrate, in the case of the assassination of JFK:

> The funeral march was embellished by an honour guard (. . .). The dignity of the ceremony and the symbolism of the funeral march were accompanied by intense feelings of sadness (. . .). Following his death, the images and memories of Kennedy became selective and more vivid as they took on sacred qualities . . . it became taboo to say negative things about Kennedy (. . .). There were no references to the narrow margin by which he has been elected, nor to fiasco of Bay of Pigs invasion, nor to the concerns of many Americans with our growing involvement in Vietnam (. . .). Many people remembered Kennedy's idealism (. . .). In popular literature and music, references were made to Abraham Lincoln in the sanctification of Kennedy as the ideal man and president.
>
> (Neal, 2005, pp. 109–111)

Collective events have the highest probability of leading to a long-lasting collective memory, or set of social representations concerning the past, when they (1) open up social changes in the long run, (2) are emotionally loaded, (3) elicit abundant social sharing among individuals, (4) are socially rehearsed by the mass media, and (5) are associated with collective behaviour and commemorative rituals (Pennebaker & Banasik, 1997). According to Jedlowski (2000), such social representations, or shared knowledge about the past, are elaborated, transmitted, and conserved in a group essentially through interpersonal and institutional communication. Social representations of the past are helpful to people for a variety of reasons. First, they maintain a positive image of the group to which they belong. Second, they preserve a sense of continuity. Third, they feed values and norms which prescribe behaviours and contribute to define what characterizes or should characterize group members (Jedlowski, 2000).

Studies have shown that events relevant for cultural values and social identity fuel both collective memories and FBMs. FBMs of the assassination of Martin Luther King (Brown & Kulik, 1977) were more common among African-Americans than among European-Americans, and FBMs of Margaret Thatcher's resignation (Gaskell & Wright, 1997) were stronger among upper-class Britons than among the working class. Presumably such differences resulted from the particular relevance these events had (i.e., for British upper-class people among whom supporters of the Conservative party are a majority; Gaskell & Wright, 1997). Although the seminal study by Brown and Kulik (1977) first stimulated FBM studies focusing on individual aspects, more recent investigations have evidenced the role played by cultural factors in the development of FBM. For instance, Curci, Luminet, Finkenauer, and Gisle (2001) compared French versus Belgian memories for the death of François Mitterrand. Similarly, Luminet et al. (2004) conducted a cross-national comparison of FBM for the September 11th attacks. In these studies, social identity was found to be strongly related to the recall of national past events and to CM (Rosa, Bellelli, & Bakhurst, 2000; see Berntsen, Chapter 9, this volume).

We conclude that the characteristics of CMs and FBMs are very similar in content and that they result from very similar conditions (see Table 11.2 for a comparison). The feature of FBMs is the fact that they mix personal and very idiosyncratic elements of private experience with the socially shared information pertaining to a collective event. Although FBM studies accented the role of individual factors in memory for public events, CMs are frequently intertwined with FBMs. Thus, in a study on memories of public events of the last 50 years, Schuman and Scott (1989) reported that, compared with young people, Americans who were direct witnesses of WWII frequently mentioned personal episodes of the war as motive for their choice of this public event. Despite this important overlapping of FBM and CM, studies that investigated these two manifestations differed in their respective focus. FBM studies centred on the personal reception context of the event, whereas CM studies were more directly concerned with the target event itself. In addition, FBM studies dealt essentially with negative or traumatic events, although no theoretical reasons led to exclusion of the consideration of intense positive events (Scott & Ponsoda, 1996). By contrast, CM studies dealt with both negative and positive events. Positive events do indeed strongly enhance collective identity and allow a more positive reconstruction of personal and national history, as was the case, for instance, for resistance in Italy during WWII.

That CM and FBM are alike is supported by many studies on the antecedents and processes related to their construction and maintenance. Factors such as high novelty, surprise, emotional arousal, high importance, personal as well as social consequences of the event, social sharing or interpersonal rehearsal, and mass media and institutional rehearsal are demonstrated

Table 11.2 A comparison of FBM and CM features

Dimension	FBMs	Collective memories
Level of analysis	Individual	Collective
Experience	Reported	Generally reported
Focus	Reception context of a public event	Public event
Type of event	Real, very specific	Real, sometimes extended (a period), or symbolic
Type of source	Other people, media news	Various, including commemorations, memorials, monuments, etc.
Number of sources	Usually few or one	Various
Target event features	Unexpectedness, personal consequentiality, emotionally loaded (negative, traumatic)	Social consequentiality (major changes or threats), collective emotions and meanings (positive and negative)
Memory quality	Concrete, vivid (live quality)	More abstract
Memory accuracy	High and specific	Variable
Memory confidence	Generally very high	High/consensual
Social group	Important	Very important
Identity level	Group, generational	Social, national
Media	Personal narratives (social sharing), mass media	Mass media, cultural products (books, movies, art), rituals, institutions, group and personal narratives
Duration	Generally long	Very long: years or generations

predictors or mediators of FBM as well as of CM. Several studies have confirmed these relationships.

A first example is the study on an unexpected collective loss that occurred in Belgium in the 1990s (Finkenauer et al., 1998). King Baudouin died from a heart attack at the age of 62 at his vacation residence in Spain in July 1993. The news was unexpected and had an enormous impact on the Belgian population. Baudouin had been king for 42 years and he had a strong unifying influence on a nation divided by cultural conflicts. Television and radio channels replaced their programmes with broadcasts on the royal family and newspapers covered the event widely. Finkenauer et al. (1998) conducted a study on reactions to the king's death in a large group of French-speaking Belgians. Participants reported FBM (i.e., the circumstances in which they first heard the news) and answered questions on importance, consequentiality, novelty, and surprise regarding the event, how they heard about the news, where they were when they heard about it, and what their ongoing activity had been when they heard of the news. They also had to remember specific details about the event itself. The event memory measure can be conceived of as an index of CM in the short term, or at least an index of accurate knowledge about a national political event. In addition, respondents rated their emotional response to the event and the frequency of sharing and of following the media.

A structural equation revealed that participants' appraisals of consequentiality and importance did not directly determine their memory for the facts and circumstances surrounding the event (i.e., CM). However, consequentiality and importance had a strong indirect influence on these memories, on recent memory, and FBM or reception context. The greater the level of emotionality, the more people talked about the king's death and followed this event in the media. This was consistent with findings from studies on the social sharing of emotions (e.g., Rimé, Finkenauer, Luminet, Zech, & Philippot, 1998), which demonstrated that the more emotionally arousing the event, the more people will share it with others and follow the event in the media. In line with the central role of social rehearsal for memory, this social rehearsal was the source of a higher amount of recall for the king's death (i.e., CM) which in turn consolidated people's memories of the reception context (i.e., FBM).

Similar findings occurred in the study of FBM for Judge Di Pietro's resignation in Italy (Bellelli et al., 2000). FBM and event memory were positively correlated, and the latter was predicted mainly by social rehearsal ("paid attention to the news"). Structural equations also confirmed in this case that "social availability" or overt social rehearsal reinforced memory of the main event, which was in turn related to the FBM index (Bellelli et al., 2000).

A third study conducted on FBM and CM of the death of the French President Mitterrand confirms the importance of social identity, of emotional activation, and of rehearsal: Compared to Belgians, emotional activation, rehearsal, and FBM were stronger among participants in the French sample and they also exhibited a better memory of the original event (Curci et al., 2001).

THE CONTRIBUTION OF COLLECTIVE RITUALS TO THE FORMATION OF CM AND FBM

Effects of social rehearsal on memory are not limited to mass media exposure and to interpersonal exchanges of information. Collective behaviours and rituals also constitute cultural devices of shared social recall (Frijda, 1997) and are thus expected to play a role in the construction of CM. Rituals are conceived as repetitive and synchronized collective behaviours, inducing the focalization of attention to a common point, by means of shared symbols, and verbal and non-verbal expressions that intensify emotions, provoking changes and convergence of beliefs and values, and reinforcing social identification and cohesion (Collins, 2004). As the previous discussion led us to conclude that social rehearsal predicted both memories for the event and memories for the context of reception, it may well be that participation in rituals could also predict FBM. The latter view lacks empirical testing. However, there are both observational and theoretical arguments in support of it. Current observation indeed reveals that paradigmatic events such as rites of passage or traumatic autobiographical events elicit among participants very vivid, emotionally loaded, and clear recollections (Wright & Gaskell, 1992). Theoretical arguments in a similar direction were recently proposed in the field of anthropology (Whitehouse, 2000, 2004).

Whitehouse (2000, 2004) addressed the relationships between religious rituals and memory in "simple" societies. He opposed two modes of religious rituals to be found in any culture: low frequency and high arousal and high frequency and low arousal. According to the author, low-frequency, highly emotional, painful, and dramatic rituals such as the initiation rites practised in many tribal cultures would be predominantly codified in participants' episodic memories, or as idiosyncratic events in their lives. The "imagistic" mode proper to such religious rituals would indeed favour the elicitation of flashbulb-style memories, which are characterized by their vividness, their emotionality, and their inclusion of the context of reception of the religious knowledge proposed in the initiation ritual. In contrast, high-frequency and low-arousal religious rituals, or rituals of a more "doctrinal" type, would be predominantly codified in participants' semantic memory, or as general knowledge about the world. The model in these two modes of religious practice clustered various psychological and social features which were considered in classic theories on religious forms—e.g., Max Weber's (1922, quoted in Turner, 2000) "charismatic" or "effervescent" versus "routinized" religious form. Some key features of "imagistic", emotion-loaded rituals and of "doctrinal", routinized rituals are summarized in Table 11.3 (see Whitehouse, 2004).

The model further proposes that the memory system prevailing in a culture influences the form of social organization that develops in this culture. Thus, cultures in which episodic memory systems are favoured by low-frequency and high-intensity religious rituals would generally manifest a high social cohesion together with a reduced centralization and hierarchy. Conversely, cultures in which semantic memory systems prevail due to high-frequency and low-intensity religious rituals would typically present centralized and hierarchical forms of social organization characterized by low social cohesion.

We can also explain the relationship between types of rituals and social organization by the association between social structure and adaptive culture. Productive structure and density of population could explain these associations, because the dominant productive system and population size have institutional consequences and induce a specific syndrome of cultural values (Hofstede, 2001). Societies promoting high-intensity and low-frequency

Table 11.3 Key features of "imagistic" or emotionally loaded rituals and "doctrinal" or routinized rituals according to Whitehouse (2004)

Psychological and social variables	Imagistic mode of religiosity	Doctrinal mode of religiosity
Dominant memory system	Episodic memory, or FBM type	Semantic memory
Frequency	Low	High
Level of arousal	High (through sensory pageantry)	Low
Ritual meaning	Internally generated	Learned
Assimilation mode	High active reappraisal	Passive rumination
Social cohesion	Intense	Diffuse
Leadership	Absent	Important and dynamic
Structure	Non-centralized	Centralized

rituals are usually hunter-gatherer societies not affording writing systems, and these factors probably induce the dominance of face-to-face and oral mnemonic systems, like emotional rituals. Because of the low density and preponderance of one type of work (e.g., hunting) in these societies individualistic values prevail and usually hierarchy is not important. In contrast, societies with high-frequency and low-intensity rituals are usually agricultural, disposing of mnemonic tools (like writing, calendars, etc), and of large population size and density. Cooperative agricultural work and coordination of large groups reinforce collectivist values. In these "simple" societies institutions are more complex, they are more hierarchical, and authoritarian values are dominant (Basabe & Ros, 2005; Hofstede, 2001).

Whitehouse's (2000, 2004) model is supposed to be valid for so-called "simple societies". However, as Durkheim posits, the same processes appear in rituals of simple and complex societies: Collective behaviour, emotional reaction, use of symbols, and changes in beliefs are common to Australian religious rituals and French political rituals, such as the Dreyfus affair demonstration (see below). In the case of more developed, urban, and centralized political states, or "complex societies", the predominance of semantic-based memory systems is expected to be hegemonic. However, as was abundantly documented by Hofstede (2001), complex societies vary in the degree to which hierarchic structures or egalitarianism prevails in their organization and they also differ in their predominant form of sociability. As Whitehouse's model rests upon such variables, it should be possible to extend aspects of this model to complex societies. It should be remembered that "simple" societies emphasizing egalitarian and individualist subjective cultures reinforce emotionally loaded rituals that not only help to create episodic memory of the ritual event, but also help to anchor religious semantic knowledge in the autobiographic experience. The model can indeed be interpreted as suggesting that egalitarian, or horizontal, cultures emphasize emotional arousal in their transmission of representations and thus favour the formation of flashbulb-like memories but also of more emotionally loaded and strong collective memories. By this token, such cultures would strengthen their social cohesion and group loyalty. By contrast, simple societies emphasizing collectivist and hierarchical values reinforce low-emotional rituals based on "quiet" repetitive rites, and are likely to anchor religious knowledge in more passive forms. This model implies that more hierarchical and collectivist cultures would de-emphasize emotional arousal, would not favour intense social rehearsal, and would stress dependent or vertical cohesion through adhesion to ideological beliefs. In other terms, because of low emotional arousal and low social rehearsal, in these societies FBM and CM should be less intense and frequent.

These predictions could be tested using two of the five dimensions proposed by Hofstede (2001). In his scheme, Power Distance (PDI) refers to the extent to which less powerful group members accept inequalities: in high PDI cultures respect and asymmetry in roles and rewards are stressed, while in low PDI cultures egalitarian norms and interdependence are stressed. Individualism (or high IDV) refers to the relative priority granted to the person and to voluntary relationships, while collectivism (or low IDV) gives relative priority to the group and to obligatory relationships. Individualist cultures could be horizontal and egalitarian, like Scandinavian nations, or vertical hierarchical, like Anglo-Saxon nations. Collectivist cultures could be egalitarian, like Costa Rica, or vertical, like China. A partial test of the predictions was provided by Basabe and Ros (2005). In this study, compared to people living in low PDI and individualist cultures, those living in high PDI and collectivist cultures reported lower levels of emotions, of mental ruminations, and of social sharing of emotion. In high PDI and collectivist cultures, experiencing and expressing intense negative emotions is indeed not socially desirable. Among members of such cultures, focusing on one's internal states is not valued, so that people's attention is less self-centred than is the case in other cultures. Emotional intensity and communication are higher in individualistic and egalitarian societies, and this could influence how people form episodic and semantic autobiographical and collective knowledge.

A cross-cultural study conducted about FBM and psychological responses to the 9/11 terrorist attacks (Luminet et al., 2004) offered a further opportunity to test the model derived from Whitehouse (2000, 2004). This study assessed among respondents of nine different nations (1) emotional arousal provoked by the events of 9/11, (2) frequency of social sharing and of exposure to related news in the mass media, (3) level of internal rehearsal or rumination, (4) memory for the event itself, or CM, and (5) recall of the context of reception of the event, or FBM (see Table 11.4). In order to test Whitehouse's model, we re-analysed Luminet et al.'s (2004) data, this time using nation as a unit of analysis. In this case talking and following the event

Table 11.4 Nations ranked by power distance and individualism by determinants of FBM and CM, and level of memory of the reception context and for event-related facts

Nation	PDI/IDV	Emotional feeling	Rumination	Social sharing	Following news in mass media	Memory for the reception context (FBM)	Memory for the event (CM)
Romania	90/30	.17	2.60	−.36	−.285	−.12	−.63
Turkey	66/37	−.65	3.58	−.56	−.250	.09	−.075
Switzerland	70/64	.11	2.60	.47	−.041	.07	.592
France	68/71	.23	3.04	.21	−.061	.14	.502
Belgium	67/72	.10	2.95	.21	−.143	−.16	−.336
Japan	54/46	−.69	2.76	−.25	.066	−.04	−.385
Italy	50/76	.50	3.40	.48	.225	.002	−.088
USA	40/91	.37	2.98	.11	.115	.08	.498
Netherlands	38/80	−.31	3.58	.37	.276	.11	.365

PDI = Hofstede's power distance score, IDV = Hofstede's individualism score.
Emotional feeling = emotional reactions (upset, shaken, affected by the event) related to September 11th news. Rumination = Repeated thoughts, memories or images related to the event September 11th ranging from 1 (never) to 5 (more than 15 times). Social sharing = Frequency of talking about September 11th. Following mass media = how often participants followed the news by TV, radio, newspapers, and Internet. Memory reception context = eight questions assessing the recall of circumstances in which participants first learned about September 11th terrorist attack. Memory event = nine questions concerning event-related facts. Optimal factor scores: higher positive means indicate higher scores on that variable. Rumination scores are raw data. PDI and IDV scores are for French-speaking Switzerland and Belgium. Disaggregated data for French-speaking nation were provided by Curci.

in the news, including in particular information about memorials and political demonstrations, can be conceived as a mediated form of ritual, because people feel empathy and identification with the victims and demonstrators (see Collins, 2004, for a discussion of this topic).

As was predicted, egalitarian (low PDI) and individualistic (high IDV) cultures evidenced higher levels of FBM and CM than hierarchic and collectivist cultures. FBM level was indeed negatively correlated to nations' scores on Hofstede's PDI dimension, $r(9) = -.65$, and positively to Hofstede's individualism (IDV), $r(9) = .67$. In the same line, PDI nations' scores were negatively but non-significantly related to the CM index for the 9/11 events, $r(9) = -.35$, whereas IDV scores correlated positively to this index, $r(9) = .57$. In addition, indices of social rehearsal were associated with both FBM and CM indices in these analyses using nations as a unit. Thus, a significant and positive correlation occurred between intensity of FBM and level of rumination, $r(9) = .73$, level of social sharing, $r(9) = .61$, and level of exposure to 9/11 news in the mass media, $r(9) = .68$ ($p < .05$). Social sharing, but not rumination, was also associated with a higher recall of this collective event (CM), $r(9) = .47$. Emotional feeling was positively, but not significantly, related to FBM and CM. The latter results thus confirmed previous findings showing that emotional response and rumination are only partially and indirectly related to memories. Finally, compared to more hierarchic and collectivist countries, more egalitarian and individualistic ones evidenced higher levels on variables determining intensity of FBM and of CM. Indeed, PDI nations' scores were negatively correlated with extent of exposure to mass media, $r(9) = -.88$, whereas IDV was positively correlated to this variable, $r(9) = .72$. In addition, IDV correlated positively with extent of social sharing, $r(9) = .80$. Thus, that egalitarian and individualistic nations manifested higher levels of collective memories of the events can be accounted for by higher levels of personal and social rehearsal among people in these nations.

To conclude, our analysis partially confirmed the predicted association between high power distance and collectivist national contexts on the one hand, and low level of processes related to FBM, such as social sharing or rehearsal, on the other hand. These results thus brought a partial support to Whitehouse's (2000, 2004) views. They suggest that a cultural context, in which egalitarian autonomous values are dominant, reinforces emotional arousal, rumination, and social rehearsal. Emotional activation and rumination reinforce FBM and CM indirectly, via open rehearsal. However, the findings are open to alternative explanations in terms of cultural proximity with the US and current political conjuncture (see Luminet et al., 2004). In addition, unequal sample sizes and the restricted number of nations involved in these analyses weakened them. Finally, the fact that the samples were all composed of university students restricted representativeness, but was useful in matching nations for social variables.

FLASHBULB MEMORIES, RITUALS, AND EMOTIONS

Whitehouse (2000, 2004) proposed that emotional, high-arousal rituals give rise to enduring episodic memories (i.e., flashbulb-like memories) which are necessary for the successful acquisition of religious knowledge transmitted in the course of rarely performed rituals. Inducing negative emotions such as terror, fear, or anxiety in a ritual can cause the simultaneous mnemonic encoding of the ritual episode (i.e., context of reception) and of the transmitted knowledge (i.e., semantic knowledge) as an emotional and special episode. Vivid, enduring, episodic memories of rituals favour long-term mental rumination about what the ritual activities meant. This generates religious knowledge based on personal rumination. Thus, high emotional activation would lead to "spontaneous exegetic reflection" or a self-generated and active thinking proper to consolidate learned religious or ideological knowledge.

Experimental studies involving simulation of rites of initiation have partially confirmed the set of hypotheses just outlined. Richert, Whitehouse, and Stewart (2005) had volunteer students who earned £20 for their participation and were asked to take part in a ritual derived from initiation rituals in the Amazon. Participants were told that the study intended to test the efficacy of certain ritual procedures and they were instructed to maintain an attitude of respect towards the proposed ritual procedures to ensure validity. They were submitted either to a low- or a high-arousal ritual. Participants in the high-arousal ritual condition reported a higher intensity of emotional responses. In addition, those who reported stronger emotional responses also reported a higher level of and deeper reflection on the meaning of the ritual 2 months later (Study 1) and a higher increase in the level and depth of reflection over a 1-month period (Study 2).

The finding that high-arousal rituals affected emotional arousal and rumination is congruent with data from our studies on the relationship between participation in political rituals, emotional arousal, rumination, and semantic memory about collective traumatic events (Páez, Basabe, Ubillos, & Gonzalez, 2007). On the morning of 11 March 2004, Al-Qaeda members perpetrated a series of bomb attacks on various commuter trains in Madrid, Spain. As a result 192 people were killed and more than 2000 were injured. During the subsequent days some 25% of the population participated in successive and massive demonstrations against terrorism. Data collected in the 2 months after the event confirm (see below) that the level of emotional arousal and level of rumination about the March 11th terrorist attacks in Madrid correlated positively with participation in rituals of political demonstrations 1 week after the collective traumatic event. Participation in these rituals in the first week also predicted higher attack-related emotional arousal and rumination 3 weeks later. Emotional arousal and rumination were positively intercorrelated, as could be expected. Participation in demonstrations, social sharing, and emotional arousal predicted a better presence of recall or event memory. Results also suggest that social rehearsal and emotional activation play a direct role in the acquisition of knowledge related to collective events. However, rumination did not predict a better recall. Thus, interpersonal rehearsal seems to be more important than intrapersonal rumination with regard to memory formation—this is at odds with Whitehouse's emphasis on rumination as a factor related to ritual effects on memory.

Whitehouse's views warrant criticism both from the perspective of psychology and from the standpoint of anthropology. As regards psychology, his model assimilated autobiographical memory with episodic memory, and personal emotional memories with FBMs. However, autobiographical memory also involves semantic information, and personal emotional memories represent a much broader domain than mere FBMs which, according to definitions, are limited to the context of reception of a public event (see Curci, Chapter 1, this volume). Also, while Whitehouse argued that emotional events provoke vivid and long-lasting memories, available empirical reviews suggested that intense and negatively valenced emotions consolidate some aspects of memory in a much more complex manner (Levine & Pizarro, 2004). Available evidence thus precludes any simple conclusion linking emotional level and the quality of memory. Finally, once a strictly psychological, cognitive framework is adopted in order to account for social rituals, the reductionism of individualist perspectives follows. No place is left for the role of social processes which might well be central explanatory factors (Knight, 2003). To illustrate, it can be speculated that factors such as economic development and demographic processes (e.g., growth of population and urbanization) generated hierarchical and centralized states, and that such processes brought on the preponderance of low-intensity, high-frequency, and semantic-based religious rituals.

In conclusion, the important role played by micro-social processes (i.e., social sharing, social rehearsal) with regard to memory formation, as well as by macro-social processes with regard to the ritual form prevailing in a culture, militate in favour of more socioculturally oriented models in this domain.

Whitehouse (2000, 2004) stressed that rituals induce negative emotions. Thus fear, anxiety, uncertainty, and terror constitute in his view essential aspects of a number of religious initiation rituals. Emotions and rituals would be central in the acquisition of social beliefs. Durkheim (1912/2001) also stressed that hegemonic social beliefs resulted from participation in rituals, that rituals generally enhanced negative emotions, and that emotional arousal is critical for anchoring social beliefs in participants. Yet, whereas Whitehouse's model is limited to religious rituals, Durkheim's model was not. The political conflict known as the Dreyfus case, which confronted anti-Semite conservatives and liberal democrats in France at the turn of the nineteenth century, was one of the paradigmatic cases that inspired Durkheim's classic book on religious rituals, *The Elementary Forms of Religious Life* (1912/2001). At that time, ceremonials, demonstrations, and collective rituals abounded, and in this context Durkheim noticed that things which were purely secular were transformed by public opinion into sacred objects. Thus, people consensually assimilated the moral superiority of notions such as "*la Patrie*" (Fatherland), "*la Démocratie*" (Democracy), "*l'Egalité*" (Equality), and "*la Fraternité*" (Fraternity). These secular notions acquired the status of sacred things that nobody could meddle with. In Durkheim's view, traditional and modern societies differed in the content of their sacred rituals, but not in their forms. In traditional societies rituals were centred on religious totems whereas nowadays their focus is on the individual's rights and on values related to individualism. However, as was the case in the past, today's rituals still keep building up shared normative beliefs and a moral community among attendants (Cladis, 2001).

RITUALS, EMOTIONAL ACTIVATION, REHEARSAL, AND MEMORY OF TRAUMATIC EVENTS

Durkheim (1912/2001) argued that collective traumatic events induce the search for social support and spontaneous bonding and sharing because people experience comfort in the company of others. The French sociologist suggested that bonding with others helps to overcome stress. Contemporary studies have confirmed that the presence of others is instrumental in reducing the impact of stress (e.g., Stroebe & Stroebe, 1995). Intensification of social sharing and social interaction is a major consequence of collective traumas or important events (e.g., Rimé et al., 1998). Support mobilization, higher levels of communal coping, and altruistic behaviour are very common consequences of collective traumas. Victims of disasters receive and provide high levels of social support. Social support is negatively related to social loneliness and social activities reinforce positive affect (Páez et al., 2005). Durkheim (1912/2001) argued that the pursuit of instrumental activities and individualistic or solitary tasks weakens social bonds and depletes energy. In line with this view, people were found to report higher vitality in social activities than alone (Berscheid & Reis, 1998). Since they gather individuals together, rituals offer a major system for the strengthening of values and for the restoration of social relationships among individuals. Rituals are instrumental in producing and maintaining solidarity beyond the spontaneous bonding and social sharing elicited by a collective trauma (Rimé, 2005). Studies confirmed that collective traumatic events provoked more emotional reactions, more social sharing and bonding, and more performance of rituals than individual events of comparable importance (Martín-Beristáin, Páez, & González, 2000).

Rituals are forms of communication through actions. They generally constitute strongly patterned and recurring forms of collective behaviour. Their manifest purpose is to proclaim values in order to influence public opinion, authorities, and social movements. Secular demonstrations define collective gathering in a public space aimed to transmit a symbolic message to an audience, with both expressive (protest against terrorists, critics of government involved in an unpopular war) and instrumental goals (claims of political changes), but they also represent internal forms of communication, supporting a we/them differentiation and thus reinforcing group or collective identity (McPhail & Wohlstein, 1983). Of course, such demonstrations in no manner imply total value consensus or absence of conflicts among participating parties. Usually protest rituals constitute forms of "sociodramas" staging the struggle for power which steps up value conflicts (McLeod, 1999). In the case of the March 11th terrorist attacks in Madrid, demonstrations expressed and reinforced the long pre-existing political conflict opposing left- and right-wing ideologies in Spain.

Rituals have a set of typical features and effects that can be listed as follows (Collins, 2004; McPhail & Wohlstein, 1983; Milgram & Toch, 1969):

- *Group assembly*: A large number of persons are gathered together which has the effect of intensifying social interactions.
- *Common focus*: Participants centre their attention on the same events and feelings, by means of verbal and non-verbal communication and by symbols (flags, slogans).

- *Emotional contagion*: Emotional displays of emotions are common; non-verbal expressive behaviours and emotional social sharing help to generate a common collective mood.
- *Reinforcement of collective representations and of respect for symbols*: Emotional behaviour and gathering increases the significance of symbols, values, and beliefs for participants, and shared knowledge is reinforced.
- *Induction of similarity*: Even if people do not actually share beliefs and feelings, they perceive consensus, and feelings of unity, common fate, and solidarity.
- *Reinforcement of interpersonal attraction and social support*: Similarity increases attraction and social identification with the group.
- *Creation of a positive emotional atmosphere and enhancement of social cohesion*: Transformation of negative feelings into feelings of hope, solidarity, and trust.

In sum, rituals reinforce emotions and strengthen social cohesion (Collins, 2004; Durkheim, 1912/2001). Finally, Durkheim (1912/2001) argued that rituals and similar social activities of shared recall and reconstruction of emotional events contribute to reinforce collective memories or shared knowledge about important events (see Pennebaker, Páez, & Rimé, 1997). In the same vein, Halbwachs (1950/1968) proposed that commemorations and rituals are a form of collective remembering which helps to consolidate memories of important events. In this sense, such social events thus constitute normative processes that provide people with the opportunity to learn and transmit a moral lesson and to hold a social identity.

Most of these various ideas were supported in a recent study conducted about psychosocial responses to the terrorist attacks that occurred in Madrid in 2004. A common response to collective traumatic events such as September 11 in New York or March 11 in Madrid involved participation in secular and religious rituals such as memorials, demonstrations, and worship ceremonies (Collins, 2004). Psychosocial effects of participation in these demonstrations by people not personally affected by the March 11th events were investigated in a longitudinal study (Páez et al., 2005). This study confirms Pennebaker et al.'s social stage model of collective coping. First, there is the existence of an emergency stage characterized by high arousal, high social sharing, and rumination during 1 month. A transition stage, characterized by high arousal and rumination but low social sharing, appears at 3 to 4 weeks after the event. Finally an adaptation stage emerges at 2 months, characterized by simultaneous decreases in arousal, rumination, and sharing (Pennebaker & Harber, 1993). Data were collected a week after the March 11 events, in the emergency stage of collective response to trauma, then again after 3 weeks in the transition between emergency and plateau stage, and finally when 8 weeks had elapsed, in the transition to adaptation stage. It was found that, compared to those who did not demonstrate, people who took part in secular rituals or demonstration manifested higher levels of (a) shared emotional responses, as was evidenced by a higher reported emotional arousal, (b) social bonding, as manifested by higher levels of social rehearsal (i.e., following news coverage by mass media or exposure to mass media) and of pro-social coping modes, (c) social identification and collective self-esteem. Participation in rituals also predicted three weeks later (a) a higher perceived similarity with others, (b) a higher social integration (i.e., lower social loneliness), (c) stronger positive shared social beliefs, and (d) a higher agreement with personal, interpersonal, and community positive reactions or post-traumatic growth. Finally, participation in demonstrations predicted 2 months later a more positive perception of social climate, which offered an index of macro-social cohesion.

As was expected, participation in rituals also predicted memory for the collective trauma as assessed 2 months later. Free recall of features of the March 11th events was measured by six open questions such as "How many people were killed?" or "Which railway stations were bombed?" Recognition memory for details of the events was assessed by 26 closed statements to be rated as true or false. Correlation between participation in rituals and correct recognition of factual information was positive and significant, $r(600) = .10$, $p < .01$. Both total true recall and recognition scores were significantly higher in people who participated in rituals ($M = 20.5$) than in people who did not participate in rituals ($M = 19.7$).

The findings from this study thus suggested that rituals reinforce emotional arousal and are related to social rehearsal, two processes that play a central role in the formation of FBMs. In addition, participation in rituals predicted a better recall of semantic knowledge about the event. However, multiple regression of recall score on emotional activation, rumination, social sharing, exposure to mass media, and rituals revealed that higher social rehearsal via mass media exposure (TV, newspapers, and radio) was the specific predictor of event memory about the March 11th bombing. In developed societies mediated participation in rituals via mass media exposure seems to be the most important way to create a collective memory (see also Bellelli et al., 2000).

CONCLUSIONS

FBMs and CMs are both elicited by novel, unique, and surprising events when these events (1) are relevant for social identity (i.e., are related to a central attitude and to previous knowledge of the person), (2) involve changes in central aspects of social life ("consequentiality"), (3) are socially shared and provoke shared emotions, (4) are associated with intrapersonal and interpersonal rehearsal, and (5) are commemorated in collective behaviours and rituals. Rituals have positive effects on FBM and CM chiefly because they constitute a form of social rehearsal. Cultural contexts stressing egalitarian values (low PDI) manifest higher levels for determinants of FBM and CM such as social rehearsal. By this token, people responding to these characteristics evidence superior memory for collective traumatic events as well as for the context in which they hear about such events. Finally, rumination and emotional arousal are less relevant for memory than social rehearsal and rituals. This suggests that interpersonal processes such as institutional and mass media rehearsal are the main causal mechanism in the maintenance and construction of CMs and probably also of FBMs, consistent with a neo-Durkheimian conception of rituals and memory.

REFERENCES

Basabe, N., & Ros, M. (2005). Cultural dimensions and social behavior correlates: Individualism–collectivism and power distance. *International Review of Social Psychology*, *18*, 189–224.

Bellelli, G., Bakhurst, D., & Rosa, A. (2000). *Tracce: studi sulla memoria collectiva* [Studies about collective memory]. Napoli: Liguori.

Bellelli, G., Curci, A., & Leone, G. (2000). Le flashbulb memories come ricordi collettiva [Flashbulb memories as collective memories]. In G. Bellelli, D. Bakhurst, & A. Rosa (Eds.), *Tracce: studi sulla memoria collectiva* (pp. 191–216). Napoli: Liguori.

Berscheid, E., & Reis, H. T. (1998) Attraction and close relationships. In D. T. Gilbert, S. T. Fiske, & G. Lindzey (Eds.), *The handbook of social psychology* (4th ed., Vol. II, pp. 193–281). Boston: McGraw Hill.

Bohannon, J. N., & Symons, V. L. (1992). Flashbulb memories: Confidence, consistency, and quality. In E. Winograd & U. Neisser (Eds.), *Affect and accuracy in recall: Studies of "flashbulb memories"* (pp. 65–91). New York: Cambridge University Press.

Brown, R., & Kulik, J. (1977). Flashbulb memories. *Cognition*, *5*, 73–99.

Cladis, M. S. (2001). *Introduction to Durkheim, E. (1912/2001). The elementary forms of religious life* (pp. vii–xxxvii). Oxford, UK: Oxford University Press.

Collins, R. (2004). Rituals of solidarity and security in the wake of terrorist attacks. *Sociological Theory*, *22*, 53–87.

Curci, A., Luminet, O., Finkenauer, C., & Gisle, L. (2001). Flashbulb memories in social groups: A comparative test–retest study of the memory of French President Miterrand's death in a French and a Belgian group. *Memory*, *9*, 81–101.

Durkheim, E. (1912/2001). *The elementary forms of religious life*. Oxford, UK: Oxford University Press.

Finkenauer, C., Luminet, O., Gisle, L., El-Ahmadi, A., Van der Linden, M., & Philippot, P. (1998). Flashbulb memories and the underlying mechanism of their formation: Toward an emotional-integrative model. *Memory and Cognition*, *26*, 516–531.

Frijda, N. (1997). Commemorating. In J. Pennebaker, D. Páez, & B. Rimé (Eds.), *Collective memory of political events: Social psychological perspective* (pp. 191–208). Mahwah, NJ: Lawrence Erlbaum Associates Inc.

Gaskell, G. D., & Wright, D. (1997). Group differences in memory for a political event. In J. Pennebaker, D. Páez, & B. Rimé (Eds.), *Collective memory of political events: Social psychological perspective* (pp. 175–190). Mahwah, NJ: Lawrence Erlbaum Associates Inc.

Halbwachs, M. (1950/1968). *La Mémoire Collective* [Collective memory]. Paris: PUF.

Hofstede, G. (2001). *Culture's consequences* (2nd ed.). Thousand Oaks, CA: Sage.

Jedlowski, P. (2000). La sociologia e memoria collettiva [Sociology and collective memory]. In G. Bellelli, D. Bakhurst, & A. Rosa (Eds.), *Tracce: studi sulla memoria collective* (pp. 71–82). Napoli: Liguori.

Knight, C. (2003). Trauma, tedium and tautology in the study of ritual. *Cambridge Archaeological Journal, 13,* 293–295.

Levine, L. J., & Pizarro, D. A. (2004). Emotion and memory research: A grumpy overview. *Social Cognition, 22,* 530–554.

Luminet, O., Curci, A., Marhs, E. J., Wessel, E., Constantin, T., Gencoz, F., et al. (2004). The cognitive, emotional and social impact of the September Eleven attack: Group differences in memory for the reception context and the determinants of flashbulb memory. *Journal of General Psychology, 131,* 197–224.

Martín-Beristain, C., Páez, D., & González, J. L. (2000). Rituals, social sharing, silence, emotions and collective memory claims in the case of the Guatemalan genocide. *Psicothema, 12*(1), 117–130.

McLeod, J. R. (1999). The sociodrama of presidential politics. *American Anthropologist, 101,* 359–373.

McPhail, P., & Wohlstein, R.T. (1983). Individual and collective behavior within gatherings, demonstrations and riots. *Annual Review of Sociology, 9,* 579–600.

Milgram, S., & Toch, H. (1969). Collective behavior: Crowds and social movements. In G. Lindzey & E. Aronson (Eds.), *The handbook of social psychology* (Vol. 4, 2nd ed., pp. 507–610). Menlo Park, CA: Addison-Wesley.

Neal, A. G. (2005). *National trauma and collective memory* (2nd ed.). Armonk, NY: M. E. Sharpe.

Neisser, U., & Harsh, N. (1992). Phantom flashbulbs: False recollections of hearing the news about Challenger. In E. Winograd & U. Neisser (Eds.), *Affect and accuracy in recall: Studies of "flashbulb memories"* (pp. 9–31). New York: Cambridge University Press.

Páez, D., Basabe, N., Ubillos, S. & González, J. L. (2007). Participation in demonstrations, emotional climate and coping with collective violence in March Eleven Madrid bombings. *Journal for Social Issues, 63,* 323–327.

Páez, D., Rimé, B., & Basabe, N. (2005). A socio-cultural model of rituals: Effects of collective traumas and psychosocial processes of coping concerning March 11 demonstrations. *Revista de Psicología Social, 17,* 369–375.

Pennebaker J. W., & Banasik, B. L. (1997). On the creation and maintenance of collective memories. In J. Pennebaker, D. Páez, & B. Rimé (Eds.), *Collective memory of political events: Social psychological perspective* (pp. 3–20). Mahwah, NJ: Lawrence Erlbaum Associates Inc.

Pennebaker, J. W., & Harber, K. D. (1993). A social stage model of collective coping. *Journal of Social Issues, 49,* 125–145.

Pennebaker, J., Páez, D., & Rimé, B. (1997). *Collective memory of political events: Social psychological perspective.* Mahwah, NJ: Lawrence Erlbaum Associates Inc.

Richert, R. A., Whitehouse, H., & Stewart, E. (2005). Memory and analogical thinking in high-arousal rituals. In H. Harvey & R. N. McCauley (Eds.), *Psychological and cognitive foundation of religion* (pp. 127–145). Walnut Creek, CA: Altamira Press.

Rimé, B. (2005). *Le partage social de emotions* [Social sharing of emotions]. Paris: PUF.

Rimé, B., Finkenauer, C., Luminet, O., Zech, E., & Philippot, P. (1998). Social sharing of emotion: New evidence and new questions. In W. Stroebe & M. Hewstone (Eds.), *European review of social psychology* (Vol. 9, pp. 145–189). Chichester, UK: John Wiley & Sons.

Rosa, A., Bellelli, G., & Barkhurst, D. (2000). *Memoria colectiva e identidad nacional [Collective memory and national identity]*. Madrid: Biblioteca Nueva.

Schuman, H., & Scott, J. (1989). Generations and collective memory. *American Sociological Review*, 54, 359–381.

Scott, D., & Ponsoda, V. (1996). The role of positive and negative affect in flashbulb memory. *Psychological Reports*, *79*, 467–473.

Stroebe, W., & Stroebe, M. S. (1995). *Social psychology and health*. Buckinhgam, UK: Open University Press.

Turner, S. (Ed.). (2000). *The Cambridge companion to Weber*. Cambridge, UK: Cambridge University Press.

Weber, M. (1922). *Wirtschaft und gesellschaft*. Tubingen: Mohr.

Whitehouse, H. (2000). *Arguments and icons: Divergent modes of religiosity*. Oxford, UK: Oxford University Press.

Whitehouse, H. (2004). *Modes of religiosity: A cognitive theory of religious transmission*. Walnut Creek, CA: Altamira Press.

Wright, D., & Gaskell, G. (1992). The construction and function of vivid memories. In M. A. Conway, D. C. Rubin, H. Spinnler, & W. A. Wagenaar (Eds.), *Theoretical perspectives on autobiographical memory* (pp. 275–292). The Hague, The Netherlands: Kluwer Academic Press.

12 Cultural issues in flashbulb memory

Qi Wang and Çağla Aydın

Flashbulb memory (FBM) encompasses vivid and long-lasting remembering of the reception context of public news events (Brown & Kulik, 1977; Luminet, Chapter 3, and Curci, Chapter 1, this volume). Such events are often shocking, emotionally intense, collectively and personally important, and consequential over the long term to a social group, be it a family, a local community, a nation, or the entire world. Apparently beliefs, goals, practices, and other cultural aspects of the social group can have profound impact on how the remembering process takes place, on the quality, content, and structure of the memory subsequently formed, and on the long-term social, emotional, and behavioural consequences of the memory for the social group and its individual members. Yet in both theorization and empirical research of FBM, the role of culture is often treated implicitly and sometimes is even taken for granted. In this chapter we put culture "in the middle" of analysis (Cole, 1996). By delineating the various ways that culture may affect the process and consequence of remembering, we highlight the central role of culture in FBM.

We focus our discussion on cultural issues in FBM, and analyse memory for public news events wherever appropriate. Although FBM and public event memory have distinct structures (Curci & Luminet, 2006; Finkenauer et al., 1998; Luminet, Chapter 3, this volume), we focus on the shared processes in which they are shaped by cultural beliefs and practices. We first briefly discuss variables in the larger cultural context that may give rise to cultural differences in FBM. In particular we discuss means of information transmission across cultures that may introduce variations in how and what types of public event news individuals receive. We then turn to the discussion of how culture operates on the individual processes of receiving, experiencing, and sharing with others the news events. We focus on three mechanisms that are commonly thought to affect FBM invariantly across cultures: the importance effect, intense emotion, and post-event social sharing. Then we move on to discuss the self-defining functions of FBM and public event memory that vary across cultures where an independent versus an interdependent self-construal is emphasized. Against this backdrop we address the relationship between autobiographical memory and public event memory across the lifespan, and analyse cultural differences in individuals' use of public event memory to construct their personal and generational identities. In several sections we report some of our most recent findings of cross-cultural differences in FBM and public event memory. While analysing data from extant literature, we discuss theoretical and methodological challenges in cross-cultural FBM research and make recommendations for future studies. We end the chapter by pointing out more future directions in this exciting area of research on FBM.

INFORMATION TRANSMISSION AND MASS MEDIA

Societies differ in the ways that knowledge, information, and news are transmitted to individuals, such as through oral transmission, written and print formats (e.g., newspapers), or television (Wright & Gaskell, 1995). Modern technological innovations further enable individuals to actively seek and exchange event information through Internet, email, cell phones, and so on, thus creating further variations in information access across cultures. Importantly, even in societies that share similar information transmission channels and technologies, there are often cultural variations in news coverage, such as the proportions of prime time allocated for reporting different types of news events, and the continuous, around-the-clock news coverage of a disastrous event. The topics of news coverage have also been shown to vary across nations. A recent media analysis (Shoemaker & Cohen, 2006) showed that the most common category in news coverage in the US is sport, which accounts for 19% of US news coverage. In comparison, sport accounts for 13% of news coverage in Germany and only 4.5% in China. Furthermore, the content of international news coverage is often determined by political and economic factors and reflects the power structure in the world. Indeed, international news coverage is found to gravitate to a few powerful nations and the US is the most-covered country around the world (Wu, 2000).

These macro-level cultural variables may have important implications for FBM. They may determine the types of news events individuals are frequently exposed to, ponder on, and share with others, which further shapes FBM as well as public event memory (Hirst & Meksin, Chapter 10, this volume). In a recent study by Wang and colleagues (2008), middle-aged adults from middle-class communities in the US, England, Germany, Turkey, and China were asked to recall within 5 minutes as many public news events as they could that took place in any period of their lives. They then provided FBM details of first learning of the events, including place, time, source, activity, and others present. The recalled events were categorized as either "domestic" if they were relevant only to the respondent's local community or country of residence, or "foreign" if the event did not take place in or intricately involve the respondent's country of residence. For example, the fall of the Berlin Wall would be coded as a domestic event for German participants but a foreign event for non-German participants. Particularly relevant to the context of media coverage, it was found that foreign events recalled by non-US participants were disproportionately about the US (UK: 54.8%, Germany: 61.4%, Turkey: 53.2%, China: 75.2%). Furthermore, non-US participants recalled significantly more FBM details about foreign events involving the US than events not about the US. These results may reflect the fact that these countries devoted the greatest percentage of their foreign news coverage, approximately 17.7%, to the US (Wu, 2000). Notably, the percentage of US-related memories greatly exceeded the percentage of US-related media coverage, suggesting that individual selective processing may be critical during encoding and retention rather than media coverage alone determining memory. We discuss the individual processes in the next section.

Research considering mass media and information transmission as a macro-level influence of culture on FBM is sparse and should be a fruitful area in future. Especially in this technological era, new means of information transmission such as websites, emails, and text messages have become increasingly important ways in which individuals seek and receive public event news. Compared with traditional methods of news broadcasting such as newspaper, radio, and, more recently, television, these innovations can introduce substantial changes to the reception context of news events and consequently influence memory for information pertaining to the personal circumstances of first hearing about the events, such as when, where, who, whom, and what. For instance, a person may first learn about a news event alone, at an Internet cafe, while surfing on the web, as opposed to learning about the news with family, at home, while watching TV. The person may then email friends to share this news, as opposed to discussing it with family face-to-face. These changes may create differences in FBM, not only between societies of different degrees of modernization and technology, but also among individuals in the same culture or society who have varied access to modern technologies. One form of such within-culture variation may be reflected in generational differences because young people are generally more receptive to new things and perhaps are more willing to make use of new communication technologies than older populations. It would be of interest to study how the use of new technologies may impact on the structure and content of FBM both within and across cultures.

CULTURAL VARIATIONS IN UNIVERSAL MECHANISMS

Research into FBM has identified critical factors that affect the quality and preservation of memories. These factors include encoding variables such as surprise, intense emotionality, and the consequentiality of the original event as perceived by the individual and social group, which may trigger special encoding mechanisms to make the subsequent memory representations vivid and long lasting (Brown & Kulik, 1977; Conway, 1995; Pillemer, 1984).

Furthermore, post-encoding factors such as rehearsal, narration, and social sharing are equally, or perhaps even more, important for the formation and maintenance of FBM, although in the meantime they may contribute to memory distortions over time (Neisser, 1982; Schmolck, Buffalo, & Squire, 2000; Wright, 1993).

These basic-level factors and processes may be universal mechanisms underlying FBM as well as public event memory, yet cultural variables may operate on the ways in which the universal mechanisms take effect, resulting in cultural or group variations. Next we analyse some of the universal mechanisms in cultural contexts, focusing on the factors pertaining to the importance effect, emotionality, and social sharing.

The importance effect

Cognitive theories suggest that the importance of the incoming information is one of the critical determinants of how well the information will be attended to during encoding and, subsequently, how well it will be remembered (Alba & Hasher, 1983). For FBM, the importance effect may be further associated with intense emotional reactions and the consequentiality of the event as well as repeated post-event rehearsals, which can further facilitate vivid and persistent retention (e.g., Bohannon, 1988; Finkenauer et al., 1998; Rubin & Kozin, 1984). Patently, the nature and salience of a particular public event may vary significantly across groups depending on the personal, social, and cultural importance of the event as perceived by respective group members. For instance, an event that happened to a group or its members would be likely to be perceived as more important by the members of this group compared with outgroup members. This, in turn, can result in cultural and group differences in memory for the personal context details of first learning of the event (e.g., time, place, activity, source, others present, and aftermath) as well as memory for the event itself.

In an early study, Brown and Kulik (1977) compared FBM for 10 public events in Caucasian and African-American respondents. The latter group reported higher frequencies of memories of hearing the news of four events that were highly important and consequential for their group, including the murder of Medgar Evers, the attempted murder of George Wallace, and the assassinations of Malcolm X and Martin Luther King. Similarly, Conway and colleagues (1994) investigated FBM for the sudden and unexpected resignation of British prime minister Margaret Thatcher in a large-scale, cross-national study. The resignation of Mrs Thatcher was significant and surprising to the British because "it marked the end of a political era during which the fundamental changes had taken place in British Society, most of which stemmed from the policies and actions of her government" (Conway, 1995, p. 53). One year after the event, 86% of the UK participants, but only 29% of the non-UK participants, still preserved FBMs. Furthermore, memories of the UK participants showed greater consistency with an initial recall shortly after the event, compared with those of the non-UK participants.

Another example comes from a study by Curci, Luminet, Finkenauer, and Gisle (2001), who compared FBM for the death of the former French president François Mitterrand, in a French and a Belgian group. French participants rated the event as significantly more important and more emotional, particularly being sad and anxiety evoking, than did the Belgian group. Correspondingly, French participants had higher levels of recall for canonical details of the reception context than did Belgian participants. And while both groups showed forgetting over time, French participants were more confident in their memory reports than were Belgians. Similarly, in a study of FBM for the 9/11 terrorist attacks, Luminet and colleagues found that, compared with non-US respondents, US respondents rated the event as more important and had better memory of the event and its reception context (Luminet et al., 2004).

The importance effect also operates on the phenomenal qualities of FBM. For instance, Kvavilashvili, Mirani, Schlagman, and Kornbrot (2003) examined Italian and British participants' FBM for the 9/11 terrorist attacks (a recent event) and the death of Princess Diana (a distant event). Presumably the two events were equal in importance and consequentiality for the British participants, whereas the 9/11 attacks might seem more important than the death of Princess Diana for the Italians. The results showed that, in spite of the different time lags of the two events (3 months vs 51 months), the British participants' FBMs for the events were equally detailed, specific, and vivid. In contrast, the Italian participants remembered the 9/11 attacks significantly better than the death of Princess Diana. A follow-up of Luminet et al.'s (2004) study by Curci and Luminet (2006) also showed that US participants reported more specific FBMs as well as more accurate event memory of the 9/11 terrorist attacks than participants in Belgium, Italy, Japan, Romania, and The Netherlands.

More important from the current perspective, the larger cultural ambience may determine which events are likely to be perceived as salient, important, and significant by individuals. This in turn may drive individuals to selectively attend to certain types of events and their reception contexts, resulting in cultural differences in memory over the long term. Recent research by Wang, Conway, and colleagues has provided evidence for this proposal (Conway et al., 2006; Wang, 2005; Wang et al., 2008). The researchers suggested that given the cultural context in the US that promotes a national egocentrism in policy, education, and aspects of daily lives, Americans would value, attend to, and further remember more information about local and national events relative to foreign events, compared with people in other countries. In the multi-national study described in the previous section, the researchers found that American participants recalled twice as many FBM details for domestic events as for foreign events, while such a difference was absent in all other groups. In addition, Americans recalled proportionally more domestic events (93%) and fewer foreign events (7%), compared with British (72% vs 28%), German (49% vs 51%), Turkish (56% vs 44%), and Chinese (62% vs 38%) participants.

Together, current empirical data suggest that the quality of FBM and public event memory is a positive function of the subjective importance of an event as perceived by a particular social or cultural group. This poses an important methodological question, as well as challenge, for cross-cultural research on FBM, where one needs to take into consideration the specific social and personal significance of the target event to respective cultural groups.

Emotional determinants

Emotion, when within the normal range of human experience, is generally thought to facilitate the remembering of event information (Christianson & Safer, 1996; McGaugh, 2003; Reisberg & Hertel, 2004). Consistent with this theoretical view, independently rated emotionality of a public news event is found to be positively associated with the recall of subsequent FBM (Bohannon, 1988; Christianson, 1989; Julian, Bohannon, & Aue, Chapter 5, this volume; Rubin & Kozin, 1984). The effect of emotion on FBM may occur via various pathways. The reception of a public event often engenders intense surprise and other more general emotional reactions, which may further trigger special mechanisms to facilitate the formation of FBM. This process may be related to or mediated by the appraisal of the importance and consequentiality of the event to one's social group (Brown & Kulik, 1977; Conway et al., 1994; Fivush, Bohanek, Marin, & McDermott Sales, Chapter 8, this volume). Furthermore, emotion may influence post-encoding mechanisms such as rehearsal and memory sharing, which in turn may help individuals solidify their memories of hearing the news-breaking event in a social context (Finkenauer et al., 1998). Indeed, individuals tend to share their emotional experiences with others and search for more information about what happened (Rimé, Philippot, Boca, & Mesquita, 1992), and more-intense emotional experiences often elicit more frequent social sharing compared with less-intense ones (Luminet, Bouts, Delie, Manstead, & Rimé, 2000; Philippot & Rimé, 1998). Mass media, especially television, may also play a role by creating "FB emotions" and "public mourning" for a tragic event, which can substantially shape individuals' feeling and memory concerning the event (Bourdon, 2003).

Given the social nature of these pathways, it is obvious that the facilitative effect of emotion on FBM cannot be reduced to a state of arousal or a mere subjective feeling state, but must be situated in a cultural context. Cultures hold different beliefs in terms of how emotion ought to be experienced, expressed, and shared. For instance, in Euro-American culture that emphasizes individuality and autonomy, emotion is often regarded as a direct expression of the self and an affirmation of the uniqueness of the individual.

Expressing one's true feelings and sharing them with others is highly encouraged and often perceived as an indication of honesty and self-authenticity. In contrast, in many East Asian cultures such as Korea, China, and Japan that put a premium on social harmony and group interests, emotion, especially negative emotion, tends to be viewed as destructive or even dangerous to ongoing relationships and therefore needs to be strictly controlled. Explicit communication of emotions is often treated as superfluous or even improper. Instead, individuals are encouraged to infer others' feeling states without being told, while restraining their own emotions through psychological discipline (Bond, 1990; Chao, 1995; Wang, 2003).

These different cultural beliefs may affect how individuals actually experience, express, and share emotions. Research has shown that individuals in cultures that emphasize self-expression and individuality often report experiencing more intense emotions than individuals in cultures that value collectivity (Fernandez, Carrera, Sanchez, Páez, & Candia, 2000; Wang, 2003). The former also report more frequent social sharing and rumination about feeling states than the latter (Basabe et al., 2002; Luminet et al., 2004). Interestingly, parents tend to use culture-specific ways of integrating emotions into memory conversations with their young children, in line with their cultural beliefs and socialization goals. When sharing memories of past experiences with their 3-year-olds, Euro-American mothers frequently talk about the causes of the child's feeling states and provide elaborate explanations as to why and how the child experienced the emotion. They are also ready to accept the child's negative emotions and reassure the child that everything was all right. In contrast, Chinese mothers often initiate little causal discussion about children's feeling states and often comment on the child's emotions in such a way as to "teach the child a lesson" about his or her negative emotional experience and rule-violating behaviour. And consistent with the belief about emotion being potentially threatening to interpersonal harmony, Chinese mothers often prescribe the child's negative emotions as unacceptable (e.g., "You shouldn't get mad at Papa") and needing to be controlled or resolved through the child's proper behaviour in the future (Wang, 2001a; Wang & Fivush, 2005). These different practices of emotion socialization may eventually instill in children different attitudes towards emotion and how it should be experienced, expressed, and shared.

Thus, although intense emotional reactions—surprise and other emotions more generally—may serve as a universal mechanism in facilitating FBM encoding and subsequent retention over time, there may be cultural variations in the degree to which this mechanism takes effect. Specifically, when the experience, expression, and social sharing of emotion in response to life events is undermined in a particular culture, individuals in that culture may benefit less from the facilitative effect of emotion and thus have fewer or less-detailed memories, compared with those in cultures where emotion and emotion sharing is prized. Recent cross-cultural findings of FBM recollection point to this possibility (Wang et al., 2008). When asked to recall memories for public events, Chinese participants retrieved the fewest FBM details and the least number of event memories, compared with US, British, German, and Turkish participants. Similarly, after the nuclear accident that occurred in Japan in 1999, only a small percentage of Japanese participants formed FBMs, regardless of whether they lived close to or far away from the accident site (Otani et al., 2005). These cultural variations in accessibility to FBM and event memory may result from different views of emotion and the related subjective emotional experiences across cultures. They may also be a function of different cultural emphases on and practices of post-event memory sharing, to which we turn next.

Rehearsal and social sharing

Repeated rehearsal following a news event is a critical predictor of the quality, content, and general retention of FBMs, no matter whether it is covert ruminations within an individual or public communications with others about the event and about one's circumstances and reactions when first learning of the event (Bohannon & Symons, 1992; Finkenauer et al., 1998; Julian et al., Chapter 5, this volume; Luminet et al., 2004; Martin & Tesser, 1996). Rehearsal often strengthens the aspects of the experience that are linked to intense emotional reactions and further facilitates the process and retention of relevant information (Pezdek, 2003). Furthermore, social sharing of FBM may provide individuals with opportunities to relive the shared experience, thus deepening their emotional involvement with the social group to which they belong, particularly when the event is consequential and emotional to the group as a whole (Pennebaker & Banasik, 1997). Sociological and psychological research has also suggested that FBM and public event memory are in most part outcomes of shared experiences that take place in social contexts (Finkenauer, Gisle, & Luminet, 1997; Halbwachs, 1992; Pennebaker & Banasik, 1997). In addition to the private rumination and social sharing of an experience, rehearsal of FBM is often influenced by media communication and involves such activities as following event-related media proceedings (Curci et al., 2001; Hirst & Meksin, Chapter 10, this volume). These cognitive and social processes of rehearsal take place in a larger cultural context and are subject to variations across cultures.

Generally, sharing memories with others is considered a valuable social practice in Western cultures (Fivush, 1994; Nelson, 1993; Pasupathi, 2001; Pillemer, 1998). Such conversations permit individuals to express their own opinions and emotions, elicit strong empathic responses that can serve to deepen intimacy between the conversational partners, and further release and regulate negative feeling states. This positive emphasis on memory sharing, particularly on relating stressful emotional experiences to others, may not be appreciated to the same extent in other cultures (Wang & Ross, 2007). For instance, in many East Asian cultures, individual expression tends to be de-emphasized and elaborate, self-focused recounting of one's own experiences is often considered socially inappropriate. Furthermore, relationships in these cultures are largely defined and governed by existing social orders and group memberships, and therefore do not require, at least not to the same extent as in Western cultures, individual efforts through practices such as sharing memories (Wang, 2004; Wang & Fivush, 2005). In addition, individuals are often expected to control their negative affect through psychological discipline and self-regulation, and not to impose their emotional burden on others (Bond, 1991; Tweed, White, & Lehman, 2004).

Consistent with these different cultural views, studies have suggested cultural variations with regard to how, when, with whom, and to what extent emotional experiences are shared (Rimé, Corsini, & Herbette, 2002; Rimé et al., 2001). Koreans reported that 20% of their emotional experiences were never shared; for US participants the comparable figure was only 5%. French and US samples also claimed to have repetitively shared a single emotional episode with others on a greater number of occasions (about five times) than did Korean, Singaporean, and Japanese samples (two or three times). In addition, Westerners reported sharing the emotional event shortly after it took place, usually after a delay of 1 or 2 days; in contrast Asians typically reported a much longer delay, for instance 4 to 5 days in the case of Singaporeans. Although people in both Western and Asian cultures reported sharing emotional memories most frequently with best friends and rarely with strangers, French and US participants were more inclined to share memories with their family members (spouse, parents, siblings, and grandparents) than were Asians (see Rimé et al., 2002).

In addition to the data based on retrospective reports of frequency and dates of memory sharing, observations of everyday interactions in the family also suggest varied practices across cultures. During a 1-day observation of Euro-American and Korean mother–child conversations, Mullen and Yi (1995) found that American mothers talked with their 3-year-olds about past events three times as often as Korean mothers did. Similarly, Martini (1996) observed that during weekday evening meals at home, Euro-American parents were twice as likely to ask their children to talk about past events as were Japanese-American parents.

What would be the implications of the varied cultural practices of social sharing of past experiences for FBM? If after-the-fact pondering, discussion, and reconsideration are indeed critical for the establishment of FBMs (e.g., Neisser, 1982), one may expect individuals in cultures such as East Asia that put less emphasis on memory sharing to have fewer or less-detailed FBMs than those in cultures that regard such a practice as paramount. Recent cross-cultural findings of FBM recollection (Wang et al., 2008) provided some preliminary evidence for this suggestion, where Western participants recalled more FBM details and, compared with Chinese adults, were able to access a greater number of memories of public news events quickly. Alternatively it might also be that, given the reduced social rehearsal, Asian individuals preserve their FBM content as more uncontaminated than their

Western counterparts, since rehearsal has been demonstrated to induce modifications and distortions in individuals' memories over time (Neisser, 1982; Schmolck et al., 2000; Wright, 1993). Although rehearsal may aid preservation of details and consistency in FBM and event memory (Julian et al., Chapter 5, this volume; Shapiro, 2006), retellings of events in social contexts often serve such purposes as garnering sympathy, expressing emotion, entertaining, and so on, rather than accurately conveying facts, and therefore can be particularly error-prone for later memory (Marsh, 2007). Obviously, further research is needed to examine the consequence of rehearsal and social sharing for the remembering of public events and their reception contexts across cultures.

CULTURE AND THE SELF-DEFINING FUNCTIONS OF FBM

FBM is inextricably connected with one's self and identity. Such memories provide clues, materials, and resources from which we build benchmarks of our lives that converge with history. Just as Neisser (1982, p. 73) claims, FBMs "are the places where we line up our own lives with the course of history itself and say 'I was there'". Indeed, we would like to posit that FBM can be conceptualized as a special form of autobiographical memory (AM), which is characterized as taking place at a particular place and time in the past, personally significant, enduring, and socially sharable (Nelson & Fivush, 2004). Thus, FBM may play just as important a role in constituting one's self and identity as AM does (Wang, 2005). Importantly, the self-defining functions of FBM may vary across cultures, further resulting in cultural variations in the quality, structure, and content of FBMs.

Memory and self in cultural contexts

Memory is functional, no matter if it is FBM, event memory, or semantic memory of the world (e.g., knowledge of history), and the function of memory lies in the significance of specific recollections in sustaining individuals' current goals, self-theories, and beliefs (Pillemer, 1998; Wang & Conway, 2004). A considerable number of sociological and psychological theories have discussed the functions of FBM as well as memory for public events in relation to the construction of self and identity (Berntsen, Chapter 9, this volume; Gaskell & Wright, 1997; Tajfel, 1982). It is suggested that FBM elements such as "who was a co-participant" help to increase group identification and group cohesion (Barrett, 2000), and the preservation of detailed and vivid FBMs may serve as an expression of commitment to the social group to which one belongs (Berntsen, Chapter 9, this volume). Furthermore, memories for public/political events may help individuals to identify themselves as members of the social group as well as to build separate personal identities, and may further serve to enhance individuals' self-esteem (Gaskell & Wright, 1997).

The self-defining functions of FBM are further manifested in the context of culture, given that the very definition of the self emerges in response to the philosophical and religious traditions and the everyday customs and practices of a culture. Typically, Western cultures, particularly European-American culture, are characterized as emphasizing the self as an independent and autonomous entity (i.e., an *independent self-construal*), whereas Eastern Asian cultures tend to view the self as primarily interconnected with significant others (i.e., an *interdependent self-construal*) (Heine, Lehman, Markus, & Kitayama, 1999; Markus & Kitayama, 1991). Cross-cultural research on autobiographical memory has further demonstrated that, compared to individuals with an interdependent self-construal, individuals with an independent self-construal have greater access to very-long-term memories such as early childhood experiences, describe their memories with richer emotions and details, and focus more on their own roles and perspectives in the past events during recall (Wang, 2001b; for a review, see Wang & Ross, 2007). Presumably such detailed, self-focused, emotional, and rich representations of one's unique past experiences can, in turn, reaffirm the self as an autonomous entity.

The cross-cultural data on autobiographical memory can shed light on FBM in different cultural contexts where culturally prevailing views of the self shape the ways in which information of public events is received, interpreted, and shared. To date, however, most studies examining cross-national or cross-cultural differences in FBM have involved only Western samples, and there were no direct measures of cultural self-construal in these studies. Studies with more diverse populations to examine the direct link between cultural self-construal and FBM should be a fertile area in future research. Conceivably, individuals with an independent self-construal may remember more details about their own actions, feelings, and emotional reactions relative to those of others when first hearing the news, compared with individuals with an interdependent self-construal. Methods that elicit extended narrations about the event reception context should prove effective such that content analysis of the memory narratives can be performed to examine the aspects of FBM that are most susceptible to cultural influences.

Another exciting research area is to examine the degree to which individuals in different cultures integrate FBM and public event memory into their life stories. A recent study by Wang and Conway (2004) may shed some light on this question. In this study, 40- to 60-year-old European-American and Chinese adults were asked to remember and briefly describe 20 specific, one-moment-in-time personal events that took place in their lives. Content analysis of the memories indicated that Chinese adults provided an average of 3.4 memories (approximately 17% of the total 20 memories) that had a reference to historical/public events, whereas Americans on average did not even provide one memory ($M = .26$, less than 1.5% of the total 20 memories). This cultural difference may reflect the greater concern with the larger collective and societal context in relation to one's self and identity in Chinese people than in Americans, whose identity construction is more dependent on self-revealing, unique autobiographical events. Such cultural difference may similarly surface across generations, in which case memories of historical events help to define each generation's identity (Holmes & Conway, 1999).

Lifespan retrieval

A wider perspective on the operations of culture on self and memory can be achieved by looking at memories across the lifespan. This approach can provide us with insights into questions such as whether cross-cultural differences, as well as similarities, in preserving FBM and public event memory may vary as a function of the age at encoding, and how and to what extent the retention of the memory is influenced by the canonical conceptions of various life periods across cultures (e.g., whether in different cultures the youth period is similarly perceived as a time for individuals to form a stable identity). Furthermore, this approach to studying FBM can be informed by research on the phenomenon of the reminiscence bump in relation to the interactions between autobiographical memory and the self in different populations (Benson et al., 1992; Conway, Wang, Hanyu, & Haque, 2005).

Briefly defined, the reminiscence bump refers to a period of marked increase in memories of autobiographical events dated to when rememberers were 10 to 30 years of age (e.g., Rubin, Wetzler, & Nebes, 1986). It is reported to be one of the most robust phenomena in cognitive psychology (Conway & Rubin, 1993). Since the reminiscence bump corresponds to a period when a stable self comes into form as the transition from adolescence into adulthood takes place, the great accessibility of memories from this period has been explained by their inherent links to this stable self that "serves as the foundation of autobiographical memory knowledge structures persisting over the lifespan" (Conway et al., 2005, p. 3). According to the Eriksonian conception of lifespan development (Erikson, 1963), individuals oscillate between identity confusion and identity formation during this period. Consequently they may allocate a great amount of cognitive effort in processing self-relevant information, which renders event memories from this period encoded in more privileged ways than those encoded at other points in the life cycle (Conway & Pleydell-Pearce, 2000; Holmes & Conway, 1999). A question of interest in the present context is: Are there any cultural differences in the reminiscence bump, and lifespan retrieval in general, that may result from different processes and milestones of identity formation across cultures? Conway and colleagues (2005) suggested that there might be differences among cultures in how to define adulthood. For instance, in some Asian societies initiation of adulthood does not occur until 30 years of age, which is substantially later than in Western societies where adulthood is often considered established following adolescence, in the early 20s. The different cultural views of adulthood might, in turn, contribute to differences in the age distribution of the reminiscence bump. In a multi-national study

(Conway et al., 2005) the researchers asked middle-aged adults from Japan, China, Bangladesh, England, and the United States to each recall 20 personal memories of specific events that took place in any period of their lives. Interestingly enough, there were no cross-cultural differences in the timing of the period of the reminiscence bump. As shown in Figure 12.1, the reminiscence bump took the same shape across all groups. A great percentage of memories were retrieved from the period 10 to 30 years, a finding consistent with many previous observations of the reminiscence bump.

What was found to be different, however, was the content of the memories. Consistent with previous findings (e.g., Wang, 2001b), people from Western societies recalled memories that focused on the rememberer, whereas people from Eastern societies recalled memories with a group or social orientation. The researchers suggested that compared with memory content that seems sensitive to cultural influences related to the nature of the self, the structural features of autobiographical memory, including the reminiscence bump, may be more susceptible to biological mechanisms such as the development of frontal networks and hormonal changes in adolescence that facilitate a greater integration of self and memory (Conway et al., 2005). Alternatively, the cultural similarities in the lifespan distribution of autobiographical memory may reflect the shared characteristics of the middle-class samples in this study. It is perhaps true among middle-class populations in all modern societies that each life period (early childhood, adolescence, midlife, etc.) is associated with similar social demands imposed by the society, and that young adulthood is an important period in life and memories from this period are crucial for identity formation and development (Wang &

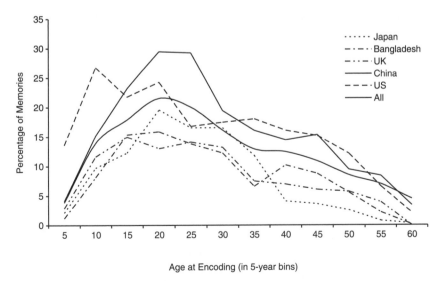

Figure 12.1 Lifespan retrieval curves of autobiographical events in five cultures. From Conway et al. (2005).

Conway, 2006). It remains an empirical question in future research to examine the relation between self and the reminiscence bump in more traditional societies that hold views and practices different from middle-class values concerning individuals' entry into adulthood.

Research on the lifespan retrieval of memory related to public events has yielded interesting findings. People are more likely to report an event as "one or two most important *public events*" in their lifetime if it had occurred during their adolescence and early adulthood than other life periods (Schuman, Akiyama, & Knauper, 1998; Schuman & Scott, 1989). They are also more likely to answer *general knowledge* questions correctly (e.g., about the Academy Awards) if the event happened when participants were aged between 10 and 30 years than between 31 and 50 years (Rubin, Rahhal, & Poon, 1998). Given that our identities are directly tied to our political beliefs and behaviours, it should come as no surprise that these beliefs and behaviours become solidified around the same time as identity formation. Indeed, it has been found that a person's partisan beliefs and attitudes, which are fairly elastic at an early age, become stable by the end of the "bump period" (Alwin & Krosnick 1991).

In a related vein, memories of political events, which are thought to be connected with individuals' political identities, are more accessible from the youth period. Interestingly, when comparing the lifespan retrieval of public versus personal event memories, Holmes and Conway (1999) observed a peak recall of public memories from when the participants were aged between 10 and 19 years, whereas there was a peak recall of personal memories from when the participants were aged between 20 and 29 years. While personal memories may help to solidify an individual's personal identity, public event memories may help to form a shared generational identity. Thus there appears to be a two-stage process of identity development: the stage of generational identity formation at around 10 to 19 years of age, and the stage of personal identity formation around 20 to 29 years of age (Conway, 1997; Holmes & Conway 1999).

According to Conway (1997, p. 29), a generational identity is formed by "shared cultural experiences of a type of event, common ways of responding to the world, common existential problems and shared conceptual knowledge". Other researchers such as Schuman, Belli, and Bischoping (1997) have also linked the Eriksonian psychosocial identity stage to both the individual and generational identities. They contend that generational identity occurs when individuals recognize that they are part of a particular social group with which they share common goals, knowledge, and memories of similar kinds of experiences. In trying to identify themselves with the group, young adults invest cognitive effort that leads to privileged encoding of relevant information into memory and thus better retention of public knowledge and memories from this period. Notably, compared with personal event memories, memories of public events are more likely to be affected by rehearsal mechanisms that occur in the process of commemoration following an event, both in the form of official commemoration such as war memorials and popular commemoration such as movies and memoirs.

Wang and colleagues recently conducted a multi-national study to examine the lifespan retrieval of public event memories (Wang et al., 2008). US, British, German, Turkish, and Chinese middle-aged adults free-recalled memories of public news events that took place in their lifetimes within a limited timeframe. As shown in Figure 12.2, when responses were plotted in terms of age of the participant at time of encoding, it was found that for all groups but Chinese, the peak recall for public events was in the period when participants were between 10 and 19 years of age, consistent with previous findings (Conway, 1997; Holmes & Conway, 1999). There was also a bump from 40 to 49 years for all groups, possibly reflecting a recency effect on recall. Surprisingly, the Chinese group had a peak recall that occurred from 30 to 39 years, which was reliably later than that of all other groups. It is not entirely clear whether and how this pattern of lifespan retrieval in the Chinese participants may be associated with the timing of their generational identity formation. Perhaps the late bump in the Chinese participants entails the establishment of a "mature" self with sincere commitment to social needs and moral rectitude—which, according to Confucian teachings, does not appear until age 30, when one can hold on firmly to what he or she has learned (*san-shi-er-li*, 三十而立). These findings suggest a complex relation among culture, self, and memory recollection. Further research on lifespan retrieval of FBM across cultures is crucial to corroborate the findings.

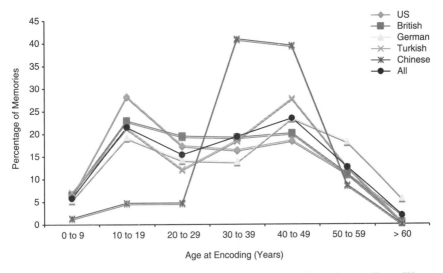

Figure 12.2 Lifespan retrieval curves of public events in five cultures. From Wang et al. (2008).

FBM AS A CULTURAL PRACTICE: CONCLUSION

In this chapter we discussed various cultural factors in the macro and micro contexts that may substantially shape the process and consequence of FBM. Specifically, the methods of information transmission and news coverage in a culture, together with the values and beliefs embedded in the larger cultural ambience, may largely determine how individuals receive public event news, as well as what types of events individuals value, attend to, and subsequently remember. Cultural beliefs and practices may further act on basic-level mechanisms of remembering, influencing the degree of importance or significance individuals perceive of an event, the type and intensity of emotions individuals experience and report upon learning about the news, and individuals' attitude towards and frequency of memory sharing following the event. These varied processes, in turn, contribute to cultural variations in the quality and accessibility of FBM. Furthermore, cultural belief systems, particularly cultural conceptions of selfhood, shape the self-defining functions that FBM as well as public event memory assume, which further affects the content, structure, and lifespan distribution of the memory across cultures.

We must acknowledge, however, that in spite of the extant theories and empirical findings, research on FBM with cultural sensitivity and methodological sophistication is still very much needed. Wherever appropriate we have suggested directions for future research throughout the chapter. In addition to what we have discussed, several issues deserve further attention. One is related to the accuracy of FBM and its cultural determinants. It will be particularly rewarding to examine whether memory distortion about public events and their reception contexts may take different forms across cultures, such that individuals in a given culture may tend to make systematic omission or commission errors for certain types of information. Moreover, in addition to examining FBM for news events pre-selected by researchers, studies need to sample a wide variety of public events that are deemed important, consciously or unconsciously, by individuals from different cultures. And in addition to examining the accuracy, quality, and long-term retention of FBMs, a great emphasis should be placed on the content of memory narratives that individuals provide, both about the news event itself and about the contextual aspects of receiving the news (Julian et al., Chapter 5, this volume). As research on autobiographical memory has demonstrated, memory content opens up a window through which we can observe cultural influences on the ways in which individuals attend to, represent, organize, retrieve, and share event information.

Patently, FBM not only takes place in a larger cultural context where the public event occurs and the news is then transmitted to and received by individuals, it also takes shape in proximal social settings during face-to-face interactions among individuals. It is thus essential to examine the dynamic interactions among individuals upon receiving the news and afterwards, and to examine how such interactions, while mediating cultural influences, shape the nature of FBM. Recent studies on collective memory, memory for conversations, and the effect of social sharing on individual memory have yielded important findings informative to FBM. For instance, individual recollections of shared experiences were strongly influenced by memory conversations in the presence of a narrator who initiated or dominated the conversations (Cuc, Ozuru, Manier, & Hirst, 2006; Gabbert, Memon, & Wright, 2006), and by the specific information the narrator selectively said or left unsaid (Cuc, Koppel, & Hirst, 2007). It follows that in cultures that promote social hierarchy among individuals, individual recollections of FBM may be more likely to conform to memories of those who hold greater power and resources in the society at large and within the context of memory sharing, compared with cultures that value equality and individuals' ownership of their experiences. This remains an interesting empirical question for future research.

Ultimately, remembering of public news events and their reception contexts is an important cultural practice. Not only do the process and consequence of the remembering vary as a function of cultural influences, such memories, once formed, also serve to constitute a shared cultural identity among individual members of a society or a social group, as well as a shared generational identity among individuals of a historical time that may transcend culture. Such memories further interweave our personal history with the history of our time and place, thus sealing our individual identities with a clear mark of culture.

REFERENCES

Alba, J. W., & Hasher, L. (1983). Is memory schematic? *Psychological Review, 90*, 203–231.

Alwin, D. F., & Krosnick, J. A. (1991). Aging, cohorts, and the stability of sociopolitical orientations over the lifespan. *American Journal of Sociology, 97*, 169–195.

Barrett. J. L. (2000). Exploring the natural foundations of religion. *Trends in Cognitive Science, 4*, 29–34.

Basabe, N., Páez, D., Valencia, J., Gonzalez, J. L., Rimé, B., & Diener, E. (2002). Cultural dimensions, socioeconomic development, climate, and emotional hedonic level. *Cognition and Emotion, 16*, 103–125.

Benson, K. A., Jarvi, S. D., Arai, Y., Thielbar, P. R. S., Frye, K. J., & McDonald, B. L. G. (1992). Socio-historical context and autobiographical memories: Variations in the reminiscence phenomenon. In M. A. Conway, D. C. Rubin, H. Spinnler, & W. A. Wagenaar (Eds.), *Theoretical perspectives on autobiographical memory* (pp. 313–322). Boston: Kluwer Academic.

Bohannon, J. N. (1988). Flashbulb memories for the space shuttle disaster: A tale of two theories. *Cognition, 29*, 179–196.

Bohannon, J. N., & Symons, L.V. (1992). Flashbulb memories: Confidence, consistency, and quantity. In E. Wingograd & U. Neisser (Eds.), *Affect and accuracy in* recall: Studies of "flashbulb" memories (pp. 65–91). Cambridge, UK: Cambridge University Press.

Bond, M. H. (1991). *Beyond the Chinese face*. Hong Kong: Oxford University Press.

Bourdon, J. (2003). Some sense of time: Remembering television. *History and Memory*, *15*, 5–35.

Brown, R., & Kulik, J. (1977). Flashbulb memories. *Cognition*, *5*, 73–99.

Chao, R. K. (1995). Chinese and European American cultural models of the self reflected in mothers' childrearing beliefs. *Ethos*, *23*(3), 328–354.

Christianson, S. A. (1989). Flashbulb memories: Special, but not so special. *Memory and Cognition*, *17*, 435–443.

Christianson, S. A., & Safer, M. A. (1996). Emotional events and emotions in auto-biographical memories. In D. C. Rubin (Ed.), *Remembering our past: Studies in autobiographical memory* (pp. 218–243). New York: Cambridge University Press.

Cole, M. (1996). *Cultural psychology*. Cambridge, MA: Harvard University Press.

Conway, M. A. (1995). *Flashbulb memories*. Hove, UK: Lawrence Erlbaum Associates Ltd.

Conway, M. A. (1997). The inventory of experience: Memory and identity. In J. W. Pennebaker, D. Páez, & B. Rimé (Eds.), *Collective memory of political events: Social psychological perspectives* (pp. 21–46). Mahwah, NJ: Lawrence Erlbaum Associates Inc.

Conway, M. A., Anderson, S. J., Larsen, S. F., Donnelly, C. M., McDaniel, M. A., McClelland, A. G. R., et al. (1994). The formation of flashbulb memories. *Memory and Cognition*, *22*, 326–343.

Conway, M. A., & Pleydell-Pearce, C. W. (2000). The construction of autobiographical memories in the self memory system. *Psychological Review*, *107*, 261–288.

Conway, M. A., & Rubin, D. C. (1993). The structure of autobiographical memory. In A. F. Collins, S. E. Gathercole, M. A. Conway, & P. E. Collins (Eds.), *Theories of memory* (pp. 103–137). Hove, UK: Lawrence Erlbaum Associates Ltd.

Conway, M. A., Wang, Q., Hanyu, K., & Haque, S. (2005). A cross-cultural investigation of autobiographical memory: On the universality and cultural variation of the "reminiscence bump". *Journal of Cross-Cultural Psychology*, *36*(6), 739–749.

Conway, M., Wang Q., Hou, Y., Kulkofsky, S., Mueller-Johnson K., Aydın, Ç., et al. (2006, July). *Public event memories: A multi-national investigation*. In Q. Wang & M. A. Conway (co-Chairs), *Memory and Culture*. Symposium conducted at the 4th International Conference on Memory, Sydney, Australia.

Cuc, A., Koppel, J., & Hirst, W. (2007). Silence is not golden: A case for socially-shared retrieval-induced forgetting. *Psychological Science*, *18*, 727–733.

Cuc, A., Ozuru, Y., Manier, D., & Hirst, W. (2006). On the formation of collective memories: The role of a dominant narrator. *Memory and Cognition*, *34*(4), 752–762.

Curci, A., & Luminet, O. (2006). Follow-up of a cross-national comparison on flash-bulb and event memory for the September 11th attacks. *Memory*, *14*(3), 329–344.

Curci, A., Luminet, O., Finkenauer, C., & Gisle, L. (2001). Flashbulb memories in social groups: A comparative test–retest study of the memory of French president Mitterrand's death in a French and a Belgian group. *Memory*, *9*, 81–101.

Erikson, E. H. (1963). *Childhood and society*. New York: Norton.

Fernandez, I., Carrera, P., Sanchez, F., Páez, D., & Candia, L. (2000). Differences between cultures in emotional verbal and nonverbal reactions. *Psicothema*, *12*, 83–92.

Finkenauer, C., Gisle, L., & Luminet, O. (1997). When individual memories are socially shaped: Flashbulb memories of socio-political events. In J. W. Pennebaker, D. Páez, & B. Rimé (Eds.), *Collective memory of political events: Social psychological perspectives* (pp. 191–208). Hillsdale, NJ: Lawrence Erlbaum Associates Inc.

Finkenauer, C., Luminet, O., Gisle, L., El-Ahmadi, A., Van der Linden, M., & Philippot, P. (1998). Flashbulb memories and the underlying mechanisms of their formation: Toward an emotional-integrative model. *Memory and Cognition*, *26*, 516–523.

Fivush, R. (1994). Constructing narrative, emotions, and self in parent–child conversations about the past. In U. Neisser & R. Fivush (Eds.), *The remembering self: Construction and accuracy in the self-narrative* (pp. 136–157). New York: Cambridge University Press.

Gabbert, F., Memon, A., & Wright, D. B. (2006). Memory conformity: Disentangling the steps toward influence during a discussion. *Psychonomic Bulletin and Review*, *13*(3), 480–485.

Gaskell, G., & Wright, D. (1997). Group differences for memory of a political event. In J. W. Pennebaker, D. Páez, & B. Rimé (Eds.), *Collective memory of political events: Social psychological perspectives* (pp. 175–189). Hillsdale, NJ: Lawrence Erlbaum Associates Inc.

Halbwachs, M. (1992). *On collective memory*. Illinois: University of Chicago Press.

Heine, S. J., Lehman, D. R., Markus, H. R., & Kitayama, S. (1999). Is there a universal need for positive self-regard? *Psychological Review*, *106*, 766–794.

Holmes, A., & Conway, M. A. (1999). Generation identity and the reminiscence bump: Memory for public and private events. *Journal of Adult Development*, *6*, 21–34.

Kvavilashvili, L., Mirani J., Schlagman, S., & Kornbrot, D. E. (2003). Comparing flashbulb memories of September 11 and the death of Princess Diana: Effects of time delays and nationality. *Applied Cognitive Psychology*, *17*, 1017–1031.

Luminet, O., Bouts, P., Delie, F., Manstead, A. S. R., & Rimé, B. (2000). Social sharing of emotion following exposure to a negatively valenced situation. *Cognition and Emotion*, *14*, 661–688.

Luminet, O., Curci, A., Marsh, E. J., Wessel, I., Constatin, T., Gencoz, F., et al. (2004). The cognitive, emotional, and social impacts of the September 11 attacks: Group differences in memory for the reception context and determinants of flashbulb memory. *Journal of General Psychology*, *131*, 197–224.

Markus, H., & Kitayama, S. (1991). Culture and the self: Implications for cognition, emotion, and motivation. *Psychological Review*, *98*, 224–253.

Marsh, E. J. (2007). Retelling is not the same as recalling: Implications for memory. *Current Directions in Psychological Science*, *16*, 16–20.

Martin, L., & Tesser, A. (1996). Some ruminative thoughts. In R. S. Wyer (Ed.), *Advances in social cognition* (pp. 1–48). Hillsdale, NJ: Lawrence Erlbaum Associates Inc.

Martini, M. (1996). "What's new?" at the dinner table: Family dynamics during mealtimes in two cultural groups in Hawaii. *Early Development and Parenting*, *5*(1), 23–34.

McGaugh, J. L. (2003). *Memory and emotion: The making of lasting memories*. New York: Columbia University Press.

Mullen, M. K., & Yi, S. (1995). The cultural context of talk about the past: Implications for the Neisser, U. (1982). Memory: What are the important questions? In

U. Neisser (Ed.), *Memory observed* (pp. 3–19). San Francisco: W. H. Freeman & Company.

Neisser, U. (1982). Snapshots or benchmarks? In U. Neisser (Ed.), *Memory observed: Remembering in natural contexts* (pp. 43–48). San Francisco: W. H. Freeman & Company.

Nelson, K. (1993). Explaining the emergence of autobiographical memory in early childhood. In A. F. Collins, S. E. Gathercole, M. A. Conway, & P. E. Morris (Eds.), *Theories of memory* (pp. 355–385). Hillsdale, NJ: Lawrence Erlbaum Associates Inc.

Nelson, K., & Fivush, R. (2004). The emergence of autobiographical memory: A social cultural developmental theory. *Psychological Review, 111*(2), 486–511.

Otani, H., Kusumi, T., Kato, K., Matsuda, K., Kern, R. P., Widner, R., et al. (2005). Remembering a nuclear accident in Japan: Did it trigger flashbulb memories? *Memory, 13*, 6–20.

Pasupathi, M. (2001). The social construction of the personal past and its implications for adult development. *Psychological Bulletin, 127*, 651–672.

Pennebaker, J. W., & Banasik, B. (1997). On the creation and maintenance of collective memories: History as social psychology. In J. W. Pennebaker, D. Páez, & B. Rimé (Eds.), *Collective memory of political events: Social psychological perspectives* (pp. 3–20). Mahwah, NJ: Lawrence Erlbaum Associates Inc.

Pezdek, K. (2003). Event memory and autobiographical memory for the events of September 11, 2001. *Applied Cognitive Psychology, 17*, 1033–1045.

Philippot, P., & Rimé, B. (1998). Social and cognitive processing in emotion: A heuristic for psychopathology. In W. F. Flack & J. Laird (Eds.), *Emotion in psychopathology* (pp. 114–129). Oxford, UK: Oxford University Press.

Pillemer, D. B. (1984). Flashbulb memories of the assassination attempt on President Reagan. *Cognition, 16*, 63–80.

Pillemer, D. B. (1998). *Momentous events, vivid memories.* Cambridge, MA: Harvard University Press.

Reisberg, D., & Hertel, P. (Eds.) (2004). *Memory and emotion.* New York: Oxford University Press.

Rimé, B., Corsini, S., & Herbette, G. (2002). Emotion, verbal expression, and the social sharing of emotion. In S. R. Fussell (Ed.), *The verbal communication of emotions: Interdisciplinary perspectives* (pp. 185–208). Mahwah, NJ: Lawrence Erlbaum Associates Inc.

Rimé, B., Finkenauer, C., Mesquita, B., Pennebaker, J. W., Singh-Manoux, A., & Yogo, M. (2001, July). *The social sharing of emotion: An overview of cross-cultural data.* In Q. Wang & M. A. Conway (co-Chairs), *Memory and Culture.* Symposium conducted at the 3rd International Conference on Memory, Valencia, Spain.

Rimé, B., Philippot, P., Boca, S., & Mesquita, B. (1992). Long-lasting cognitive and social consequences of emotion: Social sharing and rumination. In W. Stroebe & M. Hewstone (Eds.), *European review of social psychology* (Vol 3, pp. 225–258). Chichester, UK: Wiley.

Rubin, D. C., & Kozin, M. (1984). Vivid memories. *Cognition, 16*, 81–95.

Rubin, D. C., Rahhal, T. A., & Poon, L. W. (1998). Things learned in early adulthood are remembered best. *Memory and Cognition, 26*, 3–19.

Rubin, D. C., Wetzler, S. E., & Nebes, R. D. (1986). Autobiographical memory across the adult lifespan. In D. C. Rubin (Ed.), *Autobiographical memory* (pp. 202–221). Cambridge, UK: Cambridge University Press.

Schmolck, H., Buffalo, E. A., & Squire, L. R. (2000). Memory distortions develop over time: Recollections of the O. J. Simpson trial verdict after 15 and 32 months. *Psychological Science, 12*, 39–45.

Schuman, H., Akiyama, H., & Knauper, B. (1998). Collective memories of German and Japanese about the past half century. *Memory, 6*, 427–454.

Schuman, H., Belli, R. F., & Bischoping, K. (1997). The generational basis of historical knowledge. In J. W. Pennebaker, D. Páez, & B. Rimé (Eds.), *Collective memory of political events*. Hillsdale, NJ: Lawrence Erlbaum Associates Inc.

Schuman, H., & Scott, J. (1989). Generations and collective memories. *American Sociological Review, 54*(3), 359–381.

Shapiro, L. R. (2006). Remembering September 11th: The role of retention interval and rehearsal on flashbulb and event memory. *Memory, 14*(2), 129–147.

Shoemaker, P. J., & Cohen, A. A. (2006). *News around the world*. New York: Routledge, Taylor & Francis Group.

Tajfel, H. (1982). *Social identity and intergroup relations*. Cambridge, UK: Cambridge University Press.

Tweed, R. G., White, K., & Lehman, D. R. (2004). Culture, stress, and coping: Internally- and externally-targeted control strategies of European Canadians, East Asian Canadians, and Japanese. *Journal of Cross-Cultural Psychology, 35*(6), 652–668.

Wang, Q. (2001a). "Did you have fun?": American and Chinese mother–child conversations about shared emotional experiences. *Cognitive Development, 16*, 693–715.

Wang, Q. (2001b). Cultural effects on adults' earliest childhood recollection and self-description: Implications for the relation between memory and the self. *Journal of Personality and Social Psychology, 81*(2), 220–233.

Wang, Q. (2003). Emotion situation knowledge in American and Chinese preschool children and adults. *Cognition and Emotion, 17*(5), 725–746.

Wang, Q. (2004). The cultural context of parent–child reminiscing: A functional analysis. In M. W. Pratt & B. Fiese (Eds.), *Family stories and the life course: Across time and generations* (pp. 279–301). Mahwah, NJ: Lawrence Erlbaum Associates Inc.

Wang, Q. (2005, September). Autobiographical memory and public memory in self and identity. In K. Nelson (Chair), *Autobiographical memory in cultural perspectives*. Invited symposium conducted at the 1st International Congress of the International Society for Cultural and Activity Research (ISCAR), Seville, Spain.

Wang, Q., & Conway, M. A. (2004). The stories we keep: Autobiographical memory in American and Chinese middle-aged adults. *Journal of Personality, 72*(5), 911–938.

Wang, Q., & Conway, M. A. (2006). Autobiographical memory, self, and culture. In L-G. Nilsson & N. Ohta (Eds.), *Memory and society: Psychological perspectives* (pp. 9–27). New York: Psychology Press.

Wang Q., Conway, M., Kulkofsky, S., Hou, Y., Mueller-Johnson K., Aydın, Ç., et al. (2008). *The ethnocentric Americans? Long-term memory of public events in five countries*. Manuscript submitted for publication.

Wang, Q., & Fivush, R. (2005). Mother–child conversations of emotionally salient events: Exploring the functions of emotional reminiscing in European American and Chinese families. *Social Development, 14*(3), 473–495.

Wang, Q., & Ross, M. (2007). Culture and memory. In H. Kitayama & D. Cohen (Eds.), *Handbook of cultural psychology*. New York: Guilford Publications.

Wright, D. B. (1993). Recall of the Hillsborough disaster over time: Systematic biases of flashbulb memories. *Applied Cognitive Psychology*, *7*, 129–138.

Wright, D. B., & Gaskell, G. D. (1995). Flashbulb memories: Conceptual and methodological issues. *Memory*, *3*, 67–80.

Wu, H. D. (2000). Systemic determinants of international news coverage: A comparison of 38 countries. *Journal of Communication*, *50*(2), 110–130.

General conclusions

Antonietta Curci and Olivier Luminet

Thirty years have elapsed since Brown and Kulik published the first work on flashbulb memory in 1977. Since then, a considerable number of studies have been carried out, the researchers' interest in the topic being driven by the characteristics of the phenomenon as "common knowledge, compellingly curious, and lacking any scientific explanations—favourable conditions for inspiring empirical study" (Pillemer, Chapter 6, this volume, p. 127). Researchers concerned with investigating the relationship between memory and emotion have been variously confronted with the following dilemma: How can memories for mundane details of the learning context of a public news event remain vivid and unchanged even many years after the event originally occurred? Are these memories a kind of bizarre exception to the principle of economy which regulates the functioning of human memory? And if this is the case, then why is this so? This book represents an attempt to sum up three decades of research work on FBM, and at the same time to go beyond the local interest in these memory formations to provide some hints towards a deeper understanding of the general functioning of autobiographical memory systems.

In their original paper, Brown and Kulik (1977) started from a trivial observation: There is a very familiar phenomenon, which refers to the everyday experience of remembering irrelevant details of an emotional event. This phenomenon does not fit into the traditional views of memory, and does not follow the ordinary rules of cognitive functioning. The authors had some ideas on the possible determinants of FBMs, and found in Livingston's *Now Print!* (1967) theory a nice account for their data. More generally, this theory allowed the researchers to explain the enhancement effect of emotion on memory for an everyday experience as a consequence of the biological significance of that experience for the survival of the individual and human beings in general. Relevant political events, such as the death of John F. Kennedy or Martin Luther King, and every private event entailing a strong emotional reaction can be understood through this conceptualization. FBMs are emotional memories in that they derive from the activation of this special mechanism having an evolutionary value.

This was the sole mechanism available to our ancestors for retaining crucial information for the well-being of the whole community. Significant images needed to be deeply imprinted into the individual's mind to be subsequently transmitted to other members of a community. In Brown and Kulik's view (1977), all forms of rehearsal have the effect of accommodating these images into the form of narrative accounts. It follows that modifications might intervene in these accounts, but the original memory trace remains vivid and unchanged over time.

Many criticisms have been made against this speculation. Of course, contemporary research work has added so much to the general understanding of the relationship between memory and emotion. On the other hand, some intuitions by Brown and Kulik (1977) have recently been reconsidered by more complex modellings on FBMs (see, for instance, Finkenauer et al., 1998, and Luminet, Chapter 3, this volume, for a summary). But there is a fact that cannot be ignored at the present time, and it imposes additional constraints on all theoretical and empirical considerations of FBM: We live in an information society, all our lives are modelled by the mass media and new media. TV, radio, newspapers, and the Internet permeate our lives, so that the boundaries between private and public experiences are diminishing (McQuail, 1994). Personal memories flow into the realm of collective knowledge and cultural representations. What are FBMs in this society? More generally, what kind of impact can both emotional and social factors have in determining the content and persistence of autobiographical memories? This book has provided some answers to these questions, which will be summed up in the following pages.

DISENTANGLING THE SOCIAL DIMENSIONS OF MEMORY

The problem of constructing an explanatory account of FBM requires an appropriate understanding of the role of social factors in shaping memories for relevant personal experiences. The same label "social factors" subsumes a quantity of variables and processes having a different impact on the phenomenon, from mental rumination on the original experience, to social sharing processes with relevant others, the pervasive impact of the mass media, and social communication. Beneath all this there is the influential role of cultural practices and societal constraints. A reliable assessment of this multitude of factors would impose a substantial caution from the methodological point of view. For instance, the SEM approach has been variously considered in FBM research (see Luminet, Chapter 3, this volume) because of its potential to simultaneously deal with complex interrelationships within a broad set of variables. On the other hand, it has been stressed (see Wright, Chapter 2, this volume) that alternative approaches are also available to isolate the effects of explanatory variables in more controlled settings. The problem rests on the definition of what is "social" in the investigation of FBM. Every operationalization of a construct requires a convincing theoretical definition of the construct itself. In other words, it is crucial to delineate a comprehensive account of the social determinants of FBM.

First of all, it is important to go beyond the original dichotomy between emotional and social effects on FBM, as hypothesized by Brown and Kulik (1977). In their view, overt and covert rehearsal processes can have an impact on the narrative accounts of FBMs, while the original memory trace is invariable over time. A contemporary view on emotional memory leads us to conclude that emotional elicitors of FBM can be considered social in their essence (see Fivush et al., Chapter 8, this volume). Experiencing an emotion makes the individual feel the urge to give a meaning to what happened. Indeed, emotions provoke some rupture in the ordinary flow of daily life experiences. This rupture needs to be fixed, so individuals attempt to integrate what happened into their conceptual system, through a process of cognitive elaboration. This is particularly compelling when the experience has had a strong impact on the individual's life. Interacting with relevant others provides support for such a meaning-making process. Emotion sustains this process as far as the original experience continues to have an impact requiring cognitive elaboration (Curci, Rimé, Gisle, & Baruffol, 2007).

A second point needs to be considered with respect to the social aspects of FBM, which entails a broader conceptualization of the phenomenon. Social identity theory (Tajfel, 1982) considers the individual's behaviour as deeply determined by social identity issues of the self-representational system. In a study on conceptual and methodological issues in FBM research, Gaskell and Wright (1997) pointed out that memory for political events contributes to identify each person as an individual and member of a social group. As a consequence of their identification with the group, individuals exhibited a specific pattern of recall for relevant public news. The identification with a given group determines what is relevant for the members of that group, the emotional impact, and amount of public and private conversations following a public event. In this view, it is social identity rather than personal relevance that triggers the formation and maintenance of FBMs for public events (see Berntsen, Chapter 9, this volume). The activation of all emotional factors usually included in FBM modelling (emotional feeling states, appraisals, rehearsal) stems from the activation of the social identity processes.

This account represents a clear advancement for the understanding of group differences in FBM for public events (see Curci & Luminet, 2006; Luminet et al., 2004). More generally, this framework might help to explain some empirical inconsistencies concerning the role of FBM determinants. If the effect of a predictor variable appears to be significant in one study and not assessed by another, this might be due to the interaction between this variable and the social identification that participants have adopted in relation to the original event. The emotional impact experienced when hearing of the death of a former president is not the same for citizens of the president's home country and other foreign nationalities (see Curci, Luminet, Finkenauer,

& Gisle, 2001). The effect of rehearsal factors on individuals' memory is different with respect to the availability of the mass media across different societies (Curci & Luminet, 2006). If these aspects are not controlled in an empirical study, they might result in spurious relationships between the supposed predictors and FBM.

Third, the mass media represent an important vehicle of transmission of information in contemporary societies. A consideration of their role allows researchers to extend the micro level of analysis of the process of formation and maintenance of FBM to macro levels of the cultural practices and social rituals (see Hirst & Meksin, Chapter 10, Páez et al., Chapter 11, and Wang & Aydın, Chapter 12, this volume). Again, a definitional problem is imposed: Are FBMs something different from collective memories, and in what way? It has been stressed (see Páez et al., Chapter 11, this volume) that the proper feature of FBMs is their mix of personal and socially shared information pertaining to a collective event. Given this, how can researchers identify the complex set of cultural factors that affect personal memories for very idio-syncratic details of learning of public news? The problem cannot be solved by simply including some new exogenous variables in a more complex FBM modelling. On the other hand, running experimental studies controlling for these issues is rather puzzling. Culture is so pervasive that all everyday practices are shaped by its constraints. It defines the general climate of expectations, beliefs, knowledge, and attitudes in which a given event takes place. It follows that theorizations extending to cultural issues might be undetermined if not adequately sustained from the theoretical and method-ological points of view. Sociology, anthropology, political sciences, and his-toriography can concur on a broader account of human memory functioning. Of course this would require considerable efforts of integration with trad-itional psychological research.

METHODOLOGICAL CONCERNS

Considering the relevance of social issues has noteworthy implications for the assessment of FBMs. If these memories are deeply determined by the social processes outlined above, their consistency over time is rather a matter of agreement among individuals recalling the same experience under the same situational constraints. Individuals might co-construct their accounts of learning of an important news item, so that their narratives appear more consistent as time passed compared with assessments obtained shortly after the event (Winningham, Hyman, & Dinnel, 2000). As a consequence of this, alternative indices might be tested as reliable measures of memory accuracy, such as the amount of recalled details (see Julian, Bohannon, & Aue, Chapter 5, this volume). On the other hand, different memory characteristics need to be investigated in relation to specific event conditions and memory processes. Among these, the subjective feelings of confidence and memory vividness have appeared as more specific to FBM than many other indicators (see Talarico & Rubin, Chapter 4, this volume).

This latter perspective on the measurement might eventually lead the researcher to question the nature of FBMs as "special" formations. If FBMs do not have exceptional features to be distinguished from ordinary auto-biographical memories, there is no need to postulate a special mechanism accounting for their formation, since they can easily be assimilated into ordinary autobiographical memory systems. Choosing a measure for FBM is not simply a matter of convenience, but it does tell us a lot about the theoretical consideration of the phenomenon.

It is clear that methodological issues are of great concern in investigating FBMs. Advanced statistical modelling has progressively given researchers the chance to test more stringent hypotheses about the nature of FBM. To illustrate, latent variable modelling has been adopted when assuming that different observed indicators concur in the assessment of a theoretical construct (Curci, 2005; Wright, Gaskell, & O'Muircheartaigh, 1998). In the case of FBMs, categorical and dimensional latent variable approaches have been proposed, although research work on this point is still at an early stage (see Curci, Chapter 1, and Wright, Chapter 2, this volume). If a kind of dimensional model was proven to be more appropriate to FBM data than a categorical model, then the special encoding hypothesis would be more difficult to sustain, and, from the theoretical point of view, FBM would be easily located along the continuum of the ordinary autobiographical memory formations.

By contrast, arguing for a categorical model does not imply that the special encoding hypothesis is necessarily true. Finding that there is a distinct class of memories would suggest that FBMs are somewhat different from ordinary memories, but it does not mean they came from a different process. Conway pointed out (1995) that FBM can be considered as "whole" units or "local minima" in the space of autobiographical memory. Recent findings have confirmed the idea that FBMs convey an integrated form of knowledge representation, while ordinary autobiographical memories can better be conceptualized as a distributed form of knowledge representation (see Curci, Chapter 1, this volume). However, although considered as special cores of knowledge, FBMs could become associated with new details which unavoidably alter their original content (Conway, 1995). They can be affected by many changes in the interpretations they convey, associated emotional experience, and consequent verbal accounts. Their formation and maintenance can be affected by constructive processes like any other memory, but these processes apply on event-specific sensory–perceptual material, having peculiar features of specificity and vividness.

As a further consequence of what has been said up to now, it follows that findings obtained from investigating FBMs have unavoidable implications for general research work on autobiographical memory. Either assimilated or differentiated from ordinary autobiographical memory formations, FBMs cannot be considered as an isolated phenomenon, but they need to be analysed with respect to broader research questions concerning the general functioning of the individual's cognitive system.

EMOTIONAL FEATURES OF AUTOBIOGRAPHICAL MEMORY

Recent models of formation and maintenance of FBMs have tried to profit from years of research on psychology of emotion. By definition, the proto-typical elicitor of a FBM is a shocking and relevant public event. This means that all features of an original emotional experience—that is, its cognitive antecedents, the associated subjective feeling, its cognitive and social consequences (rumination, social sharing, media exposure)—are important aspects to be included in a comprehensive description of FBM formation and maintenance (see Luminet, Chapter 3, this volume). This does not mean that all the supposed emotional factors work equally well in predicting FBMs. Evidence on this point is mixed: various authors have attempted to get a unique convincing model for FBM, and this has also been done through the pages of the present book. This issue is particularly important since, as has been said in the preceding pages, understanding the process of formation and maintenance of FBMs as well as the characteristics of its content will result in a significant advancement in the general understanding of the autobiographical memory processes.

Unfortunately we can only expect to get the ultimate solution to this problem from future research work. At present we can merely rely on different lines of work, besides the traditional pathways of investigation of the phenomenon, to get more insight into the relationships between FBMs and their associated variables. First, research work on FBM can be connected with the interest in social identity issues, considering human memory formations as serving important functions for the definition of the self. In this view, FBMs would be considered for their role in the process of definition of the self, and their systematic comparison with memories for ordinary experiences (first-hand experiences, see Pillemer, Chapter 6, this volume) would require appropriate research strategies. Second, and in connection with this, the analysis of the narrative accounts of emotional experiences can provide evidence of how individuals create meaning out of their experiences (Bartlett, 1932). FBM—and all forms of autobiographical memory—can represent a significant instance for this meaning-making process across the lifespan (see Fivush et al., Chapter 8, this volume). Third, the analysis of the clinical populations might help to shed light on the ordinary functioning of the autobiographical memory system. In this field, some relevant topics—such as the formation of emotional memories for depressed and social-phobic individuals—have not been sufficiently investigated and would require appropriate methodological consideration (see Budson & Gold, Chapter 7, this volume).

Finally, on a more general level, FBM research work represents an important arena where two research traditions of cognitive and social psychology are confronted. Indeed, from the theoretical point of view, the origin of the interest in FBM can be traced back to both cognitive and social psychology, with some influence of sociology and history (Bellelli, Curci, & Leone, 2007). Researchers have decided to focus on either how groups of people differ in their memory for a single event or how different events are remembered by a small sample of individuals. In the first case, the researchers' aim has been to assess a kind of relationship between some specific characteristics of social groups (French vs Belgians; US vs non-US, etc.) and the *flashbulb-ness* of memories. Research work from this line has paid tribute to the collective memory tradition. When researchers have decided to focus on the investigation of different memories for the same sample of people, their approach has been more in line with cognitive psychology. Many of the outlined difficulties in the study of FBM reflect the problem of comparing, choosing between, or even combining the two different research approaches. This consideration makes it easier to understand the general problem of defining what a FBM is, and the related measurement issues. The solution to this problem would of course depend, among many other things, on whether the researcher belongs to one or the other of the two traditions. However, being aware of this point might help to overcome some impasses that research has sometimes faced.

At the end of this book, FBM can be considered as a label for a more complex set of interactions among variables, processes, methods of investigation, research perspectives, and theoretical accounts. This label might have a strong correspondence with a real phenomenon normally occurring in daily life; it might be something like an arbitrary classification for some observed concurrent features in psychological life; finally, FBM conceptualization might be completely pleonastic with respect to the study of ordinary autobiographical memory phenomena. However, its heuristic value for the advancement of research work on the relationship between autobiographical memory and emotion still appears undeniable.

REFERENCES

Bartlett, F. C. (1932). *Remembering: A study in experimental and social psychology.* New York: Cambridge University Press.

Bellelli, G., Curci, A., & Leone, G. (2007). Social and cognitive determinants of collective memory for public events. In J. Valsiner & A. Rosa (Eds.), *Cambridge handbook of sociocultural psychology* (pp. 625–644). Cambridge, UK: Cambridge University Press.

Brown, R. & Kulik, J. (1977). Flashbulb memories. *Cognition, 5,* 73–99.

Conway, M. A. (1995). *Flashbulb memories.* Hove, UK: Lawrence Erlbaum Associates Ltd.

Curci, A. (2005). Latent variable models for the measurement of flashbulb memories: A comparative approach. *Applied Cognitive Psychology, 19*, 3–22.

Curci, A., & Luminet, O. (2006). Follow-up of a cross-national comparison on Flashbulb and event memory for the September 11th attacks. *Memory, 14*, 329–344.

Curci, A., Luminet, O., Finkenauer, C., & Gisle, L. (2001). Flashbulb memories in social groups: A comparative study of the memory of French President Mitterrand's death in a French and a Belgian group. *Memory, 9*, 81–101.

Curci, A., Rimé, B., Gisle, L., & Baruffol, E. (2007). *Social sharing after emotion, its temporal evolution and consequences for emotional recovery*. Manuscript submitted for publication.

Finkenauer, C., Luminet, O., Gisle, L., El-Ahmadi, A., Van der Linden, M., & Philippot, P. (1998). Flashbulb memories and the underlying mechanism of their formation: Toward an emotional-integrative model. *Memory and Cognition, 26*, 516–531.

Gaskell, G., & Wright, D. (1997). Group differences for memory of a political event. In J. W. Pennebaker, D. Páez, & B. Rimé (Eds.), *Collective memory of political events: Social psychological perspectives* (pp. 175–189). Hillsdale, NJ: Lawrence Erlbaum Associates Inc.

Livingston, R. B. (1967). Brain circuitry relating to complex behavior. In G. C. Quarton, T. Melnechuck, & F. O. Schmitt (Eds.), *The neurosciences: A study program* (pp. 499–514). New York: Rockefeller University Press.

Luminet, O., Curci, A., Marsh, E., Wessel, I., Constantin, T., Gencoz, F., et al. (2004). The cognitive, emotional, and social impacts of the September, 11 attacks: Group differences in memory for the reception context and the determinants of flashbulb memory. *Journal of General Psychology, 131*, 197–224.

McQuail, D. (1994). *Mass communication theory: An introduction* (3rd ed.). London: Sage.

Tajfel, H. (Ed.). (1982). *Social identity and intergroup relations*. Cambridge, UK: Cambridge University Press.

Winningham, R. G., Hyman, I. E., & Dinnel, D. L. (2000). Flashbulb memories? The effects of when the initial memory report was obtained. *Memory, 8*, 209–216.

Wright, D. B., & Gaskell, G. D. (1995). Flashbulb memories: Conceptual and methodological issues. *Memory, 3*, 67–80.

Wright, D. B., Gaskell, G. D., & O'Muircheartaigh, C. (1998). Flashbulb memory assumptions: Using national surveys to explore cognitive phenomena. *British Journal of Psychology, 89*, 103–121.

Author index

Subject index